T0247791

SKIES OF THUNDER

ALSO BY CAROLINE ALEXANDER

The Iliad:
A New Translation

Lost Gold of the Dark Ages:
War, Treasure, and the Mystery of the Saxons

The War That Killed Achilles:
The True Story of Homer's Iliad and the Trojan War

The Bounty:
The True Story of the Mutiny on the Bounty

The Endurance:
Shackleton's Legendary Antarctic Expedition

Mrs. Chippy's Last Expedition:
The Remarkable Journal of Shackleton's Polar-Bound Cat

Battle's End:
A Seminole Football Team Revisited

The Way to Xanadu:
Journeys to a Legendary Realm

One Dry Season:
In the Footsteps of Mary Kingsley

SKIES *of* THUNDER

THE DEADLY WORLD WAR II
MISSION OVER THE ROOF
OF THE WORLD

Caroline Alexander

VIKING

VIKING
An imprint of Penguin Random House LLC
penguinrandomhouse.com

Text credits may be found on page 385.

Maps by Jeffrey L. Ward

LIBRARY OF CONGRESS CATALOGING-IN-PUBLICATION DATA

Names: Alexander, Caroline, 1956– author.
Title: Skies of thunder : The Deadly World War II Mission
Over the Roof of the World / Caroline Alexander.
Other titles: The Deadly World War II Mission Over the Roof of the World
Description: [New York] : Viking, [2024] |
Includes bibliographical references and index.
Identifiers: LCCN 2023026939 (print) | LCCN 2023026940 (ebook) |
ISBN 9781984879233 (hardcover) | ISBN 9781984879240 (ebook)
Subjects: LCSH: World War, 1939–1945—Campaigns—Burma. |
World War, 1939–1945—Himalaya Mountains. |
World War, 1939–1945—Aerial operations. |
Burma Road (China and Burma)—Strategic aspects. |
Stilwell Road (Burma and India)—Strategic aspects. |
Burma—History—Japanese occupation, 1942–1945.
Classification: LCC D767.6 .A44 2024 (print) | LCC D767.6 (ebook) |
DDC 940.54/2591—dc23/eng/20240216
LC record available at https://lccn.loc.gov/2023026939
LC ebook record available at https://lccn.loc.gov/2023026940

Printed in the United States of America
1st Printing

Book design by Daniel Lagin

To Frank,

Naval Aviator,

Officer and Gentleman
by Act of Congress

CONTENTS

NOTE TO READER

This book draws heavily on writings of the era, both private and official, and from a range of nationalities. In the interest of consistency with these sources, the geographical place-names of the era are used throughout. Thus, Myanmar is referred to by its World War II–era name "Burma," modern Yangon is "Rangoon," Thailand is "Siam," and so forth. Similarly, obsolete terms have been allowed to stand, and punctuation and spelling of the sources have been retained despite being on occasion unorthodox.

Air speed and distance is conventionally measured in knots, but the majority of sources of the era cite "miles-per-hour."

SKIES OF THUNDER

1

PRELUDE

Years ago, a *National Geographic* assignment brought me to the remote jungles of the Hukawng Valley in the north of Burma. Situated in the politically troubled Kachin State, this great, sparsely inhabited region is a wildlife protected area and has been kept off-limits to most outsiders by its formidable, rugged geography, its sparse infrastructure, and the presence of the Kachin Independence Army. Even today, access to the Hukawng can only be made by way of the old, unpaved Ledo Road. Driving north with a team of Forest Department rangers from the town of Myitkyina, at the sedate pace of twenty-five miles an hour, our jeep encountered little traffic—a few bicycles, four repurposed World War II military vehicles, and two ambling elephants.

Looming over either side of the gouged and often muddy track, the forest asserted a fearsome, unnegotiable presence, and the rangers with me in the jeep were among the very few people to have ventured into its towering greenery. The cover is so dense, they tell me, that within the forest, on even sunny days, they often cannot see the sky. In the course of their six-week-long patrols, they scout the forest for evidence of incursions—for poaching, for timber gathering, for opium-poppy cultivation. And occasionally, the rangers tell me, they have come on World War II–era aircraft crashed and buried in the jungle overgrowth and, in one stricken plane, the skeleton of its pilot.

The aircraft that are strewn throughout this jungle are US Army Air Forces transport planes that, between 1942 and 1945, ferried cargo from military bases in neighboring India to China. Some six hundred planes, I later learned, lie along the old flight route—an aluminum trail that leads from the mountainous jungles of Assam in northeast India, across the vast forbidding forests of Upper Burma, over the hump of mountain ridges that define the Burma-China border, and onto the mountains and plains of Yunnan province in southwest China. According to Air Force estimates, some 1,700 American airmen crashed and died flying "the Hump," either on impact or after bailing out and stumbling through the jungle.

The purpose of these cargo-flying missions was starkly simple: to carry war supplies to Japanese-blockaded China and so "keep China in the war." War planners in Washington, however, had paid scant attention to a few inconvenient facts: that between the route's two termini rose the foothills of the Himalayas; that the harsh and mostly inaccessible terrain did not permit navigational beacons along the route; and that a chronic vortex of extreme air systems across the route ensured the worst flying weather in the world, which no aircraft then existing could reliably overfly. The result was a litany of both deadly crashes and astonishing feats of survival, as revealed in even a cursory perusal of the most accessible source material. From the multivolume history compiled by a veterans' pilot association:

> The cloud around us was as black as a dungeon cell. . . . The air currents seemed to grasp the plane and shake it as a dog would shake a rat, and then turn us loose only to regain its grip and shake more violently than before. Snow and hail beat against the plane and the vertical currents seemed to be tossing us in a game of catch. . . . The snow and freezing rain were forming huge slabs of ice on the leading edge of the wings. . . . Cold sweat streamed down my face as I saw the small "artificial horizon" turn slowly

over its side and stay there. Without it and my other instruments
I could not tell if the plane was diving, climbing or rolling. . . .
[F]inally, as though we were a bad taste in the mouth of the thunder
god, Thor, the storm seemed to spit us out into the calm and soupy
overcast. Minutes passed before anyone spoke.[1]

From a civilian registry of crashes over the Hump:

This Air Transport Command plane was on a routine flight from
Jorhat, India to Yangkai, China. This aircraft was carrying ammunition, gasoline, and ten one thousand pound bombs. Ice began
building up and it took 53 minutes to get up to 26,000 feet. By
that time one engine had seized, a second was leaking oil, and a
third was on fire. The pilot ordered the crew to bail out, and began
a series of swallow-swoops to maintain air speed. The crew tried
to open the rear hatch, but the pins broke on the release handle.
They opened the right rear hatch and the pilot gave the signal to
go. The lone survivor Sgt. Paul Beauchamp landed safely, and with
the help from friendly Tibetan natives, walked out to the Burma
road and encountered an English missionary; He then walked on
until he reached the Chinese army, this was 38 days after the
crash of his plane.[2]

From a collection of reminiscences published by pilot Lieutenant Carl
Constein:

St. Elmo's Fire made the cockpit weird. Rain hit the windshield
and sparkling bits of static electricity fell on us as though it carried through the windshield. Sparks built up on the ends of the
windshield wipers like wet snow. . . . Suddenly there was a deafen-
ing bang. We had been struck by lightning. The radio operator
was knocked to the floor. The copilot frantically pointed to the
instrument panel. We were descending so fast the gauges were

maximum down, the engines so cold they registered almost no oil pressure. . . . We were down to 11,000 feet in an area where the route minimum was 13,500.[3]

From the US Army Air Forces Air Transport Command "Ditching and Survival" reports:

> I was radio operator of Ship 321 that left SOOKERATING 0438 on Wednesday, 24 November, bound for YUNNANYI. . . . Everything normal. Checked weather with Yunnanyi, they reported the weather bad, but getting better. At about 0500 noticed that engines started to surge, we lost altitude. Highest altitude was 19,500. I guess we jumped at 12,000. . . . Hailey went first followed by Carlson, Burrows, Beck, Kaplan, Smith and CoPilot. Nobody knows about the pilot, I remember seeing two (Smith and CoPilot probably) above me. The ship circled above us and then started in a whining dive and hit a hill, almost underneath me. It lighted up the whole country, for quite a while. I landed in a mass of high thorny vines. . . . I was in vines about 60 feet above the ground.[4]

Burdened from the outset by a stubborn disregard for weather, terrain, and, indeed, basic logistics, the Hump operation—or simply "the Hump," as it was quickly dubbed by airmen—was further hampered by being embedded in the most chaotic theater of World War II. The China-Burma-India theater, or CBI, was defined by a blur of shifting commands bristling with military acronyms, competing interests, and contradictions that exposed the fault lines between the Allies—America and Britain, Britain and China, and ultimately and most fatefully between America and China. Although a military operation, its chief purpose was political not military, a function of President Franklin Roosevelt's desire to boost the morale of Chiang Kai-shek and his Nationalist government and ensure a close relationship between the US and China after the war. Yet while strictly noncombatants, Hump airmen were fired on by Japanese planes and co-opted into the battle for Burma, a campaign that saw some of the fiercest fighting of the war and, as one historian put, it had "the elements of a great Homeric saga."

> [T]he Burma campaign took place in a fantastic terrain, isolated by great mountains and jungles from any other theatre. It went on unbroken for three years and eight months. It covered vast areas. It sucked into its maelstrom nearly 2,000,000 men. It encompassed great disasters and ended in great triumphs. It produced prodigies of heroism, patience, resolution and endurance. It brought about great suffering, but fascinated and enthralled those taking part in it, both victors and losers. It was like no war that had ever been in the history of conflict.[5]

At the heart of this epic are the experiences of the often under-trained and ill-equipped young airmen. The saga of the Hump, then, above all else, is a story of the air. Yet threaded through it is the earthbound and very muddy history of the legendary Burma Road. The building of the road as a backdoor supply route from Burma into China, the attempt to save the road, the closure of the road, the attempt to replicate the road, the reopening of the road—these objectives directly inspired most military activity in the CBI theater, including some of the war's bloodiest battles against the Japanese along the way. The airmen who flew over the band of mountains that gird north Burma were in essence flying an aerial Burma Road. The story of the historic airlift over the Hump, then, begins on the ground, with the building of the Burma Road.

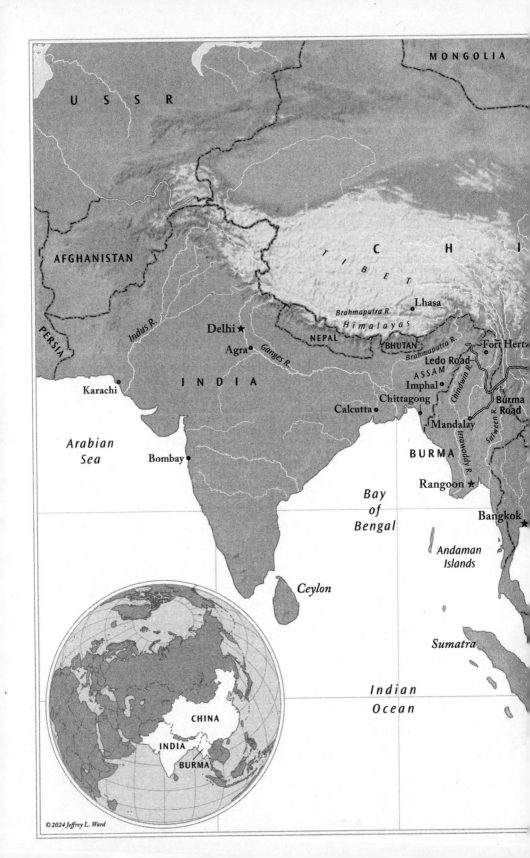

THE CHINA-BURMA-INDIA THEATER, 1940–1945

Peking
Tientsin
KOREA
Sea of
Japan
Lanchow
Yenan
Tokyo
Nancheng
Sian
Kaifeng
JAPAN
Chengtu
Nanking
Hankow
Suchow
Shanghai
Chungking
Hangchow
East
China
Sea
Kunming
Hengyang
Luliang
Lingling
Swatow
Liuchow
Kweilin
Nanning
Canton
Formosa
Hanoi
Hong Kong
Haiphong

Pacific Ocean

SIAM
South
China
Sea
FRENCH
INDOCHINA
PHILIPPINES

BRUNEI
Kuala Lumpur
MALAYA
Singapore

INDONESIA

Yellow R.
Yellow
Sea
Yangtze R.
Mekong R.

N

USAAF air bases in China

0 Miles   500   1000
0 Kilometers   500   1000

2

THE BURMA ROAD

Despite its name, the greater part of the Burma Road lay not in Burma but in China.

In 1935, the year in which preliminary work on the road was begun, Chiang Kai-shek, the leader of the Chinese Nationalist government, or Kuomintang, had recently won important victories over the Chinese Communists, the principal threat to his power. Aided by powerful figures in the criminal underworld, Chiang had fought his way to national leadership over the years following the death in 1925 of Sun Yat-sen, the revolutionary founder of the modern Republic of China. Although he controlled China's national army, Chiang's position was not secure, and he ruled with an ever-wary eye on rival warlords who controlled whole regions throughout the country's vast and still fractured land and, most especially, on the Communists.[1] In 1934, Nationalist victories over the Red Army caused the Communists to abandon their southern strongholds and march west, and north for nearly six thousand miles and establish a new headquarters at Yenan, in the province of Shaanxi.

Eager to consolidate his gains in the south, Chiang ordered the construction of a road that would allow the transportation of troops and matériel from his new capitol at Chungking, an inland port city on the

Yangtze River, into Yunnan, China's most southern province, which shared its western border with Burma.[2] The first section of the new military road from Chungking southwest to Yunnan's capital, Kunming, was soon completed. Rough work on the second leg was advanced westward from Kunming for some one hundred miles toward the Burmese border as far as Hsia-kuan, a town known for its stormy winds, the glinting snow of its distant mountains, and its flowers.[3] This second section was the fore-runner of the Burma Road.

China's need for an overland link with the outer world soon became a matter of vital national importance. Japanese forces had invaded and occupied Manchuria, China's most northern province, in 1931, unresisted by the Nationalist army, which, being the basis of his own power, Chiang had been loath to put at risk. A succession of military clashes between the two nations had continued after the occupation, and in the summer of 1937 a series of confused interactions between Chinese and Japanese troops at the Marco Polo Bridge outside Peking escalated into de facto war.[4] Shortly afterward, Peking itself was captured by the Japanese, who then executed lightning-strike attacks along China's coast, capturing key port cities. On November 26, 1937, Shanghai fell after a three-month-long onslaught from air and sea, leaving only one port of note, Canton, open to China for international trade.[5]

With the threat of a blockade, the Nationalist government scrambled to create overland lines of supply. As China historically received the vast majority of imports through the ports strung along its nine-thousand-mile-long coastline, few land routes existed, the most important being a narrow-gauge railway built by the French to service tin mines that ran from Haiphong and Hanoi in French Indochina to Kunming. To the north, an unpaved "highway" that followed a branch of the ancient network of Silk Routes for over three thousand miles across deserts and mountains led from Soviet Kazakhstan to Chungking. This Turkestan Road, as it was called, was both arduous and inefficient. In ideal weather the journey took the hardy drivers—many of whom were women—a minimum of eighteen days.[6] The extreme length of the route over uninhabited land made it impractical, for without staging stations or depots along the way, all trucks had to carry their own fuel.[7]

There existed one other "backdoor" route into China, and this was through Burma. Threading a tortuous course across mountains, jungle, and plunging gorges, an ancient mule track ran between Yunnan and Upper Burma and fed into the ancient web of Silk Routes. Traversing some of the most formidable terrain on earth, merchant caravans had used it for many centuries to carry wares of Szechuan silk, tea, and Yunnan cotton to markets in Tibet and beyond: Marco Polo described the route in his *Travels*, and the recently begun road west of Kunming toward Burma also followed this track.[8] If the old pack trail could be modernized, it was now thought, it could link Kunming to the town of Lashio in British Burma, and there connect with an existing rail line that ran directly to Rangoon, Burma's capital and a major port. As the crow flies, the distance from Kunming to Lashio was only 320 miles, but given the geographic challenges, this distance would be more than doubled. Of the road's total adjusted 717 miles of construction, 600 miles lay in China's Yunnan province. The British, who had long dreamed of a "north-east passage" overland to China, agreed to cooperate and committed to improving the relatively short section of road that lay in Burma and ran from Lashio to the Burma-Chinese border; and so in this way Burma's fate was inextricably linked to China's need.[9]

YUNNAN WAS A HIGH PLATEAU, A JUTTING SHELF OF THE TIBETAN MASSIF, pitted with wooded, mountain-ringed valleys and lake plateaus, and cleft by the gorges of some of Asia's mightiest rivers. The wild country, ribbed with steep ranges, permitted significant cultivation only in the ancient drained plateaus, fertile tracts isolated from one another by the barriers of mountains. In these private valleys, cut off from one another and the outside world, lived myriad peoples differing in culture, race, and language, and even after six centuries of Chinese rule an estimated three-quarters of them did not speak Chinese.[10] Travel and communication could be made only over rough mountain trails on foot or by packhorse, a slow and expensive business, and the inhabitants of these small valleys strove for self-sufficiency.[11] The province was ruled by the warlord Long Yun, who was ethnically a Lolo—the feared "tiger-people"—and who with his own great army, paid for by a long-established opium trade, was a source of ongoing concern to Chiang Kai-shek.[12] "There is perhaps no country, except Tibet, which is as little known to Europeans as Western Yunnan," wrote a longtime European resident of the region in 1941.[13]

To start the ambitious project, toward the end of 1937 Long Yun dispatched a small team of surveyors to scout the route. New to road construction and lacking all modern equipment, the Chinese authorities equipped the surveyors with sedan chairs and bearers and spirit levels for basic survey. Setting out from Kunming along the old caravan trail, the surveyors traversed bare uplands and an open scrub country covered with twisted pines and wild azaleas, then plunged two thousand feet to the Lu river valley, from where they stopped to ponder their first major challenge. While the caravan trail slipped out of the valley by a narrow pass and climbed the steep range of the opposite bank, this was clearly a route no motor vehicle could follow. The road out of the valley, therefore, would have to be cut from the valley cliff in hairpin bends for some forty miles. Beyond the pass, at the head of the valley, stood Hsi Shan P'o, or Western Mountain, a thick-wooded range of some nine thousand feet, crested with pine and rhododendrons, whose summit offered a few miles of level travel. Descent into the lake plateau behind it, however, would be treacherous, for the surface consisted of what was locally known as a "clay slope," soil with no stone, which devolved into pure, sliding mud in wet weather. At this point, the hardy surveyors were at the sixth of the old caravan route's thirty-four stages.

Through wild, uninhabited country, through high passes, up steep ranges and into valleys, past cavernous limestone caves, into the land of aboriginal inhabitants who spoke no Chinese, passing the fourteen-thousand-foot Tsang Shan range, skirting lakes and the junction with the old Tea Road leading north to Tibet, into the rich-fruited land of the

Salween river country, feared for its virulent malaria, the surveyors walked and were carried by their sure-footed bearers over a landscape and through populations that had never seen a wheeled vehicle, up to the village of Man Hsien, or Barbarian Limits, on the Burma border.

Meanwhile, the main task was to gather labor to build the road through one of the most sparsely populated provinces in China. While in Burma laborers were paid wages by the government, labor in China was levied and unpaid. In every district along the projected route, the newly formed Yunnan-Burma Highway Engineering Administration presented village chiefs with a quota of mandated manpower and a list of tools each was responsible for providing. As the levies were raised, a steady stream of people duly set forth from their abandoned villages on the long trek to allocated stations along the road.[14]

Yunnan had already sent most able-bodied men off to the National-ist army, thus it was disproportionally children, women, and old men who met the district quota. Dressed in their characteristic dark-blue cot-ton clothing and carrying bedrolls, the laborers trekked west, some in small family knots, some in bands several thousand strong. Often a re-gion could muster the necessary numbers only by summoning villagers from a hundred miles away, and it was not uncommon for people to walk for many days to reach their stations, surviving all the while on simple meals of rice and water from mountain streams and sleeping at night on rough ground. "Only a people accustomed to living close to the earth, in-ured to the privations of a hard simple life, and never having known real comfort could have undergone such an ordeal," managing director Tan Pei-Ying recalled.[15] Hardy or not, many died along the roadside, and many more suffered ill health—from exposure, from insects, from drinking unboiled water from the streams.

As labor stations were established farther west, the levies were raised from the Border races, as the Chinese called them, the hardy mountain people who were not of Chinese descent. From Yunnan north of the Yang-tze River came the Lolo women, dressed in snow-white tunics elaborate with embroidery and silver jewelry. The women preferred to work at night so as to tend to their families during the day, and could be seen in the darkness by the white-gleaming of their clothes in the moonlight, singing as they worked. Night was when the predators of hill and jungle ventured out, the leopard and the tiger, and fearful of these the Chinese workers stayed within their makeshift lean-tos; but the Lolo women, timid and shy among their overseers by day, were, in the awed words of director Tan, "dead shots with the bow and arrow."[16]

Near the snow-fed Yangpi River, almost halfway along the road, lived the Chinese Muslim Hui, a "tall and muscular" people, according to director Tan, his professional eye always on the lookout for potential labor. But in the wider countryside, the poverty was striking, the people stunted and weak, plagued with goiter, and most remarkably, with skin of a greenish-yellow color, perhaps, it was speculated, on account of chronic malaria.[17] As a consequence, little labor came from here.

Yet farther west, on the outskirts of Lungling, the road entered Shan territory, which extended beyond the Chinese border, deep into Burma. This, although the landscape was renowned for its beauty, would prove the most difficult and deadly stretch of road to build. The stunning scenery was notorious for "miasmic vapors," dense, choking mists that hovered from ground level to just over the height of a tall man's head, and which were erroneously believed to be the source of a virulent strain of malaria that haunted the Shan country. The road administration also confronted peculiar labor problems. So fertile was the land, so well-watered by monsoons, that the Shan girls and women, friendly, high-spirited, and eager to lend their hands, were unused to heavy physical labor. They insisted on carrying their loads of dirt and stone in a single basket balanced on one shoulder, instead of by the more efficient method of two baskets dangled at opposite ends of a carrying bar borne securely across both shoulders. If they carried baskets dangling on bars, the women protested, they would not be able to sway as they walked—they were known as the swaying people, "the pendulum people," and if they could not sway, they could not work.[18] Thwarted by this logic, the exasperated road management bent to the women's will and assigned them only light work.

Close to Burma came the headhunters, the Naga people, who knew no borders, and whose homes ranged across the mountainous jungle of western Yunnan and Upper Burma. Short and agile, of legendary toughness, they appeared dressed in rough, blue, cotton clothing, armored with rattan belts and leg greaves, their lips and teeth red from betel nuts. Emerging silently from the hills in the morning, they melted back into them at night. The social standing of a Naga man was assessed by the number of human heads hanging outside his hut, a practice that gave rise to sinister myths; it was said, for example, that a Naga's eyes gleamed like a cat's in the dark.

Officially, two hundred thousand laborers were mustered in China to build the Burma Road. In reality, the number was almost surely higher, given the many uncounted deaths along the way. Except for night workers, such as the Lolo, the working day began when morning mists had cleared, and ended at dusk. To clear land, massive trees had to be cut by hand and uprooted with ropes and crowbars. Over a third of the route had to pass through solid rock, and lacking equipment as basic as rock drills or explosives, the builders attacked the towering cliff faces with picks, hoes, mattocks, and improvised rock hammers. Cutting and chipping inch by inch, they tunneled inward to depths of as much as a hundred feet. No dynamite was available, but it was discovered that black powder used for firecrackers had some effect, and accordingly thousands of little squibs were daily set in shallow indents in the rock, and the meager debris they dislodged then patiently chipped away.

The faces of the great river gorges presented special challenges. At the Mekong River, just over halfway to Burma, cold winds arose seemingly from nowhere in the gorge below the cliffs, roaring as they blew through, the sound merging with that of the roaring river. The Chinese workers here were greatly unsettled by the profusion of butterflies drawn by riotous red and yellow wildflowers and by the anguished cry of a local species of partridge—butterflies and crying birds being symbols of departed souls. Farther west still, where the mighty Salween pounds down from Tibet, the river and its great gorge cast an almost paralyzing spell. So deep was the gorge that its black limestone face lay in perpetual twilight. The twists and turns in the tumultuous river's course caused the roar of its waters to rise and fall in an unnerving cadence, so that it seemed, to those who heard it, to snarl like an angry beast. The gorge itself harbored strange acoustical effects, and small sounds, such as the snapping of a distant twig, carried far as spooky, menacing echoes.

Working from improvised hanging platforms, dangling like spiders above this black abyss, a web of twenty thousand workers covered the cliff face to tackle this most formidable of all the rock-cutting tasks. A series of hairpin turns was required to carry the road up from its base height of two thousand feet above sea level to the seven-thousand-foot-high crest of the Salween gorge face, over a distance of eighteen miles. Blasting with firecrackers, swinging their five-pound hammers, scrambling aside to avoid the flying rock—each individual action was part of an intricate choreography, with all those on the ground dodging constantly falling debris.

Three mighty rivers and many other smaller ones cut north to south across the Yunnan plateau, which the ancient Silk Road caravans had traversed by way of rickety wooden or iron-chain suspension bridges. Newly erected stone bridges sufficed for the minor rivers across the road, but bridging the great riverways—the Mekong, the Salween, the Yangpi—required epic ingenuity and effort. The swiftness of their currents, which at times ran over twelves miles an hour, and the lack of any pile-driving equipment made it impossible to set supportive piles in the water. The bridges, therefore, would have to be suspended between the river shores, spanning distances of as much as four hundred feet.

The bridges' many structural components—beams, rods, cables, wire ropes—were custom-built in Rangoon, transported by rail to the Burma border, then carried by mule and on foot for three hundred miles to the construction sites. In the riverbeds close to shore, cofferdams were built around those places where deep foundation holes were to be sunk for the suspension towers. Constant pumping was required to keep the coffer-dams clear of water, day and night, without a moment's break. Burning vegetable oil for illumination, the night workers pumped in darkness by their sense of touch, their hearing overwhelmed by the roar of rushing water. Bucket pumps operated by foot treadle, bamboo plunger pumps operated by hand, bucket brigades—the technology used for pumping was centuries, even millennia old. When the towers were ready, swimmers were sent across carrying in their teeth long hemp lines, to which the suspension cables could be attached and hauled through the water. Swimmers were deemed preferable to rafts and boats for this task; all were likely to be dashed against rocks or the shores, but swimmers could be more readily replaced; "[A]s fast as one failed, another would step up to take his place," recorded director Tan.[19]

Women and children mostly undertook the task of hauling earth and rock away; the sturdy Lolo women easily hefted 150-pound burdens in the baskets they wore attached to carrying bands across their foreheads. The most vulnerable workers were perhaps the older women, who in accordance with ancient custom had had their feet bound in childhood, and who found such basic acts as walking and keeping balance on rough terrain perilous.[20] Much rock was repurposed for the wearing course, broken piece by piece into millions of small stones of uniform size. The desired standardized dimensions of these stones at first proved difficult to establish, the concept of measurements as such, inches or centimeters, being completely unknown to the majority of workers. Thousands of "standardized" stones were painted red to serve as working models, but these attractive products began to disappear, making as they did pretty playthings for the children. At length, director Tan established that any stone that could be passed between the circle made by a thumb and forefinger was acceptable. Scrupulous and obliging, the Lolo women made official presentations of the stones cut to the standard size, while smaller chips and shards were presented separately as gifts to the staff.[21]

Meanwhile, teams of men tamped down the loose earth of the roughly cut road with rounds of timber joined together with lifting straps and wielded by two men like a crude jackhammer. This primitive tool was called a "hang," after the sound it made as it hit the earth. The two-man teams coordinated the arduous lifting and dropping of this blunt force instrument by working to the rhythm of songs: "Work hard [hang]. . . . Grit your teeth [hang]. . . . Pull now [hang]. . . ."[22]

Once cleared, leveled, and surfaced with chipped stone, the road had to be tamped down by rolling. Enormous rollers, as much as six feet in height, were cut and shaped from blocks of limestone with hammer and chisel. Ranging in weight from three to five tons each, their size was determined in great part by the nutrition and health of the people of the district in which they were made, with rice-poor districts furnishing rollers so small they could be pulled by a single water buffalo.[23] Often, a limestone quarry lay far from the road, and the roller had to be built off-site, then hauled across mountainous terrain and through jungles to get to the place it was needed. Pulled by teams of fifty to one hundred men on the upgrades, the monstrous rollers took on lives of their own on the downslopes, which saw terrible accidents. Many victims were children, who raced playfully ahead of the runaway behemoths, innocent of their speed and power.

Toward the end of 1938, the road had advanced as far as the Shan village of Mang Shih, the last settlement of any note in China. From here it entered deep jungle, towering walls of great trees and bamboo stands, then drifted southwest into the thinly populated country of the Naga. Continuing through the small district called Chefang, the road ran on to Haishan Men, meaning Black Mountain Gate, from where it zigzagged to an obscure outpost called Wanting, which served as a customs checkpoint.[24] And somewhere just south of here, in the very heart of the jungle, a small iron bridge spanned a stream. This—sometimes guarded, usually not—was the frontier between China and the British Empire.[25]

IMPERIAL BRITAIN HAD ACQUIRED BURMA THROUGH A PIECEMEAL PROCESS and a series of wars, the last of which occurred in 1878. King Thibaw, who ruled from the royal city of Mandalay, and who had executed his eighty half brothers and sisters on ascent to the throne, had bankrupted the royal treasury. Looking to the wealthiest commercial entity in his country, Thibaw approached the Bombay Burmah Trading Corporation for funds to refill his coffers. Having already advanced considerable funds, this British timber company declined to comply and as a result was fined by the Burmese government to the tune of £230,000. Events escalated, and when the Burmese government rejected Britain's demand that the matter be submitted to outside arbitration, the British dispatched an ultimatum. This Thibaw rejected, adding by way of emphasis that he would drive the British into the sea.[26] Three weeks later, British forces traveled up the Irrawaddy River to Mandalay and informed the king he was under arrest. Although sporadic fighting with loyalists continued over the next four years, the arrest of Thibaw, Burma's last king, on November 28, 1885, effectively brought an end to the one-thousand-year-old Burmese kingdom.[27] Burma was now seen by the British as a backwater province of British India.

For half a century, Burma remained buried within the administration of Britain's most valued colonial possession. In 1937, reacting to local movements for independence, Burma was separated from the Indian government and made an independent colony with a Burmese parliament and prime minister, and a British governor, who retained authority over the so-called Excluded Areas inhabited by the non-Burman frontier tribes and the Shan States.[28] The elevation of Burma's status within the British Empire was a reassuring development to Burma's eastern neighbor, who had in the same year embarked on the building of the Burma Road. This lifeline for China, it appeared, was buttressed on every side by British imperial power. South of Rangoon lay British Malaya and the naval base of Britain's Crown Colony Singapore. To the west was India, the jewel in Britain's imperial crown. As a backdoor route to China, the Burma Road, as the saying goes, appeared as safe as houses.

British rule wrought many changes. Frontier officials posted to the Upper Burma frontier worked to abolish slavery, head-hunting, and human sacrifice. Schools and clinics were built throughout the country, and an excellent university and hospitals were established in Rangoon, which was transformed from a mud-mired outpost into a modern city with such novel features as electricity and transportation. The drainage and cultivation of millions of jungle- and swamp-covered acres in the Irrawaddy Delta resulted in a 600-percent increase in rice production that put Burma at the top of the world's rice-producing economies—although little of this revenue trickled down to Burmans.[29] Canvassing the opinion of local people living around Mandalay regarding the British, a Burmese historian found it to be generally favorable, the consensus being that "[t]he British are earnest and truthful; their 'yes' is a 'yes' and their 'no' is a 'no.'"[30]

Yet all these innovations came at a high price. The spectacle of Thibaw carried away with his family to permanent exile in bullock carts was deeply wounding to his subjects.[31] Omens were recalled that pointed to what seemed to be the cosmic significance of this loss of a kingdom—the rare blooming of the bamboo forests and a remarkable display of meteors and comets that lit the sky on the night before Thibaw's last day on the throne.[32] In more concrete terms, the collapse of the royal court shattered a way of life and traditions that had shaped Burmese society for centuries.

In Burma as elsewhere, British rule imposed a new social stratification, with British men and women at the top. Anglo-Burmans or other Anglo-Asians—the children and families of mixed race—came next, then professional classes of various ethnicities, and then the ordinary Burmese subject. Especially disruptive to the old order was the arrival of a million mostly Muslim immigrants, who followed the British from India.[33] Burma's population, exclusive of the quasi-independent states and hill tribes that were not ethnically Burman, numbered only ten million, and an influx of a new population on this scale could not go unnoticed. Eager for the opportunities offered by the opening of this ancient land, the immigrants arrived to clear swamps in the sweltering delta, to work on the docks as stevedores, and to do all this more cheaply than would the local Burmans. A caste of moneylenders from South India known as the Chettiars quickly rose to ascendancy in rural areas. Generally, money was loaned to enable a borrower to purchase land, and in the event of default on the loan, the lender acquired that land.[34] These straightforward terms gave rise to consequences Burmese villagers could not have imagined—that the very land of their country could be sold or yielded to an outsider. Thus, within a generation the newcomers had claimed not just choice livelihoods, but Burma's very soil—or so it was darkly perceived. Indians also claimed the professional class, having strong traditions in engineering, clerical work, and accounting; even the military police and army were largely Indian. In Rangoon, Burma's only real city, over 50 percent of the population was Indian. "[T]he traditions of the Burmans are of no account," a British civil servant wrote as early as 1908. "[T]he Burman who would talk with the European in the Rangoon streets must speak in Hindustani."[35]

Burmans despaired that they could not "compete with foreigners in the battle of life," wrote historian Taw Sein Ko in 1913. This sense of dispossession, of no longer being players of any importance in their own country, gave rise to friction and outright hostilities between Burmans and Indians, culminating in a series of ugly racial riots in the 1930s, in which hundreds of Indians, including women and children, were murdered.[36] All of these tensions, between Burmans and British and Burmans and immigrants, would be of enormous importance to the events ahead.

Many of the British administrators, civil servants, army officers, and entrepreneurs who came to live in Burma complained of a backwater existence far removed from sophisticated colonial cities like Calcutta and Hong Kong. Yet Burma had much to appeal to the kind of unabashed romantic who had left the British Isles in search of an adventurous life. Fully half the country was clad in forests—deep, unexplored jungle filled with fabulous animals: elephants, leopards and tigers, bear cats and bears, over a thousand species of birds and rare butterflies.[37] Even the county's economic products had a whiff of fairy-tale enchantment: Burma's natural wealth was in rubies, jade, amber, wolfram, silver, gold, and towering forests of teak.

Woven throughout all levels of Burmese society, from aristocrats to rural villagers, from university students to the unlettered, were two especially potent forces: Buddhism and witchcraft, and indeed, Buddhist witchcraft. The practice of magic extended the length and breadth of the country. In a remote village among the hill tribes of northernmost Burma, one officer conducting his annual administrative tour of inspection found a "witch" imprisoned in a bamboo cage.[38] A good wizard, it was believed, could inoculate soldiers from harm, for example, by tattooing them, or having them bathe in magically treated water. Magic enabled a soldier to shoot down an airplane by pointing a finger at it, and to walk into machine-gun fire without being wounded.[39] These beliefs were severely tested in the late 1930s, when a wizard priest crowned himself king on a jungle-covered hilltop not far from Rangoon and led his followers in an uprising against British rule. Armed with their tattoos, with needles under their skin, and with bullet-shaped amulets containing miniature carved Buddhas, the rebels advanced toward the army troops that were dispatched to confront them. When the deputy commissioner of the district ordered his troops to fire over the heads of the advancing rebels so as not to harm them, the rebels, misreading this act as proof they were indeed invulnerable, charged forward, and many then were killed. "They advanced on to our machine guns believing these things," wrote a British government official and historian, "and they continued to believe even after they were wounded."[40]

With the downfall and arrest of King Thibaw, British rule extended over the entire heartland of the Burman people, the undulating scrub country of the Irrawaddy river valley, the Arakan and Tenasserim coastal areas that the Burmans had from time to time invaded and claimed, and the Irrawaddy Delta area, which included Rangoon. Soon it further expanded over other territories outside these regions that had been little visited by Burmans. This vast frontier, amounting to over 40 percent of Burma's total area, was delineated by the high, rough, remote, jungle-covered hills that form a lopsided arc across the north of the country, from the Chin Hills in the west, northward to the Central Asian high-

land, and south and east to the massive Shan Plateau. The British presence was at first resisted, sometimes fiercely, but as time passed the hill
tribes came to regard it as protective. Non-Buddhist and nonliterate,
they had historically been regarded by the Burmans as backward,
whereas the British tended to romanticize them as being admirably
unspoiled by civilization—"men . . . free to live under their own natural
conditions," to quote one civil servant. Consequently, British rule in the
Frontier Areas, as they were officially called, left a light footprint: in the
entire Chin Hills, for example, an area larger than Wales, there were five
British officers.[41]

In outposts across the frontier territory, British officials adjudicated
in disputes between both individuals and tribes, doggedly toured the wide,
wild territories of their jurisdictions, and got to know the headmen and
villagers of the far-flung settlements, their dialects and customs, jungle
trails and mountain passes. The "jungle-wallahs," the British men who
worked in oil and timber and the mines, men who kept Burmese mis-
tresses and were not quite gentlemen, also led rugged lives, as did the small
clusters of missionaries who lived and worked across the frontier territories.[42] American Baptists in particular had long been a presence in Burma,
their first missionary having arrived in the country in 1812.[43] Established
in remote, self-sufficient stations, these missionaries were a hardy lot. Like
the British frontier officers, they were individuals who thrived in the relative isolation and hardship, and enjoyed the people with whom they had
come to live, and the wild, untamed land. The practical knowledge they
accumulated, of people and terrain, would be an asset to the struggle
ahead.

By far, the majority of European foreigners, however, lived in Rangoon.
While its foundation dated back at least to the eighth century, the bones
of the modern city had been laid by the British.[44] By the late 1930s, Rangoon
was a cosmopolitan metropolis of imposing Victorian buildings, tram-
lines, trading houses, and banks, as well as dockyards. It had smart hotels,
like the famous Strand, nightclubs and restaurants, Chinese gambling
clubs, cinemas, and leafy tree-lined neighborhoods with gardens and

gold, sweet-scented padauk trees.[45] Cars, bullock carts, and rickshaws shared the congested streets, which rang with the sound of motor horns and rickshaw bells.[46] Shops sold fashionable Western clothing, Western newspapers and books, even Western cigarettes and tobacco. Also thriving in Rangoon was a robust trade in practices collectively referred to as "vices"—gambling, opium use, and paid sex.[47] Overlooking this lively sprawl from its hilltop domain shone the magnificent, gilded Shwedagon Pagoda, the most sacred shrine in the country, and the most conspicuously Burmese feature in a city whose population and character was now overwhelmingly foreign—Indian, European, and Chinese.

While many in the rising Burmese middle class strove to adopt British speech, dress, and club practices, most did not. By the late 1930s, a new generation of young Burmans, mostly students of Rangoon University, was coming of age. Wholly familiar with Western fashions and values, they were neither in awe of them, nor felt themselves beholden to them, but rather looked toward a day when they would see their country's independence. A number of nationalist groups were formed, of which the Dobama Asiayone (We Burmans Association) would eventually prove most significant. Fractious and embracing a range of ideologies, its president proclaimed himself to be a "Hitler-dictator" and preached a doctrine of a Burman master race.[48] Claiming an honorific title traditionally used to address Europeans, Dobama members referred to themselves as "Thakin," or "Lord." The university became the hub of anticolonial movements, and the base from which frequent strikes and demonstrations were organized.

Back in the first years of the twentieth century, early Burmese nationalists had evoked Japan as a shining example of what a modern industrialized Asian nation could achieve. Japan's victory over Russia in the Russo-Japanese War in 1905 had demonstrated that an Asian power could defeat a European one. Allegedly, the first movie ever shown in Burma was film footage from that war, projected in the streets of Rangoon.[49] "The Japanese seemed to be the only eastern people that could hold its own against the West," wrote Thakin Nu, destined to be prime minister of independent Burma, "and we came to look confidently to Japan for leadership."[50] Alert to this sympathy, the Japanese scouted for likely leaders of a future nationalist uprising; Colonel Keiji Suzuki, posing as a journalist, made lengthy trips to Burma to this end. In late September 1940, one such young man, a twenty-three-year-old student named Aung San, made his auspicious arrival in Tokyo for what would be extensive military and propaganda training.[51] Japan also had a significant undercover intelligence network within Burma, and Japanese expatriates, mostly in Rangoon, working in a range of professions from barbers to prostitutes, quietly kept their ears to the ground, while other operatives paid for pro-Japanese articles to be placed in the local press.[52]

The construction of the Burma Road had done much to exacerbate racial tensions and resentment by opening the way for an even greater influx of foreign people and products. Its first convoy, of munition lorries, had set out from Lashio in December 1938, two months after the Japanese had captured Canton, China's last open port.[53] Officially, the road was for military use, yet by 1940, private traders eager to capitalize on the high prices that imported goods could fetch in Kunming and Chungking accounted for an estimated nine hundred to one thousand lorries on the road.[54] This booming trade also attracted Chinese merchants to immigrate to Burma, and soon lorries coming from China carried goods for this growing expatriate community.

Small, once-quiet towns in Burma were transformed into loud, sprawling truck stops and trading posts. By 1940, Lashio had become a munitions dump, with warehouses stockpiled with supplies that had come from Rangoon by rail and were awaiting transport across the border to China. It was also a boomtown, catering to the new flood of international traffic. Shops in Lashio were full of American goods, such as cans of Heinz and Del Monte products.[55] As one young British officer observed, Lashio was almost a Chinese-American town.[56] Driving west from Yunnan, a Chinese traveler recorded that "a 3-ton GMC truck from the United States cost about 3,500 rupees in Rangoon. The same vehicle would fetch 4,000 rupees in Lashio and as much as 6,000 rupees in Kunming." Awash in new money, the small town was now also plying a booming trade in prostitution, opium, and gambling. [57]

Adding another layer of tension was the new presence of hundreds of Chinese truck drivers. Along with reputations for being hard-charging men, they were also, relative to Burman villagers, very well paid, especially those employed by the Southwest Transportation Company, the partly private, partly government entity whose managing director was Chiang Kai-shek's brother-in-law. These drivers, the "biting dogs on the Burma Road," were proving to be highly attractive to local women in the Shan States near the border, a fact that caused much heartache and retributive brawling to follow in their dusty wake.[58] Like sailors who had lovers in every port, the truck drivers were said to have a concubine in every station along the Burma Road.[59]

How well did the Burma Road meet the military needs for which, at such high cost, it had been built? Early reports after the opening of the road in December 1938 were not encouraging. By April 1939, the only freight that had made the trip was a twenty-eight-ton trial shipment, and an estimated twenty thousand tons of munitions were reportedly backlogged on the docks of Rangoon. Light traffic, such as private cars, reportedly could make the approximately seven-hundred-mile trip from Kunming to Lashio in four days, but it was estimated that trucks would not be able to travel safely over twelve miles an hour.[60] Matters somewhat improved over time, and travelers' reports indicated that from the end of summer 1939, the road "worked more or less smoothly until the middle of 1940."[61] By this time, in the best of fair-weather conditions, the road could carry an estimated 250 lorries a day hauling an average of two and a half tons each—although a quarter of this weight was fuel for the journey itself. Moreover, a significant, if undetermined, proportion of this traffic was for private trade.[62]

By the end of 1940, however, the condition of the road and of the transport operation in general had seriously deteriorated. Rough road conditions had put many trucks out of action, and private trade had inflated freight rates to levels with which the Chinese government could not

compete.[63] Then there was the brutal reality of the driving experience itself. Two American travelers setting out in a Ford coupe from Kunming
to Burma in June 1940 found the road blocked by a crowd that had gathered at the cliff edge to observe a munitions truck lying overturned in a
stream far below. The travelers were informed that "in the three weeks
since the beginning of the rains, an average of three trucks daily had
been wrecked along the road," and the wreckage of broken or abandoned
trucks littered the route. The monsoon overtook the pair on their return
journey as they strained to race it to Kunming, with the lowering sky
turning black and clouds descending so low it seemed they could reach
out of the car window and touch them. When the heavens opened, the car
floundered through truck-tire ruts and potholes already three feet under
water. Eventually, a massive landslide brought all traffic to a complete halt,
and the travelers found themselves joining two hundred trucks queued
on the side of the road. A team of sixteen men equipped with four shov-
els was tasked with clearing the pile of soil and massive boulders that
rose thirty feet above the surface, and all the drivers resigned themselves
to a week or so of camping by their trucks.[64] Meanwhile, caravans of
mules, as many as four to five hundred together, continued to ply the old
trail.[65]

Relentless maintenance was required to keep the road even minimally
passable, and this came at a high cost. The American travelers passed one
road repair gang, "a group of fifteen or twenty men whose miserable appearance was appalling," as one of them described the small body of
forced labor. "They were scarecrows in rags. . . . [T]he wretched road gang
stared as we passed, their eyes dull as those of cattle."[66] In hard financial
terms, it was estimated that transport on the Burma Road cost over $925
a ton, compared to an estimated $200 a ton by way of the Kunming to
Haiphong rail line.[67] Of grave concern was the stunning fact that, due to
corruption and mismanagement, only an estimated one-third to one-
fourth of all goods loaded in Lashio arrived in Kunming; the rest was
peeled off for black market sale ahead of its destination or dumped in depots along the road.[68]

Nonetheless, from a practical point of view, the Burma Road was better than no road at all. More to the point, the epic story of its hardscrabble construction by the bare hands of Chinese peasantry served as a potent form of propaganda for Chiang's Nationalist cause and was widely covered by Western and especially American media. *National Geographic*, for example, ran a splashy feature that, while conceding this was not the all-weather road that had been advertised and omitting any mention of the levies of unpaid labor, was mostly full of praise. Although the *Geographic* team found the journey atrocious and were forced to turn back to Burma some three hundred miles short of their Kunming destination, the writer characterized the road as "the culminating achievement which has given China a front-rank place among road builders."[69]

INCREASINGLY, CHIANG KAI-SHEK WAS WORKING TO DRAW AMERICA CLOSER to China's cause. To this end, he possessed a number of important assets, one of which was his wife, Soong Mei-ling, a member of the brilliant, fabulously wealthy, and very powerful Soong family of Shanghai, whose patriarch had been an early and key supporter of Sun Yat-sen and the republican revolution. Educated in America, Madame Chiang was fluent in English and, like all members of her family, a Westward-looking modernist, and her mastery of English and experience with Americans made her an able agent in helping Chiang woo American support. Another potent asset was the large number of American missionaries who had worked in China and whose connections, particularly within the American media, did much to promote both Chiang, who had converted to Christianity, and China to the outer world, and especially to Americans.

As early as December 1938, the United States Export-Import Bank had enraged Japan by loaning China $25 million, which had been used in part to purchase two thousand three-ton Chrysler, Ford, and General Motors trucks and fuel destined for the Burma Road. Shipped in knockdown form, the trucks were assembled at a General Motors plant close by the Rangoon docks.[70] In 1940, the scale of American support jumped

with the news that a "reorganized" National rebel government was to be
established in Nanking under Japan's protection and nominally led by
Wang Jing-wei, a long-standing rival of Chiang's who had served twice as
the premier of China (and whom Chiang had attempted, but failed, to as-
sassinate).[71] Reacting to this development, Chiang had renewed his own
"unofficial peace feelers" with Tokyo, a move that succeeded both in stalling Japan's recognition of the Nanking government and in alarming Washington. Chiang's rationale, as he shared with the Americans, was that
he did not fear Japanese aggression so much as he did the "collapse of
[China's] national economy and society," its public morale, under the
weight of the Japanese blockade. China could not continue to fight Japan,
he declared, unless the United States gave substantial aid, including up to
one thousand aircraft and volunteer pilots. This was Chiang's first use
of what would be his habitual tactic of threatening collapse if the US did
not comply with his demands.[72] On November 30, 1940, the day on which
Japan formally recognized the Nanking puppet government, Washington approved a credit line of $100 million to China.[73]

By now, aftershocks of the war in Europe had been felt around the
world. Germany, Italy, and Japan had joined in a Tripartite Pact in September 1940, and in November Italian forces had invaded Egypt, a move
that presaged the coming North African campaigns. The fall of France
to the Nazis in June of the same year had brought swift consequences for
French possessions in Asia, with Japan soon making a formal "request"
to the French ambassador in Tokyo to close the border between French
Indochina and China. While awaiting a reply, Japanese troops moved up
to the Indo-Chinese border, and the Japanese navy entered the Gulf of
Tonkin. After a standoff of some months, the governor-general of Indochina capitulated, and the rail line from Haiphong to Kunming was terminated.[74] Similarly, to the north, the long and difficult Turkestan Road
from Soviet Kazakhstan was becoming dangerously tenuous as Moscow
edged toward a pact of neutrality with Japan.

The culling of supply routes only enhanced the importance of the Burma
Road, both to China and to its enemy. In June 1940, shortly following

the closure of the Haiphong line, Japan had extended a "friendly communication" through diplomatic channels to Britain, requesting a halt to the flow of supplies into China by way of the Burma Road. Fully preoccupied with its air war with Germany, and recognizing, as Churchill put it, that Britain "could not afford the Japanese navy being added to the German and Italian," Britain somewhat complied, and from July through September of that year the road was closed to the transport of "munitions, aeroplane parts, and petrol."[75] The three-month period of the road's closure fell squarely within the five-month-long monsoon and its annual delivery of some seventy-five to ninety inches of rain, a period of incessant landslides and mired vehicles. Although it had little practical effect, the event was hugely significant, indicating as it did that Japan had the road in its gunsights.

In late February 1941, at Chiang's request, Roosevelt's economic adviser, Lauchlin Currie, traveled to China to advise on the country's economic situation—and to inform the generalissimo that the US would be delivering $45 million worth of military equipment.[76] In the course of his trip, Currie met and interviewed numerous members of Chiang's cabinet and other officials, generals, and military personnel, as well as Communists and resident foreigners, and on his return to the US he submitted a report of his investigations to the president. A united Chinese front against Japan would be hard to achieve, he reported, for Chiang's hatred of the Communists did not spring from an ideological antagonism but from the fact that "the Communists have been the only group that he has not been able to buy off, absorb, liquidate or suppress," and the only party "which has been able to attract mass support." The generalissimo's attitude to his own people was "purely paternalistic" and undemocratic, and "he has little faith in the ability of the people to govern themselves." Even those loyal to him were "disillusioned, discontented and discouraged." The economy was worsening, and a culture of fear of being spied on was so great that Currie had been able to get "virtually nothing from an interview in which there were two Chinese present," and meetings were only fruitful when he could get one person alone, in which case the interviewees "would draw their chairs closer to mine and their voices would fall almost to a whisper." Censorship was severe, with the result that faith in the press had been largely lost. The economic situation had "reached a dangerous state," with unmanageable inflation having a serious social and political effect. Of great significance, given the recent pledge of $45 million for war matériel, was the fact that "a very important segment of Chinese military strength is not being used to prosecute the war against Japan" but against the Chinese Communists. Currie's subsequent conclusions and recommendations amounted to a blueprint both of American policy toward China throughout the war and of the pattern of optimistic disregard for known facts that attended it, and are worth quoting at length:

> I think Chiang can be held in line with a little care and attention from America. His attitude toward America is compounded partly of sentiment and partly of self-interest. He admires America, and particularly you [FDR], tremendously, and to be treated as an equal or ally would mean a great deal to him. . . . He is most anxious that China be regarded as a "democracy," taking part in the common world struggle for democracies. From the point of view of self-interest he is relying almost entirely on American help in the great work of post-war reconstruction. He reverted to this topic again and again. He bears much resentment toward the British. I think it most important, in addition to giving material aid, to go out of your way to say nice things about China and to speak of her in the same terms now used toward England. . . . One of the most effective ways of encouraging China and deterring Japan would be to go out of our way in giving evidences of friendship, close collaboration and admiration for China. This can be done both overtly and through "inspired" stories coming out of Washington. Since China really is a dictatorship, the character of Chiang Kai-shek himself is a prime desideratum in our foreign policy. . . . China is at a crossroads. It can develop as a military

dictatorship or as a truly democratic state. If we use our influence wisely we may be able to tip the scales in the latter direction.[77]

On March 11, 1941, the US Congress approved the Act to Promote the Defense of the United States, informally known as Lend-Lease, a program by which the US offered to manufacture and supply defense articles and matériel to "the government of any country whose defense the President deems vital to the defense of the United States."[78] The immediate and primary recipient was the United Kingdom, but in May Roosevelt approved the pledged $45 million for China, and two weeks later the first Lend-Lease shipment—three hundred two-and-a-half-ton trucks destined for the Burma Road—was on the way from New York to Rangoon.[79]

The ensuing shopping list of military equipment requested by China soon raised concerns in Washington. A case in point was the demand for thirteen-ton light tanks that, as was repeatedly pointed out, could not cross most bridges in Burma or China.[80] The recognition that it would be desirable to establish an American liaison team to advise on Lend-Lease equipment and monitor its use led to the formation of the American Military Mission to China (AMMISCA) under General John Magruder, whose stated duties were to "[a]dvise and assist the Chinese Government in all phases of procurement, transport, and maintenance of materials, equipment and munitions," and also "to advise and assist . . . in the training of Chinese personnel in the use" of these.[81] Additionally, in April, the Roosevelt administration authorized sending one hundred Curtiss P-40B Tomahawk fighter planes and pilots recruited from all branches of US military services for the defense of China. The pilots of this newly formed American Volunteer Group, having resigned their military commissions, sailed from San Francisco not as combatants but as "tourists." Arriving in Rangoon in September 1941, they traveled by train up to the Burmese town of Toungoo, where an RAF base on the edge of the jungle had been made available for their training.[82]

On December 7, 1941, Japan attacked Pearl Harbor, maiming the US Pacific fleet and bringing the US unambiguously into the war. Global events now moved with lightning swiftness. The day after the bombing of Pearl Harbor, Japan invaded the Philippines, Guam, and Malaya. On December 11, the Axis powers declared war on the United States.

Given Burma's strategic geographical position, natural resources—including rice—and, above all else, control of the Burma Road, it should have been obvious that Burma would soon be a target of Japanese aggression, yet its government had made few preparations for defense. An attack was one thing, actual invasion quite another, and the complacent view of those responsible for defending Burma was that the country was well protected by geography. Until the fall of Malaya and Singapore, and with them the loss of two of the British navy's most powerful battle vessels, an attack on Burma from the sea was deemed unlikely. Burma's geography, it was thought, would give protection from invasion by land, for mountainous terrain and dense and unexplored jungles lay between Burma and all bordering countries—two of which, Siam and Indochina, being neutral states.

In Burma, the civil administration undertook some preparations, such as hanging blackout curtains in Rangoon, but without much conviction. The first blackout practice filled onlookers with admiration for the beauty of the city now bathed only in moonlight. "[A] wonderful sight to behold indeed," recalled a British resident. "All the traffic naturally came to a standstill, with their lights off. . . . It was difficult to imagine war."[83] The attention of the European population, at least, had been riveted by the news of the Blitz from home, and throughout Burma fundraising events were being held to benefit victims of air raids in Scotland. Few measures were taken for an air raid on Rangoon beyond digging slit trenches along the road and in gardens. As General Archibald Wavell, Commander-in-Chief, India, was told by his superiors, "an attack in force on Burma was unlikely."[84] Unlikely or not, on December 11, Japanese planes bombed and strafed Burma's Tavoy airfield, which lay halfway down the long tail of the country's peninsular arm. Two days later, Japanese troops landed at Victoria Point, at Burma's southernmost tip. The Japanese, already in control of Vichy Siam across the border, now had air bases on Burmese soil.

THE JAPANESE AERIAL ATTACK ON RANGOON CAME OUT OF A FLAWLESS BLUE sky on the morning of December 23, 1941, when the city's streets were crowded with Christmas shoppers, and the new Excelsior cinema was about to play Bob Hope and Bing Crosby's *Road to Zanzibar*.[85] Air-raid sirens sounded the alarm, but instead of taking shelter, the untrained population went out into the streets to watch the air show. "It was all wonderfully exciting," according to one British official.[86] In fact, airpower available to confront the Japanese was negligible, consisting of a single RAF squadron, a flight of the Indian air force numbering some three "obsolete machines," and fourteen planes of the American Volunteer Group's Third Squadron.[87] Almost directly above the government's district headquarters, some six miles outside of Rangoon, two Japanese planes were brought down by direct hits from the ack-ack guns positioned on the grounds.[88] By day's end, five Japanese planes had been shot down, but an estimated two thousand civilians, mostly Indian, were killed, and almost as many wounded.[89]

Charles Haswell Campagnac, a former mayor of Rangoon, set out in his car for his office and found "the streets littered with Indian dead. . . . At several places on the road I had to stop my car and drag dead bodies to the side of the road to enable me to proceed." His son returned home that evening carrying a baby he had found abandoned on the roadside. Incendiary bombs set the flimsy wooden houses of the poorer neighborhoods on fire, and by evening a mass exodus from the city was underway. "The Burmans reacted very differently from the Indians," recalled Campagnac. "They took shelter in open drains and immediately the planes had passed over they went to their houses, packed their clothes and cooking utensils and started marching gaily out of Rangoon, to take shelter in the jungles." Passing a suburb to the west of Rangoon that afternoon, he found every house was already empty.[90]

Of the million or more Indians in Burma, well over half had been born in India, and their instinct now was to head for home. Over the next three days, tens of thousands of refugees—some estimates put the number as high as one hundred thousand—set out from Rangoon by rail and road for Prome, a town some 175 miles to the north on the Irrawaddy River.[91] Across the river, a jungle track wound through the Arakan mountains and over the Taungup Pass to the Bay of Bengal, from where it was possible to make eventual passage to India. That was the plan. But alarmed at the prospect of wholesale evacuation of Rangoon by its Indian population, who supplied almost all of the labor for the docks, as well as all municipal services—which now included building air-raid shelters and clearing the damage from raids—vigorous attempts were made to stem the exodus. Government officials and prominent Indians were dispatched to plead with the refugees to return to Rangoon, with assurances that once their duties were completed they would be safely evacuated in due order; these pleas were bolstered by orders to local officials to prevent people from crossing the river. The majority of refugees did comply and returned to Rangoon to await further directives.[92]

The aerial bombings resumed on Christmas Day. Setting out from her home for the hospital where she worked as a volunteer, Scots-born Jean Melville looked across her parents' garden to see "about 30 or 40 Japanese planes flying to the north of our house" and heard the sound of artillery and bombs. Dashing into the trench that had been dug for shelter, her household watched the planes and ominous puffs of smoke. The servants were out in the garden, she recalled, and the *mali*, or gardener, stubbornly continued his watering of the plants until the last minute, when he dashed for the safety of the trees—a small shard of memory that conjures the startling incongruity of war, the settled domestic peace of tended lawns and gardens, and the indiscriminate menace that would efface them all. [93]

An evacuation center was set up on the Rangoon racecourse and the Burma Athletic Association football pitch, where entire families waited for ships specially sent from India to collect them. During January of the new year, some seventy thousand Indians and many European women and children successfully made the voyage to Madras or Calcutta, escaping the murderous chaos that was descending on Rangoon; a "Defence Ordinance" prohibited male Europeans from leaving without explicit permission.[94]

Southeast Asia seemed to be unraveling. Hong Kong had fallen to the Japanese on Christmas Day. In January 1942, Japan invaded the Dutch East Indies, Borneo, and Vichy Siam. From Siam, Japanese land forces crossed the border into Burma and closed in on Moulmein, the second largest port city in Burma. On the last day of January, Moulmein fell, unleashing another wave of panicked refugees, who struck west to the coast and north to Rangoon.

In February, British Malaya fell to Japan, then Singapore, the bastion of British naval might, after only a week of fighting, shattering the last shard of any illusion of Britain's protective imperial power. The threat to Rangoon, the terminus of China's sole remaining outside line of supply, greatly alarmed Chiang Kai-shek, and he offered to send his crack German-trained Fifth and Sixth Armies for the defense of Burma and the road, dependent upon certain conditions being met by the British. For a number of reasons, the offer was received with a qualified response from General Archibald Wavell, who was also responsible for Burma. Wavell had been promised significant reinforcements drawn from across the British Empire, and he also had grave concerns about the difficulties the British command would face in being solely responsible for supplying a large Chinese force, which was one of Chiang's conditions. The Chinese armies typically lived off the districts in which they were stationed and were furnished with no supply, transport, or administrative services, or even infrastructure.[95] A further consideration was the history of virulent racial tension in Burma that had been exacerbated by the Burma Road and the fact that Burmese government ministers opposed having an army enter from China, a historic enemy that claimed ancient territorial rights across their border.[96] Finally, Wavell shared the robust skepticism of seasoned American observers about the abilities and reliability of Chiang and the Chinese military.[97]

Above all else, however, the British response was predicated on a reluctance to believe that Burma could fall. Eventually, Wavell accepted the offer of Chiang's Sixth Army, which was already stationed on the Yunnan-Burma border, less one division, but suggested that the Fifth should remain in Kunming, to where many observers, including Chiang, believed the Japanese might next be tending.[98] A Chinese "army" was roughly equivalent to a weak British division, or about seven to nine thousand men. Of these, only some three thousand were armed with rifles, and a couple of hundred equipped with light machine guns.

In his eventual, much-criticized dispatch, Wavell would state that "it was desirable that a country of the British Empire should be defended by Imperial Troops rather than by foreign."[99] But the blunt fact was that the British Empire had few troops in or available to Burma. In the whole of Burma, there were only eight hundred British soldiers and two brigades of the hastily raised Burma Rifles, which were afflicted by lackluster leadership, a dearth of battle experience, and a contentious recruiting policy that drew on the hill tribes to the exclusion of Burmans.[100]

James Lunt, who served as a young British second lieutenant with the Burma Rifles, recalled the tedium and humdrum routine at his undermotivated garrison, where officers complained of not having time to shoot snipe and tigers, the principal attractions to them for being in the country.[101] "During those two months before war came to Burma in 1941 I can only recall two occasions when my battalion actually practiced jungle warfare," Lunt wrote. During the second of these occasions, while conducting night exercises in the rain, the unmistakable growl of a tiger was heard. As a man, the columns of hill-tribe troops—the Kachin and Chin and Karen—turned inward toward the jungle and the growling, rifles drawn. In a panic, the commanding officer raced forward shouting, "Stop!" in Hindustani, realizing that if the tiger broke cover, "one half of the battalion would be shooting at the other." Soon the tiger "went bounding down the middle of the column, taking a swipe at the CO as it passed," and on into the darkness. The second-in-command was found sheltering in a buffalo wallow, and that was the end of night practice.[102]

In terms of Britain's needs in fighting a war that now had many fronts, Burma came last in the long line of those requesting equipment, supplies, and manpower. First were the forces defending the British homeland, followed by those in the Middle East, then those in India, then those in Malaya. Anything left over had to be divided between West Africa and Burma. Few of the many promised reinforcements were ever sent. Belatedly, the military authorities now recognized the desirability of a much-discussed jeep road from northeast India to Burma, connecting, in the original grand scheme, with the existing Burma Road. In January 1942, preliminary work was undertaken on the Indian side of the border, and food supplies for the necessary labor were stashed in stages along the route— supplies that would prove to be vital, but not for their intended purpose.[103]

IN EARLY JANUARY, GENERALISSIMO CHIANG KAI-SHEK, NOW THE SUPREME commander of the Allied China theater, had requested of President Roosevelt that a high-ranking US officer be dispatched to serve as chief of his Allied staff. Characterizing the requirements for this position, Chiang made the curious suggestion that the officer "not be an expert on the Far East. . . . [M]ilitary men who have knowledge of Chinese armies when China was under war lords, operate at a disadvantage when they think of the present Chinese national armies." This request was interpreted in Washington as suggesting that Chiang wanted an officer in Chungking who would unquestioningly accept what he was told.[104] This unenviable position was declined by the first candidate approached, but eventually, at the urging of General George Marshall, chief of staff of the United States Army, was accepted by Marshall's close friend Joseph Stilwell, a fifty-eight-year-old career army officer who, far from having little experience in the Far East, had lived in China and spoke Mandarin Chinese.[105]

On March 3, 1942, Stilwell, promoted to lieutenant general, briefly met with Chiang before flying on to Kunming, following the route of the Burma Road from the air.[106] He already wore several hats. In addition to being one of two chiefs of staff to the supreme commander of the China theater, he was commanding general of the US Armed Forces, of which there were few, in the hastily formed China-Burma-India Task Force, or CBI—an acronym that was swiftly repurposed to stand for Confusion Beyond Imagination. Of paramount importance to Chiang, Stilwell was also supervisor of Lend-Lease. His mandate from Washington was to "increase the effectiveness of U.S. assistance to the Chinese Government for the prosecution of the war and to assist in improving the combat efficiency of the Chinese Army." If in Burma, it was understood he would work to increase the capacity of the Burma Road.[107]

The straightforward tone of Washington's directives masked an astounding disregard for what were by now established facts about China's military will and preparedness. In the autumn of 1941, the AMMISCA had arrived in Chunking, and Magruder at once dispatched two officers to inspect the frontline activity and training in the war areas around the city. The ensuing report offered sobering observations that threw cold water on any illusion that Chiang's armies were fighting the Japanese. "No contact between Chinese and Japanese troops at the front was observed," the report read. "The interest of the Chinese towards any aggressive action appears to be quite negligible, regardless of their statements that all they need is airplanes, tanks, and artillery in order to drive the aggression from their shores."[108] Reporting independently, one senior American officer described Chiang's true motives: "Many small things all pointing in the same direction have caused me to have a feeling stronger than a suspicion, that the desire of the Chinese for more modern matériel was not . . . for the purpose of the war against Japan," he wrote, "but was to make the Central Government safe against insurrection after diplomatic pressure by other nations had forced Japan out of China."[109] In other words, when other nations, by force of arms and diplomacy, had driven out the Japanese, Chiang's army could use the massive stockpile of American matériel to fight against would-be usurpers. Chiang's greatest fear was of the Communists, but he was wary, too, of other warlords and factions that could unite against him. The battle Chiang was prepared to fight, then, was not for China but for his own power.

Japan's original plans for Burma had been limited to two main objectives: the seizure of Moulmein and its airfield near the mouth of the Salween River, to protect the western flank of the Imperial Japanese Army entering from Siam, and the sealing off of Rangoon, which would put a stop to all supplies destined for the Burma Road. For internal control of the country, Japan had counted on exploiting the restive, nationalistic elements already in Burma and inciting them to throw off the shackles of colonialism.[110] Alert to this danger, the Burma government had arrested and jailed influential nationalists whom they suspected of complicity, or potential complicity, with the Japanese.[111] Nonetheless, fifth columnists were embedded throughout the country, and when Rangoon was bombed it was remarked how accurately Japanese bombers targeted key assets, such as firms importing and delivering Lend-Lease trucks to China.[112]

The swift success of Japan's southern advance throughout the Pacific following Pearl Harbor, and its uncomplicated attainment of its modest objectives in Burma, prompted a recalibration of its ambitions. On February 9, new orders were issued to Japan's Fifteenth Army to occupy "important cities in central Burma," including Rangoon itself, and, moving further north, the town of Toungoo, the oil fields of Yenangyaung and to Mandalay, the capital of Upper Burma.[113]

In Rangoon, the official word to residents had been "to stay put." In late February, a motion was made in the Burmese Senate to adjourn to Mandalay—but the counselor to the governor quashed this with assurances there was no danger of the Japanese entering the city. Mere days later, on February 28, in a startling about-face, the government posted the order for evacuation of everyone except essential workers.[114] But by now, authorized or not, a mass disorderly exodus of terrified civilians was already underway, with thousands of individuals and families pushing, pulling, or driving any kind of conveyance—carriages, rickshaws, a horse-drawn hearse, perambulators—that could be piled with possessions. Many high-ranking or wealthy Indians had already left by boat for India, and the exodus now was mostly of the poorer class—the small merchants, the urban and dockyard laborers—that formed the backbone of the working city.

Swaths of Rangoon had been destroyed by air raids, but it was the collapse of civic order, the looting and arson, that held the most horror. Such remnants of order as remained were due to the efforts of one of Burma's two alotted prewar infantry battalions, which patrolled the streets shooting and arresting looters.[115] But the growing disaster overwhelmed all efforts, and throughout the city and suburbs looting was rife—of shops, of homes, of people and cars traveling the roads. On the docks, all was mayhem. "I do not think there was one single sober man anywhere," an observer wrote. "The crews of the boats alongside and the troops had looted cases of liquor. . . . It was impossible to board one boat as there had been a riot amongst the crew in which bottle[s] containing tear gas had been used as missiles."[116]

Gaolers and wardens fled, and the order was given to empty the central gaol and mental hospital of their inmates, since there was no longer means to care for them. Driving alone at night through the city, Leslie Glass, an Indian Civil Service officer who had worked on the Frontier, had a punctured tire and, by the light of the burning buildings around him, got out of his car to change it. A "macabre sensation of being watched" made him look up to see a group from the asylum watching him vacantly in the flame-light, an apocalyptic vision that came to haunt him.[117] "I can find no excuse for the Burma Government in not having the women and children from the Mental Hospital sent by steamer to India," Campagnac, the former mayor, recalled.[118] The young Indian Civil Service officer responsible for the decision to empty the prison and asylum shortly afterward took his own life. "I know I made a bad mistake," he had written in a last note. "I thought I was doing the right thing. I am . . . ," and the note trailed off in despair.[119]

Howling packs of feral dogs roamed the shuttered city, and birds of prey scoured the streets for carrion. A volunteer group was dispatched to kill all dangerous animals in the Rangoon Zoo, which had been deserted by its keepers. Tigers, panthers, and snakes were shot, while the harmless animals like deer were released to take their chances.[120] Longtime residents took last, wistful looks at their homes and the possessions they were leaving to looters. "[T]he curtains were blowing in the breeze—the pictures, covered with dust, still hung on the walls," wrote a British resident. "I cannot describe the feelings that came over me as I left all our treasured possessions in that house—things of such great sentimental value to us— things we had collected during 32 years of our married life."[121]

On the last night before Rangoon fell, Government House, the grand symbol of the authority and might of the British Empire in Burma, was all but abandoned. Governor Reginald Dorman-Smith and two aides remained, along with the cook and head butler from a staff that had once numbered 110 servants. Two journalists from London also remained to observe the last days of the old order. After a desultory dinner, the group retired to the billiard room, which was lined with photographs of the past governors of Burma, whose assured expressions seemed a reproof. The suggestion was made that these portraits should not be left to the Japanese, and one of the party let fly at them with a billiard ball. Others followed, and the result, as Dorman-Smith reported to a friend, "was a massacre."[122] The next day, they all departed by train for Maymyo, a summer hill station some four hundred miles to the north where the government had temporarily retreated.

The majority of the remnant population was mostly male British officials and volunteers who had managed to send on their families, and the city's significant population of Anglo-Burmans, who were caught, as so often, between their two ethnic identities. No plans had been made for their evacuation, and although they regarded Burma as their home, the Burmans did not want them. Writing with pride for his fellow Anglo-Burmans, Campagnac noted how many stuck to their posts as Rangoon fell, providing essential services to the end—"post and telegraph, at the water pumping and sewage stations; at the wireless stations, in the police and railway," he recorded. "Nearly all the Indian and Burman employees

of the railway had deserted but the Anglo-Burmans kept the trains running to the last."[123]

Captain Nadir Tyabji, who was in Burma as a representative for Tata
Oil Mills, an Indian firm, and had traveled extensively throughout Burma
until the outbreak of war, recalled the "grim options" available to the
majority of Indians and other foreigners, namely "whether to stay back
and make peace with the Japanese or risk the hazards of a trek some hundreds of miles with wives and children."[124] No one was sure who was friend
and who was foe. The Burmese, it was rumored, were celebrating the
Japanese victories.[125] Would they turn against their longtime neighbors—
the Indians, the British, the Anglo-Burmans, the Anglo-Indians, the
Chinese—with physical acts of violence? Would they betray the departing
refugees to the Japanese invaders? No one knew how events would turn
out. Driving the panic were the many reports of acts of barbarism that
had followed Japan's victories, from the infamous rape of Nanking in
1937 to the fall of Hong Kong only two months earlier.

ON MARCH 8, THE JAPANESE ENTERED RANGOON, HAVING MET WITH NO RE-
sistance, and without pause continued north. Now civilian refugees and
retreating soldiers alike were caught in a race to stay ahead of the rapidly
advancing enemy. Traveling by lorries and bullock carts, but mostly on
foot, the majority of refugees once again headed north and west to Prome,
then onward for a hundred miles to the Taungup Pass, which gave access
to the Arakan coast and the swiftest means of passage to India. Already,
bodies of people broken by exhaustion and hunger lay beside the road;
outbreaks of cholera had erupted in some of the camps along the route.
Once at the coast, escape depended on getting a boat to the small town
of Akyab, from where ships could complete the passage to India; but the
launches could carry only a thousand people a day, and even before the
final evacuation of Rangoon, there was a backlog of twenty thousand
refugees frantic for passage.[126] In an attempt to manage the evacuation,
the lone official on duty issued boat tickets to women and children so as

to get them out first, an initiative that was blunted by the crowd's entrepreneurial instincts. Many women sold their tickets to men and then re-
applied for others, while some men set themselves up as brokers, it being
known that the wealthier among them would pay any price to get out.
Once boats arrived, a mass stampede ensued, the strong trampling the
weak, who were crushed underfoot.[127]

The route to the coast through Prome was well known, by report if not
by actual experience, but as the Japanese advanced, panicked refugees
were driven farther north and into unfamiliar parts of the country. A
network of hastily improvised escape routes had been established by the
British authorities, and evacuees received directions as to which road,
river, path, mule trail, or jungle track could be followed to India. "[P]am-
phlets and maps were distributed showing the places of halt, evacuee
camps, availability of free rations etc.," recalled Krishnan Gurumurthy,
whose father worked for the Burma railway. As a young boy, he set out
with his family for India from Toungoo, an old, distinguished town on
the Sittang River, north of Rangoon; the base for the RAF and the American Volunteer Group aviators had been nearby, until they had evacuated
to an airfield farther north shortly before the fall of the city.[128] Business
contacts gave his father the use of a car, with which the family traveled
north for the first stage of their exodus, amid the confusion of refugee
and military traffic, to Maymyo. After resting a few days, the family—
father, mother, grandmother, six brothers and their sister—struck out
for the Naga Hills, traveling by ferry, bullock cart, and on foot through
dense forest. The family met up with a group of Sikhs going the same
route who banged drums as they walked to frighten off the wild animals
of the forest. Seven days trekking, with little food and less sleep, brought
them to the next stage of the journey. "Many unfortunate evacuees per-
ished by the way side. There was no one who cared to remove the corpses
of the dead," Gurumurthy recalled. "I can vividly remember holding my
father's hand and asking him how far still to go. He used to point at
some flickering light and say that was it. I, of course, believed him."[129]

Belatedly, the British command in Burma, now headed by General

Harold Alexander, saw the value of Chiang's offer of two armies.[130] Despite mutual mistrust, and with each party unconvinced that the other was prepared to fight, Alexander and Chiang were in agreement that, now that Rangoon had fallen, the best option available was to take a stand for Mandalay, the capital of the old Burmese kingdom, in Upper Burma. It was agreed that they would attempt to hold a line about 150 miles above Rangoon, with the British holding Prome on the Irrawaddy River, and a division of the Chinese Fifth Army holding Toungoo on the Sittang River. Chiang's Sixth Army was to stay north in the Shan States to guard the border with Siam, while the other two divisions of the Fifth Army were to enter Burma as far as Mandalay.[131]

Chiang had a great deal at stake. The two armies he was committing, ragged as they were, represented his "crack units," and if they were defeated he would have nothing with which to confront a Japanese advance on Yunnan and up the Burma Road to Kunming. His British allies had done a bad job of defending their colonies and had been defeated in all the actions they had fought so far in Burma and in the Southeast Asian arena. The Americans, too, had fared badly in Guam, the Philippines, and Wake Island—yet he was now entrusting his best forces to these same Allies to save Burma. With great misgivings and much obfuscation, he informed General Stilwell that he was giving him command over his Fifth and Sixth Armies. However, General Tu Yu-ming, in command of the Fifth, reportedly stated to Governor Dorman-Smith at the same time that *he* was in charge of the Chinese armies in Burma, "Ah, your Excellency, the American General only thinks that he is commanding. . . . the only way to keep the Americans in the war is to give them a few commands on paper." (In her diary, Lady Dorman-Smith noted: "There seems to be some confusion as to who is really C.-in-C. of the Chinese armies as various Chinese Generals arrive and say they are. And Stilwell says he is and [General] Alexander thinks he is. So it is all very muddling.")[132]

On March 19, the Japanese attacked Chiang's best Fifth Army division at Toungoo, nearly encircling them and the town. For twelve days the Chinese troops, led by General Tu, fought courageously before being ordered to break out and retreat; their battle for Toungoo represented the longest defensive stand taken by any party fighting for Burma.[133] With the capture of Toungoo, the Japanese also captured documents revealing that the main Chinese forces were just south of Mandalay. With the monsoon now looming, the Japanese revised their operational plans one last time and raced for Upper Burma.[134]

Advancing in three parallel lines—up the Irrawaddy Valley, up the Sittang toward Mandalay, and by a back road toward the Shan States and Chinese border—the Japanese, shadowed always by their aerial bombers, methodically overran and destroyed Burma's fragile bamboo-and-thatch-built towns. Magwe, where the Allied air forces had temporarily taken refuge; Yenangyaung and its oil fields, which the British blew up as they retreated, fighting in 114-degree heat under "a vast, sinister canopy of dense black smoke" over days without water;[135] Mandalay, whose graceful, ancient buildings were shattered by Japanese bombers—a city, it was said, it had taken a thousand years to build and an hour to destroy; Mauchi, with its wolfram mines—up and up the Japanese advanced, driving Allied forces before them.[136]

Burma was lost. On April 25, Stilwell and the British generals met in a small town to the south of the wreck of Mandalay. Taking measure of the situation, General Alexander gave the order for the imperial troops to retreat to Imphal in India and be kept as intact a unit as possible for what might be a battle for India itself. On April 29, Lashio—the head of the Burma Road, as well as an important center of Allied command—also fell, with its Chinese defenders simply melting into the hills.[137] For them, as for the British and Indian forces, the only recourse now was to escape from Burma. The Sixth Army, over which Stilwell had lost whatever control he had ever really had, was already heading home.[138] The Fifth Army, with the Japanese advancing to their east, found itself cut off from retreat to China.[139] Ill-supplied and possessed of little knowledge of the country in which they were stranded amid an increasingly hostile popu-

lation, Chiang's crack army joined the tens of thousands of panicked civilians running for their lives to India.

Central to the Allies' contingency plans in the event of the loss of the
Burma Road was the town of Myitkyina, where a small airfield was being
built. In early February, the US War Department had prepared a memorandum examining alternative supply lines to China. Noting that the
"Chinese Government is backed by a large, loyal, and experienced native
Army," it envisioned a number of implausible, complicated scenarios in
which supplies would be carried by rail from Calcutta or Chittagong to
Assam in northeast India, close to the border with Burma, from where
they could be floated on rivers, or carried over an old pack trail, or flown
by air to Myitkyina, and then taken by air to Kunming.[140] Local people
and military planners alike had faith that, even in the kind of crisis that
would see the loss of the Burma Road, they could count on the survival
of Myitkyina. Lured by promises of air transportation that could whisk
whole families and their possessions over the mountains and above the
jungle to India or China, the tide of refugees, now tens of thousands
strong, surged north to the town.

"[W]e had been on the run for over two weeks," recalled Stephen Brookes
of the erratic path he had traveled as an eleven-year-old boy with his English father, Burmese mother, and brother and sister from their home in
Maymyo to Myitkyina. "There was nothing north of Myitkyina except two
tiny border outposts. Beyond them were the snow-covered mountains of
Tibet and China. You did not need to be a clever adult to realise that once
we were in Myitkyina the game was up."[141] When the family at last arrived
in Myitkyina in the late evening of May 4, the Japanese were some seventy-
two hours behind them. Overhead, Japanese planes continuously strafed
and bombed the town.

On the following morning, an army jeep carried the family to the last
operational airfield in in the country, a single runway set in an open
plain surrounded by scrub and jungle some distance outside the town.
Thousands of refugees were already waiting, and the Brookes family was

informed that when a plane did arrive, the coveted seats on it would go to the first forty people who could scramble on board. Evacuation by air had been ongoing since April 7, with uneven and unpredictable success, as there were few planes available for refugees.[142]

The Brookes family waited with the other refugees all day under a cloudless sky, but nothing appeared overhead except white paddy birds. Disconsolately, they returned under the stars to Myitkyina, whole sections of which were now on fire; then at dawn they set out for the airfield again.[143] They could not have known it, but both the Chinese-American CNAC airline and US Army Air Forces planes had ceased operations the day before, fearing damage to their aircrafts by the frenzied mob of evacuees.[144] An immense crowd was already at the field, pointing toward the west. Minutes later, it was possible to make out the silhouette of an RAF two-engine Dakota, or DC-3. "Suddenly the even-tempered crowd was transformed into an aggressive mob," Brookes recalled. Fighting through the crowd, then carried by it as if by a tidal wave, he was borne toward the plane, the propellers of which continued to spin, ready for takeoff in the event the enemy appeared. Embedded in a crowd of adults who towered over him, young Brookes lost his bearings. "Suddenly, above the clamour of voices, I heard the aeroplane engines roar," he recalled. "There was more dust and the smell of petrol as the crowd began to plunge back and forth in desperation, and I knew I had failed."[145]

Rejoining his family, he huddled with them in the scrub at the edge of the field so as to escape the sun. Lying on the rough grass that surrounded the airfield, squinting into the cloudless sky as he searched for the sight of another plane, Stephen chanted to himself again and again, "I wish I could fly away. How I wish I could fly. . . ."[146] Time passed, and another RAF plane appeared. Again, the frantic crowd surged forward. Troops materialized to restrain them, while half a dozen stretchers were gently loaded onto the aircraft. The airmen on board were shouting that only women and children would be taken, but men still fought and struggled to join them. Amid the turmoil, suddenly, another Dakota landed. Racing toward it, Brookes found himself beside the wing, where an air-

THE BURMA ROAD 49

man was leaning down to grasp his hand. Safety was at last literally within reach—but from somewhere behind him, above the cries and turmoil of the crowd, he heard his mother screeching to him not to go. Paralyzed, he allowed the crowd to push him aside. The plane door was closed, the engines roared, dust swirled, and the plane moved on.

As it did, another plane with an unfamiliar profile appeared low in the sky, headed for the field. Slowly it banked to the left, revealing under the wings the two red disks of a Japanese fighter. Terrified refugees scattered in search of safety, blundering against one another, while from above machine-gun fire raked the ground. There were sounds of bombs exploding, and Brookes turned to see the two Dakotas, still on the runway, take direct hits. Racing for the shelter of the scrub, he joined his family and thousands of others who had come to the airfield with their fantasies of safety. The Japanese planes returned again, and then again. "[T]owards evening a bomber appeared over the airfield and blasted the runway," Brookes recalled. "The earth heaved when the heavy bombs went off, signalling what we had always feared: the airfield was now closed for further business."[147]

The official report eventually prepared for the British government on the evacuation of Burma noted that, on the morning of May 6, a Japanese reconnaissance plane had flown low over the airfield "with a red flag waving from the pilot's cabin," which was afterward interpreted as a warning sign of the attack to come—"a pleasing instance of humanity on the part of the enemy."[148] Apparently not everyone had seen it or understood its import. Japanese ground troops were now nineteen miles away, with no defensive force whatsoever between them and Myitkyina. For the tens of thousands of people stranded on the shattered airfield, the only remaining possibility of escape was an overland trek through the jungle and mountains of the Hukawng Valley, a path so arduous, as the official report noted, that "civilians who were not thoroughly fit were advised to remain in the town and take their chance with the Japanese rather than risk the overland routes."

By now, the horrors of the overland treks were well known. Yet, by and large, arduous as they were, most routes had been stitched together from bits and pieces of passages—by road, by river, by trail—that in ordinary times were fairly well traveled. The route through the Hukawng Valley was of an entirely different order. A vast, almost circular, jungle-covered pit of some 150 miles in circumference, the Hukawng Valley embraced all the major rivers, which combined to form the mighty Chindwin. Sparsely inhabited even by the rugged hill tribes, the valley was one of the wildest places in Burma, rarely entered by outsiders and still unexplored. It was known that, just beyond the valley, jungle paths led over the twelve-thousand-foot-high Patkai Range, which formed the border between Burma and Assam, but this was a journey that few had attempted.[149]

Refugees who, like the Brookes family, were now confronted with this last chance of escape, were parents carrying babies, grandparents, children, mostly city dwellers, people who, unlike the Frontier officers, were not outdoorsmen, nor athletic, nor remotely equipped for such a venture. Those who had clustered on the Myitkyina airfield had come with the expectation of being flown to safety; many women were dressed in summer frocks and high-heeled shoes or their best finery, by way of carrying possessions they valued out of the country.[150] "That is the reason why many women ultimately arrived in such flimsy garments," recalled one volunteer who trekked from India to help in their rescue. "[A]nd not a few were found dead at lonely spots in the Naga country, clad in the fine evening gowns which in happier times they had purchased in London, Calcutta or Rangoon."[151]

On May 12, the monsoon broke early. "The day before the road had been dry and firm but now it was a treacherous skating-rink of churned up brown slush," Brookes recalled.[152] Overnight, small streams were transformed into thundering flash floods, and the jungle, its great arboreal arms laden with rain, seemed to lean forward to assert itself. Within its green heights, the steaming humidity soared; the earth became sodden, the valley itself a vast swamp. Suddenly, the refugees were made aware that the silent trees through which they had trundled or trudged were teeming and fecund with malevolent life—malarial insects that stung and buzzed; sand flies that tortured the face, eyelids, ears; leeches that dropped with the silence of owls from trees to infiltrate even tight clothing and batten on starving bodies; the ticks that carried scrub typhus, the flesh-eating red ants, the bloodsucking dim-dam fly, which appeared at the most pleasant times of the day, when morning mists had cleared and evenings had become cool. Within this universe of jungle, it was made plain: life had evolved with an utter indifference to mankind.

Already refugees were dropping beside the trail and dying in the little makeshift jungle shelters that were their last refuges. Their disintegrating bodies, the stench of these, or a gleaming skeleton picked clean by ants remained to terrify those who struggled on. At the head of the Hukawng Valley was Shingbwiyang, a small frontier outpost with a handful of thatched bamboo huts, from which a young political officer, assisted by six or eight armed police, administered the local Kachin and Naga tribesmen.[153] At this obscure settlement the different escape routes from various parts of Upper Burma converged; some forty-five thousand civilian refugees, as well as thousands of soldiers, would pass through.[154] From Shingbwiyang, too, ran the known trails to India. "Bad as was the road to Shingbwiyang, it was after that point that the real trouble began," according to the official report.[155]

Beyond the outpost a track of red clay ran up, over, and down corrugated ranks of mountain ridges, encased in a tunnel of jungle so dense that the sky could not be seen above it. As the rains fell, the clay became heavier, stickier, deeper. Slogging thigh-deep in this morass, a strong man could advance perhaps as much as seven miles a day;[156] but few refugees were strong men, and two miles a day was as much as many could muster.[157] On the mud-slick slopes, going uphill or down, it was hard to get a footing, and so people crawled. Worst was to fall face down in mud; after this happened two or three times, the weaker gave up and lay where they had fallen, preferring to die.[158] "[W]e saw elderly men and women standing weeping at difficult corners which they had not the strength to round," a refugee recalled of advancing up a three-thousand-foot-high ridge. "[S]oon it was the same thing again, people weeping from weariness and despair and then the dead. One pair we saw where the elderly man had just died and his younger companion was wrapping himself in his blanket as we passed, to die in the same place."[159] Every hundred yards, unburied corpses lay in the mud beside the trail, or on the trail.[160] In deep mud, sometimes waist-high, people stumbled over concealed rocks and roots, and what seemed to be sandbags but were only more bodies of the dead.[161]

The veil of rain that dulled and reduced the visible world was occasionally pierced by startling, thrilling moments. "I heard the evocative call of a solitary gibbon," Brookes recalled. "He was perched in the trees of an adjoining ridge not far from two flame-of-the-forest trees which were ablaze with red blossoms. They looked like iridescent coral reefs in a calm sea."[162] In other circumstances, under fair skies, the majestic valley offered unparalleled beauty—an unimagined luxuriance of plant life, a profusion of birds and butterflies that seemed the stuff of dreams. But encountered on this death march, even the languid, gauzy butterflies were sinister. As big as plates, they flocked to the fallen corpses, blanketing them like white shrouds, and fed; then, when disturbed, rose with a humming and whirring of wings.[163]

From the raging Namyung River, which could rise or fall three feet within an hour, a three days' march brought the refugees to the foot of the Pangsau Pass.[164] Here, at last, they received the first glimmer of salvation. Coming over the pass from Assam, the Indian Tea Association planters had mobilized all their resources for rescue, clearing the trail and setting up a string of camps, often overseen by their wives, that offered food and shelter for this last leg of the journey. At the start of the evacuation, in early May, the association had been warned to expect some "9,500 Indian and 500 European food-eating persons," and had supplied the camps accordingly.[165] However, from May 18, the day they received the first refugees, until July 31, when the camps were ceded to military authorities, the Indian Tea Association counted 20,344 evacuees whom they conducted to safety.[166]

Haunting cameos stand amid the catalog of suffering: former Rangoon mayor Charles Campagnac practicing with his pistol in the jungle because he and his wife had decided that, rather than allow their daughter to fall into Japanese hands, "I would shoot her";[167] eleven-year-old Colin McPhedran's dying mother sitting in the jungle rains beneath a tree and telling her son, "[I]t is your duty to leave me";[168] the unnamed British officer who, as Rangoon fell, helped keep the road leading out of the city clear for traffic and was last seen shouting "Cheerio" at the departing trucks, "left standing there," according to an eyewitness, "for who can say what fate."[169]

Most people involved in the relief and rescue efforts agreed that "down to earth" women—tough, resourceful, and collected—proved to be the best candidates for survival.[170] As one tea planter summed it up, "[S]urvival was not a matter of brawn, but of determination and common sense. Those who could keep their matches dry and could light a fire, those who washed their stinking bodies and their dirty socks, those who started the day's march at sunrise and walked unhurriedly until midday and then camped—those were the people who survived."[171] For Stephen Brookes, the secret of surviving the monsoon was to submit to the rain, as animals do: "Fighting the monsoon led to exhaustion—whilst trying to stay dry led to insanity. The answer was calm acceptance. It was as simple as that."[172]

The official report of the evacuation conceded the impossibility of giving an accurate account of how many civilians accomplished the journey from Burma to India, by any route. Relying in part on the numbers of refugees formally received in Calcutta, the report concludes that a conservative estimate would be 400,000.[173] How many others died was even more difficult to conjecture. The official report concluded, "[A] death roll of even 10,000 would be sufficient evidence of a tragic nature of the whole wretched business," but this figure is generally believed to be greatly understated.[174]

Essentially, the population of Burma that was not wholly Burmese had attempted to leave. The fates of those foreigners who did not succeed in leaving varied greatly. Maureen Baird-Murray, age nine and of Burmese and Irish descent, was at a convent school in the Shan States when the

Japanese invaded. After Japanese officers inspected the convent and its occupants, the Sisters and their three remaining students were told they were allowed to stay but had to learn Japanese and the "Kimigayo," Japan's national anthem, and were caned if they made mistakes. But another Anglo-Burman woman to whom the convent gave shelter was beaten with rifle butts and marched out at bayonet point to an unknown fate.[175] In the town of Bhamo, in Upper Burma, many Indians were forced to work as laborers, unloading and carrying stores from the supply boats on the river, but were not otherwise ill-treated; others in the same area were allowed to go on their way and eventually arrived in India.[176] From Kyaukpyu in the Arakan, Japanese officers allowed some twenty-three thousand Indians to depart for India in specially chartered boats, and there seemed to have been an effort to treat the Indians well as "fellow Asiatics."[177] Yet at Waingmaw, a village near Myitkyina, Japanese soldiers rounded up Chinese, Indian, and Burman men, women, and children, tied their hands behind their backs, and bayoneted them.[178]

In the 1930s, Burman soldiers fighting for the rebel wizard priest had coolly walked into enemy fire, trusting in the magic power of their amulets. In a similar manner, the British had placed their trust in their own long-trusted talismans of power, entities that it did not seem imaginable could fail them. Now the Burmese people had witnessed the British Empire make a ragged exodus from their country in what was the longest retreat in Britain's own long military history.[179] The government in Burma, including many Burmese ministers, had departed the country to establish headquarters-in-exile in Simla, a hill station in India, to wait out the war. The sole British presence remaining in the country was at Fort Hertz, a remote military outpost in the extreme northeast. As for the Burmese people, yet another imperial power now controlled them. Japan, their new conqueror, offered promises of independence, but these, as events would soon reveal, were empty.

Among the many memories that would haunt those who survived the treks from Burma, was the sound of airplanes constantly droning overhead. These were not, as the refugees feared at the time, enemy aircraft.

Rather, these were Allied planes conducting food drops for the refugees and carrying supplies to China.[180] "The Japanese may cut the Burma Road," President Roosevelt had declared in April 1942, "but I want to say to the gallant people of China that no matter what advances the Japanese make, ways will be found to deliver airplanes and munitions of war to the armies of Generalissimo Chiang Kai-shek."[181] The remaining ways to be found were now extremely limited. The Japanese had long ago sealed off China's coastline. The only rail line into China was in Japanese hands. With the loss of the Burma Road, all practicable land routes to China had been terminated. In short, access to China by sea and land was closed—there remained only the air.

3

THE AIR

M an had only very recently scratched the face of heaven. The Wright brothers' first motorized heavier-than-air machine had hopped some ten feet off the earth in 1903, but something close to heaven's heights had not been attained until 1910, when Jorge Chávez, a young Peruvian man living and working in Paris, completed a record-breaking high-altitude flight to 8,127 feet above earth.[1] And from the earliest tentative dreams of flight, a military use had been envisioned. Writing in 1842, Tennyson had allowed his imagination to dip "into the future" in his poem "Locksley Hall" and saw

> . . . the heavens fill with commerce, argosies of magic sails,
> Pilots of the purple twilight, dropping down with costly bales;
>
> Heard the heavens fill with shouting, and there rain'd a ghastly dew
> From the nations' airy navies grappling in the central blue.

In reality, too, the armies of various nations had been quick to explore the new technology's military use. The US War Department had commissioned air pioneer Samuel Langley to build a man-carrying aircraft as early as 1898, and it was the British Army that had developed Great Britain's first powered flight machine in 1908.[2] Even hydrogen balloons, the precursors of heavy air machines, had been put to military use, with the first operational flight made in France in 1794, to overview the disposition of Austrian enemy forces. In a similar vein, in 1910, the Mexican government hired a group of international stunt pilots to make reconnaissance flights south across the Rio Grande to spy on rebel-held territory.[3]

And it was military innovation that gave flight technology a great, accelerating boost. During World War I, aircraft did more than seize the heights to surveil the enemy. For the first time, "aeroplanes," or "planes," were used as "fighters"—called "pursuits" in the US—and early fighter pilots carried an array of weapons, such as handguns that they fired at close range, or grenades that they lobbed onto enemy forces on the ground. Some pilots trailed grappling hooks behind them to snare the propeller of a pursuing enemy.[4]

By the end of that war, air technology was less quaint and had made fearsome advances. These included the first heavy bombers, like the German Linke-Hofmann R.I, produced toward the end of the war. Powered by four Mercedes DIVa engines, it had a wingspan of 138 feet and a propeller diameter of 23 feet—still the largest that has ever been used in flight—and was capable of carrying loads of nearly nine thousand pounds. "Pursuit" planes became more sophisticated, being faster and more powerful and fitted with better guns; the Dutch-designed Fokker D.VII could climb over sixteen thousand feet in fourteen minutes, twice the typical rate of ascent.[5]

Yet, despite such advances, when the Great War ended, there was no consensus about the virtue of investing in the development of airpower. Every nation had its passionate advocates, but on the whole the military establishments remained unconvinced; the exception was Germany, but by terms of the Treaty of Versailles it was forbidden to develop an air force and was compelled to destroy existing military aircraft. The value of airpower had been proven, but so had its vulnerabilities and limitations. Bombing campaigns had failed in their two main objectives of lowering enemy morale and disrupting industrial production.[6] The slow-moving bombers, moreover, had been easy prey to the new fighters, while field cannons and artillery had more reliably inflicted targeted damage to the trench lines, and at vastly less cost. Now in peacetime, only limited use of aircraft was envisioned. In Britain and France, military aircraft were mostly used to survey and police remote tracts of their empires, or repurposed for civilian life to dust crops and carry mail.[7]

The US had entered World War I with air capabilities that lagged behind those of the European nations. The military's dedicated aviation arm, the US Army Air Service, was a section of the Signal Corps, the military communications system established during the Civil War, indicating that its envisioned role was the old one of spying out the enemy and serving as courier—more carrier pigeon than combat arm. Although America had pioneered flight, national and military indifference stalled its development, with the result that no American-made planes were deemed fit for combat operations, and throughout the course of the war American pilots had flown aircraft bought from French and British allies.[8] American pilots, on the other hand, despite their late entry into the war, had held their own, flying more than thirty-five thousand hours over enemy lines.[9]

After the war, the US military, like its European and British counterparts, was divided as to the future role of airpower, with the "old guard" claiming that "an Air Force acting independently can of its own account neither win a war at the present time, nor, as far as we can tell at any time in the future." To its advocates, on the other hand, airpower was "not a new weapon—it constitutes a new force, as separate from land power and sea power as each is separate from the other."[10]

Outside the military, however, an enthusiasm for aviation swept the US. Stunt flying had briefly been popular before the war, and now a fleet of surplus military aircraft, along with thousands of young men minimally trained as pilots but who had not earned wings in time to reach the front, spurred the return of this form of entertainment on a grand

scale.[11] Thousands of wood-and-canvas biplanes made for military training, the Curtiss JN series, or "Jennies," originally produced at a cost to
the US government of $5,000 a plane, were now widely available for $300
each.[12] An unemployed pilot could pick up his own plane along with
bargain-priced spare parts to scrape a living barnstorming across the
country. Public imagination had been captivated by the novel role played
by fighter pilots in the war, and the daredevil "ace" had become a highly
glamorous figure. Stunt pilots capitalized on this new glamour—ironically,
given the military's ambivalence to airpower—performing and adapting
"combat maneuvers" for rapt crowds, and the most popular air shows
cultivated military themes. The annual Miami air show, second only to
the National Air Races in importance, even adopted a military-sounding
name: the Miami All-American Air Maneuvers. Here, pilots performed
mock air battles over miniature, custom-built cities, and, for added effect,
roped in old dirigibles, bombers, and antiaircraft batteries.[13] Meanwhile,
the military strove to prove its aviation arms had value in peacetime, and
Air Service and Air Corps pilots and planes served as forest rangers, border patrollers, crop dusters, and aerial surveyors and mappers, and for a
limited time, less successfully, to deliver mail.[14]

While skeptical of the need for a distinct air force, the militaries across
the globe nonetheless advanced aviation technology significantly throughout the 1920s and early '30s, creating air machines that flew faster, farther, and higher, and were capable of carrying heavier loads than had been
imagined during the last war. Infrastructure supporting long-range aviation also advanced, including for passenger services, especially in the
US, and airdromes with paved runways, night lighting, navigation aids,
and even air traffic control towers were now scattered around the world.[15]
In Germany, development of a civil aviation industry that employed former military manufacturers and airmen allowed the nation to skirt the
terms of the Treaty of Versailles and keep abreast of advancing aviation
technology, while popular flying and glider clubs trained the next generation of pilots. By 1932, the Deutscher Luftsportverband, or German Air
Sports Association, had over fifty thousand members.[16]

The Japanese military, and most especially its naval arm, had closely followed the pioneering accomplishments of the West, and, at the end of World War I, advisory missions from France and then Britain were invited to Japan to advance aviation training and technology. For the Western powers, the chief incentive in going to Japan was the opportunity to cultivate a lucrative market for their own aircraft.[17] But against this complacent expectation, the Japanese proved to be not merely good students but dazzling innovators, and by the mid-1930s, Japanese firms like Mitsubishi had designed and produced the most cutting-edge fighter planes in the world, with all parts—engine, metal sheets and tubing, propeller, instruments—made in Japan.[18] Ironically, one of the spurs to this swift advancement was a treaty that Japan had been pressured to sign that placed limitations on her construction of warships. This, the London Naval Treaty of 1930, inspired the Japanese navy to look to airpower to make up for its deficient strength at sea.[19]

IN CHINA, MEANINGFUL INTEREST IN AVIATION, MILITARY OR CIVILIAN, came late. Throughout the tumultuous 1920s, with its ongoing civil warring among regional warlords, only sporadic attempts had been made to build a national air force, while a British attempt to create a limited commercial air service ended in failure.[20] Efforts were renewed at the end of the 1920s, with the Nationalists under Chiang Kai-shek having stabilized their power base in the lower Yangtze Valley, and in April 1929, the government partnered with the US corporation Curtiss-Wright and created the China National Aviation Corporation with a view to developing a variety of air services, from mail delivery to passenger airlines. Since China lacked wholly the necessary means and infrastructure—from manufacturing planes, maintaining them, training pilots—the intention was to outsource the services to American companies. This plan, however, drew howls of criticism from the Chinese military, who argued that foreign use of Chinese airfields and airports was an encroachment of China's sovereignty.[21]

The decade ended with little progress made and the government having proved unwilling or incapable of providing financial and political support. And yet, as many both inside and outside China observed, "commercial aviation could be of more value to China than to almost any other country in the world."[22] The vastness of China and the titanic features of its terrain—deserts that took weeks to traverse and impassable mountains—had contributed to the country's backwardness. Tribes living along the route of the Burma Road had not, in the whole course of their existence, seen a wheeled vehicle, even a cart, until the coming of the road builders in the 1930s. Madame Chiang Kai-shek, an ardent advocate for the development of aviation in her country, would recall trips she had made to remote areas as she accompanied her husband on his political tours, flying in mere hours to places that would otherwise have required weeks of dangerous travel by sedan chair. In one mountain settlement, she entered a world seemingly frozen in time, in which women were dressed in the style of her grandmother.[23]

Aviation promised to be the magic carpet that would not only carry people and commerce from place to place across the country, but also whisk the Middle Kingdom out of the Middle Ages. In July 1930, a new Chinese-American aviation venture was created, also called the China National Aviation Corporation, or CNAC, a commercial airline and limited liability share company jointly owned by American investors and the Nationalist government, with 45 percent and 55 percent ownership respectively; in 1933, Pan American Airways would acquire the American interest.[24] Over the next years, the airline developed a network of air routes across the country and the region, including to Hong Kong, Rangoon, and Hanoi. Additionally, the airline's connections with Pan American and Britain's Imperial Airways made it possible to travel to and from major cities of the Western world. Its most important route was a twice-weekly service from Chungking to Hong Kong, which, when Japanese fighter planes began to menace in 1939, was flown at night or in bad weather to elude them, thus making it one of the most dangerous routes flown by commercial aviation anywhere in the world.[25] "Airline flying by night over China has no parallel," recalled one pilot who flew this route.

"There are no intermediate fields, and there are no airway beacons. . . . Also no lighted cities. . . . Radio communications are restricted, weather reports almost unavailable."[26]

Nearly a year after the creation of CNAC, in the spring of 1931, the Kuomintang government held a National Aviation Conference in Nanking, with the object of creating a program to catch up China's military aviation with that of the rest of the world. The conference resulted in a number of plans and also overtures to the US government for assistance, but little of substance was accomplished.[27] Then, in January 1932, Japanese carrier-launched navy planes joined with ground troops to attack Shanghai in what has been called the first terror bombing of a civilian population, a campaign that caused the loss of thousands of civilian lives.[28] Watching the events from his hotel room window was George Westervelt, a retired US naval captain who was in China as a sales representative for Curtiss-Wright, one of America's elite aviation companies, and who seized the moment to write to the Kuomintang's minister of finance, Soong Zi-wen, familiarly known as T. V. Soong, who was also Chiang's brilliant and entrepreneurial brother-in-law. "I take it for granted," Westervelt wrote, "that the events of the last few weeks have sufficiently demonstrated the significance of air power as differentiated from lack of air power."[29]

While the US State Department, wishing to avoid antagonizing Japan, declined to show any interest in working with China to develop airpower, the Commerce Department did not share these scruples. In July 1932, Colonel John Jouett, who had both combat experience in World War I and had an administrative background in the Air Corps, arrived in Shanghai with a small training squadron. Over the next nearly three years, Jouett oversaw the development of airfields, hangars, barracks, machine and repair shops, engine-overhaul facilities and training, and established a rigorous and successful program of pilot instruction. And "[s]ince there seemed to be not the remotest possibility that the United States would ever become involved in a war with China," Jouett noted, "everything we had learned about military aviation was placed at the disposal of the Chiang Kai-shek government."[30] The effect of Jouett's outstanding success was to arouse Chiang's suspicion and jealousy of T. V. Soong for his control over what was developing to be the most potent military force in China. Disruptions followed, resulting in the removal of Soong from that particular office, to be replaced by the less threatening General Keh Ching-on, whom Jouett characterized as "completely ignorant and uninformed as regards aviation matters and not at all prone to ask for advice or listen when given."[31]

Several other developments killed Jouett's Central Aviation School and all its successes. In America, despite the national sympathy for China that had arisen following Japan's invasion of Manchuria in 1931, the revelation that Americans were instructing Chinese military pilots caused a furor. This and the fact that Jouett refused to participate in operations against Chiang's rivals prompted Chiang to lend a keen ear to overtures from the Italians to build an aircraft factory in China and to operate a cheaper flight training school.[32] Jouett's contract was allowed to expire, and the Italians came in. As a consequence, when in 1937 the war with Japan began, it was discovered that China had few planes and few able pilots to confront the invaders.[33] Madame Chiang, observing a night mission returning to the field from Shanghai one dawn, watched with horror as five of the eleven returning planes crashed on landing. "What can we do, what can we do?" she sobbed. "We buy them the best planes money can buy, spend so much time and money training them, and they are killing themselves before my eyes. What can we do?"[34] Chiang's hunger for airpower, and his inability to lead China in developing it, even with wave after wave of outside aid, would be one of the most potent elements of the US-China relationship in the years ahead.

IN LATE SEPTEMBER 1940, FRENCH INDOCHINA CAPITULATED TO JAPAN, AND the Japanese edged closer to Lashio and the railhead of the Burma Road, heightening concerns about the vulnerability of both the road and air routes over Burma. In November, the CNAC's unflagging operations manager, William Langhorne Bond, set out to surveil an alternative route to Kunming. After flying into Lashio, he traveled north by car and train up to Myitkyina in Upper Burma to discuss with British officials the possibility of constructing an airfield in the district. "They were all interested and cooperative, but they all seemed to think we were looking a very long way into the future," Bond recorded. "The idea that Burma could ever be occupied by the Japanese was 'most amusing.'"[35] Nonetheless, the idea shortly received official approval from the governor of Burma.[36]

Returning to Lashio to continue his reconnaissance, Bond boarded a CNAC plane and directed it north up the Irrawaddy Valley back to Myitkyina, circling the area so as to survey it with an eye to the prospective airfield, then flew due north beyond Fort Hertz, the most northerly British military station in Burma. Turning west, the crew flew over the Naga Hills at the Indian border to survey their height, climbing to nearly fifteen thousand feet, then turned east toward China. Passing over the fourteen-thousand-plus-foot-high Santsung Range on the Burma-China border, he then turned southeast to pass over the Likiang and Tali Mountains, so as "to establish their exact position and altitudes as our maps were quite unreliable," as Bond later reported. "[I]n fact [they] showed some of the territory over which we flew as unexplored and there had never been an airplane flown over this part of the World before." Flying above low winter clouds, the pilot had experienced mostly clear conditions, ideal for the survey. Turning northeast, he flew on to land in Chungking.[37]

"Little of definite value could be told from one flight," Bond recorded. "We know the country is high but can be flown in weather similar to what we had, but if the weather should be much worse, with bad cross winds or a bad icing condition, or if the tops of the clouds should be two or three thousand feet higher than we saw, then it would be extremely dangerous and costly and very nearly impractical."[38] This survey flight of November 1940, flown in good weather, represented the first flight over the terrain that would be called "the Hump."

Over the following months, Bond and CNAC continued to press ahead

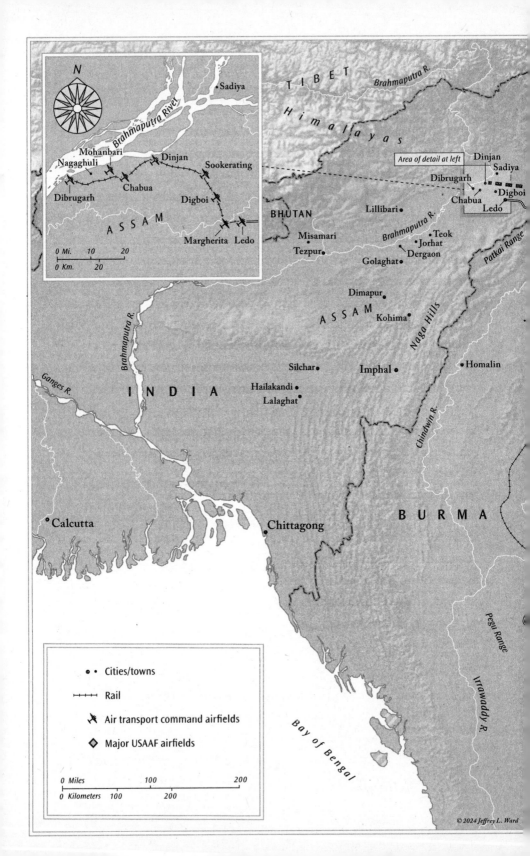

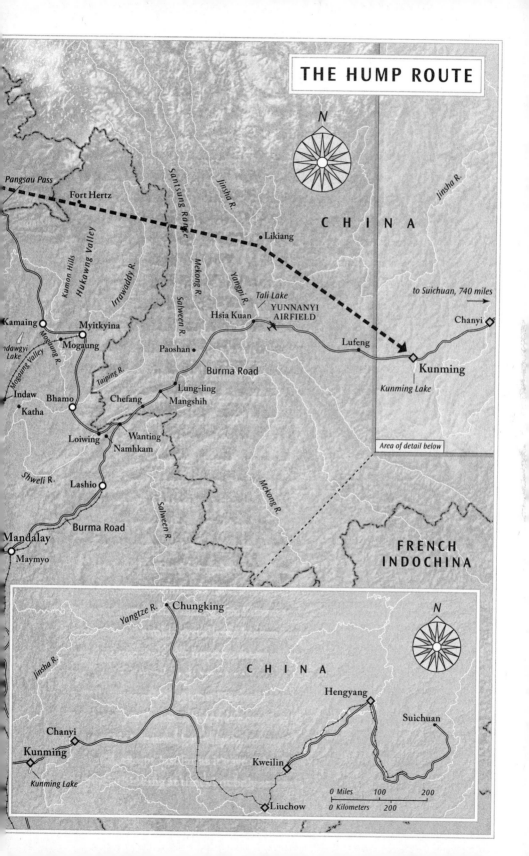

THE HUMP ROUTE

N

Pangsau Pass

Fort Hertz

Santsung Range

Jinsha R.

C H I N A

• Likiang

Kumon Hills

Hukawng Valley

Irrawaddy R.

Mekong R.

Yangpi R.

to Suichuan, 740 miles →

Tali Lake
**YUNNANYI
AIRFIELD**

Hsia Kuan

Kamaing

Myitkyina

Mogaung R.

Salween R.

Paoshan •

Lufeng

Chanyi

*ndawgyi
Lake*

Mogaung

Chefang

Burma Road

◇ **Kunming**

Mogaung Valley

Taiping R.

Lung-ling
Mangshih

Kunming Lake

Indaw

Bhamo

Loiwing •

Wanting
Namhkam

Katha

Shweli R.

Lashio

Salween R.

Mekong R.

Area of detail below

Burma Road

Mandalay

Maymyo

**FRENCH
INDOCHINA**

Yangtze R. • Chungking

Jinsha R.

C H I N A

N

Hengyang

Suichuan

Chanyi

Kunming

Kweilin

Kunming Lake

0 Miles   100   200

◇ Liuchow

0 Kilometers   200

with the exploration of an alternative aerial route, resulting among other things in a keen appreciation for how inaccurately terrain elevations were depicted on the available maps. In Washington and New York, CNAC and Pan American management met with Chinese Nationalist and State Department officials to discuss an aerial supply line—an aerial Burma Road—and presented optimistic calculations regarding the mileage, cargo tonnage, and number of planes that would be involved. While the Chinese emphasized an urgent need for more planes, Bond raised a more pressing shortfall—namely, of pilots. At that moment, he reported, writing in March 1941, CNAC had fourteen qualified pilots, and "beyond this, we have absolutely nothing, and we have no idea where we can even try to get any more." Acquiring aircraft for China in such circumstances, he wrote, "is like building air castles in a vacuum."[39] Beyond the concern to supply China, the need for a military air transport system with global reach was becoming increasingly apparent, and May 1941 saw the establishment of the US Army Air Forces Ferry Command to convey Lend-Lease planes to Britain.[40]

In the same month of May, Bond came to Washington to discuss in person the plans for China. He confirmed that all studies supported Myitkyina as being the best site for the western terminus of the new aerial Burma Road, with Kunming being the eastern terminus. Myitkyina had a good rail line, as he reported, and was north of all Japanese air bases. Bond had made careful calculations and suggested that thirty-five aircraft, preferably all DC-3s, would be required, and eight pilots would be needed for every five planes. He also had a solution for the pilot shortage and suggested that US military personnel could be released from active duty if they volunteered to fly CNAC's air cargo line—a suggestion that ignored the military's own looming need for pilots and particularly, in view of the creation of the Ferry Command, pilots for transport aircraft.[41]

Bond's report stands as the first blueprint for what would eventually become the military Hump operation. However, along with the litany of logistical facts and figures, Bond also issued a caveat. Any aerial Burma Road supply line, he disclosed, confronted inescapable difficulties.

> The country between Myitkyina and Yunanyi [an ancient town to the west of Kunming designated for airfields] is high and rugged and the country west and north of this route, where the freight planes frequently would be forced to fly during air raids, is even worse. The weather is usually bad and the country is notoriously windy. Winds of forty to seventy miles per hour prevail most of the year. In clear weather flights would have to be at altitudes of from twelve thousand to fourteen thousand feet. To the west and north of the course, but within seeing distance or about one hundred miles, are peaks and ranges more than seventeen thousand feet in height.

On the other hand, these natural hazards would deter Japanese planes and pilots, so they could be seen, as Bond put it optimistically, as "safety factors." And despite all the obvious dangers and all the difficulties inherent in running an aviation operation in China, as he proudly pointed out, "CNAC has shown, after nearly four years of such operations, that it can be done successfully."[42]

In late November of 1941, a year after Bond's first survey, CNAC made another reconnaissance flight, this one with an eye to the feasibility of a route that bypassed the need to land in Burma, from Assam, in northeast India, directly to Kunming. After some months of negotiations with British authorities, it was agreed that a small party of CNAC personnel that included Bond and CNAC's director, Arthur Young, who also served as a financial adviser to Chiang Kai-shek, along with a delegation of British air officers and diplomatic staff, would convene in Lashio for a surveillance flight. Bad weather delayed the arrival of two of the British officers coming from India, and as the rest of the party awaited them, stormy weather closed over Lashio. However, three days later, on the afternoon of November 23, the weather had cleared and the much-anticipated trip was able to proceed. "First flight" airmail stamps had been prepared for the occasion and were duly mailed from the Lashio post office before the plane took off in bright weather for Assam.

As the plane soared above Burma, passengers and crew looking down upon the deeply forested, rolling land could see occasional green streams in the jungle. Villages and the red roofs of small settlements appeared as the plane headed north, following the Irrawaddy Valley up to Myitkyina. As the plane flew toward Assam, the country below became rougher and wilder, more jumbled, with higher mountains to the north. Soon, the landscape leveled, and the party looked down upon the vast plain of Assam. The big plane landed in Dinjan, an airfield located in the tea-growing district of the Brahmaputra flood plain, and was greeted by an excited crowd of British planters.[43] Assessing the terrain with a professional eye, Bond was happy to observe that "[t]here was a large, level, open area of 2,500 to 3,000 acres there with no obstructions of any kind." Dinjan was also situated some fifty miles south of a garrison station at Sadiya, located on a tributary of the Brahmaputra River close by the Assam Bengal rail line, and so well-placed for river and rail transportation; it was, he believed, "perfect for our base for freight service over the Hump."[44]

After spending the night with friendly families of English tea planters, the party continued their reconnaissance the next morning. Climbing through clouds, they could see the lower Himalayas to the north and, in glimpses through the clouds, the first snow-capped mountains on the Assam border. The clouds, too, were mountainous, huge piled-up masses, and gave warning of the big storm that was moving in from Calcutta. Below, the Brahmaputra Valley narrowed and the mountains became higher, and soon the Irrawaddy appeared as a blue-black stream boiling in a deep gorge. As the plane crossed the snow-covered ridges ahead of the Salween gorge, the copilot came back to the passengers to urge them "not to move around" as the plane was going higher. He also took back to the cockpit three of the plane's four oxygen tanks; the DC-3 was of course unpressurized.

Flying at about fourteen thousand to fifteen thousand feet, the passengers looked down upon the mighty Salween—"a grand sight," as Arthur Young recorded. The sides of the gorge were so steep that it was mostly lost in shadow, even though it was about 1:00 p.m. and the sun was high above it. As the windows of the plane fogged with condensation, the river itself could be made out as a thin, black ribbon. As they turned east toward the Mekong, the weather cleared, enabling the pilots to avoid the necessity of flying higher; bare, rocky mountains appeared just beyond the window, and higher mountains, up to eighteen thousand feet, could be seen in every direction.

East of the Mekong, and they were soon over the Yangtze Valley, and villages and cultivated fields appeared, although on the far horizon there loomed the peaks of northern Yunnan, rising to some twenty-five thousand feet. The temple of Chang Tien, set in a broad valley, flashed gold below as the plane flew on among high mountains, over the gold-producing country around the River of Golden Sand. Descending, the plane landed at a high-altitude airfield in Likiang with the intention of rendezvousing with Joseph Rock, the renowned explorer of Tibet, whom it was agreed they would take on as a passenger. Dr. Rock, however, failed to appear, and after an hour, having received radio warnings of a storm coming into Kunming, the anxious pilots insisted on taking off. Bond and Young ran ahead to clear the rough field of local people who had gathered to see the novel sight, then jumped on board, and the plane barreled down the short track that served as a runway. Climbing through the thin air, the plane flew on toward Kunming, arriving just at dusk, and, as Young reported, "picking our way past the storms. It had been," he concluded, "a wonderful day."[45]

"The weather was perfect and we could clearly see the terrain along the entire route," was Bond's more succinct summation. "We flew at fifteen thousand feet. . . . It was beautiful scenery, but very discouraging from a safe flying point of view. Ranges and peaks in every direction were as high or higher than our flight altitude." Assessing the route, Bond and the other pilots concurred that "it would probably be a good candidate for regular service, with variations such as weather and other circumstances taken into consideration." This was the first flight made over the entire Hump route, from Assam, India, to Kunming. As Bond acknowledged, his party had experienced the route "at its best, but we could imagine it at its worst. That thought was not encouraging."[46]

ON DECEMBER 7, 1941, THE JAPANESE ATTACK ON PEARL HARBOR BROUGHT America forthrightly into the war and also gave the world yet another reminder of the unprecedented and still-evolving capabilities of airpower. Just over a week later, President Roosevelt signed an executive order for the control of civil aviation, authorizing the secretary of war "to take possession and assume control of any civil aviation system as deemed necessary for the war effort." Among other things, the order highlighted the military's reliance on commercial airlines for planes, pilots, crew, management, and operational infrastructure—and its own lack of the same. This reliance was reinforced when some months later Cyrus Rowlett "C. R." Smith, the brilliant president of American Airlines, was made a colonel in the Army Air Forces so as to direct its cargo-carrying operations.[47]

At the end of this same momentous month, events in Burma, as long feared, threatened the survival of the Burma Road. The Japanese seizure of the British airfield at Victoria Point in southern Burma, across the border from Siam, gave the enemy a base of operations on Burmese soil; two weeks later, Japanese planes bombed and strafed Rangoon. This direct threat to the source of all supplies destined for China galvanized further discussions in Washington about an aerial supply route, and, at the end of January 1942, T. V. Soong wrote an urgent memorandum that expanded on Bond's earlier proposal. "The Burma Road is placed in great jeopardy by Japanese successes in the South Pacific," Soong wrote.

To supply the Chinese armies and to sustain civilian morale to enable China to keep on fighting it is necessary that a new life line to China be opened.

Miraculously enough that new life line is conveniently at hand. From Sadiya, the terminus of the Indian Railways, to Kunming... is only 550 or 700 miles respectively, flying over comparatively level stretches. These alternate routes have been surveyed for year-round operations by Pan-American Airways which is ready to operate them, and the project has been declared feasible by the American military mission. All the necessary air bases are already established and in constant use.

Citing studies by CNAC, Soong went on to note that one hundred C-53 transport planes (which, like the C-47, was a military adaptation of the passenger-carrying DC-3) could carry a net of twelve thousand tons of supplies monthly, "working under usual service conditions." Thirty-five such planes had already been allocated to China (pulled from CNAC's passenger services) he noted, so only sixty-five more planes would be required. "There are of course competing demands for transport planes," Soong allowed, with a smooth nod to the demands of theaters of active warfare in Europe, Russia, North Africa, and the Pacific; the German capture of Crete in May 1941, in which troops had parachuted or landed from transport planes, had further underscored the desirability of possessing such aircraft and their still-unexplored potential.[48] Yet, Soong ventured to submit, "nowhere else in the world could 100 transport planes be placed to greater advantage for the cause of the United Nations."[49]

The following day, Soong was able to report to Chiang that Roosevelt's response to his memo was favorable; evidently the president had either overlooked or been wholly blind to the inherent difficulties of the "comparatively level" route described, the capacity of the DC-3, or indeed in finding one hundred planes.[50] The same day, January 31, 1942, events in Burma took an even more ominous turn when the important coastal town of Moulmein and its airfield fell to the Japanese.

Two days later, on February 2, 1942, the War Department also took a closer look at other possible aerial routes into China in the event that Rangoon was lost or became blockaded. There was now general agreement, as Soong had proposed, that Sadiya, near Dinjan in Assam, should be the western air terminus, given that it was linked by rail to Calcutta, Karachi, and Bombay—albeit by what one American adviser described as a "flimsy, one-track, meter-gauge affair."[51] "[O]ne or two more" airfields would be required, but in the meantime the airport at Myitkyina, envisioned as the eastern air terminus, was allegedly nearing completion. The many complications about transport of cargo from any of the named port cities to Sadiya—including the fact that different states in India used different gauges of rail—were not investigated closely. From Myitkyina, the plan called for supplies to be loaded onto barges and floated down the Irrawaddy River to Bhamo, from where they could be reloaded onto trucks for the long and rocky journey to Kunming along the Burma Road.[52]

On February 9, 1942, Roosevelt met with General Stilwell, who only two weeks earlier had accepted the commission to go to China as a chief of staff to Chiang Kai-shek.[53] "Saw the Pres. at noon for 20 minutes," Stilwell recorded in his diary. "Not too impressive. Just talk."[54] In fact, Stilwell had already met with Soong shortly before Soong's memorandum had been delivered to the president, and had been as unimpressed: "Dinner with Soong, Ch'u, Shên, Si. & 2 squirts from C.D.S. [China Defense Supplies]," he wrote in his diary. "Usual nonsense & froth about transport planes & crap."[55]

Only hours after meeting with the president, Stilwell joined with General Henry "Hap" Arnold, the chief of the Army Air Forces, and Lauchlin Currie, Roosevelt's economic adviser and now Lend-Lease administrator to China, to discuss the "aviation program."[56] The wheels in Washington were now grinding, and on this same day Roosevelt telegrammed Chiang Kai-shek with the news for which the generalissimo had been lobbying for so long: "We are rapidly increasing our ferry service to China," he wrote. "I can now give you definite assurances that even though there should be a further setback in Rangoon, which now seems improbable, the supply route to China via India can be maintained by air."[57]

Despite caveats from aviation professionals regarding the dangers of the proposed route, and despite ongoing reports from US personnel who visited China that there was no active Chinese-Japanese fighting front, the plans for an aerial Burma Road had acquired a momentum and life of their own. The oft-stated objective of the air ferry operation was "to keep China in the war" and, less certainly, to have a foothold in China from which to bomb Japan. Yet the vagueness as to how China's requested matériel was to be used indicates that Roosevelt's commitment to supply China by air was not directed by practical, military concerns, but rather by the recommendations set forth by Lauchlin Currie in his landmark memo: namely that "[o]ne of the most effective ways of encouraging China and deterring Japan would be to go out of our way in giving evidences of friendship . . . for China." This tension between the practical and symbolic purpose of the Hump operation was to persist throughout the war.

ON FEBRUARY 12, 1942, THE NEW TENTH AIR FORCE WAS ACTIVATED AT PATterson Field, Ohio, and shortly after assigned to India with the broad mission of establishing airpower in Asia. Specific objectives were to keep open the supply route between India and China and to prepare for possible offensive operations from China; additionally, should Stilwell so order, it would conduct missions from India and Burma.[58] On March 5, General Lewis Brereton assumed command of the force in New Delhi, "fresh from a series of defeats in the Philippines and Java," as the official historians of the Tenth put it.[59]

On March 6, 1942, the day after he assumed command of his new post, and still, surely, reeling from the tumultuous events only a little over a week behind him, Brereton wrote to General Arnold from the Cecil Hotel in New Delhi. An awareness of the audacious and daunting scale of the command assigned to him was sinking in. Apart from any other consideration was the fact that, with sea routes in the Mediterranean and Pacific closed, he was dependent upon a supply line thirteen thousand statute miles long, or a minimum of two months for each shipment from the US to India—no other military unit of such size was dependent on a supply line of such length.[60] Brereton's letter, however, focused on one particular element of his responsibilities: overseeing the aerial supply of China.

Although he had been only a week in India, it was evident, as he wrote, that the "air ferry route both to supplement or to replace the lower reaches of the Burma road is in itself an enormous problem." Fuel supply in Assam alone for the number of aircraft being discussed seemed "impossible of solution." Many new airfields had to be built, yet labor was scarce and "may become non-existent if the Japanese push to the north develops as their major effort." Furthermore, the monsoon season was approaching and, as he noted, "in the greater part of the area under consideration, the wet season rainfall is as heavy as any place on earth." Finally, although charged with organizing the new air force and the ferry command, Brereton had absolutely no idea what staff or even how many planes he would have with which to work. It was, he wrote, "essential that I receive as soon as possible, the most complete plan as to what is intended by the United States in the way of air and ground forces in India for the next year." His earlier six messages had so far gone unanswered.[61]

While Brereton fretted in New Delhi, plans for the India–Myitkyina ferry route ground ahead. In Assam, RAF engineers began work expanding the Dinjan airfield and building an airdrome, while in Myitkyina the new airfield was said to be approaching conclusion. In the US, the newly formed 1st Ferry Group, assigned to air supply of China, departed Charleston, South Carolina, on March 19, 1942, aboard the SS *Brazil*, a luxury cruise ship that up until some weeks before had catered to the tourist trade between the United States and South America.[62] The five thousand troops and medical personnel on board had not been briefed as to their destination, or their eventual duties, but had been instructed to pack every single personal item they would require for a year, down to socks and shoe polish, including clothing for every type of weather.[63] They had arrived in Charleston just as the stevedores had gone on strike, leaving all supplies, from jeeps to generators, stacked on the docks beside their ship and taking with them keys to all cargo-handling equipment. Thus the 1st Ferry Group's last hours onshore had been spent in sweating all the crates aboard by manual labor.[64] They were, so they were informed, an Air Corps Ferry Group, yet they had no aircraft; these were said to be flying over to meet them at their destination, and throughout the two-month-long voyage, daily bets were made as to where this destination might be.

The day after the *Brazil*'s departure, a distinct ferry command for the supply of China was activated. Pledged an allocation of twenty-five CNAC civilian transport planes, the Assam-Burma-China (ABC) Ferry Command was organized as part of the Tenth Air Force, which was in turn tasked with its protection.[65] Around the same time, an advance bombing detachment assigned to the new Tenth force, code-named Task Force Aquila, geared up for the long flight to India. Leading them was Colonel Caleb Vance "C. V." Haynes, a forty-seven-year-old bomber pilot of vast pioneering experience, and known as "the dean of the big ship pilots."[66] A big, imposing man, he was invariably characterized by admiring colleagues with references to forces of nature—"a big, hulking mountaineer," "Old Grizzly," a pilot who "looked like a gorilla and flew like an angel." Born in Mount Airy, North Carolina, he was of Chinese and Thai ancestry on his mother's side, being a grandson of Chang Bunker, one of the original Siamese twins.[67] Directives he carried in a confidential letter of instruction from Arnold stated that the Tenth's mission would be "to keep open essential lines of communication between India and China" and to be prepared for general offensive operations in the China area as may be directed later, and was cautioned that all movement of his force was to be conducted with the "utmost secrecy."[68] Although Haynes did not yet know this, at the heart of Aquila's formation lay a plan to bomb targets in Japan from a base in eastern China as part of a two-pronged retaliatory operation for the attack on Pearl Harbor. The second prong was to

be a carrier-launched air strike led by a Lieutenant Colonel James Doolittle. Without knowing the details, the Aquila bomber group had high
expectations of participating in a secret "dream mission."[69]

Serving as assistant executive officer to Haynes was Lieutenant Colonel Merian Cooper, who at age forty-eight had enjoyed successes as a
World War I bomber pilot, Pan Am executive, adventure traveler, screen-
writer, and Hollywood producer, including of the movie *King Kong*; allegedly, when he landed for the first time in Kweilin, China, he had exclaimed
on its "million dollar background."[70] Thriving on adventures, he had reportedly looked ten years younger when, relieved of the pressures of Hollywood, he approached the war zone.[71] At a party at his Beverly Hills home
in April 1941, Cooper had met a thirty-five-year-old Air Corps pilot named
Colonel Robert Lee Scott Jr., a flight instructor at the Cal-Aero Academy
in nearby Chino, California, who also moonlighted as a technical consultant and sometime stunt pilot for various Hollywood productions. Very
tall, handsome, and with an easygoing Southern manner, Scott was besotted with Hollywood, with flying, and with dreams of glory. Despite
his lack of combat experience and of flying a bomber of any kind, Scott
impressed Cooper, and with Haynes's support, "Coop" brought him onto
the Aquila team as executive officer. Scott would go on to write *God Is My
Co-Pilot*, a highly successful, if sometimes embellished, memoir of his experiences.[72]

On April 7, 1942, Haynes and his fleet of eight bombers and nine C-47
transports arrived in Karachi. "No one seemed to know anything," Scott
wrote of their reception on arrival. "Behind us lay twelve thousand miles,
which we had made in eight days—for what?" While Haynes flew on to
New Delhi to report to Brereton and present his instructions from Arnold, Scott and the rest of his crew remained jealously guarding their aircraft against being pulled into other service: behind their impatience
was the highly secret "dream mission" that had tantalized throughout
the long days of flight. "When we explained as much as we could about
our secret orders, smiles came to the officers' faces," Scott wrote of the

base personnel, who placed bets that the new arrivals would never leave with their aircraft.[73]

In New Delhi, Haynes was informed that the Chinese had lost the air base that was to have been used by the bombers and that the secret mission had been canceled. "We learned the worst when Haynes came back from Delhi with a face a yard long," wrote Scott. The "dream mission" was gone. There remained for Haynes and his team only the second part of the directives he carried to Brereton: "[T]o keep open essential lines of communication between India and China." The dispirited task force was ordered to leave the bombers in Karachi and take the C-47s up to Dinjan. Primed for a mission of military glory, Aquila's elite bomber pilots had been co-opted into the Ferry Command, falling in along with CNAC's civilian pilots as transport drivers.[74]

Haynes, now designated the commanding officer of the new Assam-Burma-China ferry, arrived with his team in Dinjan on April 23, 1942. The newly expanded airfield lay on a flat plain beside the Brahmaputra River, surrounded by jungle, and set within a horseshoe of formidable mountains. Visible to the north, 150 miles away, were the Himalayas, rising to over twenty-five thousand feet; to the east and south rose the Naga Hills. Breaking the jungle cover were the groomed, green swaths of the region's extensive tea estates, which had also provided the primary labor for the new airfield. The few operational buildings and all living quarters were modeled on local huts, or *bashas*, being long, narrow structures built from woven bamboo strips and roofed with palm fronds. Inside, set on dirt floors, were double rows of bunks shrouded with mosquito netting as defense against not only mosquitoes but the variety of creeping, slithering, flying wildlife that found its way within.[75] These *basha* barracks lay some ten miles from the airfield, requiring the men to rely on British ground transport to get to and from them. "Messing facilities were bad," to quote the Tenth's own history, "and the food, while sufficient in quantity, left much to be desired in quality."[76]

"When Colonel Haynes and I arrived in Assam we both considered ourselves 'shanghaied,'" wrote Scott. "I could tell, as we faced each other across the breakfast table that first morning, that things were going to be bad."[77] Given the hasty construction of the base and the ballooning crisis in Burma just over the border, the base was under-equipped, with no air defense or warning system of which to speak. Defense tactics entailed beginning the sixteen-hour working day at three thirty every morning and being airborne at dawn as the mist lifted, so as to avoid being caught on the ground in clear daylight by Japanese bombers.[78]

Two RAF squadrons, one of transport and one of pursuit, were already operating on the base. The international mix of officers were all "characters," according to Veronica Downing, who worked as a civilian cipher clerk at the base, which was near her home on a tea estate. Lieutenant Colonel William Old, serving as the base commander until the arrival of Haynes, had impressed his British colleagues with his Texan "drawl and pungent wit." Of a fighter pilot who had lost his nerve and was afraid to land, Old—a famously fearless pilot—had said, "If that goddam son of bitch don't come down, turn the ack-ack on." "Bats," a British officer, was "very immature," Downing recalled. "He used to go round, looking up in the sky, biting his nails saying, 'Where are my airqwarft' with a lisp." A South African pilot who had fought in the battle of Britain kept the love letters from his many girlfriends in his soft-topped RAF pilot's cap.[79]

Reflecting its improvised nature, the US transport operation encompassed a mishmash of personnel and planes. Haynes and his bomber pilots represented one component. Another was comprised of commercial airline pilots who had been drafted by the Air Corps when the American Military Mission to China had "requested" seventy-five captains from the commercial airlines; the co-opted pilots considered themselves to have been "kidnapped," not recruited.[80] Pilots of both groups, while experienced, had never flown in mountains or monsoons.[81] Joining these were the seasoned CNAC pilots who were familiar with the terrain and weather, some of whom had been dodging Japanese air assaults since the early days of the Japanese-Chinese war. Different numbers of planes had been allocated to the operation at different times, but the reality Haynes met with on the ground was a command strength of thirteen DC-3s, the majority of which had been diverted from service in Africa; two planes were temporarily out of action after failing to locate the Dinjan field, with one making a forced landing in a dried riverbed.[82]

To date, only one supply mission had actually been flown from Dinjan over the Hump. On April 9, William Old had led two battered DC-3s full of 100-octane aviation fuel over the fourteen-thousand-foot Kumon Mountains and on to Kunming; the fuel had been earmarked for the Doolittle raiders on their return to China (as it happened, none of the raiders made it to the Chinese bases).[83] But now, as the Japanese advanced at breakneck speed toward Mandalay, attention was diverted from China, and toward Myitkyina and other points in Burma. Thirteen hundred tons of gas and ammunition were piled on the docks in Karachi to be ferried to Dinjan, and in Dinjan seven hundred tons awaited transport to Myitkyina and onward.[84] Planes were leaving Dinjan with ammunition, aviation gas, and food, as Scott recalled, and "returning from Burma with our ships completely filled and overflowing with wounded British soldiers."[85]

Rumors of airlifts to the safety of India had lured huge crowds of refugees to the Myitkyina airfield, where in their agitation they milled around the many wounded brought for evacuation. "Those of us whose wounds or sickness were considered to require evacuation by air were taken down daily to the airfield where we were dumped on our stretchers to await the arrival of the aircraft," Lieutenant James Lunt recalled. "There was very little cover and no facilities whatsoever. The airfield perimeter was one huge latrine." In his diary, he jotted a few notes: "Aerodrome about 3 miles from town in jungle and still being built. Dry-weather 'runway' finished, 'all-weather' runway still uncompleted. . . . Foul day and bitterly cold . . . No planes came as flying conditions very bad."[86]

As the Japanese advance pressed north from Mandalay towards

Myitkyina, the air mission changed from one of supply to one of desperate evacuation. CNAC had already begun moving personnel from its base at Myitkyina to Dinjan, and on May 1, 1942, Haynes and Scott received unexpected orders to evacuate General Stilwell and his staff from Stilwell's headquarters in Shwebo some seventy miles north of Mandalay.[87]

"We flew through black storms all the way to the Mekong," Scott recorded of the flight from Kunming. "[T]hen, turning South, we found better weather, even if we were getting into Japanese-controlled skies. . . . I know that neither of us had ever been so careful at watching the skies." They were flying at almost treetop level, following the rail line from Mandalay. Columns of smoke ahead marked bombed and burning settlements and towns. "The smoke plume grew larger and blacker as we came nearer, until we could see the glow of the fires and the licking flames," Scott wrote. Spotting the field, Haynes "pulled the big transport around like a fighter," Scott recorded admiringly, "slipping her in and sitting her down like a feather-bed."[88] Shwebo had been bombed only minutes before.

Haynes left at once for Stilwell's nearby headquarters. Wafting from the burning town, the air carried the scent of smoke and burnt human flesh. Haynes shortly returned in a jeep, leaping out to report that most of the staff was behind him, but that Stilwell himself would not be going and intended to drive on to Myitkyina. With the plane loaded with some forty passengers, Haynes took off for Calcutta. "We could easily have taken from fifty to seventy," Scott observed. On arrival in Calcutta, Haynes directed another transport to Shwebo, and after quickly refueling he and Scott set out again. "Once again we ourselves flew through black rain across the Ganges into Burma," Scott wrote; "but when we landed we found that all had been evacuated except wounded British and American soldiers."[89] Stilwell and the entire company with him could have been flown to India, but Stilwell had already departed.

At the Myitkyina airfield, evacuations continued erratically, there being no schedule for flights; some planes that did land had been diverted at the last minute from other tasks. Sent to complete the evacuation of his company's headquarters, CNAC pilot Moon Chin landed to learn that the last of the CNAC personnel had in fact just left, and that the vast crowd of refugees surging toward him believed he had come on their behalf. Standing on the wings of the plane, Chin and his crew began hauling people on board, trying to select the elderly and the very young, and eventually squeezing seventy people into an aircraft designed to carry twenty-one. They were, Chin recalled, "[j]ust packed in there. Sitting on the floor. Standing up. Then we landed. We found when we opened the cargo door, we had another eight people packed in the cargo area."[90]

Days later, and two months to the day since it had departed Charleston, the SS *Brazil* tied up at the docks of Karachi, and the men of the 1st Ferry Group and ninety female nurses disembarked for duty. After a long wait under the glaring sky, the company was trucked some twenty miles inland through chaotic city trees and villages, and deposited in newly built barracks at the British-operated New Malir air base, on the edge of the Sind Desert. Dust from the desert covered everything—the ground, plants, buildings, and even, as they would discover, filled the air with a thick band of sand extending upward to over four thousand feet.[91] The next day, the exhausted, sweat-stained company learned that their intended destination had been Rangoon; but in the course of the long journey at sea, Burma had fallen.

The Japanese capture of Myitkyina and its airfield in one brutal stroke rendered irrelevant most of the carefully calibrated plans for the aerial Burma Road. All contingency plans for the loss of Rangoon and its docks, and southern Burma, had centered on Myitkyina. Nonetheless, Roosevelt had personally stated that an air route to China had to be kept open, "no matter how difficult," and had directed that "every possibility, both as to airplanes and routes," was to be explored.[92] Now it was clear there was in fact only one route available, and that was from points in Assam, over north Burma's forbidding jungle and high ranges, direct to Kunming.

Toward the end of June 1942, the very structure of the Assam-Burma-

China ferry operation, so painstakingly patched together, was dealt another blow. The Tenth's commander, General Brereton, received orders to depart India and take command of the Middle East air forces so as to support British forces under General Claude Auchinleck, following the Allied retreat to El Alamein. Brereton left New Delhi the day after receiving the order—in his diary he refers to a "quick getaway," suggesting he was not sorry to receive the new command—leaving his subordinate, General Earl Naiden, as the temporary commander, and also a trail of rumors involving attractive female stenographers and a too-close relationship with his married secretary.[93] Departing with him were the Tenth's heavy bomber units and several transport planes, along with the most experienced ferry pilots, all of which left his successor with a crippled air transport system, a bare-bones staff, and virtually no combat strength.[94]

"Bomb shell from Wash," Stilwell wrote in his diary on June 24. "Brereton to Auchinleck with B-17s & 24's. Temporary duty. Takes all our transport planes. Now what shall I tell the gissimo?"[95] The "gissimo" was Stilwell's shorthand for Generalissimo Chiang Kai-Shek. Two days later, Stilwell met with Chiang and Madame Chiang to break the news, and minutes of the meeting, both Chinese and American, record the generalissimo's bitter dissatisfaction and Stilwell's game attempt to reassure. At the end of the conference, as the American minutes record, Madame made a dramatic pronouncement. "The Generalissimo must make a speech at the end of the fifth year [of the Chinese war with Japan]," she announced. "He must tell the Chinese people the truth at that time. The pro-Japanese element is very active. The Generalissimo wants a yes or no answer to whether the Allies consider this theater necessary and will support it."[96]

This thinly veiled threat that China might go over to Japan was duly reported to Washington. From an early stage, American analysts viewed with skepticism Chiang's strategy of threatening China's imminent collapse if his demands were not met; among other things it would surely divest Chiang himself of power. "I do not think that she meant this," wrote James McHugh, an old China hand then serving as naval attaché to the American embassy in Chungking, of Madame's threat; "nor do I think that peace with Japan is possible. It is only theoretically so under three conditions: (1) that the Generalissimo do it, (2) that he retire and permit others to do it or, (3) that others force him to retire and do it. I think the first two points are absolutely out of the question and the third very unlikely."[97] US concerns to "keep China in the war" mostly arose from the fact that doing so would keep significant Japanese forces "tied up" in China. Yet even were Chiang to make a separate peace with Japan, Japan would undoubtedly have required the same forces to manage the ongoing occupation and to contend with the many regional warlords and other noncompliant factions, including the Communists in the north; Japan could not simply cut and run. Nonetheless, despite widespread skepticism about Chiang's threats, Washington continued to cater to them. This conciliatory approach well-suited Roosevelt's own management style, and possibly his own feelings toward China, which were based on personal family history. His maternal grandfather, Warren Delano, had made his fortune in the tea and opium trade in China, and his mother had grown up in a mansion overlooking Hong Kong and its harbor.[98] "Please remember that I have a background of little over a century in Chinese affairs," Roosevelt had told his secretary of state back in 1934.[99]

Roosevelt's response to Chiang came the next day and was, in Stilwell's words, "quiet & dignified & promised nothing."[100] On June 29, Stilwell met again with Chiang and Madame to deliver the president's diplomatic message, and received in return Chiang's "three minimum requirements essential for the maintenance of the China Theater of War." The Three Demands, as they became known, were that three US divisions should be sent to India to "co-operate with the Chinese Force in restoring the line of communication through Burma"; that the US air force in China should consist of "500 planes continually fighting at the front"; and "[b]eginning from August, the monthly aerial transportation should be 5,000 tons."[101]

Roosevelt's official response was presented to Chiang three months later and served to heighten national celebrations then underway in Chungking. The president's message informed Chiang that he was to receive most of what he had demanded—five hundred planes for the China Theater and an additional one hundred transport planes to increase the tonnage over the Hump to five thousand tons a month. Only the demand for US combat troops was denied.[102] Again, Roosevelt was likely guided by Lauchlin Currie's observations that Chiang could "be held in line with a little care and attention," and that "[o]ne of the most effective ways of encouraging China and deterring Japan would be to go out of our way in giving evidences of friendship."[103]

At any rate, the president had now pledged to have American pilots fly five thousand tons a month over the Hump. Basic math best conveys the scale of the enterprise to which he had committed them. From the earliest days of planning for a prospective airlift, it had been recognized that "the standard Douglas DC-3 transport," or its adapted military equivalent the C-47, could carry "two tons with only one trip daily per plane."[104] The actual carrying capacity of the C-47 had been tested and stretched to over twice the approved safe weight during the evacuation of Burma.[105] Revised calculations based on this proven, if undesirable, capacity reckoned on an average cargo load of six thousand pounds, or three tons per flight; the goal of five thousand tons, therefore, worked out to 1,666 flights a month, or 55 flights a day.

Back in November 1941, after surveilling the Assam–China route, William Bond had written that it was "very discouraging from a safe flying point of view. Ranges and peaks in every direction were as high or higher than our flight altitude."[106] The route he had sketched at that time passed over Myitkyina. North of this town, as he noted, the mountains were higher and the dangers greatly increased. Yet now the loss of Myitkyina and the Japanese occupation of northern Burma ensured that the low-elevation routes had gone, and all flights across Burma would be pushed north into the high and dangerous mountainous terrain against which he had specifically warned. Bond had also noted that if the weather were to be much worse than what he had encountered, the route "would be extremely dangerous and costly and very nearly impractical."[107] Thus it was not logistical difficulties that now defined the Hump operation, but danger. Heedless of years of careful reconnaissance, reports, and planning, the United States had committed to sending to China a ceaseless procession of overloaded planes above the jungles of Japanese-occupied Burma and through the most hazardous flying conditions in the world.

4

THE HUMP

At seventeen thousand feet and about halfway from India to China, pilot Joseph Dechene had lost both his aircraft's engines to ice. The lumbering, cargo-laden plane was now a glider. With white, ice-laden clouds pressed tight against the glass of its windows, the cockpit was like the inside of a bathysphere, a contraption of glass and metal churning in an abyss. The violence of the winds aloft had blown the plane so far off course that the pilots and radio operator had no idea where they were, knowing only that the peaks of high mountains were somewhere close below. Shining a light through the cockpit window, they could see ice building on the wings, but as they did, a lurch of turbulence, the worst the experienced senior pilot had ever encountered, heaved the plane upward "like an express train," as he reported. "We came busting out the top of the thunderhead at 20,000 feet with twenty-four tons of airplane and no engine." Above the clouds, he got the engines running again and so, eventually, safely concluded another trip over the Hump.[1]

During the fight for Burma and the terrible aftermath of its loss, the gravest difficulties facing the new Ferry Command had to some extent been obscured. Now, with no such diversion, and as the Hump operation settled down and began to find its rhythm, the monstrous scale of the undertaking and the breathtaking sweep of the inherent dangers came to the fore. Remedies for the many deficiencies—in aircraft, air bases, safety systems—might be found in the months ahead, but there was nothing that the hand of man could produce to mitigate the two most potent dangers: the terrain and the weather.

On days of pure sunlight, Hump pilots were treated to one of the great spectacles on earth. On reaching an altitude of ten thousand feet after leaving Assam, the route turned east to give a panoramic view of the great mountains that dominated the horizon. "I gasped," recalled Lieutenant Carl Constein, who was flying as copilot when his plane broke through clouds. "Suddenly, marvelously overhead in the cloudless sky was the sun, a white-hot furnace spewing dazzling brilliance over the jagged peaks in the distance. Sheer, absolute beauty—gray cliffs, some variegated in black, most topped by snow-capped peaks. A favorite Psalm flashed into my mind: 'I will lift up mine eyes unto the hills whence cometh my help....' On tours to Europe and Africa since then, I've flown over marvelous sites and panoramas, but nothing compares to the Himalayas."[2]

Directly below, as pilots crossed from Assam to Burma, rolled the vast, dense jungle of the Hukawng Valley, in which so many refugees had recently lost their lives. Farther east and the snaking Irrawaddy could be seen, then the Kumon range separating Burma from China, then the great gorges of the Salween and Mekong rivers. In the afternoon it was already night in these dark, deep-cut chasms, recalled an RAF pilot, "but at 12,000 ft the sun still shone, lighting up the clouds that, in this cooler part of the day, were forming along the ridges of the mountains. Katabatic air currents caused their silvered surfaces to curve and flow into huge, greying streamers of mist like gigantic waterfalls, their veils of spray pouring down into the jungle."[3]

In the later afternoon, however, the lowering sun created shadows of total darkness on the mountains' eastern slopes, accentuating their majesty, and also their menace. "Peering into that threatening blackness on our afternoon return flight is a chilling experience," one pilot recorded.

"As shadows turn to dark, the feeling of being lost over a great black void to which there may not be an end wells up in the pilot's mind. He wishes he had started an hour earlier so that he could arrive in daylight."[4]

North of the Hump route rose the high, true Himalayas. Nothing the pilots had met with in their careers or lives prepared them for aerial views of these epic mountains. They were traversing the heavens at heights humans had only recently imagined possible—yet through the windows of these, their historic air machines, there rose in nonchalant grandeur seemingly endless peaks that were higher than they were flying. Rumors of "lost" mountains, off the charts, never before located, became part of the Hump airman's lore. One aircraft blown off course far to the north broke out of clouds at 30,200 feet by its altimeter, yet pilot and crew claimed they found themselves looking at two mountains that stood higher than they were. Another pilot, lost and also north of course, emerged from clouds at thirty thousand feet and saw less than a mile away a towering peak at least two thousand feet above his altitude.[5] These mysterious mountains seemed to hover around the Amne Machin range in Tibet. Perhaps within their high gulfs and valleys lay some magical lost kingdom. James Hilton's *Lost Horizon*, which evoked the mythical hidden lamasery of Shangri-la, enjoyed huge success in the late 1930s and early '40s, being the first mass market paperback book ever published, as well as a popular movie. When Roosevelt was asked from where the Doolittle raid had launched, he had famously replied "Shangri-la," and a rest camp for pilots tucked away in a gorge of the Himalayas in Assam was called "Lost Horizon Lodge."[6] The hero of *Lost Horizon* stumbles on Shangri-la when the plane in which he is flying crashes among unknown mountains "far beyond the western range of the Himalayas, toward the less known heights of the Kuen-Lun."[7] The pilots flying the Hump were privileged to cast their eyes upon the most formidable and uncharted mountain terrain on earth; all below was mystery. Who knew what might be possible?

The pilots' unease and the perceived spookiness of the terrain over which they flew were heightened by the fact that available air charts were unclear and sometimes simply wrong about locations and altitudes of the mountains, with elevation errors as great as five thousand feet.[8] A war zone familiarization manual used by pilots and navigators, for example, reported that the many mountain peaks along the Hump route ranged "from 8,500 feet in the south to 16,000 feet on the direct route from India to Southern China, to 25,000 in the north." In reality, there were no peaks over twenty thousand feet along the entire India to China route.[9] Near Likiang, at a major turning point in the most northern route, a spectacular cleft mountain rose to a height estimated between eighteen thousand to twenty thousand feet, but it was not clearly indicated on any chart.[10] In view of such known inaccuracies, the pilots' word of mouth and the stories of their experiences and travails counted a great deal; and in the unsettled, monstrously turbulent conditions they routinely encountered, the mountains did not in fact seem securely located.

More deadly than this—"as villainous and forbidding a stretch of terrain as there was in the world," to quote the principle history of the CBI— was the weather.[11] The Hump route bored through the chaotic intersection of three major air systems: moist, warm, high-pressure masses spawned by the Bay of Bengal to the west and the South China Sea to the east, and frigid, dry lows that swept down from Siberia.[12] This unique convergence created the seasonal thunderstorms, monsoons, and ice that were chronic along the Hump route. Additionally, fierce winds blew out of the heart of Asia across the mountains and high tableland of Tibet, while from the west a subtropical jet stream blew continuously at high altitude. The collision of these torrents of wind with the unyielding barrier wall of the Himalayas created tumultuous roller coasters of wind-wave effects.[13]

The magic of flight, the ability to heave and sustain aloft an object massively heavier than air, derives from the fact that when air is forced or pushed to go faster it becomes less dense; and with less density there is the potential for lift. An aircraft flies because its wings are designed to exploit this potential: a wing's shape—its air foil—is fatter on the top than the bottom, ensuring that air moves faster across its top surface. The

faster air moves, the less pressure it has; less pressure across the top of a
wing than across the bottom creates lift. An aircraft's engine and propeller give it the speed to fly; propellers do this by grabbing and pushing air
back, as a canoe paddle or swimmer's hand grabs water. Pulled through
the air by the propeller, the airfoil of the wing creates lift. When these basic
principles are compromised—when an aircraft loses speed, or the shape
of its wings is altered—the magic of flight is shattered. And the phenomena that characterized Hump weather—the towering storms, the raking
winds and ice—were prime agents of such compromises.

"I had both props in high emergency rpm and the throttles full on—
and we were still losing altitude," Robert Seekins reported of his plane
being gripped by an unassailable downward force. "We were being tossed
around, up 4,000 feet per minute and down as much. . . . Both copilot
Gustafson and I had to hold the controls with all our strength to keep
the ship right side up."[14] Violent drafts of air can make an airplane's
speed irrelevant. When wind slams against a mountain's side, it can surge
up the mountain face to create a powerful updraft; riding up and over
the mountain, it creates an equally powerful downdraft on the mountain's lee. A mountain wave might be fast yet smooth, in which case the
plane can simply ride it. Flying the route in spring, when the turbulence
and storms were generally worse, one pilot was lifted eight thousand feet
in one minute as he crossed a ridge.[15] But a powerful downdraft over high
terrain gives a pilot little room to survive, while a ragged, lurching wave
can tear off an aircraft's wings.

New arrivals received scant briefing on finding their way over the
mountain ranges now known as "the Rockpile" or "the Hump." Pilot-to-
pilot reports were the most valuable source of information, and new pilots flew first missions in the right seat as copilots so as to learn the route
and ropes firsthand.[16] "My first trip over the hump I drew a newly checked
out Lt. for 1st pilot," recalled John Shaver, who was flying as copilot. "The
weather was broken clouds over the valley. . . . The scattered clouds were
building up thick, and somewhere over the Fort Hertz Valley our course
was blocked by the biggest blackest, anvil-top thunderhead I have ever

seen. It was highly charged with electricity, with constant lightning flashes." From the left seat, the pilot leaned across to ask Shaver if he had instrument training. "My reply was yes, but most were simulated instruments, very little actual," Shaver replied. "The Lt. then turned loose the wheel and said, It's all yours."[17]

As it bored into the thunderhead, the plane was seized by powerful blasts of wind that tossed it up and drove it down. Power up or power back, gear up or gear down, had no effect on whether the plane climbed or fell. Caught in a severe downdraft, Shaver had the plane at full power but still was sinking at one thousand feet per minute. Outside, lightning was so close and brilliant as to blind him, and all across the aircraft— windshield wipers, fuselage, propellers, cowling—skittered Saint Elmo's fire. "We hit the eye, had smooth flying for a couple of minutes, then battled the winds going out the other side." The plane landed undamaged in Kunming.[18]

Dinjan, with its minimum-length runway, was still the only operational air base in Assam, although work was progressing on other sites. Closely surrounded by jungle and jungle-covered mountains, Dinjan faced the Himalayas to the north and to the east the Naga Hills. Over these mountains the great storms brewed, and local people—Indians and British tea planters—had forewarned the Americans that when the monsoon broke it would be impossible to fly.[19] There were in Assam two principle seasons and one interlude: the Cold Weather, from the beginning of November until mid-March; Chota Barsat, or Small Rains, from March until May; and the monsoon, which burst around the middle of May and ended only in October.[20] The monsoon delivered in one season most of a region's annual rainfall, with downpours that could last for seven or eight hours. In some places, as much as 375 inches of rain fell in the five-month period; in Burma, it had been known to rain fifteen inches in twenty-four hours.[21] Hot, moist winds rising from the Indian Ocean and Bay of Bengal flooded over the mountains, creating the torrential rains and turbulent thunderstorms, ice and hail, and unbroken cumulus masses that reached from twenty thousand to fifty thousand feet.[22]

"The weather of the S.W. monsoon presents all the difficulties of flying in heavy rain anywhere with the additional hazards due to the intensity of the phenomena in this part of the world," read a notice from the air marshal for Southeast Asia, which went on to describe these various phenomena. There were the cyclones with wind speeds of 100 to 150 miles per hour that created turbulence "such that probably no aircraft could be handled in them," and squalls, "vertical currents of the order of 100 miles per hour." The notice also offered helpful tips for the airman: "Try to avoid the squall by flying round it or turning back" and the "best height to fly is below the base of the clouds if that is possible"—which generally it was not, given that cloud bases brushed or entirely hid the tips of the mountains.[23]

Pea-soup fog and low ceilings routinely had pilots on instruments within a minute of takeoff.[24] Between takeoff and landing were only two radio beacons on the route—one by Chabua and the other at Kunming—which lightning static rendered useless during the big storms.[25] Once in the clouds, a pilot flew blindly through the enveloping weather over the vast, undifferentiated jungle and mountain ridges of uncertain height, slogging through the churning clouds by dead reckoning, as sailors of old had made their way across the unknown oceans. Occasionally, the stress of flying blind was overwhelming. "On one occasion when I was co-pilot flying with a Captain as first pilot, he lost his nerve about 15 minutes into a very violent thunderstorm and decided to turn back toward China," pilot Stephen King recalled. "Before we got back out of the storm he concluded it wasn't such a good idea after all and turned around again."[26]

The monsoon also changed the landscape below, flooding the lowlands east of the Himalayas and with them all distinguishing features that might, with snatched glimpses through the clouds, orient a pilot. Landing strips were turned into lakes, creating further hazardous conditions.[27] The only paved area in Dinjan was its short "half runway," and the rest of the base was a quagmire of ankle-deep gooey mud, which, like the sodden thatch roofing of the *bashas*, made living conditions yet more unpleasant. While airmen and ground crew strove to push the twentieth century's technology to unexplored limits, their daily life was defined by primitive conditions. Planes were parked in the mud on high ground in the open, there being no hangars or shelters. Regardless of the season, most maintenance work was performed at night; during the monsoon this was when it tended not to rain, and when it did not rain daytime temperatures soared between 100 degrees and 130 degrees Fahrenheit, and metal surfaces exposed to the sun became hot enough to inflict second-degree burns on anyone who touched them. The excessive heat also played havoc on hydraulic lines, causing hydraulic fluid to expand and break valves and fittings, and created vapor locks in the gasoline lines. The report of a technical inspection made of one Ferrying detachment gave a picture "of almost complete lack of facilities," with gasoline being pumped by hand and the only maintenance equipment being "some hand tools and one portable air compressor." All the aircraft, it was noted, had "uncorrected defects," and housing and food were also bad. Under the circumstances, the inspector concluded, the maintenance performed was "very satisfactory."[28]

The handful of planes steaming on the airfield in Dinjan were mostly Douglas C-47 Skytrains, the military adaptation of the civilian DC-3, and the backbone of Allied air transport fleets in every theater as well as across the Hump. Since its introduction in 1935, the civilian version had revolutionized commercial air travel, and with its wingspan of ninety-five feet and length of sixty-four feet, it could comfortably carry twenty-one passengers and a full crew that included air hostesses. The military C-47 was essentially the same aircraft with adaptations for carrying cargo: a reinforced floor, a large cargo door and hoist attachment, and passenger seats pulled. A special tail feature also enabled it to tow gliders. Another, less ubiquitous military version of the reliable DC-3 was the C-53 Skytrooper, a troop carrier.[29]

Powered by 1,200-horsepower Pratt & Whitney Twin Wasp engines, the C-47 had a range of about 1,600 miles, a normal service ceiling of 12,000 feet, and a published maximum altitude of 20,000—the height of the highest mountains encountered on the Hump route. The civilian DC-3 was accustomed to carrying cargo and passenger loads up to 2,500 pounds.[30] In military practice, this workhorse was pushed well beyond the stated limits, routinely carrying 5,000 to 6,000 pounds of cargo— and sometimes even more.[31] Unfinicky, unflappable, and forgiving, the DC-3/C-47 proved itself again and again, stolidly working its way across storm-tossed heavens at the sedate speed of some 170 miles per hour. It could take off and land on grass and dirt as well as paving, and did not require a long runway.[32] It was so aerodynamic that, engines removed, it had been tested as a glider.[33] If monstrous winds knocked it on its beam end, it righted itself and flew on. One RAF DC-3 flying beneath a storm was repeatedly caught in violent, vertical-spinning updrafts, twisting corkscrews of wind that inverted the plane while hurling it upward and slamming it down before releasing it at one thousand feet. Safe on the ground, the pilot inspected the plane: "Windows out, strips torn off the fuselage, tailplane twisted, wing fillets gone, etc., etc.,"[34] as he reported. But the wings had not fallen off; the plane had not come apart at the seams. Known as the Dakota in Britain, the stoic, hardworking plane was affectionately nicknamed by American pilots "the Gooney Bird."

ON JUNE 4, 1942, STILWELL EMERGED FROM THE JUNGLE OF BURMA INTO A glare of publicity in New Delhi. The weeks between the fall of Burma and his high-profile press conference had been eventful. After refusing air evacuation from his headquarters in Shwebo, he had intended to travel by road or train to Myitkyina, where Chiang had instructed him to proceed with all haste to make contact with the Chinese troops who were to gather there. Haynes and Scott, the pilots who came to evacuate Stilwell and his staff, impressed on Stilwell the fact that Japanese forces were less than twenty miles away.[35] Why, in the face of obvious need for speed, Stilwell chose to take his chances by road or rail speaks to intractable elements of his character, among other things an infantryman's essential mistrust of airpower and a perverse need to do things his way.[36]

In the event, Stilwell's plan had failed, and he was not able to reach Myitkyina by any land route. Meanwhile, parts of the Chinese troops he nominally led were still behind him, only just ahead of the advancing Japanese. Nonetheless, Stilwell radioed to Chiang that the Chinese troops had broken into disparate parties and that "further command would be unnecessary." To General Du Yuming, Stilwell gave instructions to lead the Fifth Army troops he had with him not to China but to India. He did not inform Chiang of this directive, although he subsequently did send the generalissimo a message stating that he and his staff and others collected along the way were independently setting out for India.[37] The two messages, from Du and Stilwell, stunned Chiang. Stilwell "has abandoned my 100,000 soldiers in foreign jungles and headed off to India," he wrote in his diary. "Only then does he send me this telegram."[38]

Stilwell's own diary indicates he had cut himself loose from any sense of responsibility for the Chinese troops. Striking west toward the tracks that led to India, he was, he recorded, "ahead of the Chinese horde as yet."[39] Colonel Robert P. Williams, Stilwell's medical officer, also kept a diary of the trek and records how, at the early stage of the journey when the party was still able to use vehicles, they "reached a big town and one of the main roads. It was choked with Chinese troops and refugees. . . . To get a jump on the crowd, our party got up at two-thirty a.m. and drove until mid-morning when we came to the end of any real trail."[40]

The diverse collection of people that formed Stilwell's party numbered 114. Among them were eighteen American officers and six enlisted men; sixteen Chinese guards; the missionary doctor Gordon Seagrave and his nineteen indomitable nurses from the Burmese hill tribes; six members from the British Quaker Friends Ambulance Unit; a Chinese general and his bodyguards; a handful of British soldiers; the American Baptist missionary Reverend Brayton Case, who was the dean of a regional agricultural college and a font of valuable local information as well as fluent in many local languages; and a public relations officer and a reporter, who also took photographs.[41] Taking responsibility for this small and easily managed group allowed Stilwell to convince himself he had a duty to them, as opposed to the thousands of Chinese troops with whom he had been entrusted.

Stilwell's trek to India was to become part of his mythology. It was an arduous feat, but, within the context of the thousands of other treks undertaken by civilian refugees, not remarkable. The photographs reveal that no member of his party carried a pack, at least for any amount of time; this was because they were accompanied throughout by trains of up to one hundred porters. ("Shortly after waking on that morning of the 6th May we heard the martial tramping of feet," recalled a British Forest officer, who had been working in the refugee camps along the routes of exodus and was camped with his wife on a nearby river sandbank; "and watched General Stilwell, his staff, and about one hundred Indian labourers carrying the kit, striding down the opposite bank getting out of Burma.")[42] On the third day of the march, the RAF dropped food and medicine. At the Uyu River, rafts were prepared for the group, and the passage on the river seems to have had its extended periods of serenity. "The three days on the raft were beautiful and it was good to rest after all that walking," M. T. "Big" Bawk, one of Seagrave's nurses, recalled. "It was very beautiful sometimes and one time—early in the morning—Hla Sein stood out on the front of the raft to sing. She had a beautiful voice and the moon was still up and the sun was coming up and it was very beautiful."[43] On the second day of walking after leaving the river, the group was met by a British rescue mission that arrived with four hundred porters carrying medical supplies and food, a doctor, pack ponies, and more ponies on the way; for the remainder of the trek, those who needed to could ride.[44]

"Chinese troops not heard from," Stilwell wrote in his diary on May 21, from the British Residency in Imphal.[45] His own small party, so extravagantly assisted, had come through without death or injury. By contrast, parts of the Chinese Fifth Army that had made their way as planned to Myitkyina had been forced to march out through the Hukawng Valley with much loss of life. Total Chinese casualties for the campaign amounted to an estimated 25,000, compared to the estimated 10,000 of British and

Indian troops.[46] Some 2,700 men of the Fifth Army had wandered, lost and in starving condition in the Hukawng Valley, and were eventually located by aerial reconnaissance on the Chindwin River south of Shingbwiyang, the small outpost used as a recovery center for the refugees. Reports of violence and aggressive looting had followed the Chinese soldiers throughout their retreat, and the British authorities decided they should not be allowed to enter Shingbwiyang, where it was feared they would claim all air-dropped supplies to the cost of the other refugees assembled there. Eric Lambert, a young British police officer who had extensively explored the area as part of a survey team in 1937, was given the task of finding and leading the army out by trails that skirted the main refugee route—a commission he successfully fulfilled after a forty-three-day, round-trip trek while suffering badly from malarial fever.[47]

While the press lionized Stilwell's epic trek, and top brass in Washington, including the president, commended Stilwell, others took a different view. By air he could have been in India within hours, from where it would have been possible to give some direction to the unfolding crisis of the Chinese exodus. To Haynes and Scott, the pilots who had risked their lives to evacuate him, Stilwell's real motivation for remaining was obvious. "Well, for the life of me I couldn't see what face could be saved," Scott recorded. By their estimation, the plane could have carried up to thirty additional passengers, but departed close to half empty.[48] While Stilwell had the reputation of being a fighting solider, the debacle in Burma had been his first experience in combat, and the defeat stung.

On June 3, Stilwell arrived in Chungking and gave Chiang and Madame, as he wrote in his diary, "the full story [of the Burma campaign], pulling no punches."[49] In his view and presentation, the disasters involving the Chinese troops were exclusively the fault of the Chinese army and of Chiang's interfering communications with the Chinese generals. Stilwell's contempt for Chiang, which would come to define his relationship with the generalissimo and infect the entire CBI theater, was already apparent. "His ignorance & fatuous complacency are appalling," he wrote in his diary shortly after this meeting. "He is so dumb he's impervious to attack."[50] The following month his diary recorded his first use of his habitual name for the generalissimo: the "Peanut."[51]

In the time between the loss of Burma and his arrival in Chungking, Stilwell had devised an ambitious, sprawling plan: the approximately nine thousand Chinese troops that had evacuated to India would become the basis of a new American-trained Chinese army under his direction. These would eventually be joined by an additional forty-four thousand more Chinese troops that the already-hard-pressed transport pilots would fly from China over the Hump to India.[52] The grand plan—the Pacific Front Plan—envisioned a further twelve reformed and retrained Chinese divisions—Y-Force—advancing from Yunnan across the Salween River into Burma. Simultaneously, the American-trained Chinese divisions in India—X-Force—joined by three British and one US division, would enter Burma from India, joining Y-Force above Mandalay. The combined forces would then fan out, south through Burma down to Rangoon, and down through Siam and into Indochina. Additionally, nine Chinese divisions would be deployed along the Indochina border, destined for either Hanoi and Haiphong or Canton and Hong Kong—or both. In short, having been drummed out of Burma after two months in the field during his first combat command, Stilwell's fantasy was that he would recapture all of Southeast Asia.[53]

Realistic considerations gradually revised the plan, but basic elements remained, beginning with the retraining of the Chinese troops in India. The British were pressured to make available a centuries-old cantonment at Ramgarh, some two hundred miles northwest of Calcutta, that had recently served as a camp for Italian prisoners of war, and were also induced to foot the bill for the soldiers' maintenance, food, and uniforms.[54] Although Chiang had committed to releasing troops in good physical condition for the Ramgarh program, the men who were in fact offered were so underweight and stricken with disease that almost half were rejected by American medical officers. Within a short period of time, Chinese authorities began to send the selected men to India in an almost naked condition on the principle that it was foolish to waste money on clothing when new uniforms would be issued in India.[55]

In addition to his role as the ranking American officer in China, Stilwell also remained a chief of staff to Chiang Kai-shek and the administrator of Lend-Lease supplies in China, duties that had him shuffling on a 2,100-mile commute between his office in New Delhi and headquarters in Chungking.[56] Lend-Lease was central to Stilwell's plan, for it was this that would equip the new Chinese armies. Stilwell did not command the operation over the Hump, but given that the Hump operation existed to deliver Lend-Lease supplies, his plan had significant implications for Hump airmen. Meanwhile, the great Brahmaputra River flowing alongside the Dinjan air base was cluttered with boats full of Lend-Lease supplies that had been sent up from Rangoon when the fall of the city seemed imminent. The laden boats provided a daily visible reminder of how far behind the air supply scheme had fallen. In the month of July 1942, the 1st Ferry Group delivered seventy-three tons of supplies with thirty-five planes, or an average of about two tons per plane. These figures were so far below the target five thousand tons a month as to be risible, and also compared dismally with CNAC's operation, which delivered 129 tons with ten operational planes during the same period.[57]

OUTSIDE THE CBI'S JUNGLE AND MUD-MIRED ARENA, THE US NAVY WON A hard-fought battle at the island of Midway in June 1942—the first momentous reversal of Japan's fortunes in the Pacific. Field Marshal Erwin Rommel's capture of Tobruk at the end of the same month, however, was a disastrous Allied setback, and by summer's end the Germans had advanced to Stalingrad. Particularly in view of German success in damaging Allied sea-lanes, all these vital, active fronts were in sore need of transport aircraft—so much so that Roosevelt had pressed parts of the US commercial airline fleets into military service.[58] Within the CBI, the anti-British independence movement in India, further inflamed by Japanese and German propaganda, had led to civil unrest that came to a head when British authorities ill-advisedly arrested leaders of India's Congress Party, including both Jawaharlal Nehru and Mahatma Gandhi. Strikes and organized acts of sabotage in the aftermath of the arrests greatly unnerved American officers headquartered in New Delhi and stationed in other parts of India, as they worked to build and extend major infrastructure projects.[59]

In the Assam Valley along the Brahmaputra River, which seemed to point like a finger northeast toward the Hump, work on the new air bases was sufficiently advanced to begin moving to them in August. Like Dinjan, Chabua, Mohanbari, and Sookerating were carved out of British tea plantations. All were situated some thirty-five miles from Dinjan under the ostensible protection of the 51st Fighter Group transferred from Karachi. August also saw a shuffle of leadership within the CBI, and command of the Tenth Air Force was handed to Brigadier General Clayton Bissell, a World War I ace credited with shooting down five German planes over the Western Front and Stilwell's air adviser. Attacking the many defects weighing down his new command, Bissell had every available aircraft assigned to the Assam-Kunming route and made aircraft maintenance as high a priority as was possible, including by transferring service personnel to Dinjan and the new Assam bases.[60] His efforts showed evidence of progress and, in the month of August 1942, the Assam-Burma-China Ferry Command and CNAC planes carried 708 tons to China.[61]

The Japanese, meanwhile, had withdrawn most of their airpower to the Malay Peninsula, so as to use the rainy season for improving night flying and aerial combat skills, while their army divisions were dispersed among the region's more salubrious areas—Yunnan, the Shan States—for rest and retraining.[62] Deep in the jungle along the Siam-Burma border, however, the Japanese had been at work since June on construction of a rail system to support a future offensive into India. Built from the slave labor of 61,806 Allied prisoners of war and as many as 269,948 forced laborers from across Southeast Asia, this, the notorious Death Railway, would come to represent one of the great atrocities of the war. In August, the Imperial Headquarters approved a plan for its southern army to prepare for a campaign to occupy Assam and the Chittagong region along the eastern coast of the Bay of Bengal, and to terminate the supply line to China.[63]

Thus far, Assam's only defense against enemy attack had been the weather, and there was a keen expectation that once the rains ended, the Japanese would emerge from their bases across north Burma.[64] Still lacking any normative air defense systems, the command decided to seek cover again in nature by attempting a night flight over the Hump, substituting for the monsoon's turgid clouds the night's darkness. On September 12, 1942, Captain John Payne, a tall, rangy pilot from Paducah, Kentucky, departed Chabua in a C-47 with a handpicked crew for Kunming. Before joining the Air Corps, Payne had for nine years been a pilot with Eastern Airlines, flying between Chicago and Atlanta; he had "let down" so many times in the smoke and fog of Atlanta, he said, that the weather of Burma didn't trouble him much. Payne had shown his skill during the evacuation of Burma, landing his C-47 on a hilltop runway just nine hundred feet long.[65] Now, flying over the mountains, he was guided, in his words, by "hell and destiny." The moon was up but obscured by severe thunderstorms that kept him on instruments all the way, while an inch and a half of ice on the wings forced him to a lower altitude than he would have liked. But eventually, out of the pitch-black darkness, the runway at Kunming appeared, dimly outlined by small smudge pots. A psychological as well as practical landmark, the night flight was widely reported in newspapers back home.[66]

Ten days after Payne landed back at Chabua, another landmark was reached. Having delivered their cargo in Kunming, Pilot Harold J. Folkers, with First Lieutenant George Humphrey Hadley as copilot, both of the 1st Ferry Group, prepared to head back over the Hump to Assam. Hadley, age twenty-five, described on his draft card as being a strapping six foot two, and having a ruddy complexion and brown hair and eyes, was the son of Presbyterian missionaries and had been born in Peking. After graduating from Williams College in Massachusetts, he had briefly taught at the Mount Hermon School for Boys and then enlisted in the Air Corps.

He had been commissioned as a pilot less than a year earlier, in December of 1941, and after training in Colorado and California, had been assigned to transport service over the Hump. It is fair to imagine he was gratified to be offering service to the country of his birth.

Folkers, also twenty-five, stood six feet tall and, at 145 pounds, was of slim build, with a ruddy complexion and brown hair and blue eyes. He had grown up in Wichita, Kansas, and from a young age had been raised by his aunt and her husband following the death of both his parents. At the age of eleven he had inherited a portion of a family legacy, some $8,000 (about $140,000 today), from his grandmother. Six years later, at the age of seventeen, he enrolled in the Spartan School of Aeronautics in Tulsa to train as a transport pilot. On graduation, he was employed as a copilot for Braniff Airways, flying out of Wichita, before induction into the army.

Taking off from Kunming, with the experienced Folkers in the pilot seat, the C-53 flew for an hour and a half—then dropped out of all radio communication. The plane simply disappeared, never to be heard from again, most likely somewhere over the mountains that marked the China-Burma border. No remains of the plane or its only two occupants were ever recovered, and it was speculated that ice was the most likely cause of the loss.[67]

This, the first fatality on the Hump route, was reported on in the pilot's hometown newspaper in October. The effect of the news on his family can be gleaned from a second local story that appeared nearly two months later, reporting that Captain Folker's aunt claimed she had seen her nephew in an AP wirephoto of wounded American troops arriving home from the African campaign. There—there in the front lower bunk, as seen in the photo—there was her nephew! She was going to inform "government officials" for confirmation.[68] None was forthcoming.

In early October, as the monsoon season waned, the move to the new air bases had advanced to the point that Bissell was able to report to General Arnold that the 1st Ferry Group was now prepared to operate seventy-five transports—whenever the aircraft were made available.[69] Meanwhile, the India Air Task Force was activated under the command of Caleb Haynes for the defense of the new fields, and included all combat units in India—all of which, however, were so far below normal strength as to render the activation "negligible."[70] With the end of the monsoon looming, and with it loss of protective cover from the enemy, concerns for the vulnerability of such aircraft as there were became acute. While it had been proven that the Hump could be flown at night by a confident and first-rate pilot, the inadequacies of navigation aids were still too great to make this a general practice.[71] In any case, more vulnerable than individual planes in flight were the small fleets of aircraft parked in the dust and mud at the makeshift air bases. Apart from a few antiaircraft guns and a handful of fighter planes, the bases were undefended, yet the Japanese were only some eighty miles distant from Chabua, just over the Naga Hills.[72] That the Japanese had kept closely informed of the progress of the new bases had been made clear by the almost daily appearance of their reconnaissance planes while Chabua was being built. One pilot, who became familiar enough to be given a nickname—"Photo Joe"—had impudently buzzed the field at the end of his survey.[73]

The Japanese attack came toward the end of October. Despite having been long anticipated, the enemy planes appeared over the Assam airfields so suddenly that warning of their approach had only just been received. Three American fighters happened to be already airborne, and these, joined by six others, represented the defense of the fields against the approximately one hundred Japanese bombers and strafing fighters. Dinjan, Chabua, Sookerating, and Mohanbari were all hit, with severe destruction to the hardscrabble-built runways, the flimsy buildings, and, most seriously, aircraft on the ground. Twelve aircraft, transports and fighters, were destroyed, and seventeen badly damaged. The following day, October 26, Japanese planes appeared again, and again without warning, but did less damage and lost two of their own planes to ground fire. A third raid occurred on October 28, also resulting in little damage. In the wake of the raids, aircraft were rushed to Assam from other parts of India, but all remained quiet for some time.[74]

THROUGHOUT THE MONSOON MONTHS, STILWELL CONTINUED TO HAMMER
out his plans, which with Chiang's compliance had expanded from training and equipping thirty Chinese divisions to sixty divisions, or about six
hundred thousand men.[75] Along the way, wise heads in Washington advocated retaking the Burma Road as an "essential" part of a future Burma
campaign, so as to boost the amount of supplies delivered to China and,
in some as-yet-unspecified way, support future Pacific operations.[76] In October 1942, as the monsoon waned, Chiang urged Stilwell to begin planning for a March 1943 start for the new Burma offensive, to which he had
agreed to commit X- and Y-Force troops—subject, however, to substantial
preconditions. Before any overland advance by Chinese divisions could take
place, Chiang stipulated, a large-scale amphibious campaign—utilizing
three to four British naval battleships and six to eight aircraft carriers—
would have to capture Rangoon, secure control of the Bay of Bengal, the
China and Java Seas, and occupy the Andaman Islands, while air domi-
nance was to be gained over the region.[77]

Stilwell's attention next turned to the British, whose commitment and
resources his plans had assumed. But now General Wavell drew attention
to basic realities that had so far been overlooked or ignored. Firstly, he
claimed, current circumstances were not conducive to a major offensive—
aircraft, troops, and equipment intended for India had been diverted
to the Middle East, facilities in Assam were still bogged down by the
monsoon—and in light of these circumstances, "any advance in force
against Northern Burma could not start by March 1" of 1943.[78] Wavell
was also skeptical that two Chinese armies could be rebuilt and supplied
within the few months before that date, and was concerned about the logistics of the operation. For example, merely moving X-Force troops from
the Ramgarh training base to Ledo, the designated point of entry into
Burma, would require eight hundred trucks, which were not available,
carting two hundred tons of supplies a day over a 350-mile line of communications, a process that by some estimates could take up to nine

weeks. Then there was the monsoon: an advance in March would leave at the very most only two and a half months before the next monsoon broke, and based on recent experience it was not clear how troops could be supported in north Burma through a monsoon season.[79] Moreover, he ventured, the generalissimo's agreement to Stilwell's proposal was hedged with so many preconditions that it hardly amounted to an agreement.[80] Nor was it likely that these preconditions could be met, given that US and British resources were stretched by the battle for Guadalcanal, the impending campaign in North Africa, and the seaborne supply of Russia.[81] He did not see how an amphibious operation to capture Rangoon could take place before the autumn of 1943.

Instead of a big offensive, Wavell proposed a "small combined operation" down the Arakan coast in western Burma, to take Akyab on the Bay of Bengal, where there was a port and a former RAF air base. The initial objectives of the offensive would be the northern Arakan, the rugged Chin Hills in northwest Burma, and the upper Chindwin. The whole would serve as the first stage of a later offensive to take Rangoon.[82]

Underlying all discussion about the next course of action was the fact that, beyond the mutual desire to defeat Japan, the long-term regional interests of Britain and the US did not coincide. The British looked southeast toward Rangoon and beyond—to the lost colonies of Singapore, Malaya, and Hong Kong. The Americans looked northeast across Burma solely toward China.[83] Neither party accepted or entirely trusted the other's intentions. "The British appear to have no intention of attempting to retake Burma," wrote Stilwell's political adviser, John Davies, as early as July 1942. "The reason would seem to be the conviction that no Asiatic possession is worth any appreciable diversion of strength from the British isles; that the war will be won in Europe; and that lost possessions will at the Peace Conference revert with clear title to the British if those colonies remain up to the termination of hostilities under enemy possession, whereas if those possessions are re-occupied with Chinese and American assistance, British title may be compromised."[84]

The British in turn viewed Washington's uncritical and unqualified support of Chiang and the Kuomintang with similar skepticism. "The President and his circle cherished exaggerated ideas of the military power which China could exert if given sufficient arms and equipment," Churchill would write in his memoir of the war. "They also feared unduly the imminence of a Chinese collapse if support were not forthcoming. I disliked thoroughly the idea of reconquering Burma by an advance along the miserable communications in Assam. I hated jungles—which go to the winner anyway."[85]

While Stilwell and the British focused on the details of a military campaign, Roosevelt was focused on the big, postwar picture. In his vision of the new world order, a powerful China—pro-American, democratic, and no doubt an eager trading partner—would fill the vacuum left by the collapse of British and other European as well as Japanese influences in the region and be a buttress against the Soviet Union. "After this war we shall have to think of China, America, Britain and Russia as the four 'big policemen' of the world," Roosevelt informed Chiang. Helping America to maintain order in the Pacific, China would play a special role "in certain colonial areas" of the southern Pacific and Southeast Asia, as he elaborated.[86]

While Roosevelt's own familial "China connection" seems to have colored his views, these were also encouraged by others close to him, both inside and outside of his government. His senior adviser on Far Eastern affairs, Stanley Hornbeck, who had lived and taught in China, was passionately "pro-China," while Chiang's well-connected brother-in-law, T. V. Soong, used his high-placed connections in government and media to lobby for China[87]. More broadly, public opinion in the US staunchly supported the Chinese citizenry, whose brutal treatment at the hands of the invading Japanese had shocked the world, and whose stoicism had inspired instinctive compassion. As time passed, this sympathetic support had been massaged by a determined pro-China media that idealized Chiang Kai-shek as a high-minded leader battling against all odds for the salvation of his country. A leader in this mythmaking was Henry Luce, the powerful publisher of *Time* and *Life* magazines and the *March of Time* films and radio broadcasts. The child of missionaries, Luce had been born in China, where he lived until the age of fifteen, and this experience had fostered, in the words of a biographer, "a fervent faith in America's God-ordained global mission in Asia," a cause for which he lobbied relentlessly before, during, and after the war.[88]

Pulitzer Prize–winning war correspondent Leland Stowe traveled extensively in Burma and China between July 1941 and December 1942. "The Burma Road," he wrote, echoing other journalists who had made similar investigations, "was the greatest racket in the Far East." Accepting the official line that "the Chinese armies could never stage a large-scale offensive against the Japanese" without the vast quantities of Lend-Lease supplies supposedly carried over it, he undertook "a fact-finding expedition which soon proved to be the most discouraging and depressing experience I had had anywhere, in dozens of countries, since the second World War began."[89]

His thorough investigation revealed egregious excesses from the very beginning of the operation. In addition to trucks, gasoline, airplanes, and artillery, Chungking had ordered and acquired "a rolling mill to be constructed at a cost of $1,000,000—estimated to be capable of production only after approximately two years"; and a vast array of industrial equipment, "which could not contribute to the prosecution of the war within from one to three years *after* this equipment was delivered over the Burma Road." These included a large steel and iron works, with conveyors and a water-supply system, at a cost of $4.5 million; a steam power plant, a blast furnace, more than twelve hydroelectric plants of various sizes, and "machinery and installations for the Ki-kang iron mines." ($1 million in 1941 is the equivalent of about $17.4 million today.) Machinery had been received for plants that did not exist, and for which China had no engineers to direct them if they did.[90]

The two thousand General Motors trucks and automobiles, the new Buick car that could be sold in China at over six times its US price, the six hundred armored cars that could not be used on local terrain—Stowe's investigation ran for pages. On the docks of Rangoon were piled Lend-Lease supplies amounting to an estimated value of $30 million—the equivalent of about $510 million today. Undisclosed at this time was the evidence that the Soong family network was siphoning off Lend-Lease funds at the source—for example, a freighter transporting sixty American tanks and other matériel was reported to have "sunk" before it reached China, when the freighter had never left the US West Coast.[91]

Back in Rangoon, Stowe typed up his detailed, four-part report for the *Chicago Daily News* and the fifty or so US and Canadian newspapers that subscribed to its foreign service. When he went to the cable office to file his stories, he reported, the British press censor "looked definitely upset," sighing, "I really can't take any responsibility for them, you understand." In Chicago, the report was read with alarm. "On urgent suggestion higher-ups publication remainder China series suspended pending upclearing present crucial situation stop," Stowe was cabled. "The 'higher-ups,' as I suspected," he wrote, "were in no way connected with my newspaper."[92]

FEW INDIVIDUALS BENEFITED SO MUCH FROM AMERICA'S UNQUESTIONING pro-China media as Claire Lee Chennault, a retired captain in the old US Air Corps who was to contribute to the conflict and confusion of the vexed CBI theater. Chennault had first come to China in the summer of 1937 as one of a number of former US Air Corps airmen recruited by the Nationalist government as instructors for the Chinese Air Force, which Chiang Kai-shek was attempting, once again, to rebuild. Chennault's military career in the US had not been remarkable, its pinnacle being employment as an instructor at the newly established Air Corps Tactical School (ACTS) from 1931 until 1936.[93] Along the way, he had become a skilled stunt pilot and formed a three-man team, the Three Men on a Flying Trapeze, that performed to acclaim at air shows representing the army.[94] These stints as a performer, his biographer wrote, allowed him to "escape from the intensity of ACTS," while the stimulation of admiring audiences was especially welcome, as "Chennault had a childlike need for approval."[95]

Chennault was retired from the Air Corps on April 30, 1937, being "incapacitated for active service on account of disability."[96] Stone deaf, possibly as a result of flying in open cockpits, in increasing ill health, as well as in low spirits and chronically aggrieved, he was by the time of his mandated retirement restricted to flying two-seat training aircraft under the careful watch of a safety pilot.[97] The year before retirement he had been in correspondence with a former Air Corps friend already in China, through whose connections he eventually negotiated a two-year renewable contract, with a salary of $12,000 a year (about $200,000 today), to come to China as an instructor.[98] Chennault was in China by May 1937, and the following month met Madame Chiang Kai-shek in her capacity as secretary general of China's Aeronautical Commission, to whom he was introduced as "Colonel Chennault," a quick-witted advancement from his actual rank of retired captain.[99] Some months later he was briefly put in charge of the training and operations of the Chinese Air Force; how long he held this position is not clear.[100]

Chennault arrived in China ahead of some of the most brutal and consequential events of the Sino-Japanese War, which included the fall of Shanghai and the massacre of Nanking. The ineffectual Chinese Air Force could do little in the way of defense (and indeed bombed Shanghai in error), and by early 1938 had almost ceased to exist. For a while, the air defense of China lay with the Soviet Russians, who sent three hundred planes, both fighters and bombers, and combat-ready units of pilots and crew. An attempt was made to build a mercenary air force, the Fourteenth International Squadron, from a motley assortment of foreign soldiers of fortune under the direction of a shadowy character named Vincent Schmidt, described in regional press as an "intrepid veteran of many wars." For a few short months, Chennault supervised their training, but the effort soon fell apart, largely due to internal discord, or as it was officially termed, "lack of homogeneity."[101] Eventually in the summer of

1940, Chiang sent his brother-in-law, T. V. Soong, to Washington to lobby for an idea that had been kicked around by various parties for some time, namely acquiring American planes and pilots to fly them. "It would assist in convincing authorities here if program transmitted were supported by Colonel Chennault," Soong cabled Chiang from Washington, and, accordingly, Chennault was dispatched by Chiang to join the lobby for an American Special Air Unit.[102]

Their pitch was attractive: American air support on a moderate scale, as Chennault outlined in a memorandum prepared for the presentation, could "easily recapture Canton and Hankow"; a striking force "based on Chinese air fields near the coast would, by its threat to Japan proper, Formosa, and their newly acquired bases in Hainan, act as a most effective deterrent to the Japanese designs on Singapore and the Dutch East Indies." The Special Air Unit "need not exceed 200 modern bombers and 300 pursuits" and, critically, "[t]here are 136 airfields available in China, more than half of which are in excellent condition, and all serviceable for both bombers and pursuits," some being within striking distance of Japan, and "so located that they are not easily vulnerable to army attacks." In short, the "Special Air Unit could operate in conjunction with the Chinese army," elsewhere described as "hardy and seasoned," and so supported "could effectively take offensive actions against Canton, to relieve Hongkong; against Hankow to clear the Yangtze Valley; or again the Unit could operate independently in attacking Japan proper, Formosa and Hainan."[103]

After lengthy negotiations, the lobby succeeded in getting a commitment for one hundred Curtiss-Wright Tomahawk P-40 fighters originally destined for the RAF, along with one hundred pilots—a great deal less than Chiang had wanted, but all that could be reasonably spared for what was in essence a covert operation, in which the War Department had little faith. In February 1941, the first planes were shipped, disassembled in crates, to Rangoon. The first contingent of pilots of what was now called the American Volunteer Group arrived in Rangoon in late July. Although recruited from the army, navy, and marines, the pilots had been decommissioned so as to travel as civilians, thus nominally skirting international laws of neutrality.[104] Apart from the chance of adventure, the primary lure to signing up for this covert operation was the pay: $600 a month, or double to three times what each man was then receiving, and a bonus of $500 for each Japanese plane shot down, a sum of about $9,000 today.[105]

The original plan to reassemble the planes in Rangoon and have the pilots fly them on to China was quickly jettisoned, as it turned out that in the whole of China no airfield was ready to receive them. Monsoon rains would turn "the grass-covered airfields of Yunnan into quagmires," Chennault reported in his memoir, but no explanation appears to have been offered about the unworthiness of the other 135 fields, more than half of which had been alleged to be "in excellent condition."[106] Accordingly, the eventual ninety-nine pilots were dispatched to an RAF base loaned by the British near Toungoo, in south-central Burma, to begin a regimen of training—much needed, as evidenced by the high rate of crashes. By December, the AVG was down to sixty-two planes and eighty-two pilots, the other seventeen men having either been killed or departed for home.[107]

Chennault arrived in Toungoo from Chungking to meet the first wave of pilots only in late August, and from his diary it is evident that he spent relatively little time here or in Rangoon.[108] This may have been a good thing, judging from some of the eyebrow-raising advice he gave his pilots as recorded in his memoir, such as the recommendation that pilots "in a tight spot . . . lock their heavily braced wings with the Jap fighters, open full throttle, and they would undoubtedly tear off the Jap's wing while retaining their own."[109] Further insight into the training regimen comes from a transcript of the debriefing of AVG pilot Noel Bacon on April 22, 1942, by a panel of three aviation officers, and is suggestive:

Q: Could you explain something of the system of training you had?

A: The Colonel gave—he guided us, of course, but he left an awful lot up to the units themselves. Shortly after we got there we were divided into three squadrons, most of which we did again by our-

selves [with] the Colonel's permission, and we made up our training program of indoctrination, which would hinge on an awful
lot of combat [training].[110]

Chennault's real talent would be for inspiring the men he commanded.
In this, he was aided by some natural gifts: his physical appearance—tough,
firm-jawed, intense—and deafness, which endowed him with an aura of
stern and inscrutable remoteness. Mostly, though, he had a "common
touch," the ability, arising perhaps from his own up-from-the-backwoods
background, to relate to his men in a personal way that evoked their af-
fection as well as respect. Under Chennault, the young adventurers who
made up the AVG, characters drawn to leave the safer path of orthodox
military careers to become soldiers of fortune, were having the experience of their lives. Quickly dubbed "the Flying Tigers," they enjoyed a freedom unimagined in any normative military outfit that also reaped them
financial reward, fame, and even glamour.

The AVG first saw combat following the Japanese attack on Rangoon
in late December 1941; it ceased to exist on July 4, 1942. Just how successful it was during the roughly six months of its activity is controversial,
with estimates of the "kills" credited to the group varying wildly; of these
estimates, those of Chennault were at the highest end, claiming nearly
three hundred "confirmed" against only fourteen planes lost.[111] The AVG's
most scrupulous historian, Daniel Ford, after combing Japanese records
as well as extensively interviewing any participant he could find over a
decade, concluded that the Japanese "lost about 115 aircraft to the American Volunteer Group in Burma, Thailand, Vietnam, and China" on the
air and on the ground.[112] Against this, the AVG lost 86 of the 116 Toma-
hawks and Kittyhawks it eventually acquired "to enemy action, accident
and abandonment."[113] From the early days of their activity, there was a
well-attested rumor that pilots of the RAF sold victories to AVG airmen
and split the bonuses, and despite dogged spadework by subsequent historians, the rumor has not been convincingly dispelled.[114]

The AVG's skirmishes over the doomed city of Rangoon, and briefly over Kunming, were quickly reported in the American press, where they ballooned into legend. In late December 1941, *Time* magazine ran a pithy article with the catchy title "Blood for the Tigers," which told how, thirty miles outside Kunming, "the Flying Tigers swooped, let the Japanese have it. Of the ten bombers . . . [f]our plummeted to the earth in flames. The rest turned tail and fled. Tiger casualties: none." The single photograph showed "lean, hard-bitten, taciturn Colonel Claire L. Chennault."[115] Promotors of the AVG in Washington approached Disney to design a logo for the new air group, originally envisioning a flying dragon, but somewhere along the line it was suggested—whether by the China Defense Supplies president or the ubiquitous T. V. Soong is unclear—that the icon be a tiger.[116]

Life magazine soon followed with a splashy photo essay, "Flying Tigers in Burma" ("One shining hope has emerged from these catastrophic months of war . . .") with the stunning headline: "Handful of American Pilots Shoot Down 300 Jap Warplanes in 90 Days."[117] These big national stories inspired a welter of articles and columns in local press across the county, each adding new details to the growing legend.

> Now we've had a lot of American heroes since this war started, and there's gonna be more of 'em pop up as time rocks on, but for pure fighter-cussedness, for honest to goodness ability, you're going to be a long time finding the superior of Claire L. Chennault in charge of our air forces in China. Why bless you, he almost knocks Jap planes out of the sky by focusing his hard black eyes on 'em. . . . He is full of ideas. That's why he got cashiered out of the United States Army in 1937. He knew more than his superiors. . . . [118]

Hugely enabling this mythmaking was Chennault himself, who was not the least discomforted by some of the more outrageous claims made in his name. Possibly, he truly believed two articles of his faith: that the Flying Tigers had bought time for Rangoon and had stopped the Japanese advance into Yunnan at the Salween River. In fact, as Japanese records show, the December attacks on Rangoon were only diversions from the real campaign—the capture of Singapore—to keep British forces on the defensive.[119] Similarly, the Japanese Fifteenth Army had never intended to cross the Salween into Yunnan but was looking only toward India; no ground offensive had been planned toward Kunming.[120]

Genuine misinterpretations apart, Chennault was by nature indifferent to facts. "Unfortunately, there were to be . . . [c]ases in which numbers grew, in which interpretations were contrary to prevailing opinion," his most careful biographer, Martha Byrd, wrote, describing a litany of misrepresentations. "Sometimes he succumbed to the temptation to inflate his successes. At other times he was simply careless about facts and figures."[121] Chennault would later be credited with insights and innovations that were not his own, and his deft blurring of lines is evidenced in a characteristic passage, to choose one, from his memoir: "Studying the documents of World War I, I discovered that many of the theories I had evolved independently in Hawaii had been developed earlier by the Germans. . . ."[122] Especially troubling were his claims of combat. These were hinted at privately to individuals and then allowed to spread by word of mouth; publicly he presented a face of honorable reticence, refusing to speak of his "experiences" directly, yet his most diligent biographers report that Chennault's closest associates "denied that he performed any more hazardous duty than scouting enemy positions."[123] Chennault's lack of scruples in committing factually inaccurate statements to paper would have a direct impact on decisions made in the CBI theater as a whole, and the Hump operation specifically. Moreover, the outsized publicity he garnered in the US caused the military to feel constrained by the passionate public opinion in his favor; as stated by the news story above, the growing legend was that "[h]e knew more than his superiors."

On the same day the AVG was disbanded, the Army Air Forces China Air Task Force was formed out of its components, under the command of the now general Chennault, and headquartered in Kunming. For aviation fuel, parts, and matériel, it would be entirely dependent on what could be flown over the Hump and would be defended only by Chinese ground forces. "Under ordinary circumstances this deployment would have been considered tactically unsound," as the Army Air Forces official history summed up the matter, "yet in this instance there was ample reason for the apparent gamble. Because this was the only possible way at that time to fulfill American promises of air aid to China, the risk involved was overbalanced by the importance of encouraging Chinese resistance."[124]

Apparently unconcerned about the purely political nature of his appointment, Chennault moved aggressively. In October 1942, Wendell Willkie, who had run unsuccessfully against Roosevelt in 1940, was in China on part of an extensive goodwill tour and met with the famous former leader of the Flying Tigers. Impressed with what he was told by Chennault and his airmen of their exploits, Willkie requested that Chennault write a report of his ideas that could be taken to the president.[125] In much of his correspondence, Chennault was greatly aided by the fact that among his small staff was Joe Alsop, a well-connected Washington-based columnist and a cousin-by-marriage of Roosevelt. Alsop, who described his role as Chennault's "back-room boy," not only composed much of the fluent, persuasive prose of Chennault's many memoranda but also, through his family connection, ensured they got to Roosevelt outside of normative military channels. In the case of the Willkie letter, Chennault's biographer, Byrd, sees the hand of Merian Cooper, the aviator turned Hollywood producer and briefly Chennault's chief of staff, noting the letter's "short, emphatic punch-lines" and the "cumulative excitement of a script."[126] In any event, Chennault's letter, burning with conviction and untinged with any element of uncertainty or doubt, was delivered to the president in October 1942 as the Allies debated their options in the face of renewed enemy activity following the end of the monsoon. An enlargement of his original pitch for the AVG in 1940, Chennault's plan to defeat Japan called for an independent, China-based air force under his command. "1. Japan can be defeated in China," began the infamous letter.

2. It can be defeated by an Air Force so small that in other theaters it would be called ridiculous.

3. I am confident, that given real authority in command of such an Air Force, I can cause the collapse of Japan. . . .

4. I speak with confidence, but, I believe, not with egotism. The reason for my confidence is based on the fact that since 1923 I have believed firmly in the possibility of Japan making war on the United States; I have devoted the best years of my military life to the study of this subject; I have for five years been unofficial adviser to the Chinese Air Force. . . . for the last year I have commanded first the A.V.G., then the China Air Task Force. . . . This tiny fighter force under my Command has destroyed over three hundred Japanese aircraft confirmed and about three hundred more probably destroyed—I believe the total to be about six hundred—with the loss of twelve A.V.G. pilots and four China Air Task Force pilots from enemy action. . . . I am now confident that given full authority as the American military commander in China that I can not only bring about the downfall of Japan but that I can make the Chinese lasting friends with the United States. I am confident that I can create such good will that China will be a great and friendly trade market for generations. . . . To accomplish the downfall of Japan, I need only this very small American Air Force—105 fighter aircraft of modern design, 30 medium bombers, and in the last phase, some months from now, 12 heavy bombers. . . . My reason for stating that I can accomplish the overthrow of Japan is that I am confident this force can destroy the effectiveness of the Japanese Air Force, probably within six months. . . ."[127]

His tactics would be those of Scipio Africanus, he stated, and, somewhat closer to home, General Sherman—to strike at enemy supply lines.

When the Japanese air force attempted to defend these vital lines, Chennault's air force would destroy it; then it was a simple matter of bombing Tokyo and the Japanese home islands.[128]

The reaction of military professionals to Chennault's plan ranged from skepticism to incredulity: "nonsense; not bad strategy, just nonsense," from General George Marshall.[129] Among other things, basic math exposed inconvenient realities. One gallon of fuel was burned for every gallon ferried to China, and eighteen tons of supplies and matériel were required for every ton of bombs that could be dropped on the Japanese—wildly inefficient ratios.[130] Moreover, as AAF General Arnold had pointed out, after gasoline and supplies had been ferried from Assam to the Kunming terminus, the fuel delivered was still "about 1,500 miles distant from a suitable hop off point for attack against the Japanese mainland."[131] Once in China, there were other complications, such as the fact that the many airfields referenced by Chennault were still being built. Then there were the significant ground transportation problems within China, which lacked utterly the road, rail, or river systems to transport onward supplies that had been delivered to Kunming; yet, as Chennault himself described the situation, "most important fighting bases lay 400 to 700 miles east of Yunnan."[132] And finally, there was the all-important matter of ground defense: given that any effective airpower would be based within striking range of Japanese-occupied areas, retaliation in force for successful air strikes was to be expected—in which case, the fate of all US air bases ultimately lay in the hands of the Chinese army.

It soon became apparent, however, that Chennault's plan had won key support, both in Washington and in China. It tantalized Roosevelt and greatly appealed to Chiang Kai-shek, who saw yet another opportunity to obtain an air force in China, this one entirely at the expense of the US government, which would supply planes, pilots, parts, fuel, and maintenance. Moreover, the doctrine that Japan could be defeated by airpower alone blunted the mounting pressure on him to reform his army.

The Chennault plan was disseminated as the War Department continued to deliberate over the prospective Burma campaign. Meanwhile, the British Akyab advance was to proceed, going overland instead of from the sea as first planned, owing to a severe shortage of landing craft. In turn, the Americans stated their own "great objective": the buildup of air operations in China with a view to "carrying out destructive attacks against Japanese shipping and sources of supply," and the opening of a land route, so as to supply the American-China Air Task Force "in increasing quantities."[133] In essence, Chennault's plans for the air and Stilwell's plans for the ground had converged.

THROUGHOUT ALL THESE DELIBERATIONS, TRAFFIC OVER THE HUMP SLOWLY advanced, and in October the AAF's 1st Ferry Group and civilian airline CNAC together transported 1,016 tons.[134] The essential threats to air traffic, however, were undiminished. On November 17, 1942, a CNAC C-47 heading back to its home base at Dinjan made a hasty departure from Kunming after being warned by the tower that enemy aircraft were incoming. Piloting the plane was Captain John Dean, a former navy pilot who before signing on with CNAC had flown with the AVG and been decorated by the Chinese Air Force for shooting down three enemy planes; with Dean was copilot James "Jimmy" Browne, who had flown bombers to England for the Ferry Command before joining CNAC, and radio operator Kwang Liu Yang. Eager to get underway, they left before their cargo of billets of semi-worked tin, weighing over a hundred pounds apiece, could be fully secured. An hour out from Kunming, flying the high northerly route, they met with bad ice, and Dean radioed a fellow CNAC pilot who was flying east to inquire about conditions on the southerly route. This was the last that was ever heard from the aircraft; but high on the thick-wooded flanks of Mount Tali, a local hunter looked to the sky to see an aircraft plunging at a steep angle, spewing objects as it spiraled in, before crashing into the bowels of the mountain. Weeks later, a villager searching for medicinal herbs on the mountain heights was attracted by the cries of many birds just below the summit. Drawing nearer, he saw they were scavenging among metal wreckage scattered across the steep slope. He recognized an aircraft wing, and that the scavenged material was human remains. There had been two to three people, he estimated, and some of the bones were larger than those typical of Chinese people.[135] The loss of CNAC #60 marked the second fatal crash over the Hump.

With the approach of winter came an increase in winds and violent turbulence over India and Burma and, over China, freezing rain. As winter wore on, clouds and ice conditions also increased, with icing levels beginning as low as eleven thousand feet, which meant, given the terrain, a plane could not fly in the warmer air below. Ice kills planes in five essential ways: its weight can slow the aircraft so that it struggles to maintain its speed and altitude; accumulated on the leading edges of the wings, ice distorts the airfoil, thus thwarting lift; ice clogs engines and hampers propellers; and ice on windows and windshields robs all visibility, so the pilot flies completely blind.

Most ice is caused by the rising of warm air into colder heights; the moisture content of the air and how vigorously it is lifted determine how the resulting ice will be dispersed. In stratus clouds, ice tends to form in bands of only a few thousand feet in depth, but with an extensive horizontal reach. In cumulus clouds, bands of ice tend not to extend far horizontally, but can be deeply vertical: across the Hump, unbroken levels of ice had been reported from 12,000 to 29,500 feet.[136] A pilot's escape strategy is directed by the type of ice encountered: in stratus clouds, an ascent or sometimes descent of a few thousand feet is in order; in cumulus clouds, it is best to turn around.

In Assam, aircraft were equipped with two standard anti-icing features. Inflatable rubber casings fitted to the leading edges of a wing when activated would, in theory, expand to break the ice. De-icing boots must work perfectly, however, if they are to work at all. Boots that work on one wing but fail on the other, or only partially inflate, can render an aircraft less stable than if they had not been used, and Assam's rough stone runways and rotting humidity quickly shredded the rubber boots to tatters.[137] The aircraft were also fitted with a system that fed anti-icing fluid, when available, to the propeller hubs, so as to be dispersed across the blades as they whirled around. Dislodged and flung from the props, the ice slammed against the fuselage with the sound of shrapnel—a sound both terrifying and comforting as audible proof that this system, at least, was working.[138]

Conventional wisdom and experience about ice did not prepare pilots for all conditions over the Hump. Water, as it turns out, can exist in a liquid state at well-below-freezing temperatures. Suspended sometimes in clouds, sometimes below clouds, sometimes in clear air, these supercooled large droplets retain a liquid state—until they come in contact with an impurity or object; touching a sixty-four-foot-long metal and glass aircraft they are transformed, instantly and massively, into ice.[139] Flying back to Assam from China at sixteen thousand feet, Captain Anthony Bally picked up what he regarded as a normal load of wing ice; then, as he recalled, the plane "hit a solid sheet of ice, just like water freezing as it comes out of the faucet." His left engine cut out, and losing altitude he turned back toward Yunnanyi and the nearest airfield. Putting the plane into a sixty-degree bank, he spiraled down over the field, breaking out of the overcast at three hundred feet, with ice still stuck on the propeller blades and engine.[140]

From the blur of weather-related incidents and accidents reported in diaries, memoirs, or mission debriefings, the many references to violent turbulence and ice stand out:

> **Pilot report:** Over the first range of mountains on the India-Burma border there was a line of thunderstorms formed by the hot, moist air mass moving from west to east. The lightning was blinding and turbulence was bouncing the plane around. . . . As I watched the line of squalls, the lightning leaped from cloud to cloud and from cloud to the ground, lighting up the churning clouds. When we approached the line of storms there was no opening between them. . . . I buckled up as [the pilot] slowed the plane to 100 miles an hour, so it wouldn't feel like we had run into a mountain when we hit the dense, black part of the storm.

He turned the rheostats to the cockpit lights up to maximum so they would be the brightest, and thereby to reduce the size of his pupils. In that way he hoped the lightning wouldn't blind him, as it was essential to be able to read the instruments. . . . We weren't more than a couple of plane lengths into the black cloud when the plane bucked, jumped and started up. When a bolt of lightning exploded on the right, I saw the wing was flexed up three feet. . . . [141]

Pilot Report: [A]t daybreak one morning we entered a solid cold front at 16,000 indicated. Our wing boots had been removed and as there was no de-icing fluid available, we flew bare. Suddenly the entire plane began to vibrate . . . What we saw was a thick build-up of clear ice. . . . The altimeter took a nose dive and I ordered the crew to prepare to bail out and I would remain and attempt to get rid of the ice, as we were by this time, I was certain very close to the mountain tops. . . . suddenly it sounded as if the engines were coming apart and were entering the fuselage just behind the cockpit area. We had entered the warmer air and the clubbing props were letting loose large chunks of ice. . . . The ice also began erupting from the wings in large sheets, and again we were flying, just skimming the tree tops at 9,800 feet. This entire episode took less than five minutes. . . . [142]

Pilot Report: Took off from Kunming headed for Chabua ran into ice and turbulence west of Mt. Tali. Started losing power and altitude with bailout order at 14,000 [feet]. Plane stalled out and went into steep spiral before we could get out of the airplane. We were all plastered to the floor with the gravity pull and had a terrific struggle to get to the rear cargo door that had been opened. [Radio operator Sergeant] Bowman, who had been on his knees, by the door was thrown out when the ship went into a spiral.[143]

IN THE SUMMER OF 1942, THE AAF'S FERRY COMMAND HAD BECOME THE AIR
Transport Command (ATC) and merged the responsibilities of ferrying
and air supply into a single streamlined operation across all the theaters
of the war. A massive operational system, comprising over 200,000 personnel and 3,700 aircraft, and spanning continents, the ATC was more
akin to a commercial airline company than to a military aviation unit,
and indeed had been ably shaped and advised by a stream of civilian airline executives and managers. Of these, the most outstanding was C. R.
Smith, the former president of American Airlines and now the deputy
commander of the ATC. Surveying the lagging efforts over the Hump,
Smith recommended to General Arnold that the ATC take over the Hump
airlift from the Tenth Air Force so as to provide the operation with a
much needed "singleness of purpose."[144]

Consequently, on December 1, 1942, the Tenth Air Force's 1st Ferry
Group became the India-China Wing (ICW) of the Air Transport Command. While the Tenth was no longer responsible for the Hump airlift,
it remained responsible for its protection.[145] Since ATC operations were
controlled by headquarters in Washington, the ICW took orders from
General Arnold and ATC commander Harold George, and not from the
New Delhi headquarters of the Tenth, or from Stilwell's CBI headquarters
in Chungking.[146] This arrangement ensured that the coveted and much-
needed transport aircraft could not be "poached" for other needs by the
Tenth or by Stilwell.

It also ensured, as the US Air Forces historians dryly observed, that
"the already complex command structure of CBI would be made more
complicated than ever."[147] The Lend-Lease supplies destined for China
passed through a complex chain of command. War planners in Washington determined the stipulated tonnage.[148] The army's Services of Supply
handled the physical receiving and storage of cargo in Karachi, and transfer onward to Assam. The day-to-day operational oversight of the Hump

airlift was the responsibility of the ATC's newly appointed India-China Wing commander, Brigadier General Edward Alexander, who had been serving as Stilwell's air adviser. Setting up headquarters in Chabua, the principal air base in Assam, Alexander was in the anomalous position of commanding an organization stationed within CBI but, taking orders from Washington, was technically independent of the CBI command. In turn, as the Tenth Air Force was responsible for the defense of the Hump route, its commander, General Bissell, felt that as need arose he had the right—which in fact he did not—to direct cargo to his India-based bomber and fighter units, a misunderstanding that was resolved only when Bissell was transferred in August 1943. Finally, Stilwell remained, as before, the Lend-Lease agent for China, with the authority to determine when and where cargo was delivered within the CBI theater.

In the following months, similarly momentous decisions were made that directed the actions and energies of the theater for the years ahead. In early January 1943, the generalissimo informed President Roosevelt by radiogram that he was unilaterally withdrawing from the planned offensive in north Burma, on which Stilwell had hung such high hopes, and reiterated his position that any "attempt to retake Burma must be a combined overland and seaborne operation." Possibly he had always known that the British lacked the stipulated resources for a seaborne operation, their Eastern Fleet at this point possessing little more than obsolete battleships. "[I]t will be better to wait a few months longer, or even until the monsoon season ends next autumn," Chiang advised, then passed on swiftly to what would appear to be the heart of the matter. "The remarkable potentialities of an air offensive in China have already been demonstrated," he wrote, "the return, I predict, will be out of all proportion to the investment."[149]

"What a break for the Limeys," Stilwell growled on getting the news; the British would be delighted to be off the hook for a campaign they never wanted. "Chennault's blatting has put us in a spot; he's talked so much about what he can do that now they're going to let him do it."[150] But ten days later, perhaps having reflected on the state of unprepared-

ness on all fronts for a major jungle campaign, Stilwell was more philosoph-
ical. "Damn good thing Mar. 1 is off," he wrote in his diary on January 18.
"We'd have been hung."[151]

Stilwell had written his entry while the next major Anglo-American
conference was taking place in Casablanca, between January 14 and 23,
1943. Here, after weighing the many needs in other theaters, from the
small island garrisons across the Pacific to British cross-channel operations, definite plans for a Burma campaign were at last pinned down. The
stated objectives of the campaign were to keep China in the war, to retake Rangoon, to maintain pressure on the Japanese in the China-Burma
arena, and to establish airpower from Chinese bases that would damage
regional Japanese lines of communication. A variation of Stilwell's plan,
using his X- and Y-Force Chinese armies, was endorsed, as was the establishment of an air force in China under Chennault, for the supply of
which, American planners reiterated, it would be necessary to supplement
the tonnage over the Hump by reopening the Burma Road. The target
date for the start of the campaign was now November 15, 1943, with a
consensus that it needed to be over by May 1944, ahead of the following
monsoon.[152] The operation's code name was Anakim, an impenetrably
obscure reference to a race of giants described in the Hebrew Bible as
inhabiting the land of Canaan.

Following the conference in Casablanca, and further discussions in
New Dehli of logistics and structure of command, a delegation of Amer-
ican and British top brass set out for Chungking to present Chiang Kai-
shek with the proposed Burma operation. Heading the delegation was
General Arnold, who came, as he thought, bearing much good news for
China, including a commitment to have 137 transports available for the
Hump operation by April, as well as a group of B-24 bombers in India to
protect it.[153] Joined by the Tenth Air Force's commander, General Bissell,
Arnold flew from New Delhi to Dinjan for an inspection of fighter squad-
rons and antiaircraft units, then met the newly appointed head of the
ATC's India-China Wing for dinner. At just after 6:00 p.m., Arnold and
Bissell set out for their plane; Stilwell and Field Marshal Sir John Dill,

the British representative of the Combined Chiefs of Staff, had left some hours before them.[154]

"Well sir, what a night this was," began Arnold's diary description of the flight. "We climbed to 19,000 feet and all became more or less goofy from the altitude until we took oxygen." For the next two hours, nothing at all could be seen outside the aircraft. Eventually, Arnold was informed the plane would be landing shortly, in some twenty minutes. An hour passed; "then some more," and still they were flying. "Then I learned there was considerable apprehension among our combat crew as to our locality," as Arnold put it, and snapped to attention, asking the navigator if he was taking oxygen. The reply was negative, and Arnold ordered him to do so, then summoned the pilot. "I called the pilot back to the seats where General Bissell and I were and started talking with him," Arnold recalled. "While he was standing there, he crumpled to the floor. No oxygen."[155]

With the loan of Arnold's oxygen mask, the pilot was soon "back in shape," but the plane was still lost. Realizing that the Japanese could well be plotting the plane's course by radar and "must have known where we were, even if we didn't," Arnold ran over the options. "If we turn back into the wind do we run out of gas in the mountains? Do we jump? If so, when? Will we be captured over Mandalay? What should we take with us if we have to jump? What will the people back home think if they hear that the Commanding General, U.S. Army Air Forces and the Commanding General, 10th Air Force and others with us have been taken prisoners?"[156]

Assuming command, Arnold told the pilots to reverse the course they had taken and told the navigator to get a position; the radio operator was picking up only Japanese and Chinese stations. The company was now five hours into the two-and-a-half-hour flight and, having been at nineteen thousand feet without oxygen for most of it, were all again getting "somewhat goofy." Eventually, a fix three hundred miles east of their destination was obtained, and at 1:45 a.m. the plane landed in Kunming. An hour later, Arnold and his party were in bed in the old AVG barracks; at 6:00 a.m. they were woken by a barrage of firecrackers celebrating the Chinese New Year.[157] The next day, Arnold and Sir John Dill left on a CNAC plane for Chungking, where they were scheduled to meet with Chiang.

Chungking, the Nationalists' ad hoc capital, was an ancient city standing on a rocky plateau above the convergence of the Yangtze and Chialing Rivers, whose waters were crowded with square-sailed junks and rusting steamers, and whose wharves thronged with barefoot crowds of ragged workers. A car collected Arnold and his small party for their appointment, and under light snow the drive took them down many slippery hills, past the city's ancient walls, past buildings blackened by Japanese bombings and pulverized rubble. At the river, the party crossed by ferry, then continued to drive up more steep hills to the base of the plateau, where they transferred to sedan chairs and were carried by struggling bearers up nearly four hundred rock-cut steps to the summit. Here at an elevation of some two thousand feet, with views over the rubble of the city and the junction of the rivers, stood Chiang's residence, Huang Shan, or Yellow Mountain, set behind high stone walls in a garden whose trees in the bitter cold were caked with snow[158]—"Peanut's" Berchtesgaden, as Stilwell dubbed it.[159]

After a few minutes, the generalissimo entered the room. By appearance he was well known, for photographs of his lean, upright figure and expression of unruffled confidence had been widely published in the international press, as had images of his beautiful, American-educated wife. Yet few Westerners had met him and taken his measure in person. Now, Arnold formally presented a letter of introduction from Roosevelt, and the delegation settled down to a discussion of the Burma campaign and airpower in China. Dill gave "a very well-prepared talk on the situation in Burma," Arnold recorded in his diary, answering questions from the Chinese and Chiang "in an exceptionally able manner."[160] The house was so cold, Arnold noted, that he shivered throughout the nearly three-hour meeting, although hot tea was served every five minutes. Over an excellent lunch, the conversation focused on Chiang's main preoccupation—the creation of an independent air force under Chennault. Dutifully, Arnold took notes of the many reasons Chiang presented for this: "Chennault is the only one who can handle operations on account of the many complications; Chennault is the only one who has the confidence of the Chinese. . . . Chennault is the only one who can handle the Chinese Air Force. . . . Chennault was the one outstanding tactician and strategist in the Far East."[161] Diplomatically, Arnold told Chiang that he would give a "full report on this matter to the President," but privately he summarized his impression that Chiang would not listen to logic or reason when it came to the realities of the logistics, and that both Chiang and Chennault "glossed over these things with a wave of their hands."[162]

The next day, Arnold awoke in a house so cold its water pipes had frozen, and water was carried to him in wooden buckets. During breakfast, T. V. Soong joined him to say that the generalissimo had summoned him for a private meeting—"no one must accompany me," as Arnold recorded in his diary.[163] ("Arnold had private 'audience' with MAJESTY," Stilwell wrote facetiously in his own diary on the same day.)[164] Outside, snow covered the ground and trees and was still falling. At the top of the long flight of stone steps—no sedan bearers this time—accompanied only by Soong, who was to serve as an interpreter, Arnold was met by the generalissimo, who began the audience without ado. "I am going to be very frank with you, more so than I usually am," Chiang said, according to Arnold's diary transcription of their meeting. "The conference so far has been a failure and I want you to tell the President so for me. It has accomplished nothing."

In anger and amazement, Arnold listened to Chiang's lengthy tirade of complaints and demands: "We have gotten no supplies from anyone. Our movements have been made by our own legs; we have had no trucks. . . . Why do we not receive supplies? . . . Russia gets convoys even though they get sunk. You give them battleships and cruisers to protect them. I want you to tell the President that we are entitled to at least a regular flow of supplies. . . . This conference has been a failure. I have asked for things and the only answer I get from Bissell is why we can't get more tonnage, cannot operate more planes. He cites the railroad up to Assam, the river traffic, and states that the airports will not be able to handle more planes;

excuses, more excuses. . . . Tell your President that unless I get these three things I cannot fight this war and he cannot count on me to have our Army participate in the campaigns. . . . 1. Independent Air Force in China who will be directly under me. . . . 2. 10,000 tons a month over the air transport route into China. . . . 3. 500 airplanes to China operated by U.S.A. or China by November."[165]

Speaking with careful restraint, Arnold reminded Chiang of some of the determinations that had been made at the conference, including the pledge of four thousand tons of supplies a month over the Hump and a total of 137 planes with which to deliver them. As for the bomber squadrons and fighters, he reminded Chiang that "500 planes in themselves mean nothing but when they have gasoline, bombs, fields from which to operate and American and Chinese combat crews, that is something else."[166] The audience ended and "the crowd" came in, which included Stilwell, Sir John Dill, Chinese aviation ministers, and Chennault. Chiang asked Dill a few questions about Burma, and then Dill in turn "smoked him out" by asking directly, and publicly, if he would be taking part in the November offensive. Chiang's response was that he would—but without the stipulated monthly ten thousand tons of supplies and five hundred planes, he could not vouch for its success.[167] Chiang then allowed Arnold "to ask a few questions of Chennault as to air transport." These did not go far, Arnold recorded, "as Chennault professed profound ignorance."[168]

Following this final congregation, Arnold hurriedly left with Stilwell and three Chinese ministers for the airport, from where they departed separately, with snow still falling, for Kunming, where, at the end of this momentous day, Arnold crystallized his reading of Chiang's character. "The Generalissimo does not impress me as a big man," he wrote in his diary.

> [H]e casts aside logic and factual matters as so much trash. Apparently he believes his power can force from his subjects the impossible. He never gave any indication of thoughts of the outside world, except insofar as it gave aid to China. He gave evidence of quick thinking at times but only at times. He did have an orderly

mind, one capable of arranging details and asking pertinent questions. However, the effort died after the first question.

Apparently he has had the power of life and death so long that he expects and his subjects give him the answer he wants. Accordingly, he does not have to think things through. It makes no difference as long as he has his way.[169]

"Arnold and Dill had their eyes opened," Stilwell wrote in his diary of the Chungking summit. Privately, Arnold had told him, "I'll be God-damned if I take any such message back to the President."[170]

But in fact it was Chiang who wrote directly to Roosevelt to present his new demands. He did not repeat the threat that he had made to Arnold—that he could not be counted on to participate in the November Burma campaign—and the letter's last paragraph repeated the lukewarm assurance he had given to the Chungking delegation.[171] Roosevelt, surrounded by pro-China advocates whose embrace of Chennault's airpower plan was fervent, and against the advice of his own War Department, acceded to most of Chiang's demands: Chennault was to command his own air force, which would be built up to 500 aircraft as rapidly as Chennault believed he could support them; the ATC would work to build up to 10,000 tons a month flown over the Hump; until the 10,000-ton figure was reached, Chennault's air force must be allocated the first 1,500 of the projected 4,000 monthly tons that it was believed would shortly be achieved, with Stilwell retaining what was left over for his Chinese army training program. At this time, in March 1943, the actual, as opposed to projected, tonnage carried over the Hump was 2,278 tons.[172]

The extent of Roosevelt's ignorance of the key logistical facts of supplying any venture in China, let alone a new air force, is revealed in a telling memorandum that he wrote, through his chief of staff, to Marshall and Arnold toward the end of February:

The President this morning directed me to inform you that his tentative agreement with the proposed number of cargo planes to be sent to China, 137, was made with an understanding that one bombing plane could carry on one trip sufficient gas and munitions to make four bombing expeditions against enemy targets.

He now understands that understanding to be in error and he therefore now wants the number of cargo planes increased by 30 to a total of 167 and he wants the increase to be without delay.

The President is sure the additional planes can be found.[173]

Evidently, Roosevelt had mistakenly transposed the numerical elements: in reality, four trips across the Hump were required to carry fuel and munitions for one bombing expedition—not the other way around.

MARCH OF 1943 SAW ACTIVATION OF THE FOURTEENTH AIR FORCE—THE only numbered air force created during the war for political rather than military purposes—and Chennault accordingly promoted to command it.[174] "News of 14th A.F. & Maj. Gen. Chennault," Stilwell wrote in his diary. "Christ."[175] To the distress of Chiang and Chennault, however, although the new air force was independent of the Tenth and its commander, General Bissell (whom Chennault despised), Stilwell remained in command of the CBI theater, and over Chennault.

Roosevelt's original purpose in extending Lend-Lease supplies to China had not been for any particular military objective, but rather to offer Chiang and his government a tangible token of America's goodwill, and to indicate to Chiang—and his rivals—that he had America's support. The ambitions of the two CBI American commanders had transformed how these supplies were viewed and would be used. While war planners in Washington stipulated the tonnage to be delivered over the Hump, Stilwell and Chennault now openly competed for the allocation of this tonnage between them. Supplies "for China" came last.

The creation of the 14th Fourteenth Air Force further curdled the relationship between Stilwell and Chennault and their respective supporters.

To Chennault, Stilwell was an infantryman of the old school, stuck in the World War I model of trench warfare, with no clue as to the capabilities, or limitations, of airpower.[176] To Stilwell, Chennault was possessed of grandiose ideas of what airpower alone could achieve, and lacked utterly any comprehension of the logistics required to support and defend it.[177] It was a tragedy of the CBI theater that events would prove both men right.

Meanwhile, spring had come to Assam, bringing the towering thunderstorms and violent mountain winds that made it the most dangerous of all the seasons for flying. By the end of April, nine more aircraft had crashed over the Hump, resulting in the death of thirty-six more crew. Then April ended and it was on to the next monsoon.

5

THE VALLEY OF DEATH

Ten miles outside of Karachi, on the edge of the Sind Desert, the New Malir Cantonment was home to some twenty thousand US service members.[1] New Malir stood starkly on the sandy plain with no other features around it. Sand blew into the stone and tented barracks, settling on every surface so that it was difficult to determine where the garrison ended and the desert began.[2] When sandstorms, or *lous*, arose, blown sand permeated all things, including food, and anyone venturing outside had to throw a cloth over their face and mouth.[3] In Karachi itself, hotels and civic buildings had been appropriated to serve as billets and staff headquarters for US military personnel. American engineers had expanded the port with their wharves and warehouses, and the air force had taken over the Karachi Airport. Vast numbers of shipments of aircraft, crated in disassembled parts, arrived at the busy docks, then were trucked to an RAF maintenance base near the airport, or to a mammoth hangar in Malir that had previously been built to house a dirigible, to be reassembled for delivery to points in India and to China. For most US military personnel, the Karachi docks or airport were their first sights of India, and the desert cantonment was their first base in the country; for

Hump airmen, it was from here that, like the aircraft, they were dispersed to air bases in northeast India.

A standard feature of aviation training at the garrison was a briefing session for airmen on the use of all the items contained in the parachute escape kits they were issued: the fishhooks and line; pocketknife with a can opener; vitamin capsules; iodine to purify water from jungle streams; a polished-metal signaling mirror to flash from mountain peaks and dense forests; a detailed silk map of the terrain they would be flying over, indicating rivers, mountain contours, and elevations; a pocket compass; waterproof matches; mosquito netting; a container of "atabrine tablets to reduce the effects of malaria"—all items necessary for survival in the vast, humid, verdant, dripping jungles of northeast India and Burma.[4]

For most airmen, introduction to the jungle came here, in the desert of Sind. Assam lay some 1,700 miles distant from Karachi, across the breadth of India with all its variety, while Burma, of course, was even farther afield. Yet the distance of these jungles from the airmen is best measured not in miles but in leaps of imagination. Most US airmen in India had never previously been outside their own country. The sights they met with in Karachi, as recorded in diaries, memoirs, and reminiscences, both riveted and horrified them—the camels ambling in the city's dusty streets, the strange people in strange clothing, the many maimed and deformed beggars, the lepers crouching in doorways.[5] The sights, smells, and sounds of the desert city assailed all senses; and for those sitting in the shade of a lecture room listening to words that described yet another unfamiliar landscape, it is likely that the jungle seemed very far away.

Few Americans had entered the great forests of the north, and most printed information about the jungle and jungle survival disseminated to the American airmen came from British sources; one particularly popular publication was the facetiously titled booklet *Under the Greenwood Tree*, and the unmistakable British tone of this and other such instruction undoubtedly inserted yet another element of strangeness into the proceedings:[6]

So many officers think of the jungle as dark and forbidding: lacking in interest and incapable of supporting human life. If left to their own resources in heavy jungle, they are very likely to become as lost and bewildered as an aborigine would be in London. Whereas the latter might, conceivably, attempt to catch and eat the pigeons in Trafalgar Square instead of going to a restaurant, the former are pretty sure to do something equally ludicrous in the jungle.[7]

Delivered in a bluff, no-nonsense military manner, the directives contained in the pamphlets and lectures give a wide array of disconcerting advice: for sleeping in the jungle, consider how birds sleep, with head under wing, and cover your own head with a blanket; get used to eating rice; you may prefer sandals, or *chaplis*, to rubber-soled gym shoes; beware of *Wesa*, a disease of the feet meaning "eaten by sand," which is caused either by sand working into the pores of the skin or by a parasite, but "in any case, especially during the early rains in Northern Burma, if you walk for long periods with wet feet and across sand streams, you are very likely to find the soles of your feet pocked with holes and finally eaten away, till you are crippled"; wear your oldest and floppiest hat; dye your clothes leaf-green, then blotch them with black and brown; bamboo can be used for boiling water, cooking, making a raft, making *panjis* or spears, and for drying racks for meat; "a well-trained dog may be a most efficient sentry, and, even, messenger to your base. Carrier pigeons are invaluable aids to scouting parties working far behind enemy lines: and through their use it is conceivable that you may bring our aircraft very quickly over enemy targets that you may discover."[8]

Perhaps of more concern to the assembled noncombatant airmen was the advanced instruction on jungle warfare:

Now, gentlemen, before I proceed with this talk, I want you to visualize a ¼" map of some of those areas in BURMA, about which

I was telling you yesterday and the day before and to imagine that
you are about to conduct a one-man reconnaissance, for a period
of about a week or more, through such country. . . .[9]

The actual, as opposed to imaginative, journey from the sand-blown
desert classroom to the jungles of Assam was often made by train over
many days and required tedious changes from station to station across
the breadth of India, as the unstandardized rails switched from broad-
gauge to meter-gauge. The Sind Desert with its camel caravans was left
behind, and the domes of New Delhi, buried in trees and vegetation,
appeared; then south to Agra and perhaps a glimpse of the Taj Mahal;
southeast to Calcutta on the great Hooghly River; then north and east
to the Brahmaputra River, which was crossed by ferry; and into the monsoon rain, the mud, the paddies of rice, and the tea gardens of Assam.[10]

From the air, the journey across India passed over the Great Indian
Desert that reminded the pilots of the Middle East, which they had overflown on the outbound crossing to India. Below them, small towns the
color of the desert clustered along the flanks of the great rivers. Winds
sweeping the dry, barren land carried the sand aloft, creating a haze of
sand and making navigation so difficult that to locate airports en route
required diligent searching. In contrast, the airfields of Assam were easy
to spot, set as they were in the flat plains of the cleared valleys.[11] To many
arriving from the desert, lush, verdant Assam seemed fresh and beautiful;[12] but once settled into the bases, taking the measure of the scale and
closeness of the jungle that hemmed the valleys, the young airmen confessed to a sense of claustrophobia. Even on the tea estates, where most air
bases were set, the jungle felt too near, and this despite the many decades
of cultivation and domestication.

Yet it was only from an airborne plane, as pilot and crew were carried
over the dense, green ocean of forest, that the unsurmountable scale of
the jungle universe was made apparent. "Below us was jungle," recalled
pilot Don Downie of his departures from Chabua. "Personally I would
sweat out this part of the trip even more than over the actual mountains.

At least if you hit a hill, you had no struggle to get out."[13] By "getting out," he meant surviving a crash or bailout in the jungle and having the duty to try to walk out. It was specifically for this eventuality that the jungle craft and survival lectures had been given, and for which the parachute escape packs were equipped. "We were issued side-arms," Downie recalled. "[A] Colt .45 and three clips of ammo. One clip was bird shot for finding food. The others were heavy slugs for protection against tigers and other wild animals of the jungle that lay below the first third of our run."[14]

The first bailout had occurred on November 18, 1942, on a return flight from Yunnanyi, the airfield 130 miles west of Kunming, en route to Sookerating in north Assam.[15] Having delivered its cargo of gasoline and equipment for the Fourteenth Air Force, the C-47 was returning with twenty-four Chinese soldiers destined for Stilwell's training program in Ramgarh, as well as the usual crew of pilot, copilot, and radio operator. As was typical, the plane carried parachutes only for the crew.

"The airplane ran into a very severe storm," recalled radio operator Matthew Campanella. "[I]t was completely engulfed with fog plus heavy icing conditions." Amid the ice and fog the plane was soon lost, unable to pick up the homing radio beacon on its liaison set. Ice flung from the propellers crashed against the fuselage, and amid the whiteout and lost bearings, the lurching and crashing, it seems the pilot panicked. "The pilot, his face ashen bluish-gray from lack of oxygen and strain, ordered the co-pilot and myself to bail out," Campanella reported. "He would stay with the ship and the passengers. We wanted to stay also, but he said 'get out, get going.' The co-pilot asked, 'Is that a request or an order?' 'It's an order,' the pilot answered."[16]

As the plane lurched and slipped, losing altitude, and ice exploded against the aircraft's metal flanks, the two men hurriedly put on their parachutes. They were at about sixteen thousand feet. Campanella grabbed his .45, a flashlight, a unit of K rations, and a canteen, while the copilot, Lieutenant Cecil Williams, radioed that, by order of pilot Captain Owens, they were bailing out. At the rear of the plane, the men fumbled with the door, fighting to get it open, then stood in the gaping space—there is no record of how the watching Chinese troops reacted. Whiteout conditions completely obscured whatever lay below, whether mountain peaks or the vast jungle. "I asked, "Who's going first? The Lt. answered, 'We'll jump together.' We interlocked arms. The Lt. looked back at me and asked, 'All set?' 'Set,' I replied."

As the men jumped, Campanella was instantly knocked out, perhaps by striking the door or even the tail of the plane, briefly gained consciousness, then blacked out again. He came to his senses on top of a tree some seventy-five feet above the ground with no memory of having opened his parachute. From the darkness, Williams was calling to him, and the men realized they were in the same tree. As Campanella unbuckled his chute, he fell to the ground, where his landing was cushioned by underbrush and vines. Williams climbed down—a painfully slow process in the darkness, taking hours. By midnight, both men were on the ground together, unharmed.

In morning light, they took stock of their situation and realized that they had lost much of their equipment in the jump; Campanella had left his jungle kit in the tree, Williams had lost his shoes and one of his flying boots. From Williams's kit they had those essentials—fishhook, quinine, iodine for water, matches—that had been the subject of the jungle survival demonstrations.

Over the next twelve days, the airmen wandered in the forest. Both were city boys; Matthew Campanella, age twenty, was from Atlantic City, New Jersey, and a bookkeeper in civilian life; Cecil Williams, age twenty-eight, was from Uniontown, Pennsylvania, and, unusual for a pilot, was bespectacled. In daylight, they followed a mountain stream—painfully in the case of Williams, who was walking with one flying boot and a leather glove over his other foot. At night, they huddled in leaves, listening to the jungle sounds. By the fourth day, they had exhausted their rations, the iodine, and the matches, and, having failed to catch fish with the provided line and hooks, had killed one by firing Campanella's .45 into a school of them. The rest of the ammunition was spent shooting at three deer the men spotted wading in the stream; unafraid, the deer stood still to watch them as Campanella emptied his gun, and then they ran off. Wild lemons became abundant, and the men gorged on the fruit that was so potently sour it caused their lips to chap and bleed and their eyes to run with tears.

The stream became a river bounded by towering cliffs, and in swimming across, Campanella lost his own shoes. Both barefoot now, the men hobbled along on makeshift crutches, until one day, as Campanella reported, "we fell to our knees and prayed to God that this day we might see people and civilization of some sort." That afternoon, two local men appeared in the forest and, after an exchange of sign language, led the lost Americans to their village, a tiny compound comprised of four bamboo huts inhabited by some forty souls. "They appeared to be of a mixed Chinese-Indian type," Campanella reported. They had "slanted eyes and high cheek bones, like the Chinese, but somewhat darker. They seemed to speak a Hindustani dialect."

Hospitably received and generously fed, the airmen recovered. On their third day in the village, runners bearing notes written by the airmen were dispatched to they-knew-not-where; and on the eighth day the roar of a low-flying plane was heard overhead. From the sky above, supplies rained down on the village—shoes, food, blankets, rifles, ammunition, field jackets, flying boots, cigarettes—and the following morning, a second, very small plane appeared, a PT-17, a little biplane used as a trainer. Shortly after it had been spotted, a white man in a flying uniform walked through the village. Shaking hands with the two ragged airmen, he introduced himself as Major Paul Droz. He had made a precarious landing in a small buffalo pasture just beyond the village, but for the return flight it would necessary to clear a longer runway for takeoff. The plane was so tiny that it could not carry both men on one trip. The airmen also learned from Droz that the pilot of their plane had eventually landed safely after they had bailed out.

Once safely back at Sookerating, the rescued men learned that the village runner had brought their message to Fort Hertz, which, by air, was only some sixty-five miles away from where they had fallen from the sky.

The men also learned that it was now December 10, that they had been lost for twenty-three days, and that their names were inscribed on the memorial list posted on their squadron bulletin board.

THE STORY OF THE RESCUED AIRMEN GAVE DRAMATIC DEMONSTRATION OF the first lesson of survival in the jungle, namely that salvation would not depend on fishhooks and instruction on edible plants but on the good fortune to fall in with the people who called the jungle home. The villagers who rescued Campanella and Williams were Kachin, one of the many hill tribes who lived in the harsh mountain ranges and jungles that form the great horseshoe-shaped arc across the top of Burma, and included the Chin and Naga of the hills that bear their names on the Indian border; the Shan of the Shan Plateau to the east and south, abutting China; and the Karen of the Karen Hills on the Burma-Siam border. While the geographical place-names commemorated the most numerous tribes, there were many others who were little visited or even known by outsiders: the Wah, the Abor, the Mishmi, the Dafla, the Duplan, the Ngolok, and Lolo.[17]

Of all the people inhabiting the remote forested highlands, the Kachin and Naga were most closely associated with the Allied war effort. The name "Kachin" is in fact a misnomer for the Jinghpaw and related tribes that are known by different names in different regions—Jinghpaw in Burma, Singpho in Assam, Jingpo in China. The common language of all is Jinghpaw, and Jinghpaw—meaning "a man"—is the term of reference all would accept. The term "Kachin" may be a Burmese corruption of *ye-jen*, Chinese for "wild" or "jungle men." If so, the term is in fact a slur, but so well established, and by such a range of writers past and present—including those who are "Kachin"—that it is impossible to avoid.[18] According to their own tradition, they came into Burma following the Irrawaddy River from a place called Majoi Shingra Bum, meaning "naturally flat mountain," which has been taken to refer to some part of the eastern Tibetan plateau.[19] In the many histories written about them, whether by Kachin,

Burmese, or European authors, certain traits are invariably emphasized: their love of independence and liberty, their truthfulness, vengefulness, and hospitality.[20] "They are simple, amiable, and even hospitable to those who seek shelter under their roof. They are also capable of reacting to hostility with vengeance," according to one Kachin writer. "There is no rule of civil conduct in fighting. It is always brutal, ugly, and often savage."[21] Insults or injuries were never to be left unaddressed, and if a man did not obtain satisfaction in his lifetime, the debt of vengeance was passed on to his children.[22] These warrior traits were greatly respected by and of great benefit to the several Allied paramilitary entities with whom the Kachin worked in the jungles of Burma; the honoring of vengeance in particular would cost the Japanese dearly.

The people closest to the Allied bases, and most frequently referred to in any news press about the CBI theater, were the Naga, who inhabited the rugged country around and over hills that bore their name on the Assam-Burma border. They were, as the jungle instruction pamphlet *Under the Greenwood Tree* put it, "a very tough crowd indeed."[23] In fact, they were headhunters, and while this practice, along with slavery and human sacrifice, had been suppressed under British rule, it had not been eradicated, and evidence of the practice was not difficult to find, despite an order to burn all stockpiles of human skulls. Villages still retained their skull racks and massive war drums, made from entire tree trunks up to fifty feet long, which traditionally were beaten in triumph when victorious raiding parties returned with their trophy heads, and certain articles of dress, such as cowrie shells and human hair, were worn only by warriors who had taken heads.[24] The heads were not, as might be expected, those of other warriors, but were often of women and children, as the age, sex, or status of the victim had no bearing on the desirability of their heads. Moreover, as death in battle was seen as a disgraceful and inglorious fate, a would-be warrior who felt that raiding another village was too dangerous could purchase a slave and take that person's head with no diminishment of prestige.[25]

Very few outsiders achieved intimate glimpses of actual Naga village life, and it was the old characterization of head-hunting savages that prevailed. "To the Nagas, human life has no more value than a most paltry household utensil," was the summation of Surendra Majumder, a medical officer working in Naga country in the 1920s, and who, while knowing the Naga better than most, still lived apart from them.[26] Yet Ursula Bower, a young English woman who lived among the Zemi Naga for many years, described how her friend Haichangnang appeared one day in her doorway, his face "disfigured by weeping," begging her to give him any medicine she might possess that would poison him; his small daughter had died, and he could not bear for her "to go the long, dark road of the dead alone."[27]

In their tours of the remote villages of Burma's mountain arc, British frontier officers had come to know the chiefs, the customs, and the languages of many of the hill people. Yet despite the diligence of these officers to scour and know the land of their administration, so vast was the area and so difficult to access that there remained unknown peoples who were only encountered when American airmen fell upon them from the sky; as happened when CNAC pilots Camille "C. J." Rosbert and Charles "Ridge" Hammell crashed on their way to China amid the remote Mishmi Hills on the border with Tibet.[28]

Rosbert, copilot Hammell, and radio operator Li Wong had taken off from their base in Assam, entering thick fog from the moment of departure. It was April 1943, some weeks before the monsoon, yet within minutes after takeoff "monsoon rain was flooding down the windshield in torrents" Rosbert recalled, and at twelve thousand feet the rain turned into snow. Rosbert was one of the few former AVG pilots who had signed on as a CNAC transport pilot when the AVG was wound down. Hammell, the copilot, was a master of desert flying, having come from CNAC's "Africa Corps," and the flight was to be his initiation over the Hump. According to Rosbert, Hammell "distrusted this land of three-mile-high-peaks," but as the heavy-laden C-47 climbed through the snow and fog, he relaxed, and reached back to pat Wong on the back, saying, "We're okay now. Another thousand feet and we'll be clear of the hump."[29]

As he spoke, a film of ice was spreading over the windshield, then over the wings. Within minutes, the film had turned to a block of six-inch-thick ice. "We started to drop," Rosbert recalled, "not in a dive, but slowly. Then we lost the last slit of visibility." Encased within the frosted capsule, the men were flying blind. Pressing his hand against the glass, Rosbert was able to melt a small wormhole of visibility. They were in a cloud. Suddenly, this opened to reveal a jagged peak dead ahead. Grabbing the controls, Rosbert banked the plane sharply. "A dark object swept by. A terrible scraping noise tore under the cabin; an explosive crash struck right behind me; the engines raced into a violent roar." An uncanny stillness followed, and then silence. They had hit the mountain at 180 miles per hour.

The radio operator's station had been "crumpled like tissue paper," and Wong lay dead, his neck broken. Wounded as well as shaken, the two pilots collected their strength to examine their situation. Outside, the silent snow was swirling in a bitter wind, and the plane lay at a thirty-degree angle on a mountain slope. They were, they estimated, some sixteen thousand feet high somewhere in the Himalayas near the Tibetan border. Both men suffered injuries to their legs, Hammell with a badly sprained ankle, Rosbert more severely. Looking down, he noted, "I seemed to be standing on my leg bone, and my foot was lying at right angles to it." In the night, a howling wind buffeted the plane, causing it to rock gently on its mountain perch. In the clear light of morning, they saw that the plane sat within a basin of snow, surrounded by three towering peaks, one of which reared not more than two hundred yards directly before them, like a wall of ice and snow. "Even on a clear day like this, no one could put a plane down in this spot and get out alive," Hammell said.[30]

For three days the two men rested, nursing their wounds and surviving on emergency rations in the plane. Venturing out at dawn on the fourth day, they studied a timberline some five thousand feet down the mountain, knowing that if they set out they would need to reach its shelter by dark. Ice-encrusted peaks glittered all around them; the plane was buried under two feet of snow, invisible to any aircraft searching for it.

Splinting their legs with plywood torn from the plane floor and bound with strips of parachute silk, the men floundered helplessly in the snow for half the day, then retreated back to the plane, defeated. The next day, however, they hit on a daring plan, and rather than attempting to walk they skidded and rolled down the mountain to the forest.

Once inside the tree line, the men crawled and hobbled down the mountain for eight more days, as hunger, pain, and exposure made them daily weaker. On the ninth day, they came upon faint, barely discernable evidence of a human presence—saplings that had been notched to mark a trail. Four days after this discovery, the men stumbled into a clearing, in which stood the remains of a hut that had burned to the ground. Dragging themselves over another hill, they came upon an intact, thatched hut made of bamboo and standing on stilts some four feet off the ground. Throwing themselves through the doorway, the Americans fell into a room filled with such dense smoke they could hardly see; but as their eyes adjusted to the murky light, they saw they had not only crashed into the strange hut, but into a prehistoric time.

The inhabitants of the settlement were Mishmi. All were barefooted and had long, matted hair. They were sparsely dressed, the men in loin cloths and sleeveless jerkins, the women in blankets, and adorned with ornaments made of animal teeth, beads, and what appeared to be coins. Living far from easy sources of water, they were caked in a lifetime of dirt. No words exchanged between the two parties were intelligible to the other, but the pilots were reassured by the friendly nodding and smiles of the tribesmen. Eventually, the villagers led Rosbert and Hammell over the hill to another settlement, where the pilots were carried on pallets into the corner of the large room of another house that seemed to be the home of a sprawling, extended family. "There, in that primitive smoke-filled hut, deep in the heart of the Himalayas, Ridge and I held court for two incredible weeks," Rosbert recalled. Many things about their hosts astounded the Americans, including their apparent immunity to pain; men and women took hot pots from the fire with their bare hands and passed them unhurriedly from person to person, and the men would sift through red-hot embers with their hands, searching for a tinder to light their pipes. One day, a male villager carefully examined the pilots' damaged ankles, then ran his hands over his own by way of comparison. Discovering a bump on his anklebone, he "simply drew his knife, sliced off the bump with one deft blow, and with the blood streaming down his foot, returned the knife to the scabbard and kept right on talking to us as though he had simply brushed away a fly," Rosbert marveled. Mostly, the airmen were astonished at the depth of generous and kindly hospitality they received at the hands of these strangers.

One evening, an elderly trader, who had come from the Tibetan hills, turned up in the village. On meeting the airmen, he pointed urgently to their pencil, one of the few artifacts from their former lives the pilots still carried. Reluctant to part with it, they shook their heads, and the trader left visibly disappointed. Days later, however, his son appeared, bringing gifts of tea and food—and also gestured urgently to the pencil. "To keep in his good graces, since his father might be the one to get word to the outside, I tore off a corner of my flying map and wrote this note: We are two American pilots. We crashed in the mountains," Rosbert recalled. The boy snatched the paper away and disappeared.

Four days later he was back again, visibly exhausted. Beaming, he presented the Americans with a sealed envelope. "With hearts beating like hammers, Ridge and I clawed the envelope open," Rosbert recalled. "It contained a message from a Lieutenant W. Hutchings, the commanding officer of a British scouting column about a four days' march away. He was sending rations by the messenger, and a medical officer with aid would follow shortly." An hour or so later, porters arrived carrying supplies, followed some days later by the medical officer. "He told us that no white man had ever set foot in this country before, and, had it not been that the British column, because of the war, had penetrated even as close as four days' march, we might never have been found. It was one chance in a million." The trader's son had made the eight-day trek, there and back, in four days.

It took the party another sixteen days of hiking to get free of the mountains. Safely returned to their base in Assam, the pilots used maps to retrace their course and found, as Rosbert observed, "[t]he strange world we had come from was only ninety minutes—flying time—from our base at Dinjan."

THE EXPERIENCE OF THE CNAC PILOTS WAS REMARKABLE FOR MANY REA-sons, the primary one being they had survived a crash into a mountain. Mountain crashes were not unusual, but generally they were fatal, and rarely did anyone walk away from the crumpled wreckage that lay strewn below the Assam-to-China flight path, dubbed with dark humor "the aluminum trail." Most airmen who "walked out," walked out of the jungle. Logically, then, it would be expected that the mountains would hold most terror for a pilot, and yet this was not the case. Perhaps this was because a mountain crash could be expected to result in a clean and immediate death. Perhaps, too, mountains were, in the broadest outline, familiar to American airmen, who could at least muster some point of reference—say, the Rockies—from the sum of their experiences, whereas nothing in the whole of North America offered any clue that a phenomenon like the vast jungles of Burma existed on planet earth.

Airmen met the jungle on arrival in Assam, where the thick, humid air that made a misery of daily life seemed to be exhaled from the surrounding forest, which thrived and grew luxuriant on the enervating moisture. Stories about what lay inside circulated the air bases, drawn from reports of downed airmen, foot soldiers, and tea planters. To follow a trail through the jungle, it was said, was to step into a dense, green tunnel, a gloomy, half-lit vault infused with uncanny silence, where the most audible sound was the stealthy drip-drip of moisture through the vegetation. The sky far above might be a piercing blue, but one would not catch a glimpse of it from within the jungle, except when standing on the bank of a broad stream or river. The canopy was so high and so dense that rainfall on it could take fifteen minutes to be felt below. Beneath the canopy, cables of vines and lianas and impenetrable stands of bamboo created a screen of undergrowth so dense as to impair movement, vision, even sound. Fifteen yards ahead was the farthest a man could expect to see within deep jungle, and two hours of sweating effort might advance him a mere six hundred yards.[31] Report after report from surviving airmen cited an unnerving phenomenon of jungle acoustics, of men who had bailed out together and landed only 150 feet apart yet had been unable to hear one another's voices—the jungle simply swallowed the sound.[32]

Dropped into the jungle, a man was surrounded by vigorous, vegetative life, and yet his great fear would be starvation. Underfoot, the dank earth was blanketed with decayed vegetation, and from foliage at all levels—around, beside, above, and on the trail—leeches—brown ones, green ones, tiger-striped ones—sniffed for blood, stretching, even propelling themselves toward their prey, dropping from above to fall down the shirts of the bypasser, climbing up trouser legs, slipping through shoelace holes and, most dreadfully, as the worst jungle-survival stories told, into bodily orifices from which, swollen with blood, they were extracted only with the most painful difficulty.[33] The abundant insect life—giant centipedes sixteen inches long, malarial mosquitoes, and the tormenting sand flies—was ever-present, but the apparent absence of major wildlife was striking and unsettling, even if one knew this was because one's own panting, blundering presence frightened such life away.[34] Nonetheless, intruders in the jungle knew not to drop their guard. The high-pitched screams of unseen monkeys gave warning they were being watched, and reports of unexpected encounters abounded: one British patrol was ambushed by a wild boar that exploded toward them from out of the jungle murk.[35] A downed American pilot was shadowed over two days by a tiger that strolled along the opposite side of a steam, stopping when he stopped, moving on when he moved; eventually the pilot concluded that the big cat was merely curious about him. Other airmen were gored by water buffalo on the outskirts of the jungle, and impaled and thrown by an elephant.[36]

As the sun went down, the jungle was briefly filled first with eerie shadows, then with a jumble of sounds—humming and rasping insects, croaking frogs, the howling and coughing of animals unknown, and the rustle of leaves as some creature of the night slipped past.[37] Since the air bases of Assam had been thrown up in clearings hacked raw from this same jungle, they, too, were penetrated by its sounds. "The night was pitch black, the jackals were howling, the rain was pouring down," an airman recalled of night guard duty at Chabua, "and I was scared."[38] Giant moths, like the great Atlas with its snakeskin-patterned, ten-inch wingspan, flitted through windows, and creatures of the jungle, insects and snakes, infiltrated the primitive *basha* barracks where the airmen lived—even into their beds, despite the shroud-like mosquito netting under which each man slept. One night, a tiger leaped into the pen where a tea estate manager near the base kept his prize Brahma bull, which the tiger stunned with a swipe of its paw—then carried the fifteen-hundred-pound animal over the enclosing fence and back into the jungle. This was the kind of incident that tended to capture attention and make its way into the Hump airman's lore.[39]

Addressing the special dread with which the jungle was held, air force higher-ups began to conceive the idea that it was unfamiliarity that needed to be addressed, and that if the jungle's "dark mystery" were explained, all would be well.[40] This theory informed the otherwise inexplicable decision to allow a young amateur herpetologist to create an extensive collection of deadly snakes in the heart of the Chabua air base. Corporal Wesley Dickinson, a medical technician working on malaria control with the Ferry Command, had become interested in snakes while in high school in Long Beach, California, where he made the acquaintance of a Mrs. Grace Wiley, who ran a snake farm in that city, and whose literal and physical embrace of deadly snakes had won her much press notoriety. By chance, Dickinson's superior officer at Chabua, Colonel Don Flickinger, was also from Long Beach, and so when, in March 1943, Dickinson arrived at his office for his first interview wearing a huge python draped around his thin body, Flickinger recognized him.

The two men caught up on hometown news, then veered off to the subject of snakes. Dickinson had purchased the python in Agra on his way to Assam, and had come to realize that here, in this jungle clearing in India, close to the border with Burma and its vast, pristine jungle habitat, lay opportunities beyond his dreams to pursue his peculiar passion. By another happy chance, Dickinson's immediate superior was also a herpetologist, and between the three men it was agreed that, as long as Dickinson could stay abreast of his official duties, a snake farm would be a "very useful educational facility to the over-all survivor program for air crews."[41]

So it came to be that a large *basha* was constructed adjacent to the medical office and dispensary to create a combined medical supply center and snake pit, paid for with medical supply funds. Indefatigably, Dickinson searched out for purchase or discovery prize specimens of every variety he could attain, thus bringing into the naked light of day creatures whose natural home was the murk and dank shadows of the unknown jungle; and in doing so he allowed airmen, whose greatest terror was that jungle, to confront animals they had not known they had to fear.

The brightly banded krait, for example, infuses its victims with a neurotoxin so potent as to make it one of the most deadly serpents in the world. Mostly nocturnal, the krait allegedly presented little danger in daylight hours—but then it was the jungle night that airmen most feared, and it was at this time, as they now learned, that the krait ventured out and became aggressive. A krait bite causes tremors, spasms, and eventually paralysis, and death by suffocation usually occurs six to twelve agonizing hours later, when the body's breathing mechanism shuts down. Kraits were not generally met in the course of ordinary life, but the Indian cobra (*Naja naja*) were common sights; these could inflict their neurotoxic venom by spitting, as well as with their fangs. Deadly bamboo snakes, with their coffin-shaped heads, were found on the tea estates, where their pale yellowish-green coloring blended with the young tea bushes.[42] Most terrifying was the hamadryad, or king cobra, the largest venomous snake in the world, which attacks on sight and can travel over ground faster than a man can run. Typically, these grow up to thirteen feet in length, but Corporal Dickinson could show the airmen a remarkable specimen, jet-black and twenty-two feet long—the longest ever recorded in or outside of captivity. Pythons and boas were also fairly easy to obtain, including the Burmese python, which grows up to twenty feet in length and uses its great constricting muscles to suffocate its prey before consuming it whole.

Dickinson also used the opportunity to educate himself about the snakes and studied them carefully. The fruits of his observations resulted in a publication in the scientific journal *Herpetologica* regarding spitting and non-spitting cobras that sheds light on Dickinson and his methods as much as on his snakes: "I had the snake out in the yard to take some pictures," he wrote of the four-foot-long *Naja naja*, which was captured in the Sundarbans south of Calcutta.

> I advanced my foot, protected by long pants and heavy shoes, to within striking distance. The snake would then pose for a short time. After doing this several times it stood up and spread, but not as much as usual. Again I advanced my foot. This time the snake struck with a sharp hiss, and there were two lines of venom on my pants leg. I again tasted this and found that it was apparently venom. I saw the snake strike, but not in the usual way of the spitting cobras, but rather in a way which I have seen many times in the cobras from this area. In striking they tilt the head back until the under side of the head is uppermost, then they come forward almost with a snap. I usually fear for the life of the snake when it strikes like that, so sharp is the jerk. . . .[43]

Dickinson claimed that fear, not venom per se, was the cause of many fatal snakebites. He was able to test this assumption when the king cobra, now named Black Don, bit him—by accident, as Dickinson was anxious to have it known, after the reptile had misjudged his hand for some hand-fed delicacy.[44] True to his creed he did forgo antivenom treatment, but fortunately for him a gifted surgeon at the base supervised his convalescence and was later credited with saving his life.[45] Despite such travails, Dickinson's enthusiastic diligence created a collection of over one hundred snakes garnered from throughout the theater of operations, and became famous enough to warrant special tours for visiting VIPs. How the collection served its original purpose of uplifting the morale of fearful airmen by the instruction it offered, however, cannot be ascertained. By early January 1944, as Colonel Flickinger observed, "it became obvious that soon something would have to be done with this collection." A brief survey of the great zoos around the world yielded the realization that none had a collection that rivaled that of Corporal Dickinson, and it was decided to offer it in its entirety to the Smithsonian Institution's zoo in Washington. Arrangements were accordingly made, and eventually an old bomber was enlisted to carry Dickinson and eighty-eight snakes to Washington, DC. At the back of the unheated plane, Dickinson huddled with his charges throughout the long flight, at the end of which it was discovered that twenty-eight snakes had died of cold, including the magnificent twenty-two-foot-long king cobra.

THERE WERE IN ASSAM ANY NUMBER OF ENGLISH-SPEAKING INDIVIDUALS available to give firsthand jungle instruction. The most accessible were the tea planters, who had proven their resourcefulness and hardiness during the great evacuation from Burma, when they had trekked over the Patkai Range to assist refugees struggling out of the Hukawng Valley. "Impeccable as their manners might be, they were a rough-and-ready frontier lot," according to an officer with the Office of Strategic Services, or OSS, America's fledgling special operations and intelligence unit.[46] These were people who made excursions into the jungle, often with their young families, for pure pleasure, taking picnics beside jungle streams and admiring the profusion of butterflies and wild orchids and the delicate ferns that clustered on the tree branches. The planters managed large estates and the thousands of Indian laborers, male and female, who worked on them, and doing this job well entailed learning languages and getting along with a variety of people, as well as tackling problems peculiar to the region, such as incursions of tigers, elephants, and the many snakes. Most managers had come out to India from Britain to learn a trade and work their way up the ranks of the profession, but Tea, as the industry was familiarly called, also looped in "characters."[47]

Many men who had worked in Burma as frontier officers or foresters in the rugged Burmese hill country—the jungle-wallahs—were also seasoned outdoorsmen, multilingual, and at home in the forest. The most outstanding of these were quickly recruited to the war effort. Oliver "Oscar" Montague Beauchamp Milton had worked as a forest assistant for Steel Brothers, a major trading house and exporter of rice, teak, and oil. As Burma fell, he had led a group of one hundred women and children through the jungle and hills to safety ahead of the Japanese advance; after depositing them at Fort Hertz, and he accompanied the Chinese 96th Division on its two-month-long retreat to Kunming, and "thence," as he recalled, "to Calcutta on a very uncomfortable flight."[48] A gifted linguist, Milton claimed he could read and write twenty-eight languages and was also an amateur botanist and ornithologist, as well as a photographer and painter; he was said to be a descendent of the poet John Milton.[49]

Father James Stuart of the Catholic Columban order came from Derry in Northern Ireland, but had lived and worked in Burma since 1936, first on the upper Irrawaddy River, and then among the Kachin in the wild northern "Triangle" that lay between the two rivers that converged to form the Irrawaddy. In his new mission settlement, he made few converts but many friends. News of the Japanese invasion had been slow to reach him, but when he did learn of it, his actions were decisive. On receiving word of a terrible Japanese assault on Kachin villagers and of the deliberate cruelties inflicted on them, he set out on jungle trails to help the survivors, leading hundreds to safety through the early monsoon. Over many months he ran interference with the Japanese, with whom he played the holy fool. "Are you Chinese?" he asked innocently on encountering the leader of a Japanese patrol.

"No, we are Japanese," was the reply. The officer spat on the ground. "Are you English?"

"No," Father Stuart replied, spitting on the ground. "I am Irish."[50] Throughout the war, Stuart used his jungle lore to rescue terrorized villagers, and served as a liaison between the Kachin and Allied special forces. Other missionaries with intimate acquaintance of the Burmese jungle were the Morse family, American evangelists who had first come to Burma in 1927 after trekking overland with two other missionary families from Yunnan. The family eventually settled in Western China, but the family patriarch and his sons moved continually across the China-Burma border by way of jungle trails and, like Father Stuart, were recruited to the Allied cause.

Francis Kingdon-Ward was one of the last of the great line of explorer botanists, or "plant hunters," and made a series of major expeditions amid "the tangle of mountain ranges" where Assam, Tibet, Burma, and China all converge.[51] When the Japanese invaded, he was in Putao, in the region of Fort Hertz, and decided to walk north. Crossing the fifteen-thousand-foot Diphu Pass, he turned west and strolled into Sadiya, in Assam, having covered a distance of some four hundred miles of rugged terrain.[52] Once in Assam, he was asked to give lectures on jungle survival to the Assam-based airmen. His survival tips seem to have been condensed to five main points: show local residents you are friendly; conceal any firearm; never refuse food that is offered, regardless of what it might be; never enter a village at night; and never touch a woman or her garment.[53]

An attempt to garner and coordinate the expertise of this disparate group had been made as early as April 1942. As Burma teetered, General Wavell had ordered the creation of a secret guerrilla force to disrupt the Japanese lines of communications if the Japanese advanced beyond the Burma border into Assam. Modeled along the lines of the Assam Rifles, a paramilitary force operating across the Naga Hills, the new force was to cover the one-thousand-mile-long northern frontier between India and Burma, recruiting locally from the Kachin and Naga villages. The operation was referred to as Plan 5, designated with the Roman numeral V and, subsequently, due to a misreading of the numeral, dubbed "V Force." The clandestine and somewhat freewheeling nature of the new order attracted adventurers like the jungle-wallahs, many of whom had used their consummate survival skills to escape Burma as the country fell, often leading others out with them.

Also recruited to V Force was Ursula Violet Graham Bower, the young English woman who had settled among the Zemi Naga in a village in the Barail range that sprawls across Assam into Nagaland. She had entered Naga life as an amateur anthropologist and photographer, but these were less vocations than excuses to live the life she wanted among people she had come to love, and she probably knew more about Naga culture than any outsider alive. A V Force captain, she was entrusted with raising and commanding a scout unit to operate through the northern hill country.[54] She also offered jungle survival courses for RAF and US airmen, aided by her Naga colleagues, who acted the part of "hostile natives" gleefully chasing "downed aviators" through the jungle. Bower described one "R.A.F. chap" charging strongly up a steep hill—"quite a fit little man," as Bower, who was five foot nine, observed. "The chap thought he was doing well, then all of a sudden, a hand reached out and tapped him on the shoulder. . . . The Naga had overtaken him at something like twice his speed." From Bower the airmen learned that if they met a tiger in the jungle it would probably not harm them, but it was best to creep away if they heard it growl. They learned to burn leaches off their bodies, to boil water in bamboo, and to set impaling bamboo spikes in the ground to thwart an advancing enemy. Years afterward, one RAF recruit recalled Bower's lessons and her "English rose charm": "'Good morning boys. Have you had a good breakfast?' 'Yes thank you Ursula.' 'Today you're going to learn about defence. How to use the bamboo as a weapon. . . .'"[55]

In the event the Japanese did not advance to India, and after Burma fell, V Force served as an intelligence-gathering entity and organization around which the many hill villagers loyal to the British could rally; it also undertook to look for downed aircraft, both Japanese and Allied.[56] For almost a year, it remained the most seasoned, jungle-savvy Allied entity operating in Assam and Burma, guiding the first American operatives into the jungle. One of the first Allied missions undertaken was to create an outer network of air-warning stations beyond the small, inner-circle network already established in the valley around the Assam air bases.[57]

V Force also guided and served with Detachment 101, a precursor of the OSS, which was, in turn, the precursor of the CIA. Detachment 101 had been created in Washington in April 1942, with the idea that its raw recruits would soon be operating in the jungles of Burma behind Japanese lines. The eager team had arrived with firearms, explosives, and spyware, such as miniature cameras, but had overlooked some basic facts. "We did not take into account the problem of communication," OSS agent Richard Dunlop recalled ruefully; "that is, the ability to speak the language of the country and particular dialect spoken in the locale of the operation. Nor did we consider the geography of the area, the knowledge of its people, its economy, its sociology, and a myriad of other details which compose a working knowledge of the area."[58]

In early 1943, still thrashing around to find a clear mission and means to implement it, the agents were pondering the difficulty of even parachuting behind Japanese lines, given the shortage of aircraft and the reluctance of the ATC to divert planes from the Hump for any other purpose. Then they had an epiphany: as many as forty-five men a month were bailing out over the Hump route and, given that the India-China Wing had only 70 aircraft and 112 crew at any one time, these losses were significant.[59] Pilots were flying hard, averaging over one hundred flying hours a month, or one round trip over the Hump about every other day.[60] Airmen, as well as aircraft, then, were precious commodities, yet no party was responsible for mounting rescues for the survivors. This meant, as Colonel William "Ray" Peers, Detachment 101's commanding officer, said, that "[w]e were in effect surrendering the crews of these planes to the forest or to the Japanese, because we saw no way of getting them out of a huge, primitive, multi-dangered area full of tigers, snakes, mountains and Japanese."[61] Detachment 101, then, would offer to rescue downed airmen in exchange for the ATC making planes available for their own operations.

While a number of entities, from V Force operatives and their allied tribesmen to British political officers stationed in the hills, had undertaken to search the jungle for missing aircraft and crew, Detachment 101's overture represented the first attempt to organize a standing rescue operation for downed airmen.[62] And as the months passed, crashes, fatal and survivable, were becoming more frequent, not less, and the summation "aircraft missing in flight" had become a refrain. In great part, this was due to the chronic difficulties of weather, terrain, and maintenance, and above all the fact that new pilots were arriving undertrained and with little instrument experience. Another reason was the introduction of new aircraft. The Consolidated C-87 Liberator Express, a cargo version of the respected B-24 bomber, was a twin-tailed, four-engine aircraft that could fly at twenty-eight thousand to thirty thousand feet and had four times the cargo capacity of the C-47. The first batch of C-87s had arrived in India in January 1943, and by August all six had been lost, "three in accidents that we understood, with the other three disappearing without a trace," as one pilot noted.[63] "The record showed: C-87 #3791 lost over Hump on 9 April, '43, never found, six dead; C-87 #3696, lost over Hump on 28 April, never found, five dead; C-87 #3669, lost over Hump on 7 May, never found, five dead."[64]

On paper, the C-87 looked ideal for the Hump, yet pilots feared it. To some degree, this was on account of their unfamiliarity with four-engine aircraft, which among other things required a daunting multiplication of instruments to master;[65] but partly the mistrust was due to peculiarities of the C-87 itself, of which it was said that "the assembly of parts known as a 'C-87' would never replace the airplane."[66] Ernest Gann had come to the Hump as an experienced commercial airline pilot with many hours flying for American Airlines before volunteering to join the ATC. He was also a skilled writer (and the author of the classic evocation of aviation, *Fate Is the Hunter*) and eloquent in capturing the disdain and even hatred with which pilots regarded the aircraft. "They were an evil bastard contraption," he wrote, "nothing like the relatively efficient B-24 except in appearance. In time they betrayed each of us in various ways.... No one knew yet, that the C-87's could not carry enough ice to chill a highball."

The aircraft had a much-admired wing design, with a thin profile that yielded a laminar, or evenly layered, nonturbulent airflow across its surface—an early test of the design had entailed strapping a flat board to the top of a Packard owned by actress Norma Shearer's brother and driving it at high speed along the back roads of Southern California.[67] In normal flying conditions—and in wind tunnels—the wing had performed well, but not so well, as it turned out, over the Hump, as even a minimal deposit of ice disrupted its efficient airfoil. Moreover, while the aircraft's high flight ceiling had at first offered the hope that it could be flown above weather, this proved not to be the case, as it was discovered that the towering weather systems continued up and up, far above the reach of where even four turbocharged engines could take the plane. Once caught in the violent, roiling, sheering masses of air, the wings of the plane were observed to flap like a bird's, while the aircraft's extreme gyrations twisted and stretched the fabric of the plane, causing the gas tanks that were built into the wings to leak.[68] The C-87 was moreover not a friendly aircraft. Its controls were heavy and insensitive, and its landing gear did not function in the cold. The beloved C-47 was the pilot's friend, loyal and forgiving; the C-87 was mean-spirited, ill-lit, difficult to heat, and uncomfortable, as if maliciously trying to make its crew's life unpleasant, as well as dangerous.[69] The C-47 loved to fly; the C-87 did not climb well— and could not handle the soft runways of many of the Assam fields—and had to be tricked and coaxed to get aloft. "We have developed a rather peculiar method of persuading C-87s to leave the ground," Gann wrote. "We stand hard on the brakes and then shove the throttles forward. We hold hopes and position until the snout of the airplane attains the attitude of a bull at point of charge. This creates some fifteen seconds of noise and turmoil which is perhaps more heartening to the crew than of technical value. Finally the brakes are released and if the C-87 has any guts whatsoever, it lunges forward in a reasonable facsimile of a mechanism promising flight."[70] In his memoir, Gann claimed to have had a near miss with the Taj Mahal when the C-87 he was flying made a particularly lumbering climb out of Agra.[71]

Over time, fear of the C-87 was overcome by familiarity and catering to its quirks, although the aircraft was not to be widely used over the Hump.[72] The arrival of the C-46, however, was more disastrous. Also known as the Curtiss Commando, it was designed by Curtiss-Wright to be a military version of a pressurized, thirty-six-passenger commercial aircraft that first flew in 1940. Impressed with its carrying capacity—double that of the DC-3/C-47—superior speed, and range, the air force had placed a large order for a military version shortly afterward. So many modifications were required to adapt it, however, that by the time the United State entered the war, there were only two actual examples in existence.[73] At 76 feet long and with a wingspan of 108 feet, the C-46 was the largest twin-engine aircraft in the skies. Fully loaded, it had a top speed of 240 miles per hour and a comfortable ceiling of 25,000 feet, which was both faster and higher-flying than the C-47.[74] The cockpit was designed for comfort, as one pilot recalled, "with plush, throne-like seats, adjustable headrests and solarium-like windows that gave good visibility."[75]

Early reports of the aircraft were highly favorable, but by August 1942, major problems were being reported. Fifty-three immediate modifications were requested, and forty-six additional changes were deemed "desirable." Eventually, Curtiss-Wright would report an astounding 721 required changes in the model. Meanwhile, the India-China Wing of the Air Transport Command had pinned its hopes on this higher-capacity aircraft, and, in May 1943, the first C-46s were delivered to India without having been fully tested, and accompanied by a list of difficulties for the overworked mechanics to address. In the words of the Army Air Force's official history, "the plane was a killer."[76] Engine failure accounted for many crashes, or was the speculated cause of the many crashes that had no survivors to tell the tale. Another quirk, as the air force history division chronicler blandly put it, was that "[t]he fire hazard of the C-46 appeared very early to intensify the pilot's distrust of the aircraft."[77] In other words, many planes caught fire and blew up in flight. Investigations eventually revealed that excessive torching of the exhaust was igniting gasoline leaking from the riveted tanks.

Within five months of their delivery, some 20 percent of all C-46s had been lost.[78] One cause of some of the many malfunctions was a failure to take into consideration the range of conditions in which the aircraft would operate. In the hot moist air of Assam, fungus grew on the radio wiring, disabling communications, while the extreme change in temperature, from the steaming heat at the bases to the severe ice conditions over the Hump route, wreaked havoc on joint seals, causing them to expand and contract and fail.[79] The aircraft fuselage, to quote again the official Air Force history, "leaked like a sieve" in the monsoon rain.[80] Engine loss to ice was another chronic problem. In theory, each aircraft was equipped with a pump system designed to spray antifreeze onto the carburetors, but these were often inoperative or sometimes just missing.[81] Finally, although more capacious than the forgiving C-47, the C-46 was finicky about weight and balance and had to be loaded with precision. Allegedly, a pilot could feel the plane's center of gravity shift if someone walked fore and aft.[82]

ONE POWERFUL MOTIVATION FOR GETTING THE C-46 IN OPERATION WITH all due speed and without regard for its fatal mechanical flaws was the renewed commitment made in May 1943 by the American and British Combined Chiefs to increased tonnage over the Hump. Convened in Washington, DC, the conference, dubbed "Trident," was presided over by Roosevelt and Churchill and was primarily focused on operations in Europe. The North African campaign had only just ended, with the defeat of the Axis powers. The Allies now turned to the upcoming amphibious invasion of Sicily, ahead of the planned Italian campaign that was intended, among other things, to draw German action from the hard-pressed Russians. The requirements of the Italian campaign, particularly in landing craft, pushed back the planned cross-Channel invasion of France by a year, until May of 1944. After these weighty deliberations came the question of China and Burma.

Both field commanders of the CBI, Stilwell and Chennault, were in attendance, along with the Combined Chiefs of Staff. The White House had summoned the American generals to Washington expressly to have them put forward their opposing views regarding the future course of action in the dysfunctional CBI theater. Ahead of the conference, Stilwell and Chennault together met privately with Roosevelt to plead their respective cases: Stilwell for reorganizing and training Chinese army divisions for a ground campaign to reopen the Burma Road—and to warn against a China-based air campaign that he predicted would provoke a Japanese offensive to shut it down. Chennault's pitch was essentially the same as that outlined in his memo of October 1942, only with estimates of required aircraft and tonnage revised upward.

Stilwell's diary and other written private musings are full of his famous fire and venom, but when confronted man-to-man, he had a tendency to backpedal. Whether this was because, as his biographer represents, he was constitutionally unable to promote himself or, more prosaically, because his public bluster was only part of a role he played for effect, at this most important meeting with his president, Stilwell sat with his head down, tongue-tied and subdued, mumbling half-hearted answers; his performance was so lackluster that Roosevelt inquired if he were ill.[83] Chennault, on the other hand, rose to the occasion and gave his pitch, crisply presented with projected dates: in July, his fighters would embark upon operations to gain air superiority from Japan; two months later, air superiority having been obtained, his bombers would commence an anti-shipping campaign targeting the major coastal and river ports; the campaign would then fan outward and, by the end of the year, in other words, six months hence, he would be bombing mainland Japan. Presented with unswerving confidence, these apparently professional projections charmed Roosevelt.

"He was particularly appreciative of the strategic possibilities of shipping strikes in the Formosa Straits and the South China Sea," Chennault wrote of Roosevelt. "The President asked if a China-based air force could sink a million tons of Japanese shipping a year. I replied that if we received 10,000 tons of supplies monthly my planes would sink and severely damage more than a million tons of shipping. He banged his fist on the desk and chortled, 'If you can sink a million tons, we'll break their back.'"[84]

Once the conference was underway and turned to the question of China and Burma, discussion focused on Operation Anakim, the ground campaign to support the rebuilding of the Burma Road agreed to at Casablanca. Very quickly, the intractable fault line between the two Allies was once again exposed.[85] The British were focused on the logistics of a taxing ground campaign in the jungles of Burma, the Americans on China's morale, which they warned "was weakening." The British dwelled at tedious length on such matters as the challenges of supply, the state of existing lines of communication, the limitation of forces and equipment, and the effects of the monsoon, but all such remarks were taken by the Americans as merely excuses. "Br[itish] poor mouth," Stilwell wrote in his diary of the discussions. "Can't—can't—can't."[86]

Again, American objectives veered between the practical and the symbolic. On the one hand, a plan had evolved for a pipeline for fuel to be laid apace the building of the road, but the road itself, like the Hump, served mostly as a talisman of American support for China. When General Wavell pointed out that, in addition to the enormous demands of a ground campaign, the road would not be ready until early 1945, after which "it would take from six to nine months to develop it to a capacity of 10,000 tons a month," Stilwell, speaking for the American view, responded that "the psychological reaction" in China on knowing the road was being built would "keep them from cracking."

Supplying the ground campaign and the considerable workforce of engineers building the road would also divert supplies from the attempt to build up the air force in China. As Wavell stated, "More supplies could be sent to China by air alone in the next 18 months than would be the case if the air transportation was required to use much of its capacity for operations leading to the construction of the Burma Road." Somewhere in the course of these exchanges, Roosevelt, who had mostly remained quiet at the final, key session, sensed an opening for both the outcome he desired—a commitment to the tonnage demanded by Chiang Kai-shek as a symbol of American support—and a compromise between the air-versus-ground debate. He had never accepted the low tonnage figures over the Hump, he now stated, and "it must be divided up between the Air and Ground equipment. Why should not sufficient be conveyed for both?"

The conference concluded with the consensus, more or less, that Operation Anakim would not be immediately abandoned and, as Churchill put it, "preparations should continue provided they did not hamper the development of the air route." For the Hump airmen in Assam, the practical outcome of the conference conducted twelve thousand miles away in Washington, DC, was a more strongly stated commitment to the monthly tonnage they were to haul to China in their fleet of fickle aircraft. President Roosevelt himself had now sternly set the terms: seven thousand tons a month was to be ferried over the Hump by the first of July, and ten thousand tons by the first of September.[87] Meanwhile, the tonnage achieved for May 1943, the month of the Trident Conference, amounted to 2,334.[88] And between May and September stretched the monsoon season.

BY NOW, THE AIRMAN'S LORE CONTAINED A MULTITUDE OF "WORST FLIGHT" stories, as told by those who lived to tell them. But there was also a growing body of stories whose endings were unknown. Occasionally these were heard as the events were unfolding, through the radio communication system while narrator and listener were in the air: "We heard Lt. Hunter calling for a bearing. He had engine trouble and was low on fuel. His radio pleaded for a fix . . . transmission was terrible. Lt. Hunter called that his port engine had quit . . . Silence . . . then came the call we knew would come . . . 'We have had it, we are going in' . . . complete silence from our crew. We landed in Chabua, gassed and went home to Misamari. Then came the shakes and tears of 'grown men crying.' We had lost another to the Hump."[89]

By midday, all outgoing aircraft in Assam should have departed for China; by late afternoon, all inbound aircraft should have returned. If an airplane was missing, the first hope was that the crew were RON, or Remained Overnight, at Kunming, perhaps with some mechanical difficulty, or had diverted to land at a different Assam field. "We ask other returned pilots for information about the missing flight," pilot James Segel recalled. "If we hear that he left earlier, then we get that gnawing feeling that we may have a missing airplane. We use our very faulty telephone system to call the other local fields. . . . We are not even sure that he made the first half of the trip to Kunming safely, as we have no established reporting method, except by a list brought by the last flight of the day leaving China."[90]

On occasion, the wreckage of a plane was spotted by another plane flying over the crash site in clear weather. One CNAC flight returning from Kunming went down while taking a shortcut through the Pimaw Pass on a ridge delineating the China-Burma border, and two months later its remains were spotted from the air on the east side of the mountain just below its summit. It also lay in Japanese-held territory. Had the crew been killed on impact? Had they bailed out, leaving the plane to crash? Had they been taken captive? Were they still alive and even now limping through the jungle or resting in a village somewhere in Burma?[91] "There was no accounting for their disappearance," Segel wrote of a lost pilot friend. "Just silence."[92]

June ended with a total monthly tonnage of 2,382—the best record to that date, but far short of the 7,000-ton target stipulated at the Trident Conference. A detailed special report submitted in early July by Brigadier General Edward Alexander to ATC headquarters cited operational defects that ran for pages: failures in maintenance; lack of facilities such as hangars, finished airfields, paved runways; lack of supplies including even basics such as lightbulbs; massive backlogs of cargo piled on the docks of Calcutta; lack of radio communications required to establish an efficient and safe air traffic control system needed for letdowns in poor weather; lack of aircraft; lack of personnel from pilots to mechanics; and lack of spare parts—all of which had been promised by the War Department in the wake of the Washington conference under a newly initiated program called Project 7, the sole purpose of which, as the report noted, "was to ensure the monthly tonnage goals were met." Another obvious shortcoming was that the incoming maintenance personnel and crew were substandard. Of the first ten radio operators destined for C-87s, two had failed their course of instruction, most had never been on a plane, and none had actual operating instruction; and especially damning, one had been airsick on the way out on a smooth flight.[93]

Of utmost concern was the fact that the new pilots were not, as the training command had pledged, twin-engine pilots who were the "cream of their classes." Most incoming pilots had little experience with flying in weather—or mountains—little instrument instruction, and had never flown multi-engine aircraft, let alone the revolutionary, untested, complex C-46.[94] In mid-July, another special mission was created to address this inadequacy of pilot training. Project 7-A consisted of a contingent of twenty-five American Airline flight crews and maintenance and operational personnel assigned on an emergency basis to go to India to train the wet-nosed aircrews destined for the Hump.[95]

The first Project 7-A plane arrived in Tezpur on August 1, 1943, to a monsoon-flooded field and barracks that had formerly housed cattle and goats. For civilians used to some creature comforts, the canned food, heat, mildew, mud, insects, and primitive latrines were hard to take. The day after arrival, the first Project 7-A crew flew the Hump. "There was no training, no indoctrination, no briefing," pilot J. D. "Ted" Lewis stated in a written report. Arriving as they did in the monsoon, the pilots flew for a month before they ever saw the mountainous terrain over which they were flying. Project 7-A remained in Assam for four months, flying hard—they made 1,075 Hump crossings—and helped the ATC become more professional.[96] But they also lost two planes and their crews—and not to pilot error but to engine failure.

Dark rumors had begun to circulate that many airmen were now too quick to jump at the first indication of engine trouble, rather than attempting to troubleshoot at the of risk going down with the plane; there were, of course, apart from Fort Hertz to the north and Yunnanyi, 130 miles west of Kunming, no airfields along the route that permitted an emergency landing. The suspicion that airmen were too quick to bail was difficult to counter, as only sketchy records were being kept of the number of airmen who had in fact bailed. Detachment 101, which had made good on its pledge to seek out downed airmen, claimed that they rescued "25 to 35 percent" of those who parachuted out, and speculated that the rest were killed on landing, captured by the Japanese, or died of starvation when lost in the jungle.[97]

AUGUST 1943 MARKED A TURNING POINT IN THE OFFICIAL APPROACH TO THE fate of downed airmen. On the second of the month, C-46 #2420 departed Chabua for Kunming in clear weather with a crew of four and seventeen passengers that included eleven American servicemen; two Chinese colonels; the State Department's John Davies, who was the political adviser to Stilwell; an OSS officer; and the celebrated war correspondent and CBS's Washington bureau chief, Eric Sevareid.[98] As the plane rose smoothly into the blue sky, the passengers could look down upon streamers of delicate white clouds that drifted over the densely green world beneath them. Relaxed, they read books, looked out the windows, tried to sleep, or, in Sevareid's case, took notes. About an hour into the flight, a young corporal stumbled over the correspondent's legs and leaned toward him. "Know what?" he shouted. "Left engine has gone out." Yet the plane seemed to be flying smoothly—then sunlight flashed into the cabin from a different angle than before, and it was clear the aircraft was turning back.[99]

"A sudden blare of noise and light filled the plane," Sevareid wrote. The crew chief had materialized to tear the cabin door from its hinges, and was shouting, "All passenger baggage out!" As men shoved and pushed around him, Sevareid thought, "My beautiful new bags! The perfect outfit that it had taken me weeks to gather in Washington!" Soon all baggage had been jettisoned, whistling as it descended out the door. The plane seemed to be flying in circles and flying much lower, with peaks and ridges passing "very close" below. Then, without an announcement or a command, the decision to jump was made known "by a brief, bustling scene forward."[100]

"I felt all my body stiffen," Sevareid reported, "and a great weight pressed on my lungs. Blood was pounding in my head, and it was hard to breathe. For a moment there was utter suspension of thought, and I existed in a vacuum. There were no articulated thoughts, only emotional protest. 'Oh no, no! Oh, no! This can't happen to me.'" One by one, in various degrees of panic and determination, the men jumped, and Sevareid was suddenly aware that he was one of only two or three passengers remaining. "I thought: 'We're still flying level. She'll stay up, she'll stay up!'" But the pilot was running toward him shouting, and then the plane pitched. "There was no interval between the realization that the pilotless plane was going into a dive and the action of my body," Sevareid reported. "I closed my eyes and leapt head first into space. The mind ceased to operate, and I have no recollection of thought. I do not know whether the air felt cold or warm, but instantly there was a terrific rush of wind. Some part of me was calculating, for I waited a long second before pulling the ring with both hands. A terrible blow struck my body, and my eyes opened."[101]

In the "crushing silence," he watched as below him a green mountain spurted a "geyser of orange flame"—the plane exploding as it hit the mountain. Other parachutes were visible, mostly drifting toward the trees.

Below was a brown river in a trackless valley, and the grass huts of a small village were visible a few miles away. The flames on the mountain seemed to be advancing toward him; he could distinguish individual leaves of bushes below, then everything went dark.[102]

All but the copilot, Second Lieutenant Charles Felix, survived, but as the entire party had been scattered into separate groups, this was not immediately known. The dark undergrowth into which Sevareid and his immediate companions fell was like a "dark, suffocating prison" that closed in around him as he struggled to get to his feet. "Each time I rose and plunged forward the brush closed in again and beat me to my knees," Sevareid wrote. After fighting through the bush for a short distance, he heard other members of the party, and, reunited, four men joined to climb shakily up the hillside to the wreck of the plane. The impact had cleared about half an acre of undergrowth, and the point of impact was indicated by a deep, great pit surrounded by mounds of wet, black earth. The pilot, "a very young boy with the rank of Flight Officer," seemingly sunk in depression, was staring blankly at the wreck of his once beautiful machine. A small jungle bird, damaged, its feathers seared off, was stirred by Sevareid's boot, and, taking a stick, Sevareid killed it, "the effort requiring all my courage."[103]

But the "geyser of orange flame" that had erupted on this exceptionally blue-skied day turned out to be a great boon, for it was seen from the air, and within an hour, incredibly, the small knot of men beside the wreckage heard "the glorious sound of airplane motors" drumming through the valley. This was the work of the radio operator, Sergeant Walter Oswalt, Sevareid recorded: "the man who had repeated our distress signal and our position over and over" as the plane went down. "It was his work and that of a relenting God who had provided us with a clear, sunny day in the midst of the monsoon season."[104]

Events moved now with bewildering swiftness. Local tribesmen appeared, fifteen or twenty in number, "short men with deep chests and muscular legs, coffee-brown in color and quite naked save for narrow black breechcloths." All carried long, metal-pointed spears and wide-bladed knives. The Americans strove to appear relaxed and made no sudden moves. Sevareid, with some instinct "born no doubt of the Wild West novels of childhood," stepped forward with his hand raised to say, "How!" while at the same time recognizing how comical this was. The villagers appeared friendly, although there were individuals among them who seemed surly, and the Americans felt they could not drop their guard. "*Naiy gaw American; Kurrum oo*"—I am American, help me—Harry Neveu, the pilot, ventured, reading from the cardboard list of "Useful Phrases in Kachin and Burmese" that the army provided all Hump flyers; but the tribesmen only shook their heads, uncomprehending.[105]

Sevareid's party was conducted to their hosts' village; planes appeared overhead from which were hurled bales of supplies—guns, ammunition, knives, cigarettes, rations, a radio transmitter, blankets, mosquito netting—accompanied by streams of written directives: it was important to stay where they were, the typewritten instructions stated, as they were in Naga territory and it was believed that many of the villages in their vicinity were hostile. The nearest British agent was trying to identify their position and, the directives cautioned, might take him "a week or more to get to you." "So these were the famous Nagas!" Sevareid exclaimed—the notorious headhunters; and the British agent couldn't locate them, meaning they were deep in Naga territory—hostile Naga territory.

Meanwhile, returning planes were raining down bales of supplies with such zealousness that the Americans on the ground feared that someone would be struck by one and killed; "two enormous boxes of tea," recorded Sevareid, who was taking notes all the while; "three and a half pair of socks; two pair underpants; and a hundred and ten *undershirts!*"[106] Most miraculously of all, there appeared out of the twilit sky three descending airmen. Amazed, Sevareid ran toward them, arriving as the first one landed and was folding his parachute and brushing dirt off his clothes. Slim, trim, about thirty-five years of age, the heaven-sent new arrival had cropped hair and "vivid dark eyes in a brown, taut face." This was Lieutenant Colonel Don Flickinger, flight surgeon for the ATC's India-China Wing, chief medical officer of Chabua base, recipient of the Distinguished Flying Cross for work at Pearl Harbor and in the Philippines—and the architect of Wesley Dickinson's snake farm. "Saw you needed a little help," Flickinger said, and with his appearance and matter-of-fact confidence and competence, the problem of discipline and organization of the shaken party was settled.[107] Flickinger established a roster of duties for everything from retrieval of the bales of supplies, to bartering with the villagers, to night watches, to the directive to Sevareid that he keep a daily log and preserve all the messages that wafted down from the planes. Housed in a specially built *basha* away from the center of the village, the men settled into a routine as they waited for deliverance.

On August 13, Sevareid had just begun reading an Agatha Christie novel, one of several books and magazines discovered in the bales that continued to fall like magic from the sky: "*As the butler handed round the soufflé, Lord Mayfield leaned confidentially toward his neighbor on the right. . . .* —when someone yelled 'airplanes!'" as six Japanese fighters sped overhead without appearing to notice them.[108] The days dragged on, passing most slowly when drizzling fog and gloom confined the men to the *bashas*. Yet some days offered spectacles that Sevareid understood he was privileged to witness: "Late at night a good moon, streamers of white mist moved down the mountain slopes like fairy glaciers in motion. We have seen a sight few men ever see—a perfect rainbow by moonlight, arched across our valley."[109]

Obedient to the stern instructions they had received from the Wing base in Chabua, Sevareid's party remained in the village to await rescue. In the interval, typewritten updates of the progress of the rescue plans and party continued to rain down from the sky: "*The British political agent is with us this morning, trying to identify your position from the air. The land party will start out as soon as we know where you are*"; "*You are within eight miles of what is called British control territory, some sixty miles southeast of Mokokchung. There is a British subdivisional officer there. . . . He is known to the natives as the Sahib of Mokokchung*"; "*Trip in and out of Mokokchung will require between two or three weeks"*; and more alarmingly—*"You are to put your party under cover at all times that aircraft are heard until you positively identify them as being friendly. . . . Believe it advisable for you to dig slit trenches in unexposed area. . . . Do not worry, our fighters are covering the area."*[110]

On August 14, twelve days after the crash, the Sahib of Mokokchung strolled into the village. He was, as Sevareid recorded with some awe, a "tall, slim young man wearing a halo of shining fair hair, carrying the mystery of civilization in his casual posture and soft blue eyes." Dressed in a pale-blue polo shirt, blue shorts over his bronzed, firm legs, and walking shoes, he "bore a striking resemblance in face and manner to the actor Leslie Howard" and had covered the eighty-five-mile trek from Mokokchung in five days. A long cigarette holder dangled from his lips. At the back of this *burra sahib* were unnumbered Indian porters, sixty near-naked, spear-bearing Naga guards, and two American service members who had been working in remote air-warning stations, where they had come to know the jungle. While preparations were made for the group's departure, Sahib Philip Adams made himself comfortable in a *basha* with "his peppermints, his jug of rum, and his chess set."[111]

The party set out at last on August 18 in rain and fog on a trek that saw them trudging up to eighteen miles a day. They were, they had now learned, somewhere along the Patkai Range that delineated the border between India and Burma. Through the thick, dim, towering jungle, the party advanced in a long procession that now numbered some 120 people. The heat and steep, testing hills, the party's blistered feet and aching untrained muscles laid a number of them low, to the extent that they had to be carried by porters in bamboo sedan chairs. At night, the exhausted men collapsed in villages and makeshift camps that Adams had had built on his outbound journey to them. "Horrible night, almost no sleep," Sevareid recorded in his notebook; "fleas maddening, pigs rooting under cots, rat runs over my chest, squawking hen lands my face."[112]

On August 21, only three days out, Sevareid, who was fit and in good health, collapsed. "This was the worst. I could not do it again," he recorded.[113] The heat in the suffocating jungle had been merciless, the trail had run steeply uphill, and Flickinger had repeatedly warned the men under his care against "trying to keep up with Adams." At the end of this day, the support planes dropped bales "all over village" where the party was staying the night, "causing cattle to stampede, women to run for lives with babies in arms." Several *bashas* were hit, including theirs, smashing the fragile shelters and the possessions in them. Two days later, as if in contrition, the planes dropped a case of Pabst Blue Ribbon beer.[114]

On August 24, the party reached Mokokchung, "a lonely, primitive outpost, connected with civilization by a single strand of telegraph line and a broad foot trail," where they rested for a day.[115] Arrival in the village, remote as it was, signified that the party had reached "safety" and, accordingly, celebrations were held: a delegation of locals welcomed them with a rousing rendition of "God Save the King" in their own language, and ATC planes dropped a feast of hot tomato soup, hot fried chicken, gravy and mashed potatoes, hot biscuits, and ice cream and coconut cake for dessert, "all done up beautifully in aluminum containers."[116]

Two days later, the group completed the last leg of their long trek and arrived in Mariani, no more than a stop on the railway line, where a small cluster of US newsmen were waiting, from the safety of the journey's end, for a scoop. "The American tradition of adventurous journalism has not entirely died away," Sevareid noted dryly, and observed his colleague *New Yorker* writer St. Clair McKelway collapsing in a cot after he had "plodded up the hill. . . . For some years, Mac's physical exercise had consisted in walking from the door of '21' to a taxi at the curb." Burdened by his backpack, McKelway endeavored to recruit a bypassing Naga boy to carry it for him. "The meticulous master of English prose gestured eagerly and said: 'You—coolie.[117] Carry pack. Carry pack. Five mile. Give much rupee—much rupee. [Jingling of coins in pocket.] You help um white man, no?' The boy regarded him gravely and replied: 'No. I am on my way to the Christian high school and I'm just as fatigued as you are.'"[118] From Mariani, waiting trucks carried the rescued party along the unpaved and rutted Assamese road to the Jorhat airfield, from where they were flown by hospital plane back to Chabua, the origin of their arduous journey.

Looking back on his extraordinary experience, Sevareid confessed to "a pang of unreasonable regret." Hugely relieved to be safe and returned to civilization, he had also had a glimpse—largely, as he acknowledged, informed by Adams—of an intriguing and entirely different way of life lived in those mysterious mountains that formed a jagged blue line on the horizon behind the airfields.[119] He had also reviewed the chain of events that had led not only to the mass bailout but to the death of the young copilot, who, as it seemed, had not been able to jump clear of the plane. Sevareid bleakly speculated on the circumstances that could have brought about a different outcome. If the passengers had not crammed in fear and confusion at the open plane door, perhaps precious seconds would have been saved. Or, as he reflected, one could "move the point of responsibility farther back: If there had been definite orders for and organization of the passengers, all of them amateurs; if the passengers had been briefed on the ground; if the C-46 had not been used for passengers in the first place; if Washington had not ordered these planes to the Hump run before they were perfected. . . ."[120] Sevareid had carried other evidence of the slipshod nature of the Hump operation on his person; the much-touted "jungle-kit," neatly stowed in his parachute backpack, was, as he discovered on being dropped into the actual jungle, "quite empty"—a victim of the endemic pilfering that plagued air bases, especially in Kunming. "The knife, rations, mosquito netting, and first-aid kit were gone," he reported. "Another illustration of the state of discipline at the Chabua air base."[121]

As Sevareid knew, the celebrity of his party accounted in some great degree for the enormous effort and expense that had been channeled toward its rescue. Never before in aviation history, he learned once back at Chabua, "had so many passengers, amateurs at that, successfully bailed out of a stricken plane." Sevareid had filed a story about his adventure for the United Press and CBS from Mokokchung, and the other newsmen had of course filed theirs, with the results that the events in the jungle of Burma became well known to American listeners and readers. Therefore, as the air force was keenly aware, millions of Sevareid's fellow citizens now knew that the failure of a military aircraft engine had been the cause of his sensational ordeal and, although not always robustly emphasized, that his rescue was to be attributed in great part to a British political officer. "The 'Sevareid' story," as the air force history of search and rescue put it, mostly stood out "because it involved a prolific professional narrator, and because—for that same reason—it did much to focus public attention on the flyers and the dangers of Hump flying." The history also reports, with a touch of sourness, that when radio contact with the stranded party had been achieved, one of the first messages transmitted out was—allegedly—from Sevareid to his business manager:

Contact *Saturday Evening Post* and *Reader's Digest* and close with one offering largest sum.[122]

WHETHER AS A RESULT OF THE ORDEAL OF THE TWENTY-ONE SOULS OF C-46 #2420, or of the story about it, the military's interest in the fate of downed airmen increased in its aftermath. In early September, the India-China Wing produced the first in a promised series of "intelligence bulletins" that included "Tips on Bailing Out": airmen learned that crew members should jump in rapid succession, that Brazilian boots will not stay on, that they should secure their pistols in their holsters, and inspect themselves every half hour or so for leeches—the sort of information already dispensed in the jungle survival courses to uneven effect.[123]

More heartening to airmen than yet more instruction on how to preserve their own lives was the establishment, on October 25, 1943, of a small unit dedicated to their rescue. While Detachment 101 had previously agreed to search for airmen in exchange for transport aircraft, this had not been its primary mission, and by its own estimation it had found only 25 to 35 percent of all men who bailed.[124] The new Search and Rescue Squadron (S&R), based in Chabua, was a single-purpose unit. Working closely with the Wing Intelligence and Security sector that was responsible for compiling reports of any evidence of crashed planes, its four pilots and eight to ten crew obtained the necessary variety of aircraft: two B-25 Mitchell bombers and two "weary" C-47s for surveying reported crash areas and dropping supplies to survivors, and two L-5s, extremely light and agile two-person aircraft that could handle short, makeshift airstrips.[125] As the "Sevareid story" had demonstrated, the most challenging part of a rescue effort was the removal of a party from the area in which it was stranded. Few of Sevareid's party had been injured in their bailouts, and only one seriously, and so all survivors had been able to walk or be carried out. Other bailouts, however, or crashes where a crew went down with the plane, could be far more damaging, and the L-5s offered the hope that injured airmen could be flown to safety.

The improvised rescue of Sevareid's party had demonstrated the different elements that were required for a dedicated rescue effort—search planes, supply planes, supplies, medics, communication systems. The person now credited with pulling all of these together into an organized, operational unit was Air Corps captain John L. Porter, known as "Blackie" for his dark eyes and black hair. A former test pilot, he had wide aviation experience in twenty-three different types of aircraft, including the C-87, which he had flown across the Hump. Prior to the formal creation of S&R, he had voluntarily undertaken searches for locally missing planes, and it was said that he was driven by a desire for revenge against the Japanese for the accidental death of his brother, who had been killed on takeoff during the attack on Pearl Harbor—a curious and wholly untrue story that undoubtedly did touch upon some truth of Blackie's character. In reality, his brother had died in March 1943 of a self-inflicted gunshot wound while on a ship at anchor in North Africa.[126] One can only speculate; perhaps the fact that Blackie could not save his brother was what drove him to save young men who were like him.

Thrilling reports of the exploits of "Blackie's Gang" quickly spread through the Wing. Blackie and his pilots were celebrated for flying aggressive, risk-taking sorties, skimming the jungle at treetop level as they sought for signs of life beneath the jungle canopy, flying "hair comb" patterns up and back across the top of the vast sea of forest, and sweeping low through river valleys. Occasionally they landed the L-5s on tiny airstrips that their ground crews, after parachuting in, built with local village labor.[127] Some histories refer to Blackie as "a former stunt pilot"—one of the several questionable stories about him, but which can be read as a tribute to his panache and skills. He was, as one ATC commander recalled, "a dashing, excitement-seeking fellow [who] surrounded himself with barnstorming types."[128] The very existence of the unit greatly boosted morale. Recounting his own ordeal, Sevareid had described his emotions when he saw Don Flickinger parachuting down in the twilight: "[E]verything inside my chest seemed to be melting. I began to run, digging at the tears in my eyes with my fist, like a child. This was wonderful—and impossible. Of their own free will, men were coming to help us, voluntarily casting their fate with ours."[129]

So outsized was Blackie's reputation that it comes as a shock to learn that his "Gang" was only in operation for seven weeks, for, on December 10, 1943, Blackie was killed. Responding to a Mayday call from a C-47 under attack from Japanese planes, he and his crew had raced from Chabua in one of their B-25 bombers up to Fort Hertz, where they saw the aircraft burning on the runway. Spotting two Japanese Zeros in the vicinity, Blackie rashly dove his bomber at them, triggering a dogfight. One of the bomber engines caught fire, and Blackie gave the order to bail. Only one man made it out, and the rest went down with the plane—needless casualties, for the C-47 crew they had come to rescue were safe on the ground. Among the fatalities were Blackie himself and Sergeant Walter Oswalt, the radio operator who had survived the bailout with Sevareid.

The Search and Rescue Squadron continued to operate and grow, a testament both to the determination of its agents and the ongoing need, but it would be another year before it evolved from an ad hoc "cowboy operation" run out of Chabua to a fully staffed professional outfit that had pinpointed every visible piece of wreckage along the Hump route. This last task was necessary to avoid wasteful investigation of "cold" sites long abandoned, for, as the ATC's commanding general noted, "[a]luminum was scattered the length and breadth of the route."[130]

By the end of 1943, the combination of local ad hoc rescue efforts, Blackie's Gang, and the Search and Rescue Squadron that continued to operate after Blackie's death was credited with having saved or contributed to the rescue of 127 Allied airmen from fifty-eight known lost ATC aircraft. They had also located the remains of sixty-one "Total personnel known dead." The magnitude of their task, however, is evoked by the fact that the number of "Total aircraft still unlocated" was opaque enough to be designated "Unknown."[131] It was these inconclusive stories that haunted. At the same time that Sevareid's party was trekking to safety, two survivors of an earlier crash were believed to be struggling to survive in the Hukawng Valley. C-87 #1907 had departed Jorhat on July 19 for Kunming under clear skies, never to be seen again—but search planes had spotted two men on the ground in mountainous jungle terrain close to a reported crash site. Supplies had been dropped to them, but the weather closed in and search teams on the ground failed to locate either the men or the site.[132] Military correspondence indicates that as late as mid-August the men were still believed to be "at present in an inaccessible jungle trying to get out."[133] The coordinates of the site at which the aircraft's two surviving crew had last been seen were securely known—97°0' E, 26°50' N—yet even so, it had not been possible to wrest them from the jungle.[134]

6

NIGHT FLIGHT

On August 9, 1943, a C-87 pilot en route from Jorhat to Yangkai, China, radioed that "a fighter was on his tail" and that he was going into the clouds for cover.[1] Radio operators from two other aircraft heard the call, and then the aircraft was never heard from or seen again, leaving the Air Transport Command to conclude that "it looks as if the enemy may have shot down the first of our transports."[2] Hometown news coverage of the crew evoked the range of their backgrounds and a snapshot of what was typical of any given ATC flight. Floridian Captain Tom Perry had led his golf team at Duke University; the copilot, First Lieutenant John Tennison, from Missouri, had worked as a clerk in a general office before enlisting. The navigator, Second Lieutenant John Funk, had worked for Bank of America in California and was divorced; Staff Sergeant Alvin Lenox, the radio operator, had already served in the army for three years before reenlisting in September 1942; Corporal Donald Johnson, also from Florida, had been a stock clerk. All men were in their twenties. While it was immediately understood that there was high probability the crew had been killed, the airmen continued to be reported as "missing" for some long time, and two years would pass before they were officially declared dead.[3] Two days after this attack, a CNAC transport flying east was observed by another aircraft to be flying off course with a smoking engine. The engine was then seen to fall from the thickening smoke, followed by a severed wing as the plane spun out and crashed in flames. The observers saw no parachutes, and it was assumed the crew was lost.[4]

Fear of enemy attack on the Hump traffic had loomed over the operation from its outset, but although Japanese planes occasionally harassed the air bases, no aircraft in flight had yet been a casualty of enemy action. Now, in August 1943, a month that saw many consequential developments, there was a flurry of concerning incidents and at least one confirmed loss to enemy action.

The Japanese had suffered many reverses by this autumn of 1943, with defeats at Midway in June 1942, at Guadalcanal in early 1943, and in the Aleutian Islands at the gateway to the northern Pacific in August 1943. "Isn't there any way we can confront the United States forces somewhere and beat them?" Emperor Hirohito had plaintively asked his aide-de-camp.[5] Psychologically, the nation had been shattered by the death of its greatest war hero, Admiral Isoroku Yamamoto, the architect of the attack on Pearl Harbor, whose plane had been shot out of the sky over the Solomon Islands by US Army Air Corps pilots in April 1943 ("POP GOES THE WEASEL," read the celebratory message that announced the news to US admiral Halsey).[6] Of graver, more practical concern was the fact that the nation and armed forces were severely undersupplied due to a crippling lack of raw materials and the toll that US submarines were taking on Japan's limited merchant marine.[7] In Burma, the Imperial Japanese Army's 5th Air Division was supplied with ammunition and fuel dispatched from a depot in Singapore to Rangoon, and as early as the end of 1942 it was reporting a lack of planes and parts due to enemy "hindrance." By the autumn of 1943, frequent interceptions by Allied planes and submarines ensured that "not even one third of the supplies required by both air and ground forces in Burma could be transported."[8]

Japan's position in Burma was complicated by the fact that it had never intended to take the entire country. Japanese forces had originally

entered Burma with the objective of taking Rangoon and its port, through
which supplies destined for China had to pass. The unforeseen collapse
of British defenses had induced them to keep moving north, until they
had claimed the entire colony. After their retreat, many of the British
forces were sent to Imphal, the capital of India's Manipur State situated
some fifty miles from the Burmese border, and which became the Allied
base and headquarters for the Burma front. The Chinese forces had retreated, some back to China by way of the Burma Road, some to India
where they were regrouped and sent on to Stilwell's training center at
Ramgarh.

But the Japanese had stayed in Burma, pondering their next move in
this country they never planned to take. In the wake of the Allies' flight,
some Japanese officers had urged immediately pressing their advantage
and continuing the offensive drive into India, but General Shôjirô Iida,
who had led the Fifteenth Army to its success, recognizing that even victorious troops needed rest, had called a halt ahead of the monsoon. Both
sides had taken advantage of the rains to rest and regroup, and little action was seen until the end of 1942, when the British embarked on what
was planned as a limited, morale-boosting offensive in the Arakan, the
mountainous, jungle-covered region along the Bay of Bengal. The objective was the island of Akyab, which had both a port and an airfield that
would allow bombers to reach Rangoon. This campaign, too, however,
had turned into another debacle, and the British had been forced to retreat north into the protection of another monsoon. Ahead of the same
monsoon, in February 1943, a small, new unit of unconventional British
forces—officially a "long-range penetration brigade" but unofficially
dubbed "the Chindits"—embarked on a campaign to disrupt Japanese lines
of communication using newly honed, jungle-trained guerrilla tactics.
This expedition had some limited success, but when the last of the forces
retreated in April 1943, it was discovered that the cost had been high,
with one thousand casualties of the original three-thousand-man unit.

The Japanese now focused both on their own next offensives and
on attempting to read the Allies' plans. Regarding the latter, Japanese

reports made after the war revealed that from an early stage they had surmised that there would be an attempt to invade northern Burma from the Ledo area in India with the aim of reopening the Burma Road—Stilwell's planned offensive—and they were quick to learn from a Chungking government news source the exact route this would take. By April 1943, they were aware that Chinese recruits were being transported across the Hump from Kunming to join Stilwell's X-Force in training at Ramgarh, where "they were receiving thoroughly U.S. style training." And they knew that the US was equipping and training the Yunnan Expeditionary Force—Stilwell's Y-Force—under the command of General Wei Li-huang in the Yunnan area, but that its organization was only 40 to 50 percent complete and was likely to be short-supplied; previously, Japanese planners had dismissed the "Chungking Army" as lacking combat strength to be effective. Interpreting this intelligence, the Japanese had correctly concluded that "the expected counteroffensive against Burma would be a large scale three-front drive by British, United States and Chinese forces," from the Arakan, Ledo, and Yunnan, respectively.[9]

In late March of 1943, the Japanese had organized the new Burma Area Army, commanded by Lieutenant General Masakazu Kawabe, to serve as the higher headquarters for the seasoned and victorious Fifteenth Army, to which other units were to be attached. In mid-June, the Fifteenth Army and Burma Area Army met in Rangoon to study "the grand strategy" for upcoming offensives with the overall objectives "to bring about a decisive result in the political trend within India and the severance of air transportation between India and China."[10] At the heart of these plans was an assault on Imphal, in Manipur State, through a "coordinated series of sudden attacks."[11] Once in possession of this first Japanese-occupied Indian territory, a provisional puppet government representing the anticolonial Quit India movement would be established with the aim of enabling political destabilization of British rule. This followed the same strategy already employed in Burma, which internal documents drafted as early as December 1941 had spelled out with chilling clarity: "[The Burmese] shall be induced to rise up and destroy the

British defense forces in the areas. . . . The new regime shall have on the surface the appearance of independence, but in reality it shall be induced to carry out Japanese policies."[12] Ahead of the invasion, aerial bombardments of key ports, especially Calcutta, would disrupt or break vital Allied lines of communication. The advance into India would also cut the ground supply lines that led from Calcutta's port north to Assam, and with it the source of all supplies for China over the Hump. The offensive would commence "no sooner than the early part of 1944," and ahead of the monsoon.[13]

Meanwhile, the Allies, too, had been calculating the enemy's plans, noting with alarm that, while their own resources in Burma were being reduced by demands in Europe, those of the Japanese were increasing. To the four Japanese divisions already in Burma were added a fifth from Java, a sixth from Malaya, and later, at the end of the monsoon in November 1943, a seventh from Siam.[14] Although Japanese air strength had been steadily decreasing in contrast to the Allies' strength, which was growing, it had not entirely surrendered air supremacy and had successfully supported its Fifteenth Army in the Arakan campaign, while making occasional attacks on Kunming and points in East India.[15] The Japanese air force had also mostly completed an ambitious program to improve its network of airfields in Burma, and by August 1943 had increased the original fifteen or sixteen airfields to a hundred.[16] Japanese fighter units were kept artfully concealed in locations across Burma, while heavy bombers were stationed out of Allied range on the Malay Peninsula and in Bangkok, advancing toward Burma at twilight and returning safely to base after missions.[17]

In the eyes of the British and Americans, the Japanese enemy, so unpredictably successful and rarely actually seen, had acquired a powerful mystique, attributed with special abilities and assets. It was said, for example, that they had set up dummy stations and beacons that used regular homing frequencies to lure transport planes off course and into the mountains; while there were confirmed cases of this ruse, rumors of such events outpaced actual incidents.[18] In their seizure of the Chinese coast,

as one British general wryly noted, the Japanese "had shown a disconcerting ability to land in places and at times that our experts had declared impossible."[19] Above all, the Japanese were credited with being
natural jungle fighters, peculiarly adapted to survive and maneuver in
the dark and fearsome forest as Europeans were not. Their skill in operating in the jungle had been displayed not only in the lightning-swift advance through Burma in 1942, but more recently in the disastrous Arakan
campaign, where they had briskly marched over the precipitous jungle-
covered Mayu Range that the British had decreed to be impenetrable.[20]
The primary boast of the Chindit operation was that it had shown that
Europeans, too, could operate within the Burmese jungle.

Toward the end of August 1943, Roosevelt, Churchill, and their top military brass met again in conference, this time in Quebec. The immediate
topic of discussion was the European war and the implications of Italy's
anticipated surrender. Attention was then turned to the Pacific and Far
East, and for the first time a combined plan for the defeat of Japan was
ventured to follow the defeat of Germany, expected in the autumn of
1944. The plan, a reshuffling of old elements long discussed along with
new ones, envisioned three lines of advance by sea and land to converge
at Hong Kong or, depending upon the circumstances at the time, the island of Formosa. While the Americans advanced through the Gilbert
and Marshall Islands from the east, the British were to advance from the
west through the Strait of Malacca and the China Sea. All the while, efforts would be ongoing to increase Allied airpower in China by stepping
up the airlift over the Hump and rebuilding the Burma Road. With the
land route to China reestablished, the American-trained Chinese armies
would then advance along it through Yunnan to meet the other Allies in
Hong Kong. Here they would seize and hold the area required for air
bases, from which the new, very-long-range B-29 bombers would strike
Japan.[21] Preparatory to the grand overland advance would be the clearing of north Burma ahead of the construction of the road, as had been
agreed to at the earlier Trident Conference in Washington—and as surmised by the Japanese. To this end, commencing in the dry season, the

British and Stilwell's India-based Chinese army—X-Force—were to attack from different points in northeast India into Burma, while the second re-formed Chinese army—Y-Force—would do the same from Yunnan.[22]

The discussions about the Burma operations inevitably exposed the difference between American and British views of China's value. Yet even the American-approved plans were peppered with caveats and qualifica-tions about China's role, emphasizing the need for flexibility "if China should drop out of the war or prove less effective than we now hope." Spe-cifically, it was agreed that there would be no advance overland if Chi-nese assistance were to disappoint, in which case the "main effort would be concentrated in amphibious operations along the China coast."[23] This possibility had led the British to suggest that China, and therefore oper-ations in Burma, could be bypassed altogether; for, they argued, if China were lost as an active ally, "we can re-establish our position in China by amphibious assaults and seize the area required for the air offensive."[24] But Washington was not swayed.

The conference, dubbed "Quadrant," saw several other developments of note. It was agreed that long-range penetration groups would conduct a second and far more ambitious guerrilla operation ahead of the general advance into Burma, so as to disrupt Japanese lines of communication.[25] Modeled on the Chindits, the brigade groups would include British, In-dian, and American forces—the first American ground forces in the arena. Also affirmed was a commitment to the construction of a 1,900-mile-long pipeline from Calcutta to Kunming that could deliver an estimated 54,000 tons a month of fuel to air operations in Assam and Kunming.[26] Amid the tangle of shifting and sometimes contradictory objectives and plans thrashed out in this conference, the most consequential would only be appreciated later, and this was the decision to have the Americans ad-vance toward Japan by way of the Pacific Islands.

Also finalized in Quebec was the creation of a new combined com-mand, the South East Asia Command, or SEAC, to replace the ad hoc co-alition of Allied headquarters thrown together in 1942 as disaster rolled through Burma. This move had been initiated earlier in the summer of

1943, inspired by American and British mutual dissatisfaction as to how operations in Southeast Asia were being conducted. The new command would encompass Burma, Ceylon, northern Sumatra, Siam, and Malaya, and also oversee the development of the India-China air route. Given that America did not yet have combat troops within this sphere, it was agreed that SEAC's Supreme Allied Commander would be British. The Americans dismissed a number of candidates put forth for the position before settling on Vice Admiral Lord Louis Mountbatten, known to close friends as "Dickie," a forty-three-year-old career naval officer with a record of both successes and failures (such as the disastrous raid on Dieppe in 1942) to his credit. Born His Serene Highness Prince Louis of Battenberg, a great-grandson of Queen Victoria and a cousin of the king, Mountbatten was handsome, glamorous, cosmopolitan, and, through his wife's vast fortune, very wealthy, and it was a secret to none that he owed his rapid professional advancement to his royal connections.[27] British political reaction to his appointment was close to "stupefaction," according to the historian Frank McLynn, who reports that one rival at least "consoled himself with the thought that it must surely be the end of the upstart Mountbatten's naval career."[28] He was, however, the one British officer who it was believed could get on easily with Americans—a movie lover, Mountbatten had friends in Hollywood circles and could speak to them charmingly in their own idiom—"a kind of military version of David Niven."[29]

At Quebec, Mountbatten had stunned if not dazzled the Anglo-American Combined Chiefs with his enthusiastic endorsement of the virtues of "Habbakuks," which the staid minutes of the Combined Chiefs of Staff were compelled to describe as "floating seadromes or giant aircraft carriers" made of pykrete, a substance that was "a frozen mixture of diluted pulp and water," or in other words ice and sawdust. A Professor Bernal then demonstrated the various qualities of pykrete, but it is fair to say this was less memorable than Mountbatten's own demonstration, described by General Alan Brooke in his diary.

Dickie now having been let loose gave a signal, whereupon a string of attendants brought in large cubes of ice which were established at the end of the room. Dickie then proceeded to explain that the cube on the left was ordinary pure ice, whereas that on the right contained many ingredients which made it far more resilient, less liable to splinter, and consequently a far more suitable material for the construction of aircraft carriers. He then informed us that in order to prove his statements he had brought a revolver with him and intended to fire five shots at the cubes to prove their properties! As he now pulled a revolver out of his pocket we all rose and discreetly followed behind him. He then warned us that he would fire at the ordinary block of ice to show how it splintered and warned us to watch the splinters. He proceeded to fire and we were subjected to a hail of ice splinters! "There," said Dickie, "that is just what I told you; now I shall fire at the block on the right to show you the difference." He fired, and there certainly was a difference; the bullet rebounded out of the block and buzzed round our legs like an angry bee.[30]

The creation of SEAC also added to the bewildering tangle of commands that already encompassed three geographic arenas, the conflicting interests of four nations, and all three services of land, sea, and air.[31] It was, as General Marshall described it, a "necessarily abnormal organization."[32] The new command was Anglo-American; India remained under Britain's India Command (with responsibilities in the Middle East); the China theater remained under command of Generalissimo Chiang Kai-shek; while the CBI—which operated in all three command areas— remained a distinct American operational theater under Stilwell and was not subordinate to SEAC. Yet Stilwell, now SEAC's Deputy Supreme Allied Commander, was subordinate to Mountbatten. Some time had been taken in Quebec to spell out the tangle's implications for Stilwell, who commanded the Chinese army in India, within the India Command;

had oversight of the American Fourteenth Air Force, based in China but supplied from India; and, with the initiation of the dry-season offensive, would be fighting in Burma directly under SEAC. By virtue of his position as one of the generalissimo's chiefs of staff, Stilwell also served as Chiang's liaison with SEAC.[33] Affected, too, was the US Army Air Force command structure, with General George Stratemeyer now appointed the commanding general of the India-Burma Sector, which in practical terms meant little more than the control of the US Tenth Air Force based in India.[34]

While the selection of Mountbatten to lead the new command was an eccentric choice, it could be said to be no more eccentric than the creation of the actual command. And Mountbatten brought with him genuine assets, such as a pleasant eagerness and agreeable desire to "get on" with people, which in the toxic and vituperative arenas with which his new command overlapped was as welcome as fresh air. On meeting Chiang, whom Stilwell now taunted with open contempt, Mountbatten had expressed his humble desire to "lean on his vast experience for help and advice"; to Madame Chiang he gallantly presented a Cartier vanity case emblazoned with her initials set in diamonds.[35] He was also instrumental in saving Stilwell's job. Chiang, seizing on rumors that Stilwell was intriguing against him, had demanded his recall. Mountbatten in turn ensured that the generalissimo was informed that the new Supreme Allied Commander had no desire to use Chinese troops if the officer who had commanded them for two years was to be removed.[36] "Mt.B. is no giant," wrote Stilwell in his diary on meeting him, "but he's energetic & willing to do anything to make it go."[37]

The establishment of SEAC was shortly followed by a shakedown of the Hump operation, which remained under the Air Transport Command's India-China Wing, and which continued to disappoint. Only 4,447 tons were delivered to China in August—far short of the goal pledged at the earlier Trident Conference in Washington of 10,000 tons a month by September 1.[38] "I am still pretty thoroughly disgusted with the India-China matters," Roosevelt wrote to Marshall in October. "Everything seems to go wrong."[39] The alarm over the shortfall prompted several inspection tours of the Hump's operational management, all resulting in reports of passive, lackluster leadership.[40] As a result, the decision was made to replace Brigadier General Alexander, who had led the Wing since its inception in December 1942.

Colonel Thomas Hardin, his replacement, was anything but passive, and most references to him refer to his "hard-charging" character. Before the war, he had been vice president of TWA, and was later commanding officer of the ATC's Central African Sector.[41] "[He] proved to be a hard driver," as the air force's official history states. A skilled and fearless pilot, he was respected for the fact that he never asked of others what he himself was not prepared to do. Piloting a well-worn B-25, often solo, he tirelessly made inspection tours of all the air bases, in all degrees of weather.[42] Hardin was to initiate many innovations, but it was his immediate decisions that had the greatest impact, psychologically and physically, on pilots and crew. Taking command in October 1943, he made clear that the Hump operation would no longer be managed like a pilot-run airline, in which the decision to fly or not to fly in particular conditions—such as adverse weather or the presence of enemy aircraft—lay with the airman. Henceforth, only headquarters, not pilots, could "close the Hump" on account of weather, and pilots who refused to fly would face discipline. It was said that Hardin had issued a curt directive: "Effective immediately, there will be no more weather over the Hump."[43] Whether or not his words were apocryphal, it was a fact that the Hump operation now embarked on the most perilous phase of its existence.

IN ASSAM, THE HUMP AIRMAN'S TYPICAL DAY BEGAN WHEN HE WAS SHAKEN awake before dawn by the CQ, or charge of quarters, the service member charged with overseeing the *basha* barracks. Carefully pulling aside the mosquito netting around his bed so as not to dislodge any creatures that might have descended on it through the palm-thatch roofing in the night, and stepping warily onto the concrete or beaten-earth floor, the airman fumbled for his muddy boots and wrinkled, damp clothing and got dressed. After dressing, he picked up winter clothing—a leather sheepskin-lined jacket and pants, a leather helmet, mittens, and fur-lined boots—and perhaps a blanket for the unheated cockpit, along with his survival kit, gun belt, and trench knife, in the event he had to bail out in the course of the journey. Flashlight in hand, he made his way through the mud and clinging mist to the truck or shuttle that delivered him to the base ops, where he was told his destination—most often Kunming—and met the men who would be his crew for that particular flight. The same crews rarely flew together, adding one more factor of uncertainty to increase anxiety ahead of every flight, for available pilots were of uneven quality. Most aircraft carried three-man crews: pilot, copilot, and radio operator. The C-87s had an additional seat behind the pilot for a crew chief or navigator, but these were not always used.[44] At base ops, the pilot was also given the cargo manifest. This was usually fifty-five-gallon drums, often leaking, of gasoline, but it could be anything: nitroglycerin, five-ton trucks, road graders, jeeps, toilet paper, Chinese paper money printed by the Philadelphia Mint, spare parts, desks, typewriters, new uniforms, and occasionally crates containing the fruits of Madame Chiang Kai-shek's American shopping sprees and even her grand piano.[45] The radio operator checked out an Identification Friend or Foe (IFF) set, which issued a signal identifying the plane to Allied troops as a friendly aircraft.

In the briefing room, the pilot was given his briefing folder and maps and filed his flight plan, then proceeded to the weather office, where he could read reports from pilots who had recently arrived from China. When their aircraft was loaded and ready, pilot and copilot were driven to it in the murky predawn light. Sloshing ankle-deep in mud, with the smell of warm oil and rainwater rising from the asphalt, the pilots performed their walk-around inspection, examining cowling fasteners, landing gear struts and wheel wells, seeing that rudder and elevator locks were removed, checking for leaks, checking the tires for cuts inflicted by the harsh gravel runway surfaces in China, while the radio operator installed the IFF in the aircraft's tail.[46] The pilots then embarked, and the crew chief, or mechanic, oversaw the starting of the aircraft engines. If a mechanic was lacking, the crew improvised. "We were flying out of Jorhat one day in a C-47," recalled radio operator Douglas Devaux. "It was pouring rain and the ground was wet and muddy." Arriving at the plane, they discovered the right engine starter was not working. There were no mechanics about. The pilot, looking at the co-pilot, said, 'Someone will have to get out and crank up the right engine.' The co-pilot, looking at me, said, 'Someone will have to get out and crank the right engine.' I've never done anything like that," Devaux protested, but nonetheless exited the aircraft with a long-handled crank into the rain and mud and successfully started the engine.[47]

From the cockpit, the pilots began talking to the tower, which in Chabua was located in a tall tree, essentially a tree house, overlooking the field.[48] In theory, all crew members were issued oxygen and parachutes, which served as seat cushions during flight, but which in practice might be missing or be so mildewed as to be useless. Slowly, the big plane was turned to taxi toward the runway, where it held short and took up position in the warm-up circle, while the pilots began the sacred ritual of running up the engines one by one. All around the muddy airfield, other aircraft were getting loaded, starting engines, taxiing out—the C-46s lumbering in their characteristic heavy, pitching movement like heavyweight drunks—as the air shook and rumbled with their sound.[49] Ahead lay the runway, black, bordered with uncertain lights, and often vanishing into mist.[50] What happened next depended in great part on that particular day's weather and the particular pilot's temperament. If ground fog obscured the end of the runway, there might be delays; to go or not to go was at each pilot's discretion. Meanwhile, jeeps stationed alongside the positioned aircraft were on alert to clear the runway of any roaming cattle hidden in the mist. Pilot and crew had little idea of what lay ahead beyond the veil of fog and the line of hills immediately before them, as the weather reports they had received from incoming pilots were now irrelevant. Clear conditions could change within hours into ice-bearing storms, and all that a pilot really knew of the weather was what he saw above his head.

As the sun rose and burned off the morning ground fog, the temperature in the cockpit also rose; later in the day, pilots would need gloves to handle the red-hot metal controls. Cleared by the tower for takeoff, the pilot lined up on the runway and locked the aircraft tail wheel. With the pilot at the controls and the copilot monitoring the throttles, the aircraft charged down the runway, while the crew prayed that at this most critical moment none of its engines would fail. As the plane rose ten to fifteen feet above the runway, the pilot called for "gear up," and the plane was airborne. Even in clear weather, bands of haze and dust hung off the ground, and a pilot had to be prepared to be on instruments immediately after takeoff. For minimally trained pilots, the swift change from visual to instrument conditions could be overwhelming, and how a pilot handled this early test would give his crew an indication of the kind of ride they might be in for.[51] Many airmen had their own "weirdo pilot" story. A copilot flying out of Mohanbari pulled the gear lever after takeoff. "Nothing happened," he recalled. "The landing gear remained down and locked. I was shocked when Lt. Lemon (we'll call him) turned to the departure heading and proceeded across the Hump! I asked why he didn't call a Mayday and land. He said he did not have a turnback on his record and wasn't going to get one."[52] There being no special instrument flight training program, senior pilots instructed the copilots along the way.[53]

Laboriously, the overloaded aircraft clawed its way upward, while the pilots watched the altimeter wind from 1,500 feet, to 2,000, to 2,500, continually adjusting power throughout the long climb. At three thousand feet, pilots and crew relaxed. As the aircraft climbed, the temperature in the cockpit dropped, and the crew reached for their winter flying gear. Fully loaded, a C-87 could cross the Hump at twenty-two thousand feet, and returning empty it might ascend as high as twenty-eight thousand feet, with the temperature in the unheated aircraft dipping below zero.[54] Some aircraft, like the C-46, had gasoline-driven heaters, but many airmen preferred to suffer the cold than take their chances with the heaters' open flames coming in contact with fumes from the leaking fuel drums carried as cargo.[55] One pilot recalled discovering a leaky gasoline drum in the plane nose oozing fumes into the air that were strong enough to cause the crew's eyes to smart. One spark would have blown the plane sky-high, so the crew had not used even their radio; they had all witnessed a plane explode near Misamari, lighting the sky from twenty-five miles away.[56] At twelve thousand feet, the crew were supposed to use oxygen, as hypoxia, or insufficient oxygen, was proving to be a significant problem, possibly accounting for many cases where pilots inexplicably wandered off course or made bizarre moves when coming in for a landing.[57] But once a crew was airborne, there was little that could be done to enforce this rule. Oxygen masks were heavy and uncomfortable contraptions with hanging rubber bags that inflated like balloons, and many pilots chose to "tough it out." Moreover, wearing a mask prohibited one's ability to smoke, something deemed necessary for warmth and nerves. "We figured that nothing would burn at that height without the oxygen," Devaux recalled. "After reaching cruising altitude, 22,000 to 25,000 feet, we would sometimes unhook our oxygen masks on one side so that the oxygen could spill out just enough to keep the cigarette burning."[58]

Climbing out of the Assam Valley, the aircraft headed east and soon crossed the First Ridge, the Patkai Range, into Burma and set course for the Fort Hertz radio beacon, the only marker on route and which might or might not be in operation—on occasion, this most northerly ground station had been overrun by Japanese troops. Lying so far north, the station served mostly as an off-the-wing landmark and possible site for an emergency landing. Radio operators stayed on frequency for the duration of a flight and so could monitor exchanges between any plane and the control towers, and in this way receive information about conditions ahead, including Mayday distress calls.[59]

Across the Kumon Mountains, the aircraft continued over the vast, feared jungle of Upper Burma and over the Irrawaddy River. In clear weather, peaks to the north and south were starkly, even gloriously visible, gleaming with inviolate snow and their flanks green with covering forest. Looking down upon this spectacle, pilot and crew took in the knife-edge peaks that could split a plane in two and the fathomless sea of imperturbable jungle.[60] "Always know where you can put down in an emergency," pilots were instructed, but looking down from nineteen thousand feet, pilot and crew knew the closest place they could now land was the airfield of Yunnanyi, west of Kunming and hours away, and that in an emergency they would not land, but have to bail.[61]

Crossing the Salween and the Mekong river gorges carved into the Santsung Range, the main "hump," the plane approached the route's first important checkpoint and roughly halfway mark, the eighteen-thousand-foot-high Likiang Mountain, where the course sharply "turned the corner" to the southeast. When visible, the mountain was a magnificent sight, flaunting a plume of high-flying snow like a shimmering banner off its distinctive jagged summit. Best of all, the worst of the mountains were now behind. The land became gentler and rigorously cultivated—the first evidence on the route of a significant human presence. Near Mount Tali, an ancient Buddhist monastery rose like a spire on the ten-thousand-foot-high summit of Cock's Foot Mountain, a comforting talisman to mark that the journey to Kunming was three-quarters over: moreover, not far from Mount Tali was the Yunnanyi airfield. Yet, accidents could and did happen here. One clouded day, as he flew almost directly over Mount Tali, Lieutenant John Finey watched from the copilot seat as "a column of very black smoke came up out of the cloud and formed into a huge mushroom shape as we passed." A month later, approaching Mount Tali in the late afternoon from China, when its southern slopes were clear of cloud, he saw "the tail section of an airplane on the west side and just below the crest with a large black area in front of it."[62]

In clear weather, the descent to Kunming revealed the foothills around the city, fields of rice paddies gleaming gold in the reflected sun, and the sprawling Lake Dian to its south.[63] More often, though, the weather was soupy with drizzle and fog, and arriving aircraft were forced to join a long, vertical queue that could reach to twenty thousand feet above the field. Stacked five hundred feet apart, as they flew holding patterns, the planes were released by the ground tower, one by one, to make a blind descent, perhaps through storms and violent turbulence, to the field.[64]

"Fly downwind, descending for 30 seconds past the approach end of the runway and start a timed turn (3 degrees per second) back to the airport," pilot Downie logged. "At the end of that 180 degree turn, you should have the runway in sight over the nose." If not, the pilot kept descending until the aircraft broke out of the low overcast or reached the minimum allowed for a nonvisual descent, in which case he powered up again for a missed landing and went back for another try, or sometimes to another field.[65] Official directives called for a touchdown stall at seventy-seven miles per hour for the C-46, but pilots aimed closer for a hundred miles per hour. "[T]hese airplanes were pretty well beat up, instruments were not all that accurate, and gross weights were frequently in excess of the legal limit," Downie wrote; "so you added another 10mph more for the wife and each kid."[66]

With a slight jar and the sound of crunching gravel, the aircraft was safe on the ground. Instructions from the tower and a "follow me jeep" guided it to its place on the unpaved ramp. The pilots shut the plane down and disembarked, leaving the radio operator on board to guard the plane against the theft and sabotage that were entrenched facts of life in China and Kunming. "China Is Not for the Timid," read a sign behind the operations counter. It was known that the Japanese paid Chinese saboteurs to put sugar in the gasoline tanks or a detonator in the landing gear, and personal possessions left inside the aircraft were lures for theft.[67] Parachute survival kits in particular held many treasures, including American cigarettes, money, and first aid kits, which included syringes loaded with morphine.[68] After turning in their paperwork, the pilots made their way to the egg shack at the other end of the building for a much anticipated breakfast of fresh eggs—hard to come by in India—fried potatoes, unidentifiable meat, and strong coffee, after which one of the pilots went to relieve the radio operator standing guard. When the aircraft had been unloaded, and after their breakfasts, the crew geared up for the return trip. Fuel tanks were drained down to a specified number of gallons, calibrated to allow just enough to return safely to Assam on the premise that every drop of fuel was needed to help China fight the enemy. The calibrations took into account the wind strength forecast on the route, and the crew had to hope forecast conditions did not change.[69] The short rations of fuel were one reason why so many crashes occurred toward the end of the return flight, over the Burma jungle.

In Assam, there were cement ramps and even some paved runways, but at the Chinese airfields, including Kunming, the runways were gravel and constantly undergoing repair and reconstruction. On-site at all times were squads of "coolies"—thousands of thin, underfed men, women, and children of all ages, who smashed rocks into gravel by hand and dragged massive stone rollers to smooth the runways. Despite these efforts, gravel was routinely dislodged and flung by the roaring aircraft to lacerate tires and foul the ice shields that covered the carburetors. Another factor that made departures from Kunming nerve-racking was a belief among the local workers that a dash across the path of a departing plane could, if timed just right, ensure that the plane's propellers cut to pieces the bad-luck dragon that shadowed them; if the dash was badly timed, however, it was the worker who was cut to pieces. "We were well into our takeoff roll, tail up and about 60 mph," Don Downie recalled, "when a coolie darted out of a crowd of hand laborers on the runway and headed out in front of us." The copilot reached to cut back on the throttles, but Downie locked his hand on top of his to hold the power open. "No," he said, explaining, "I didn't want to wreck all three of us to keep a suicide-bent coolie from losing his personal dragon. We tensed up, but felt no thud and later, on landing . . . we could find no blood stains on the ship."[70] The most frequent and distressing deaths were of women with bound feet, who were unable to run even as fast a child can walk.[71] No less horrifying to the aircrews were the howls of laughter from the doomed runner's friends as they watched the carnage from the sidelines. In China, as Americans so often had to observe, life was cheap.

Kunming stood at 6,220 feet above sea level, but even at this altitude takeoffs were not difficult, as the aircraft were now mostly empty—although a cliff face across Lake Dian bore the scar of a bomber that had forgotten to make a critical left turn.[72] The lighter aircraft could fly at higher altitudes on the return flight, but headwinds made the journey somewhat longer—in unproblematic weather, it was about three and a half hours going out and some four hours returning from Kunming—but any kind of weather created anxiety that the tightly rationed fuel might run out.

Approaching Chabua, or another Assam base, the radio operator searched for the signal from the high-powered radio station that served as a radio beacon for the airfield. As this also doubled as the Armed Forces Radio station, a crew might find themselves letting down to the accompaniment of the Andrews Sisters. If descending in low overcast, a pilot looked for a red light fixed to a bamboo pole some fifty yards short of the touchdown area, then for the runway lights, and then "squashed down" in the mist. On the ground, a jeep led the aircraft to its place on the ramp, where the crew shut the plane down and exited into a wall of heat so fierce it was like standing in front of an open-hearth furnace.[73] Another jeep took the crew to the base ops to turn in the paperwork. Then it was on to the dispensary to receive the traditional shot of whiskey to calm the nerves, after which a waiting truck took the crew to their *basha*, where most instantly fell asleep.[74]

FOLLOWING THE CASABLANCA CONFERENCE, GENERAL ARNOLD HAD DOUbled the number of transports for the Hump to 124 planes. This number, he calculated, could realistically achieve the four-thousand-ton monthly commitment stipulated at that time.[75] His calculations had been upset shortly afterward by Roosevelt's insistence at the Trident Conference that the ATC meet Chiang's demand for ten thousand tons monthly. As a consequence, Arnold and the ATC worked tirelessly and with as much ingenuity as they could muster to accommodate this directive. New urgency was given to the expansion and improvement of airfields in Assam, which had been entrusted to British authorities and was far behind schedule, a fact that the British attributed to monsoon conditions and labor shortages, but that the Americans viewed darkly as foot-dragging.

B-24 bombers were already tasked with carrying their own fuel and supplies over the Hump to stockpile for future operations in China, while the program to replace the dependable C-47s with the larger capacity C-46s and C-87s was pushed aggressively.[76] These efforts did produce an increase in tonnage—7,240 tons in October 1943, and 6,491 in November—but they also gave rise to an attendant, steady increase in fatal crashes; eleven in October, seventeen in November.[77] For a small fleet struggling to build its numbers, the write-off of twenty-eight aircraft in two months was a high rate of attrition—yet these material losses were overcome, and the transport fleet continued to grow.[78] The human cost of these losses, however, is evoked by the air force's Aircraft and Accident Incident Reports:

23 August 1943. Aircraft model: C-87 Aircraft No. 42-107274. Purpose of Flight: Routine Cargo Mission. Took off from: Tezpur, India. Total Pilot hours: 7000 Hours per month last 3 months: 100 Statement of Station Manager Whitford: The ship taxied out to NE-SW runway position and pulled off the runway to run up the engines again. At 5:15 A.M. the wheels started rolling for take off and I observed the ship leave the ground and start to raise the landing gear. . . . Within a minute and a half or two minutes I noticed a glow at the end of the runway. . . . The tower operator had been unable to contact the ship and the glow indicated a fire to the left of the NE-SW runway about one mile away . . . probable cause of the accident was loss of power on one or more engines immediately following take off.[79]

Sept. 15, 1943. AIRCRAFT: Type and model: C:46. Place: East of Ft. Hertz Co-pilot Statement concerning ship No. 41-1-2309: On Sept. 15 at about 8:15 our right engine started icing up. We were at about 19,500 ft. and started to lose altitude. Both engines started cutting out so at 16,500 [pilot] Idema ordered us to put on our chutes. We all got our chutes on and were in the back going to jump out when the plane made a violent maneuver and threw us to the floor. In the excitement it is difficult to determine who left the ship in order. . . . Lt. Idema's chute evidently never opened or he never pulled the rip cord. [Radio operator Pvt.] Baize found him and had the natives bury him. His chute was torn from his body and there was no evident check to his fall. . . . We landed in the mountains and a few miles from some native villages and were treated well.[80]

15 September 1943. Place: Tezpur, Assam, India. AIRCRAFT: Type and model: C-47; A.F. No. 41-38597 FIRST PILOT HOURS: Instrument time last 6 months: None: Instrument time last 30 days: None. Night time last 6 months: None

1. No details are known regarding this aircraft as it is missing on routine flight from Chengkung, China to Tezpur, India. 2. The surviving member is still hospitalized and have been unable to get statement from him. Recommendations: Judging from the figures available at this office we feel that all first pilots on multi and four engine aircraft should have more experience before flying as 1st pilot on tactical missions between Assam, India and China.[81]

29 September 1943, C-87 #0555: This aircraft encountered severe icing conditions and dropped from 20,000 feet to 13,000 feet in an uncontrollable descent. The pilot ordered the rest of the crew to bail out. Meanwhile, he struggled to regain control of the gyrating ship, was unable to do so, and moved toward the escape hatch. On the way he saw the navigator lying unconscious on the floor but was unable to aid him as he fought the centrifugal force which prevented him from leaving the doomed plane; he jumped finally, and as he was drifting down, he saw the plane blow up in mid-air. Lt. Holmes, the pilot, spent 26 days of rain, cold, and hunger in the jungle before arriving at a native village in the Naga hills. Delirious and physically exhausted he was led to a food station by the friendly Nagas, and from there was speedily removed

to Ledo Hospital. He was suffering from malnutrition, scrub typhus, malaria, pneumonia and uremia, was down to 85 pounds
from 185 pounds . . . No word was ever received of the remainder
of the crew.[82]

Oct. 3 1943. Place: Kunming (4 mi. NE). AIRCRAFT Type and
model: C-46 A.F. No. 41-12422 October 3, 1943, instrument conditions existing at Kunming, C-46, NR. 41-12422, called Kunming
Tower and was assigned a position at 17,000 ft, then 15,000 ft, then
12,000 ft, then 11,500 ft., and at approximately 0230 GMT, was given
permission to make instrument let down which call was answered
by the pilot. Tower from this time on was unable to contact the airplane in question. At approximately 0330 GMT, Chinese reported
to ATC via Fighter Control, that transport type aircraft had exploded North of Kunming. An investigating search party of ATC
Officers, after search, located wreckage. . . . By means of Chinese
speaking ATC Officers an eyewitness account was gleaned from
several Chinese Air Corps Officers. To summarize, the airplane
when first seen was in the clear at approximately 1000 ft., descending, engines apparently functioning properly, wheels up, then explosion in midair. . . . The entire crew was killed, bodies unrecognizable.[83]

The majority of crashes were caused by the chronic Hump hazards—
weather and engine failure—but the month of October 1943 also saw an
unusually high number of losses due to enemy attack. The Japanese had
been closely following the increase in cargo-carrying traffic over the Hump
and in this month commenced an operation to thwart it. Operation Tsuzigiri, or "Street Murder," was part of a wider campaign to establish air
supremacy in the region and to support the Fifteenth Army, which was
now dug in across north Burma.[84] Two days—October 13 and 23—each
saw the loss of three transports.[85]

With this spate of attacks, the enemy emerged into the open, but only
briefly. An attack by Japanese fighters on two formations of B-24 bombers

sent from China to serve as temporary transports ended badly for the enemy, with the loss of an estimated three of their fighters. More to the point, though, hunting for individual transport planes was difficult and costly. The nature of the terrain restricted the use of radar, and a fighter pilot had to visually locate his lone prey as, through intermittent clouds, it traversed the vast air. Patrolling the skies in quest of a single target burned a lot of fuel, which was in short supply. As noted, Allied air and submarines were so successfully blocking seaborne supplies from Singapore to Rangoon that not even a third of what the Japanese air and ground forces needed was getting through.[86] Operation Tsuzigiri was therefore short-lived, and the enemy reverted to focusing primarily on the air bases that made much easier targets.

Nonetheless, the attacks triggered a development that Hardin had broached when he first took command: night flying. Night, like clouds, offered cover against enemy fighters.[87] Initially, the new directives extended only to takeoffs before dawn and landings in India shortly after dusk, but very quickly a twenty-four-hour schedule was imposed. By November 1, planes were flying continuously night and day, and by mid-November night flying was standard operational practice from both India and China.[88]

Commercial aviation had been operating night flights since the mid-1930s, but the experience was still new enough to be regarded with trepidation; for many pilots destined for the Hump, even crossing the Atlantic at night on the way to India had been cause for fear. "I can recall that heading into the pitch-black darkness, to cross a huge ocean was a frightening event for a young pilot with only about 500 flying hours," Segel recalled. "Many planes and crews were lost because of faulty navigation."[89]

The human eye is imperfectly adapted for nocturnal vision. Two kinds of light-sensitive nerves located at the retina connect to cells of the optic nerve that communicates with the brain: cones, which detect color, faraway objects, and details; and rods, which are used for peripheral vision and shades of gray. Both cones and rods are used in daylight and low light, but night vision is a function only of the rods. Unlike cones, rods are not

located directly behind the pupil, and while they can see objects periph-
erally, they experience a blind spot when looking directly ahead. This is
why, if one searches at night for a faint constellation, such as the Pleia-
des, one will sight it best by looking askance at the general area. A pilot's
vision at night, therefore, is both less detailed and clear than in the day and
also inherently defective. Night darkness also creates illusions, such as
masking the horizon that aids a pilot's point of reference, or conjuring a
false horizon from layers of cloud. Distant stationary lights can appear
as stars or the lights of other aircraft, while a pilot staring at an actual
star will "see" it move. One pilot coming in for a night landing in Kunming
radioed to the tower that the field lights were "moving around," then
crashed shortly afterward.[90] To land in a "black hole," a place where runway lights are the area's only illumination, is extremely difficult, for the
pilot lacks all orienting features and is given the illusion that the aircraft
is lower than it really is. Additionally, by another quirk of nature, the rods
at the retina are especially sensitive to hypoxia; pilots were advised to use
supplemental oxygen when flying at night above six thousand feet, but,
given the ongoing difficulties in enforcing even the daylight directives
for oxygen use, there could be little confidence this advice was followed.[91]

Like everything else about Hump flying, the equipment for night operations was rough and ready, or, as the air force's own history put it,
"night radio communications and navigational facilities were decidedly
inferior to those available by day and . . . field-lighting equipment was
poor."[92] Electric field lights were shipped to a few fields in China, but
their generators required precious gasoline, which was begrudged. Recalled one pilot, it "took many hours of arguing that the expenditure of
gasoline for this purpose would be saved, in the end, by reduction in the
fuel burned by an airplane seeking a place to land while coolies lit the
torches." The lights were to prove unreliable in any case, as fungus and
damp played havoc on the wiring.[93] Night fading-out effects of radio
waves compromised navigation, and often planes could pick up signals
only when within twenty-five miles of a transmitting station.[94]

For the pilots setting out into the mountain-ringed darkness of Assam, however, the heart of the matter was not facts of ocular physiology or aviation equipment, but the prospect of the massive, jagged maw of the Himalayan night. "Flying at night—that was the clincher that terrified everyone," one pilot recalled. "The wandering around high peaks with no landmarks."[95] Pilot after pilot sought to evoke the absoluteness of the darkness. "After the moon set, it was as though we were flying into an ink bottle."[96] "Black, the black of a black leather chair."[97] "Everything is totally black over there, it's like flying inside of a cave; when you have the runway lights behind you—you're in nothing. . . . When you took off at nighttime and you passed the end of the runway and the runway lights ended, it was like going into a closet and closing the door."[98]

In the earliest days of scouting for routes to China, the director of CNAC, with all that airline's experience of flying the region's terrain and weather, had cautioned that monsoon weather was "too bad for night flying."[99] But now, to the growing body of pilots' worst-flight stories were added those that took place at night. Pilot William Ramsey, newly arrived in CBI, set out for Assam one early evening as the shadows lengthened. "Towering cumulus cloud ahead began to attract our attention," he wrote. "Lightning was visible in all quadrants, and heavy rain was falling underneath the lower clouds. As the aircraft entered the clouds, Ramsey recalled, it "was immediately buffeted about by the wildest gyrations I had ever seen up until that time. The din of rain hitting the fuselage in torrents, and the racket of hailstones made it almost impossible even to shout across the cockpit." The plane's air speed fluctuated from stall speed to above "the red line" that marked an aircraft's maximum safe speed, the rate of climb was veering from below to above the safety stops, while the instrument panel was shaking so severely it was difficult to follow the artificial horizon that indicated the aircraft's attitude in the air. The plane was also picking up Saint Elmo's Fire, which the newly arrived pilots had never seen. "[O]ut my side window . . . the right prop was a huge fiery circle running in the darkness and lit up intermittently by massive flashes of lightning. We were picking up a pretty good load of wing ice, and the very windshield seemed to be on fire." They were also having great difficulty in keeping the aircraft in what they believed was right side up. All power was off, and yet the aircraft was hurling upward at six thousand feet a minute—when suddenly the storm spat the plane out into calm air and a clear night over the Assam Valley. "I nearly cried I was so happy," Ramsey recalled. "There was Sookerating in the distance, and the lights of Dinjan over toward the Brahmaputra River." Once on the ground, the crew bolted out of the aircraft and hugged one another, and Ramsey "stooped over and kissed that hot, steamy, wet tarmac."[100]

Night flying, in good weather, when the pilot had leisure, invited reflection, encouraged perhaps of the anonymity bestowed by darkness. To pilot Peter Dominick, the urge in the cold and blackness "to shrink into the fleece-lined coat and go to sleep was almost overpowering," as he wrote. "I wonder whether death is so bad. Maybe it's something like this. Flying through blackness into blackness, and away from blackness. No sun, no clouds, no earth, no trees, nothing but silent figures and blackness. If only we could just accept it, it would be so much easier. Just fly and fly and fly like automatons, and after a while the ship, the engines, the people, knowledge itself would fall into black nihilism, and everything would dissolve. . . ."[101]

ON A CLEAR NIGHT, FLYING WEST TO ASSAM, BRIGHT STARS SHONE FORTH high above, and below little lights from hundreds of fires burning in the Chinese villages twinkled like fireflies.[102] The world seemed at peace, and pilot and crew could look down from the dark heights and know that, after all, other human beings were below them.[103] Flying east in the still-dark hours before the dawn, pilots might see the bright "passing light" of another aircraft coming at them that turned out to be the planet Venus, and planes that set out late might find themselves flying into the very dawn.[104] Mountain peaks, sanctified by moonlight, shone in grand and ghostly ranks. Under a full moon, dissipating thunderclouds lit by the moon's strange, orange-tinted light rose like massive pillars, upward from the undercast into the black vault of heaven.[105] Looking down on a row of thunderstorms, a crew might see lightning flashing through the darkness as it raced across the tops of clouds.[106] Some pilots even claimed it could be safer to fly at night than in the day, as the stark lightning flashes gave guidance as to where a storm lay.[107]

But flying west or flying east, no comfort was to be had as the plane launched across the vast abyss that was the Burmese jungle. Blacker than the ocean they had crossed on the voyage out, devoid of any feature or reflective light, the great jungle claimed all earth and space beneath them, and many planes that skittered in the shifting air above this void, shoved by winds off their fragile courses, became lost. Monitoring the Mayday frequency east of Fort Hertz Valley, pilot John Shaver and his crew caught a conversation between a lost pilot and Chabua station, which was trying but failing to get a fix on the plane. "[W]e called the pilot and told him that we would turn on all of our lights and for him to look for us," Shaver recalled. "We lighted our ship up like a Christmas tree and starting doing 360's. He spotted our landing lights, he was about 10 miles off to the south of us. I gave him the heading and distance to Sookerting [*sic*], the closest landing strip, and he made it in okay. In fact, we passed him on the taxi strip. He had beat us to Sook., then run out of gas taxiing in."[108]

Most aircraft lost over the jungle, however, found themselves swept from all effectual aid and very much alone. Lacking communication of any kind with any station, beacon, or other plane, a crew could only frantically dial the radio compass and try to estimate from wind speeds and compass readings where they might be headed. The carefully rationed fuel allotted to them in China left little margin for any error, and many lost planes simply burned through all reserves. Then there remained two choices: to bail into the darkness and leave the abandoned plane to flutter and spin down to its destruction, or to go down with it.

Father Harry Wade, chaplain and captain in the US Army based in Jorhat, had believed that the only way he could speak meaningfully to the airman's fear of the Hump was to fly it himself.[109] "Sure Father! Be tickled to death to have you along," was the enthusiastic response of pilot Bob Seimoneit to Wade's suggestion that he ride along. Thus it was that, one calm evening, Father Wade took off at dusk from Jorhat in a C-87 transport loaded with drums of one-hundred-octane gas. As the plane climbed through the dusky twilight, he was able to enjoy the scenery below before darkness fell. Higher and higher the plane climbed, while the increasingly high terrain below gave the illusion of rising to keep pace with them. From cruising altitude, he looked down on mountain summits that glowed with the last fiery rays of the dipping sun, before it dropped behind the earth's horizon. "From then on," Father Wade recorded, "we flew in darkness!"

Some three hours later, the plane emerged out of the darkness and approached the lights of the Chinese town and airfield, which stabbed through the night like "tiny flashlights." Within one hour of landing, the plane had been unloaded, the crew had grabbed a cup of coffee and were back on board again, "roaring down the runway for India."[110] As the airfield lights faded in the distance, darkness again enveloped the plane and crew. From his seat by the navigator's table, Father Wade observed the comforting sight of their youthful faces dimly lit by the instrument panel's fluorescent lighting, and with the engines purring steadily, he went to sleep.

Three hours later, at 1:00 a.m., he woke to see pilot and copilot "talking to each other, checking the instruments, and looking out of the side windows." Clearing frost from the little window beside him, Father Wade looked out and was taken aback to see through the moonlit broken clouds, not the expected approach to the Assam Valley but high peaks below. Peering to the flight deck, he saw the pilots, radio operator, and crew chief were all busy checking instruments, consulting maps, scribbling on notepads. "I sat back without a particular thought in my head, and sleepily watched the proceedings," Father Wade recalled. Another hour passed, and there was no sign the activity on the flight deck was letting up."[111] Suddenly, the crew chief was standing by his seat and saying, 'I believe we are plenty lost, Father.'"

Incredulous, Wade tried to process these words. "How much flying time have we?" he asked. "About an hour, Father." Surely this was reassuring; surely, within an hour all would be put to right. Outside the window, the jumble of peaks that had previously risen high enough to pierce the clouds were now diminishing, and then were gone entirely. "Through a break in the moonlit cover, a black void was all that was visible," Wade recorded. "A closer and more concentrated inspection revealed faint traces of a rolling mountainous jungle." More time passed, and the crew chief was back again: "Father, let's go into the back of the ship and get your chute on." Dazed, Father Wade observed that the propellers were still turning, the plane was still flying strong and steady. "Father," said the crew chief, reading his thoughts, "this is it!" Buckled into his parachute, Father Wade stood by the door as, unexpectedly, the crew chief, a Catholic, asked him for absolution. "*Misereatur. . . . Indulgentiam. . . . Dominus noster Jesus Christus. . . .*"—fervently, Father Wade pronounced the familiar words. The crew chief pulled the emergency lever on the door, which immediately dropped and fell into the darkness, and "cold, misty, moonlit night air rushed into the ship. Never in all my flying experience had a plane seemed so comfortable as this one. To have to leave it through that door at 22,000 feet above God only knew what—didn't seem rational!"

"Where are we?" asked Father Wade.

"We haven't the slightest idea, Father."

As he prevaricated, the plane suddenly shook, the engines coughed and sputtered, and it was time to go. Out into the black night jumped Father Wade. Something large and even blacker passed overhead, and he knew it was the tail of the plane. Down into the cool and frosty moonlight he wafted, down through clouds, then, swinging helplessly, down through clear black air, and down again through another layer of clouds, through which could now be seen "the dark, evil-looking jungles."[112] To his right, in the distance, the wing lights of the big plane spiraled below, then exploded into flames. All five men jumped safely from the plane, landing in different places in the jungle, from where each made his way alone. Father Wade was rescued seven days after jumping; the pilot took three days to reach a US-British jungle post; the copilot and radio operator were sixteen days in the jungle, for eleven of which each man was on his own until the two stumbled upon each other; and the crew chief whom Father Wade had given absolution wandered for thirty-nine days before reaching an outpost. Naga tribesmen guided all the men to safety.

CASUALTIES CONTINUED TO MOUNT THROUGH THE END OF 1943, AND ALONG with the eleven transports lost that month were eight bombers that had been on missions to points in China and north of Rangoon; the bombers, victims of enemy attack, carried larger crews than the skeleton crews typical of the transports, and the loss of personnel was high. Two crews—one that had bailed from a C-46 en route from Kunming to Chabua, and one that survived, though badly burned, the crash landing of a B-24—were captured by Burmese villagers and turned over to the Japanese. In late November, a copilot who had successfully bailed out when two of his C-87's engines had failed, folded into his official report some advice on bailing out at night: "If at night, the crew should jump from an exit visible to the pilot or co-pilot, to be sure that there is no slip-up in knowing who has jumped. Before the jump it would be advisable to have the crew stand where they would be visible at all times."[113] In the confusion of his own exit, it appears that no one had seen him go.

Night flying added another component of apprehension and stress to the airmen's long days—for all crew members, not just the pilots. "Reaction to the dangers was different for the pilots than it was for the radio operator," reported Douglas Devaux, who, as a radio operator, sat in the "back seat" behind the flight deck. "We were unable to physically fight the storm with our hands and minds as the plane gyrated and bounced in all directions. . . . Unless our pilots wanted us for some extra task, we would keep our place on watch, seat belt tight, and hope and pray for the best."[114]

Back on terra firma after a round trip over the Hump, airmen generally retreated to their *bashas* to sleep, or to rejoin the endless poker games that served as each base's major form of entertainment. A miasma of cynical indifference now enfolded the bases like ground fog, and morale on the ground was as low as it was in the air. Visiting Chabua, the principal and best-equipped air base in Assam, Eric Sevareid, who had traveled widely through the theaters of the war, was appalled. "When I saw the American establishment at Chabua, where hundreds of Americans and thousands of natives slaved in scorching sun or dismal rain to get supplies to China," he reported, "I could not help feeling a certain resentment of the Chinese resentment over the inadequacy of these supplies. Our men were killing themselves and being killed every day in the effort."[115] Save for a few officers, the men lived in "shocking conditions" amid the sodden *bashas* with no amenities—no lounging place, no PX store, "nothing cool and refreshing to eat and drink," no nearby place to visit for respite, nor, as at other US bases in India outside Assam, Red Cross girls who served ice cream and hamburgers with friendly smiles. Canned food—fruit and Spam—eggplants, bananas, and tough water buffalo meat were the usual fare.[116] Chabua, wrote Sevareid, "was a dread and dismal place" that smelt of fear, its overworked men haggard with dysentery and malaria, unshaved and unwashed.[117]

Such amenities as existed were the products of the airmen's entrepreneurial improvisation. The bar at the "officers' club" in Chabua, for example, was built of glass bottles of varied colors, stacked and set in concrete and then artfully lit from behind. Soda water was produced by a contraption created from a twenty-man oxygen bottle, pressure gauge, and gas-stove fitting.[118] Accomplished scavengers had found that shipping crates provided lumber for desks, tables, and rudimentary chairs, and local rugs of felted goat hair softened the beaten-dirt floors.[119] Indian "bearers," assigned to each *basha* or tent, cleaned and tidied and performed general housekeeping chores such as pumping water into the storage tanks that served the latrines and showers, the latter used mostly in the dry season; in the monsoon it was easier to lather up and step outside.[120]

Life and morale on any given air base was conjured in a play written by two theater-minded airmen, probably sometime in late 1943 or 1944, titled simply *The Hump*. One of the writers was Howard Marshall, who, after graduating from Dartmouth College, had worked as a freelance writer for *Life* magazine and as a reporter and photographer for New Hampshire's *Union Leader*. From 1942, he had served first in the Coast

Artillery and then as an Army Air Corps aerial navigator, as which he was sent to CBI, where he flew some forty missions.[121] Richard Woodworth, the second playwright, had been born in Missouri as Myron Gale Woodworth, the son of a Baptist preacher who, at least as captured by local news stories, seems to have had a somewhat rocky career. ("Pastors who are not supporting the community building with their means are Rev. M. S. Woodworth . . . [who has] made use of the pulpit in denouncing the building of the hall. . . . Rev. Woodworth is extremely militant. . . .")[122] Myron/Richard had enlisted in the Army Air Corps in 1942, received his "wings" in 1943, and was posted to transport command as a navigator.[123] On enlisting, he had cited his civilian occupation as "Actor."[124]

THE HUMP

The curtain rises on three rooms of a basha—the half grass, half bamboo building which is the quarters for a group of American fliers in Upper Assam, India. It is toward the end of a rainy day, and though it is not raining at present, the sound of water dripping from the roof and the dull, gray light make the air heavy with wetness. . . . [125]

WHITE

First pilot?

COURTNEY [WHO HAS JUST ARRIVED IN ASSAM]

No sir. Just a co-pilot.

BAILEY

You're lucky. You might not have to fly for a while.

(The bottle is being passed up the table and as it comes by BAILEY he reaches for it.) . . .

WHITE

Take it easy, Bailey. You're on to-morrow.

COURTNEY

What did you mean by saying I was lucky?

WHITE

He didn't mean anything.

BAILEY

(He looks steadily at White and speaks with sarcasm.)

No, I didn't mean anything.

(To Courtney)

How much time you got in twin engine ships?

COURTNEY

About a hundred hours.

BAILEY

Okay. That's what I thought.

(He drinks again.)

[The men continue their game of poker.]

BAILEY

I'll tell you about the weather. You see how it is outside to-night?

> COURTNEY

Pretty wet.

> BAILEY

Yes, wet. And you have about fifty feet of ceiling, the thickest stuff you ever saw. Even the goddam birds are walking. Do you think you could set down on a muddy landing strip tonight?

> COURTNEY

Gosh—no!

> BAILEY

This is the kind of stuff you fly in. There's a ship about due in now. You'll hear it in a minute.

. . . (*The players ante, and as MCLEOD starts to deal there is the faint, far away drone of an airplane. The plane is very low and it does not take long to come over the barracks with a roar. The newcomers look instinctively overhead, but the plane passes on and the sound of its engines is almost lost in the distance.*)

> WHITE

That's Jackson, isn't it, McKinley?

> MCKINLEY

I believe it is, Sir.

> WHITE

He couldn't be up there on a worse night.

COURTNEY

How about his radio, sir? Can't he gèt in on his radio?

WHITE

That depends. In a rain like this your radio acts up pretty
much. And his radio can only bring him in over the field—it
can't get him down in soup like this. He might get under the
ceiling and still never find the runway.

COURTNEY

Well—what can he do? Jesus what can he do?

WHITE

(sighs and shrugs)

Of course—they'll light flares along the runway and try to
talk him in. Sometimes it works. There's nothing we can do
for him.

(a pause)

Let's play poker.[126]

THE AIRMEN'S KEEN AWARENESS THAT THEY WERE THE FBI—FORGOTTEN
Bastards of India—at the end of the line not only for supplies but also the
concerns of their countrymen, exacerbated grievances over such matters—
promotion, pay, and getting home—that were endemic to service members everywhere. Also wearing at morale was friction between experienced
senior pilots who had come from the airlines and the Air Corps recruits.
A second lieutenant's base pay, including housing and family allowances,

was about $386 a month.[127] The figure mattered less than the shortfall it represented when compared with that of "mercenary" pilots who flew for CNAC, which was still contributing to the Hump traffic. A fully checked-out airline captain received a base pay of $800 per month, with the possibility for overtime and end-of-year bonuses that were capped at $1,200 a month.[128]

Another point of resentment was the system of seniority that kept junior pilots junior and delayed their discharge to go home. In the early days of the Hump operation, it had been decreed that airmen would rotate home after a certain period of time, which was understood—although not clearly stated—to be a year. Hardin, however, had proposed that the period of service be calibrated not by time served, but by hours flown, and suggested that one thousand hours would be the appropriate number—equivalent to roughly 140 normative India-China round-trip flights. This figure had shocked even other air force brass, and after some to-ing and fro-ing, including with the surgeon general and the India-China Wing's chief doctor, the figure was adjusted to 650 hours over the Hump; for Western Sector pilots flying the trans-India routes, the figure was nine hundred hours before rotation.[129]

This magical figure—650—became a fixed talisman in every pilot's heart and mind. As a result, senior pilots pulled rank whenever they could, so as to rack up their hours and get out, with the result that many second lieutenants were only beginning to get qualified flight time when higher-ranking colleagues who had arrived at the same time as them were on their way home.[130] Yet another setback resulted from the usual Hump woe—lack of equipment and supplies. The ratio of pilots to planes was greatly disproportionate, so that at some bases each pilot was able to fly only every eleven days.[131] Diminished flying hours also ensured that many pilots remained not fully trained; and it was this fact—the lack of training and experience—as much as any other element of the Hump experience that most eroded morale.

A number of strategies were undertaken to address the critical deficiency in training, from using commercial airline pilots as mentors under Project 7-A, to the establishment of transition training schools, where new pilots and mechanics became acquainted with the C-46.[132] As time went on, much hope was also placed on the Link Trainer, a flight simulator set up to replicate the conditions of "flying blind." Sitting in a cockpit attached to the top of a movable pedestal, the pilot looked out through a black hood instead of a glass canopy and flew simulated flights on instruments, with particular attention paid to the landing patterns used at different air bases.[133] The Link system did little to prepare a pilot for conditions over the Hump, however, and the more-seasoned pilots in particular were unimpressed—with Link and with the flight schools in general. "Haven't learned a thing," Peter Dominick wrote in his diary, "don't like their school or their procedures for flying, won't use them, extreme inefficiency on set up, but I have fair food and cold drinks and occasionally ice cream."[134]

From the highest levels of the administration to the ground crew—every participant was aware of the critical lack of training and its direct bearing on the high incidence of crashes. The policy, much resented, of using revolving as opposed to fixed crews ensured that no one ever knew in advance with whom he would be flying, with the result that each crew scrutinized its pilot with lynx-like assessment, and stories of bad flights with bad pilots made the rounds of the bases. Lloyd Gray had arrived in Sookerating in September 1943, as a mechanic, but very soon his duties were expanded to include those of flight engineer, which meant flying as crew. A month after arrival, he was already feeling the strain. "Lousy pilot," he recorded in his diary on October 16, of the return leg of what had been a straightforward outbound trip to Kunming. "There was an overcast, and we went up at a steep angle until airspeed dropped to 80 MPH. I was plenty scared. Finally got on our way, by way of Lake Tali again. Going up the valley from Kunming to Yangkai flew very low." Stopping in Yangkai, the crew decided to stay overnight, as Japanese planes had been spotted at their intended next destination; reading between the lines it also appears that the spooked pilot was glad to defer a night flight for a stop at this base, where the crew enjoyed "a good supper" and several shows, including *Casablanca*. Departing very early the next morning, they retraced their path to Tali, an orienting landmark, then proceeded as before toward Assam. Back at last at Sookerating, Gray slept eleven hours, noting he was "really tired when my nerves let down."[135] There had been no emergency situation, no storm or loss of engines, just the strain of flying with a "lousy pilot."

"The kids are flying over their head," warned deputy commander of the ATC Brigadier General C. R. Smith. "[W]e are asking boys to do what would be most difficult for men to accomplish; with the experience level here we are going to pay dearly for the tonnage moved across the Hump."[136] Deficient training and experience ensured that pilots not only operated with insufficient skills, but that they flew in fear. "[A] cold chilling fear," as pilot Jack Pope summed up his experience over the Hump. On any given flight, he felt "a cold steel knot in my stomach—that is like a lead weight." The knot in Pope's stomach would become blinding pain, and out of fear he had on occasion regurgitated into his oxygen mask. The fear was not associated with any one flight but, like a shadow, was always with him—in the air and on the ground, before each flight and after flying. Between flights, he would sit in the officers' club drinking, and ahead of a flight would lie on his bunk, eyes wide open, waiting for the inevitable duty officer to touch his shoulder and say, "Time for your flight, sir." Then the pain in his stomach would increase. Standing like an automaton he would dress, and with feet of lead walk toward the jeep that would carry him to his aircraft.[137] At the end of every flight, he counted down the hours toward his freedom.

Jack Pope would successfully complete his 650 hours of flying time and survive to go home. The fear never left him, but he learned to manage it, as not all pilots could. "Had two ships lost," Peter Dominick recorded laconically in his diary. "[O]ne went in on final at Chungking due to pilot error due to too much flying."[138] One investigation of a C-46 crash, from which the crew had safely escaped by bailing out, revealed that the abandoned plane had flown steadily on autopilot until it hit a mountain. Why, then, if all was well with the aircraft, had the crew bailed? As part of the investigation, the pilot was given "a check ride to assess his flying skill," as the check pilot himself reported. "After less than an hour into the flight, this pilot became extremely emotionally upset. His unreasonable fear caused him to cry." The investigation eventually concluded that the "pilot apparently gave the order to bail out because of his inordinate fear of adverse weather conditions. It was determined that he could not discern the difference between the sound made by ice flying off the props and crashing in the fuselage and an engine cutting out."[139]

As the days and weeks ground on, stories of this kind proliferated and were quickly spread by word of mouth across the different bases, contributing to the "legend of the Hump," and so increasing fear. "I considered some of the pilots I flew with to be, shall I say, questionable," recalled Lieutenant Carl Constein of his days flying the Hump as copilot.[140] Drawn to flying because of "the unspeakable beauty of the earth viewed from my cockpit" and the peace aloft, Constein vividly memorialized his feelings of impotence and terror when a pilot he was flying with "lost it."[141]

"We got to altitude without incident," he recorded of the pure, crystal clear afternoon on which he flew as copilot back from Kunming, with the Himalayas dazzling him with their snowcapped beauty. "Suddenly the plane veered sharply left," he recorded. "The captain yanked off his oxygen mask. 'Holy Hell,' he shouted. I looked past him and saw out the left window a trio of motionless paddles where propellers should be whirling. The red oil pressure light confirmed complete engine failure."

Sitting erect, the pilot called out: "No chance to restart this bastard." Following correct procedure, he feathered the props, shut off the fuel, turned off the switches, and came to an idle cutoff. Then "[h]e threw out his arm and yelled, 'Help me trim her. Tell the radio operator to call a Mayday. Quick! Quick! And for Chrissake, fasten your chute.' . . . I was shocked at how scared he looked," Constein wrote. "I'd flown with him once before and judged him to be cool under pressure. I was wrong." "I'm taking this bastard into Yunnanyi," the pilot barked, while Constein's mind briefly flashed to his wife at home. "Without hydraulics, it'll take us both to land her, so I want you to get your ass into it. Goddamit, are you listening?" The captain had become "a madman," and Constein's every word and gesture only triggered another dangerous, distracting outburst. Staring straight ahead, he prayed the pilot would "hold together" long enough to land, but another outburst followed: "'You weak-kneed son of a bitch, I want you to sit there and not do a Goddamned thing. Do you understand?'

I nodded.

'Jesus, take your Goddamned mask off and strap your chute on. You act as though it's your first trip.'"[142]

As Constein's head pounded, the Yunnanyi tower radioed that an incoming plane had a Mayday emergency and forbade them to land: "C-87 on approach, do not land!" The tower operator's voice was tremulous. "Repeat. Do not land. We have a plane on Mayday."

"Jesus Christ," the captain shrieked. "I thought he was going to cry" was Constein's impression. "I felt hot around my ear, my neck, my face. My throat was tight." The captain was now staring ahead, motionless, his hands off the pedestal, sitting back in his seat. "Was he reconciled to crashing? Had he given up?" Cautiously, Constein took over the controls, remembering there was an old field north of Yunnanyi that had once been used by the Flying Tigers. After finding the field, he lined up the plane for landing, when the pilot sat up, saying, "I'm alright now." He landed badly, skidding off the runway strip, but nonetheless men and plane were safe on the ground. "That was a close one," the captain said as the crew disembarked. "You're a great co-pilot."[143]

It was impossible to know how many pilots cracked in flight, and how many of the crashes attributed to mechanical failure or weather were ultimately caused by the pilot's failure to manage such emergencies. "Loss of judgment" due to hypoxia was already a matter of grave concern and the speculated cause of many accidents in which the pilot's actions just did not make sense, such as when a landing aircraft flew directly over the Kunming field to crash into a mountain a mile away.[144] While pilots knew that insufficient oxygen could make them "goofy," many failed to understand that this was an unassailable physiological fact, not merely an inconvenience that could be overcome by determination, and that supplemental oxygen was strictly necessary and not just an annoying recommendation from the higher-ups. Belatedly, yet another cause of psychoses was discovered: the proscribed anti-malaria Atabrine tablets, it turned out, triggered auditory and visual hallucinations, delusion, and occasionally "disorientation," in addition to memory loss and a "manic-like reaction."[145]

Still, the most widely recognized, and rumored, cause of pilot error was fear. "I had a bad month," wrote one CNAC pilot in the privacy of his diary. "I did some stupid things and lived through them. I get scared, and when I do, I wonder whether I should be flying the Hump. I use all my flight training, experience, and instincts, but sometimes I'm not sure where I am. Sometimes I'm not absolutely positive that I'm not letting down into a mountain."[146] A court-martial of an ATC pilot found guilty of being "grossly drunk and conspicuously disorderly in station in the presence of officers, enlisted men and civilians" revealed that the accused "had been working long and hard hours" and "had been hospitalized with typhus fever. . . . When admitted to the hospital he had been in the theater fourteen months without leave." With regard to the night in question, he had been unable to sleep despite taking sleeping pills and accepted the offer of a drink because, as he said, "I thought perhaps a drink would do me good."[147]

Army Air Forces medical professionals who made a study of the "problems peculiar to Hump pilots" had no difficulty in cataloguing the causes of the condition, which airmen, at least, now knew by several names—"Humpitis," or being "Hump Happy."[148] Acknowledging that all too many pilots were "fair weather" pilots, who had taken up flying on a whim and were not suited to the profession, the doctors nonetheless agreed that Hump pilots were exposed to "real hazards" that included the "possibility of death, injury,—of bailing out and walking back— . . . Icing, weather, Japs, night and instrument flight, motor failure at high altitude," as well as the "environmental conditions under which personnel must live."[149] Additionally, the Hump pilot had operated with certain psychological disadvantages that were unusual in military service. Unlike fighter pilots, for whom "flying of the airplane was secondary in importance to proper maneuvering in order to get in the first shot," an ATC pilot's "primary mission was to fly the plane." Combat pilots knew "they were an essential part of the war" and "saw the damage their bombs did or the enemy plane they shot down." The Hump pilot did not; he simply "flew a load of cargo over the Hump."[150]

The army's eventual comprehensive history of neuropsychiatry in World War II included a special appendix titled "Psychiatric Casualties in Pilots Flying the China Hump Route." Hump pilots, the study reported, could be divided into two groups. The first pilots to arrive in the theater "were stable individuals who had flown hundreds of hours over the 'Hump' in poorly serviced planes and who had experienced one 'close call' after another"—in other words, good pilots who had been frayed by extreme experiences. The second group that came into focus later as the "cream" of the flight schools was drawn down were "service pilots," who typically had many hours of flying time, but only under ideal conditions. These pilots "were in an older age group and did not have the desire or the courage to fly the most hazardous route in the world"—an observation that speaks as much of Army Air Forces attitudes as of the condition.[151]

The report's concise list of the nine "Anxiety-Producing Factors" stands as an elegant distillation of the Hump experience. Factors cited included poor weather, lack of confidence in the aircraft, "the possibility of death in the jungle," group morale, susceptibility to what was by now "the legend of the Hump," pilot self-confidence, and—very telling—"[t]he ultimate disposition of urgent supplies which they had to fly over the 'Hump'; that is, material either stolen or not used after the destination was reached."[152] This fact was stated even more bluntly in an internal India-China Division medical study that noted that in the majority of cases a pilot did not know of what use his cargo would be "and sometimes feared, with reason, that most of it would be wasted by the Chinese."[153]

War-weary pilots, fatigued pilots, broken pilots were usually sent to the large general hospitals in Karachi or Calcutta, or to Chabua, where they were treated to the best of the staff's skill and ability. The medical department of the CBI theater, as the army recognized, "was deficient in personnel, central authority, specialists, staff consultants, rank, and policy."[154] No neuropsychiatrists were assigned to the theater for the first three years of its operation, with the result that "Anxiety-Alleviating" treatments were somewhat improvised.[155] These included such measures as daily interviews, sedation at bedtime, and, in more severe cases, "narcosynthesis," or the administration of a narcotic drug to stimulate the pilot's recall of traumatizing events followed by a discussion that "synthesized" the recalled experience with his waking life.

Another common-sensical therapy was to send the pilot to a "jungle rest camp" for relaxation. Hacked from the jungle, usually beside an attractive stream, the camps allowed the airmen to experience Assam as the tea planters did, as a place of great peace and beauty, although few seemed to drop their guards against the feared jungle. The activities—swimming, canoeing, fishing, making campfires, playing volleyball, playing cards—were much the same as at a Boy Scout camp, except for the inevitable jungle leeches and hopeful tiger hunts that happily almost always ended in the tiger's favor.[156] "We just hung around," Douglas Devaux recalled; as a radio operator he, too, like other crew members who were not pilots, had become "fatigued." "[We] really rested, because there was no being awakened in the middle of the night for another wild ride."[157]

Sixty percent of pilots treated, the study claimed, returned to fly the Hump. The fates of the 40 percent that could not be salvaged was mixed, with some returning home, some sent to fly less hazardous routes, some grounded.[158] Men in the last category often remained to work as ground crew at their Assam bases, where their failure of nerve was daily visible to their colleagues. At Chabua was an "older" pilot in his mid-thirties, married with two children, who had come to India with the very first group of transport pilots and "was a very skillful but scared pilot," James Segel recalled. "On his third trip across the Hump he encountered extreme turbulence, icing, periodic engine failure, and was so close to total disaster that he was convinced he would never see his family again. He

made it back, a shaken man, and was found unfit to continue flying duty."
He was given the job of operations officer, also a stressful job, and became
the butt of cruel jokes, such as telling him that he had been returned to
flying status. The "old" pilot's panicked reaction to such jokes suggests
that ground duty had not brought about his recovery.[159]

Little is known about the 20 percent of fatigued pilots who were
deemed beyond treatment and sent home, but a sinister little ditty written by a field correspondent for the *CBI Roundup*, the theater's official
newsletter, is ominous:

"Wail of a Beaten Woman"

My war-weary Willie is back home again,
Decidedly psychoneurotic.
Afflicted with strange paranoiac desires
Acquired in locations exotic.

Embittered, frustrated, he cannot relieve
His desperate nervous condition
Unless he is staging an amateur bout
With me on the floor of our kitchen.

The eminent experts explain that I must
Be patient and most understanding,
Regardless of where my anatomy's hit
Or how I got battered in landing.

So beat me, dear daddy, sixteen to the bar,
my floating ribs part from their mooring.
Oh, cave in my clavicle, shatter my shin,
Assured that my love is enduring.[160]

TOWARD THE END OF NOVEMBER 1943, THE ANGLO-AMERICAN LEADERSHIP
convened two other conferences, the first with Chiang Kai-shek in Cairo
to discuss the war against Japan, the second with Marshal Stalin in Tehran to discuss the war against Germany. Although the objectives of the
sessions were distinct, the outcomes would be intertwined and together
represented, in the words of the official historians of the CBI theater, a
"watershed."

In Cairo, meetings were held in the Mena House, the spectacular former hunting lodge of King Farouk set almost in the shadow of the pyra-
mids, which stood "out in the morning sun like mountains," as General
Arnold wrote in his diary shortly after his arrival in Cairo. "I can almost
reach out and touch the largest one." The following evening, with Admi-
rals Ernest King, US chief of naval operations, and William Leahy, the
president's chief of staff, he joined the British Chiefs of Staff for dinner.
"Excellent food, good wine and splendid service," he recorded. "Discussed
history of the world: Genghis Khan, Kubla Khan, the Knights Templars
of Malta, Carthaginians, the Turks conquering the shores of the Mediterranean."[161] Preliminary presentations by the Joint Chiefs of Staff, as
he noted, had covered "England, Russia, China, India, almost the whole
world."[162]

For this, his first face-to-face meeting with the American and British
leadership, Chiang, briefed by Stilwell, had come prepared with offers
and demands relating to the long-planned Burma campaign. His offer
amounted to the proposal to train and equip ninety Chinese divisions—
up from the originally planned thirty divisions and the later proposed
sixty—that would be deployed in stages over time, with the last thirty divisions being made available by January 1945. A portion of these would
advance, as previously agreed, as the much-discussed X- and Y-Forces into
Burma. Chiang also proposed that "[n]ecessary airfields will be built and
maintained" by China. As was now typical, these commitments came

with weighty demands. He expected the ninety divisions, and additional armored divisions, would be trained, supplied, and equipped by the US; that the US would continue to maintain and supply the Fourteenth Air Force; that the Americans would reinvent and build to strength the Chinese Air Force, including with medium and heavy bombers; that thirteen US infantry and armored divisions would be made available for an offensive against the Japanese in central and northern China; and that throughout all this the "ferry route will be maintained at a capacity of at least 10,000 tons a month."[163]

Anxious for confirmation of the generalissimo's participation in the north Burma campaign, Roosevelt, rashly, had arranged for Mountbatten to present SEAC's plans at the first formal meeting in which all three heads of state and their staff were present, before the plans had been fully vetted by the Combined Chiefs of Staff. These plans, following the outlines long-discussed, amounted to an advance in stages from India into Burma, both down the Arakan and as far southeast as possible and at least to the Chindwin River. The operation would conclude with the seizure of Indaw, through which the important rail line to Myitkyina passed, ahead of the monsoon. The long-range penetration groups were to operate throughout the monsoon, and if warranted the general advance could continue after the rains. An amphibious operation would also be staged in the Bay of Bengal, details of which were to be forthcoming.[164] Mountbatten took pains to underscore the difficulties the operation faced, with lines of communication that ran through one of the most rugged landscapes in the world, "in thick jungle and across mountains running north and south across the line of communications."[165] Following this overview, Mountbatten "then gave certain logistical information for the air route over the 'hump.'" The anticipated tonnage for November and December was 9,700—not far short of the pledged 10,000 tons—but would drop to 7,900 in January and February, before rising again in March; these adjustments were necessary to supply the land campaign.[166]

The proposal, which had been shared with the Chinese delegation weeks before, immediately met with Chiang's criticism. The operation described was too restricted, in his view, and did not approach the "all-out air-land-and-naval effort" he desired to reopen the land route to China.[167] He wished for the southeast advance to extend all the way to Mandalay and that it be conducted simultaneously with "a naval action and a naval concentration in the Bay of Bengal."[168] His views on the reduction of tonnage were made clear the next day by his staff, who took pains to emphasize that "the Generalissimo was insistent that, whatever the needs of the land campaign, the air lift to China must not drop below 10,000 tons a month," as "the pressure exerted from China on Japanese forces must be maintained."[169]

At this point, the conference minutes suggest that Mountbatten's tone sharpened as he pointed out that it "was illogical to demand in the same breath that this extensive plan should be carried out and a 10,000 ton air lift to China maintained." Moreover, he continued, it was his opinion that "the U.S. Air Force had achieved miracles in reaching their present capacity over the 'hump.' It was essential that the Chinese should make up their minds whether to insist on a 10,000 ton lift to China or whether they wished his present operations carried out."[170] Smoothly overriding their reiteration that "10,000 tons a month was an absolute minimum, essential to maintain and equip the Chinese Army," Mountbatten went on to observe that "in order to make the airline safe or to open the Burma Road, it was essential to put everything into the present battle" and made the pointed suggestion that "the Chinese, at this stage, should only equip troops which would actually take part in the present battle and that tonnage designed to equip or maintain the remainder must be foregone until the battle had been won." General George Marshall then stepped in to point out, also forcefully, as it appears even in the minutes, "that the present campaign was designed to open the Burma Road, for which the Chinese had asked, and that the opening of the Road was for the purpose of equipping the Chinese Army. . . . Unless this road were opened there could be no increase in supplies to China at this time since no further aircraft or equipment could be provided from the United States due to commitments elsewhere to meet serious shortages." Stilwell's report of Marshall's outburst in his private notebook records more passionate language then the minutes suggest: "Now let me get this straight. You are talking about your 'rights' in this matter. I thought these were American planes, and American personnel, & American materiel...."[171] Smarting, as it seems, under these remarks, General Shang Chen volunteered an astonishing statement, amounting to an admission of what the other Allies suspected; the ten thousand tons were "necessary for the China area. These supplies would not be hoarded or sold."[172]

The conference stalled as Chiang continued to vacillate. "Message the G-mo would come," Stilwell recorded in his diary of an impending meeting. "That he wouldn't. That he would. Christ."[173] Instead, the generalissimo sent his aides, who then refused to speak, stating that they only wished to listen. Pressed to give any opinion, they whispered among one another and repeated that they wished to listen. An excruciating silence followed. Brooke, urging them forcefully to venture some comment, in Stilwell's view, became "insulting," yet, as he conceded in his diary, the Chinese delegation had made a "[t]errible performance. They couldn't answer a question."[174]

After meeting with Mountbatten, who was dispatched to try to bring the generalissimo around to an agreed plan, Chiang announced that the Hump tonnage could be maintained if an additional 535 transports were made available. Duly, Mountbatten put the preposterous request before the Combined Chiefs, who duly stated the aircraft could not be found.[175] Over the five days of the conference, Chiang consented to support the campaign in Burma on three occasions, and on three other occasions withdrew his support.[176] As Mountbatten noted in his diary, the leaders of the free world had at last met Chiang and "have been driven absolutely mad."[177] Late on the last night, as weary participants were getting ready for bed, "word came that General [Shang] had changed our account of the meeting with the Generalissimo," Arnold recorded; dressed in his robe, he had been in the middle of packing. "Outside of the fact that it committed me to putting about 13,000 tons a month over the Hump,

2,000 more than I could possibly carry, the change meant little." Arnold amended the document and went to bed.[178]

According to Chiang's biographer, who drew on the generalissimo's own diaries, Chiang had "saved his real negotiations for his talks with Roosevelt."[179] As he later told Mountbatten, "The President will refuse me nothing. Anything I ask, he will do."[180] In private conversations with Roosevelt, and with Madame Chiang acting as a wily interpreter, the two heads of state had discussed the postwar world, China's role as a great power in it, the return of territories to China, the end of colonialism, and Britain's end of empire.[181] The Chiangs departed Cairo buoyed in the belief, as Chiang recorded in his diary, that "the various negotiations had brought about the anticipated results."[182] He had, as he thought, succeeded in wresting a commitment from Roosevelt for much of what he had asked: the ninety trained and equipped divisions; his long-desired amphibious operation, now named Buccaneer and redirected from Rangoon to the Andaman Islands so as to intercept Japanese supply lines; and a commitment to an increase of tonnage over the Hump.

Although the principal dignitaries of the conference had departed, with Chiang and Madame returning to Chungking by way of Ramgarh, where they stopped to inspect the American-trained Chinese troops, and the American and British leadership continuing on to Tehran, it could not be said that the conference had been concluded. No plan had been agreed upon and no commitment secured from the generalissimo, and the aftershocks of the various meetings and sessions continued to reverberate— through the meeting in Tehran with Stalin, and through the follow-up meeting between the Americans and British on their return to Cairo.[183] Emerging from the inconclusive confusion, however, one thing became clear, and that was the fading importance of China and Chiang himself to the other Allies' war effort. A key development was that Roosevelt, despite his affability with Chiang, was in fact greatly perplexed by his meeting with the man he had so long and unflaggingly championed. Elliott Roosevelt, who accompanied his father to the conference, reported that the president told him that he had learned from the Chiangs about "the war that *isn't* being fought," that "Chiang's troops aren't fighting at all—despite the reports that get printed in the papers." Chiang's explanation was that his troops "aren't trained, and have no equipment." But, the president mused, "it doesn't explain why he's been trying so hard to keep Stilwell from training Chinese troops. And it doesn't explain why he keeps thousands and thousands of his best men up in the northwest—up on the borders of Red China," where the Communists were encamped.[184] Also unexplained was how China could spare manpower to mass troops to menace the Tibetan border, a fact that Churchill had angrily raised at the Washington conference back in May.[185]

MEANWHILE, EVENTS IN THE WIDER WAR ARENA WERE ALSO INEXORABLY shifting attention away from China. On November 20, 1943, only a few days before the start of the Cairo Conference, US Marines had landed on the Gilbert Islands, forging a route to Japan through the Pacific Islands—a route that would sideline China as the base from which Japan was to be assaulted. In Tehran, Stalin heartened the Anglo-American contingent by reiterating a pledge that, once Germany was defeated, the Soviet Union would be able to send reinforcements to Siberia and make it possible "by our common front to beat Japan."[186] Toward the defeat of Germany, Stalin pushed for a committed date for the all-out cross-Channel assault—code-named Overlord—and landing in southern France (Operation Anvil). Back in Cairo for follow-up meetings with the Anglo-American command, Churchill pounced on these developments, declaring that Stalin's pledge to join the war against Japan "would give us better bases than we could ever find in China," and that "operations in Southeast Asia must be judged in their relation to the predominating importance of Overlord."[187] Churchill's loathing of Buccaneer had never been concealed.

After much resistance, Roosevelt surrendered Buccaneer on the premise that the resources allocated to it would be better used to bolster Overlord. It now remained to notify the generalissimo. In Cairo, Chiang had exasperated everyone with his unreliability, fickleness, and suspicion, yet it now proved that the other Allies were the more unreliably fickle and had justified his suspicions. Quite where this left the campaign in Burma or policy toward China was now unclear, but the downgrading of China and Chiang's importance cracked open doors to other possibilities, as Stilwell discovered at a meeting with Roosevelt before he departed Cairo for Chungking. This most consequential fact was slow to emerge from their discussion, brilliantly captured by Stilwell at his writerly best:

> J.W.S. [Joseph W. Stilwell]: I am interested to know how this affects our policy in China.
>
> F.D.R.: Well, now, we've been friends with China for a gr-e-e-at many years. I ascribe a large part of this feeling to the missionaries. You know *I* have a China history. My grandfather went out there, to Swatow and Canton, in 1829, and even went up to Hankow. He did what was every American's ambition in those days—he made a million dollars, and when he came back he put it into western railroads. And in eight years he lost every dollar. Ha! Ha! Ha! . . .
>
> J.W.S.: I take it that it is our policy to build China up.
>
> F.D.R. Yes. Yes. Build her up. After this war there will be a great need of our help. They will want loans. Madame Chiang and the G-mo wanted to get a loan now of a billion dollars, but I told them it would be difficult to get Congress to agree to it. Now, I'm not a financial expert (!) but I have a plan. . . .

Then, suddenly, Roosevelt changed tack, asking Stilwell abruptly, "How long do you think Chiang can last?" On Stilwell's replying that the "situation is serious," Roosevelt made a suggestion: "Well, then we should look for some other man or group of men, to carry on."[188] This was evidently not just a passing thought, for a month later there would be rumblings in Washington to the effect that it would be possible to "break Chiang Kai-shek by withdrawing American support," or by "buying one of his competitors with an expenditure of $100 million."[189]

Years later, Stilwell's aide, Lieutenant Colonel Frank Dorn, whom Stilwell requested to keep a record of events, made an astonishing revelation in his memoir. Shortly after his return to China, Dorn recorded, Stilwell met at him at his headquarters in Kunming and reported that he had been "shocked by a verbal order he had received at Cairo." Reluctant to continue for a few moments, Stilwell had then "shrugged his shoulders, sighed, and said: 'Well, an order is an order. I have no choice but to pass this one on. . . . Here goes, then. I have been directed to prepare a plan for the assassination of Chiang Kai-shek.'" The directive was only to *prepare a plan*, Stilwell emphasized, not to execute it. Roosevelt, as Stilwell told Dorn, was "fed up with Chiang and his tantrums" and had told Stilwell "in that Olympian manner of his: 'If you can't get along with Chiang and can't replace him, get rid of him once and for all. You know what I mean. Put in someone you can manage.'"[190]

According to Dorn, after hours of "whispered talk" and "dozens of ideas," it was decided that Chiang would be lost on a flight over the Hump, en route from China to inspect his X-Forces troops training in Ramgarh. Before taking off, the American pilot would be handed sealed orders that instructed him to crash the plane; Chiang's parachute—and Madame's, were she to be in attendance—would be "fixed" by carefully unraveling the shroud lines; "So when his chute opens, old C.K.S. drops like a plumb bob."[191]

Meanwhile, Roosevelt and Washington continued their support of Chiang, if now with little faith. There were no obvious candidates for his replacement; perhaps more to the point, the effort required to locate, cultivate, and manage yet another Chinese faction was difficult to imagine, let alone summon. China's position in the world after the war mattered more to Roosevelt, in any case, than its role in the war against Japan. And a certain degree of goodwill with and control over Chiang could be leveraged in a highly cost-effective manner—by increasing tonnage over the Hump. The canceling of Buccaneer and the downgrading of the Burma offensive freed up supplies and planes that could be allocated to the air ferry, and in December Roosevelt confirmed his commitment to increasing the Hump capacity to twelve thousand tons a month.[192] The air bases were cheap to maintain, after all, with their basic living conditions, chronic lack of supplies, parts, and planes, and their untrained airmen.

THE MONTH OF NOVEMBER CLOSED WITH A DISPIRITING 6,491 TONS DELIV-ered over the Hump, but in December the long-elusive 10,000-ton mark was reached and surpassed: 12,590 tons were hauled over the mountains to China, and for the rest of the war the tonnage dipped only once below 10,000, and indeed was to soar.[193] This success was in great part to be attributed not so much to the new round-the-clock schedule, as to efforts to address the most glaring inefficiencies: better loading strategies, clipping the turnaround time in Kunming (it was reported that "crews were remaining too long in the coffee shop at Kunming"), attempting to ensure maintenance was available most hours, and addressing the paralyzing congestion at both termini. Many problems could not be solved, such as the rat-borne typhus in Kunming that caused personnel to call in sick—although, as the Wing surgeon reported, "those typhus cases which existed were mild" and "he was not particularly alarmed over the situation."[194]

Notwithstanding the improvements, the attainment of the tonnage goal took a high toll, with 155 major accidents occurring between the months of June and December 1943.[195] That night flying specifically contributed to this toll is suggested by the fact that, in November, when night flights became routine, the number of accidents attributed to pilot error jumped from around five per month to nineteen.[196] The airmen had no doubt that the "hard-charging," round-the-clock flying schedule was the cause of these casualties. "Haynie and McClean today," Dominick wrote in his diary, referring to the loss of two pilot friends; "a Jorhat ship yesterday, Misamari's Chief Pilot the day before, two more almost gone today and me almost gone 4 days ago! This business of Hardin's 24 hours a day schedule regardless of weather is bringing what we all expected!"[197]

Many airmen, pilots and crew, had taken to recording privately the almost daily disasters. "We lost [plane number] 171 somewhere in the Valley yesterday," Lloyd Gray, the mechanic and flight engineer wrote in his diary on November 8, 1943.

> 9/11/43 Routine flight to Kunming. Left landing light out and made a bad landing, brakes didn't work right, and right engine caught on fire. Finally unloaded and made repairs, and flew on back here. Left landing light out again, but made good landing. Left brake locked, and we left runway and cracked up against a C-47. . . . Ruined our right wing, and their nose section.

> 11/11/43 Routine day. Worked on line. Crew of [plane number] 172 located walking out of Hump.

> 14/11/43 Changing shifts. Worked all day, and then a night shift after five hours. Three planes washed out today. . . . Pilot took tail out of 410 on taxi, 408 came in on nose. 308 clipped a tree in the fog, then landed at Dinjan. Slept all afternoon. Chicken for supper.[198]

One noteworthy fact emerging from the statistics is how rarely transport aircraft were lost to the enemy. In 1943, twelve aircraft were reported as "destroyed by known enemy action," six of these losses being in October, the month of Japan's short-lived Operation Tsuzigiri, and, all in all, enemy action accounted for an estimated less than 5 percent of transport losses.[199] Analyzing the crash sites of the transports that were hit, however, Hump historian John Plating made a revealing discovery: all were well south of the approved safe route that arced thirty to forty miles north of Fort Hertz over the high mountains of northern Burma and beyond Japanese activity. Plating then expanded his search to include all transport crashes in 1943 for which crash coordinates were known. With only two exceptions, these, too, fell well south of the route that was secure from enemy attack. The implications were clear and stunning: it was not the enemy that pilots feared but the Hump.[200]

7

NUMBER ONE AIR COMMANDO

As noncombatants, transport pilots sat on the lowest rung of the military aviation hierarchy. A Hump pilot was a "Hump driver," a cargo carrier, a bus driver; Air Transport Command's acronym, ATC, it was said, stood for "Allergic to Combat." The lowliness of the transport pilot's status could be driven home in a highly practical manner, as was the case for Robert Boody of the Tenth Air Force's 90th Fighter Squadron.

In the summer of 1943, Bob Boody had arrived in New Malir, Karachi, where he briefly enjoyed practicing strafing and dive-bombing over Indian villages with his squadron.[1] Two and a half months after arrival, however, he had rashly decided to fly over to Assam to visit his fiancée, who was a nurse in a military hospital situated on a former tea estate, and on return to his own base six days later, discovered he had been written up as AWOL. His protests that he "was under the impression it had been agreed to between me and my 90th Fighter Squadron" that he was cleared to make the excursion did not advance his case. Ten days later, he was informed that he was being transferred to Air Transport Command "as punishment," and that "by The Brass's 'judgement,' I'm not suitable as a fighter pilot and would do better in multi-engine ships," as he recorded in his diary of this dark day. "B.S.!" he exploded. "It sort of hurts my fighter pilot ego a bit to be so ignominiously demoted by a 'new,' rank-happy colonel for his own misunderstanding."[2]

Boody, now permanently demoted, began 1944 with another lengthy visit to Ledo and the 73rd Evacuation Hospital, where his fiancée was based. The months since his transgression had been eventful. After a brief stint of flying reconnaissance missions for the ATC, he had been diagnosed with jaundice and spent nearly three weeks in the hospital in Jorhat. A severe earthquake had hit the base one night and destroyed the stone hospital in which he was quartered "around our ears," as he wrote in his diary. On discharge, he had reported to his former squadron and received "some surprise orders" for transfer to the 2nd Troop Carrier Squadron on detached service at Dinjan. Catching a flight on one of the shuttle planes that were now in operation between the air bases, Boody was in Chabua by late afternoon, where he spent a transitional night in a tent on the polo grounds, from where a short jeep ride brought him to Dinjan the next morning.[3]

Once settled in Basha #3, Boody began to familiarize himself with his new duties, but in the evening he drove to Ledo to see his fiancée, Jean—his first visit to her since the unauthorized trip that had prompted his demotion. The last time, there had been dancing at the Hospital Officers Club, Sunday service in the new hospital chapel, an evening party at a Scottish tea planter's house overlooking the Burhi Dihing River, and his actual engagement with Jean, to whom he had given a specially made star-sapphire ring.[4] This time, "[s]he and I both seem very distant and unaffectionate," he recorded, and speculated that "[w]e're both probably musing on the circumstances surrounding my surprise transfer from Fighter in P-40 single engine ships to Troop Carrier (Air Supply Droppings) in C-47 twin-engine transports."[5]

Robert Boody was born in 1920 into a close and comfortably off Staten Island family. A snapshot of his settled prewar life is gleaned from the account he gives in his diary of hearing the news that Pearl Harbor had been bombed. "I had returned to my parents' home on Staten Island, New York from attending church services—had finished luncheon and was listening to N.Y. Philharmonic concert music on CBS radio. . . ." Studying for the Army Air Corps ground prep school by day, Boody had worked the graveyard shift at night manning American Airlines' reservation department at LaGuardia Airport. The day after Pearl Harbor, he quit his job to enroll in flight school and departed shortly afterward to Maxwell Field, in Montgomery, Alabama. Patriotic, hardworking, and disciplined— the portrait that emerges from Boody's diary is of a confident young man who believes in the maxims and rules-to-live-by adages that pepper his diary: "Commitment is what transforms a promise into reality"; "Personal Responsibility In Daily Effort"; "There are Nine Requisites for Contented Living."[6]

Boody and army nurse Second Lieutenant Mary Jean Parks had met in May of 1943 at the Camp Kilmer Officers' Club in New Jersey, and shortly afterward embarked together on the HMS *Mauritania* moored in the Hudson River and bound for India. She had graduated from nursing school in Pennsylvania in 1940 and served as a US Army nurse since 1942.[7] In the course of the nearly seven-week-long voyage to Bombay, the two had fallen in love. For obscure reasons, Boody nicknamed the "vivacious and pretty little brunette" Little Butch, perhaps because she was petite but tough.[8] In Bombay, Parks and her 22nd Field Hospital had continued by rail to Assam, and eventually to the 73rd Evacuation Hospital in the jungles of Shingbwiyang—a hard posting—while Boody had gone on to the New Malir base in Karachi for training. His own eventual posting was in Tezpur, Assam, whence, the day after arrival and four months after meeting Parks, he made his impromptu visit to see her. Thus, fate and Boody's determination had brought the two together in Assam, where their respective professions, air-supply pilot and nurse, would be key in the north Burma campaign ahead: air supply was to support the unfortunate ground troops who would be laboring through the jungle, and medical care would be necessary to tend the anticipated diseased and wounded.

Boody flew his first food-dropping mission shortly after being discharged from the hospital. The day before he did so, a pilot friend crashed and burned with all crew killed on a similar mission, and Boody was able to fly over and photograph the wreckage.[9] The speculated cause of the C-47 crash was engine or propeller failure in an area known for vicious downdrafts.[10] Air supply missions required the usual crew—pilot, copilot, radio operator, perhaps a navigator cum chief—plus a drop crew of three quartermaster "food kickers," whose task was to get the supplies out the door. When the plane reached the target area, identified by coded radio signal or panels of cloth spread in a coded signal on the ground, the copilot raised his left hand for the food kickers to see as they crouched by the open doorway. "At the split-second time for dropping," as Boody described, "the pilot raised the tail of the ship" and the containers—of food, weapons, medical supplies, even personal mail—attached to parachutes, were shoved out. Twelve to fifteen passes at a target were needed to unload a C-47, Boody noted, and as the targets were in sites of military activity, the transports often drew enemy fire.[11]

While transport planes and crew were diverted from the Hump to air supply of the new Burma campaign, the regular Hump operation continued as before, as did its litany of disasters, with losses attributed to the usual causes—engine failure, thunderstorms, becoming lost and running out of fuel or into terrain. Three fatal crashes occurred on the last day of January: a C-87 went missing in bad ice conditions; a C-46 "went out of control in a thunderstorm"; and another C-46 departed for Kunming and simply disappeared, but was believed to have been lost to bad weather.[12] Air supply pilots like Boody bounced around between routine Hump missions and the increasingly dangerous food drops.

ALTHOUGH THE CONFERENCES IN CAIRO HAD CONCLUDED WITH MANY UN-answered questions, as well as a lack of united conviction as to the value of the effort, the broad purpose of the north Burma campaign had been well stated by Roosevelt. Briefing Stalin at their meeting in Tehran on the Allied strategy in the Pacific, Roosevelt had informed him that in the western Pacific the one great object was to keep China in the war, "and for this purpose an expedition was in preparation to attack through north Burma and from Yun[n]an province." The president had also pointed out that "although these operations extended over vast expanses of territory the number of ships and men allocated for the purpose were being held down to a minimum." In other words, the campaign was being undertaken for a strictly political purpose and would be run on the cheap.[13]

Following the conference, Roosevelt had telegrammed Chiang Kai-shek to inform him that the schedule agreed to in Tehran for ending the war with Germany had forced the cancellation of Chiang's cherished amphibious landing in the Andaman Islands; there would be no Operation Buccaneer. The president offered two ways forward: to advance the land campaign as planned but without Buccaneer, or to postpone operations until November, when the competing campaign in Europe would, it was hoped, be concluded, at which time it would be possible to mount the desired amphibious operation. In the meanwhile, all air transport would be concentrated on increasing the tonnage flown to China.[14]

Chiang's anxiously awaited response arrived on December 9. If the president's message were to be reported to the Chinese army and people, Chiang wrote employing his standard threat, it would so dishearten them that he feared "the consequences of China's inability to hold out much longer." The defeat of Germany would undoubtedly advance the global war effort, but "on the other hand, the collapse of the China theater would have equally grave consequences on the global war." With regard to the two options he had been given, Chiang chose to postpone the campaign to November 1944—yet, as he stated, he feared China could not hold on until that time. To prevent the collapse of morale of the Chinese people and army, it was necessary to assure them, he told Roosevelt, "of your sincere concern." The only way he could see to do this was for the US to make "a billion gold dollar loan to strengthen [China's] economic front" at a set exchange rate of twenty Chinese dollars to one US, when the actual rate on the black market was 240 to 1.[15] (Chiang "has struck us for more money and for modification of our terms on which we are helping them," wrote Secretary of War Henry Stimson in his diary. "I do not fear that the Chinese are going to drop out of the war now that we are so close and I think that their present demands show a good deal of the Chinese bargaining.")[16] Additional demands shortly followed. The number of US planes in China should be doubled and all new airfields to be built for the long-discussed B-29 very-long-range bombers must be paid for entirely by the US, at an estimated cost of two to three billion Chinese dollars, or about one hundred million US dollars.[17] "2 to 3 BILLION!" Stilwell raged in his diary. "My God. 50 million gold to build the fields & 50 million gold squeeze!"[18] Additionally, Chiang demanded that "the total of air transportation should be increased, as from February 1944, to at least 20,000 tons a month."[19]

When the dust settled, the loan was declined and the B-29 airfields were built by Chinese labor. To the surprise of everyone, Chiang telegrammed Roosevelt to say that, notwithstanding that the amphibious operation was postponed, "preparations for an offensive against Burma next spring should proceed at full speed as originally planned." This endorsement of the road-building north Burma campaign was in distinction to the "general offensive against Burma," which Chiang said *should* be postponed until November and the attending amphibious landing.[20] To Stilwell's own greater surprise, the generalissimo gave him full command of X-Force, now renamed both the Chinese Army in India (CAI) and the New Chinese Army.[21] Chiang's stipulated new target for the Hump—twenty thousand tons a month—was revised downward to twelve thousand tons.[22]

The Burma campaign was in fact already underway when the conferences in Cairo were being held, for in late October three regiments of Stilwell's CAI had been transported from their training base in Ramgarh to the town of Ledo in Assam to begin their trek into Burma. Detailed plans of the operation—code-named Albacore—had designated December 1 as the speculative D-Day, but Stilwell had given orders for elements of the 38th Division to advance before the Combined Chiefs of Staff had in fact authorized the offensive.[23] This rash act of insubordination, according to his biographer, was "conceived of as a jerk to the sleeves of his allies" to get on with the campaign.[24] Fred Eldridge, Stilwell's public relations officer, writing after the fact, was more expansive. When Stilwell was ordered by Mountbatten to delay his advance because of the general state of unpreparedness—supplies could not be guaranteed, one of his divisions was still in "the basic training stage," the American long-range penetration group would not be ready or in position until February—Stilwell ignored the order and directed the advance to commence anyway, "hoping against hope that his showing would be so good that he would literally shame the British into action."[25] If true, it was an ominous way for Stilwell to embark on a campaign that placed heavy reliance on his British allies.

AFTER SO MUCH DISCUSSION, AND THE MANY TWISTS AND TURNS AND ADjustment of plans, the Second Burma Campaign of 1944 was at last under way.[26] This was now composed of four major operational elements. The first of these was Albacore, Stilwell's ground campaign to clear north Burma so as to give advance cover for the construction crews engaged in building the new Burma Road—now dubbed the Ledo Road—as it advanced from the Indian town of Ledo through north Burma as far as the Mogaung-Myitkyina area and the Myitkyina airfield. There, it was hoped, Stilwell's New Chinese Army would meet up with the second element, the Yunnan Expeditionary Force—also known as Y-Force—coming from Yunnan, although Chiang Kai-shek had not confirmed its participation. The third element would be the twenty-three-thousand-strong British long-range penetration brigades known as the Chindits, who would be supporting Stilwell by working behind enemy lines to disrupt Japanese lines of communication. A similar, but much smaller, American special force numbering only three thousand was also to lend similar support. The major operations, however, were not those in Stilwell's Northern Combat Area Command, which were focused only on protecting the new

Ledo Road, but rather the two more southerly advances to be conducted by the British Fourteenth Army. The first of the advances would attempt, once again, to secure the strategic Arakan coast and its airfields and gain a staging area for a future assault on Rangoon; the second, on the main front, would proceed from its IV Corps headquarters in Imphal, India, southeast to the Chindwin River, toward Mandalay.[27] These two southerly advances would serve Stilwell by tying up three Japanese divisions and preventing the enemy from reinforcing the single division that confronted him.

The components of this uneasy campaign differed from one another greatly in terms of composition, leadership, and conviction. General William "Bill" Slim, commander of the British Indian Fourteenth Army, gave, characteristically, the most crisply stated overview of how matters stood. Many people, he wrote, "did not think that the Ledo road would ever repay the expenditure in men and resources that would have to be devoted to it."

> Indeed, at this time, Stilwell was almost alone in his faith. . . .
> [t]hat it would be the most potent winning factor in the war against
> Japan. His vision, as he expounded it to me, was of an American-
> trained and -equipped Chinese force [that], under his command,
> would drive through China to the sea and then with the Ameri-
> can Navy strike at Japan itself.[28]

While agreeing with Stilwell that the road could be built and that Chinese forces could be effective, Slim, as he wrote, doubted the war-winning value of the road, and believed that America's island-hopping strategy in the Pacific would bring "much quicker results than an overland advance across Asia with a Chinese army yet to be formed."[29] Both points of view held by the two Allies, he allowed, were reasonable, and both "could easily be distorted": Americans could accuse the British of hoping to use American efforts to regain a British possession; the British could allege that "several Chinese divisions and great logistical resources, devoted to an unsound and largely political American objective, were being held by one Japanese division, while the British fought the main enemy forces."[30]

William Slim was fifty-three, born in a village on the outskirts of Bristol to working-class parents. Too poor to go to university, he had worked as a schoolteacher in the slums of Birmingham and as a clerk in a metal factory, but always harboring dreams of a military career. In 1912, he enrolled in an officers' training course at the University of Birmingham, where his brother was a medical student, and in doing so was able to obtain a commission when the Great War broke out. Wounded twice in action, at Gallipoli and in Mesopotamia, he had been awarded the Military Cross. Between the wars, he had married, served in India, and written novels and short stories under the pseudonym Anthony Mills (roughly "Slim" spelled backward) to supplement his army salary. The stories, characterized by his biographer as "more a matter of craft than art," drew on his experience in India and the North-West Frontier ("... *then a muffled tramp, tramp, and the leading troops, the Sikhs, were approaching the gate and the perimeter* ... ").[31] On the outbreak of war in 1939, still in India and now a colonel, he was sent to Sudan and then Ethiopia as the commander of the 10th Indian Infantry Brigade. Wounded yet again, he was sent back to New Delhi and, after recovering from his injuries, was again put in command of the 10th, which he led in Iraq, Syria, and Persia.[32]

Back in March of 1942, as Burma toppled under Japan's attack, Slim had been given command of such loose ends of British military and paramilitary elements as were available to scrape together a defensive force—the Burma Corps, or Burcorps, at the head of which, like Stilwell, he had been forced to retreat to India.[33] Now he was put in command of the newly formed Fourteenth Army and tasked with the recapture of Burma. Built primarily from the Indian Army, some three-fifths of the new Fourteenth's total force of half a million were men from regions across India—Sikhs, Dogras, Pathans, Mahrattas, Rajputs, Assamese, Punjabis, Madrassis—as well as English, Irish, Welsh, Scots, various tribes of Gurkhas, and East and West African infantry battalions. Working with the army were militias drawn from the Burmese hill tribes—Naga, Kachin, Chin, Karen, and Shan. Perhaps not since Herodotus described Xerxes's great Persian army had so many different peoples speaking so many different languages marched forth on a united military venture—the largest volunteer army the world has known, as one Indian Army veteran boasted.[34] Slim, as befitting an Indian Army officer, spoke fluent Urdu and Gurkhali.[35]

Slim was revered by his men and peers as the exemplary soldier's soldier. Unflappable and undramatic, he had demonstrated at personal cost that he understood the role physical courage had to play in warfare, but he did not build campaigns around this. Strength and courage, he knew, arose from health and good morale, and his campaign plans paid close attention to such unglamorous elements as lines of supply, not "guts and glory." Though a careful commander, he was also aggressive and could not be faulted for "holding back" when the opportunity to strike arose. He was also a consummate professional, accepting the orders he was given. "It was not for me to decide the merits or demerits of the Ledo road," he wrote; ". . . we in Fourteenth Army got down to helping Stilwell in what we knew was a tough assignment."[36]

The originally envisioned structure of command had placed Stilwell in charge of the Ledo Road advance and of the Yunnan forces, if they materialized, and Slim in command of the Fourteenth Army, so as to operate as two army commanders under SEAC's commander in chief of ground forces, General Sir George Giffard, who was British. This, as Slim wrote, "would have been the logical and militarily sound organization of the command."[37] But Stilwell despised Giffard, and his refusal to accept this obvious chain of command resulted in one of the many dramas with which his brief combat career was strewn.[38] Mountbatten was compelled to convene a special conference, and after Stilwell had twisted, turned, and sulked, he suddenly "astonished everyone" by saying he would come under General Slim's operational control—until he reached Kamaing, a village some fifty miles west of Myitkyina halfway down the Mogaung Valley.[39] And so the dilemma was resolved.

While Slim prepared for the Arakan offensive, elements of Stilwell's

New Chinese Army had entered the Hukawng Valley at Shingbwiyang, the outpost at which so many refugees had been trapped by the monsoon and died during the exodus from Burma in 1942; at that time, the place had become known as a "charnel house." Advancing into the valley, the leading regiment followed what was now known as the "refugee trail," which despite the passage of time was still strewn with evidence of that tragedy. Human skeletons lay sprawled around every water hole, at the foot of every ascent, scattered up the hills, huddled in makeshift shelters in the jungle, many clad in rotting clothing—khaki shorts, English dresses, and saris, whose fine fabrics had rotted away leaving only their gilt-and-silver embroidery to spangle the jungle foliage like tinsel on a Christmas tree—their bleached skulls still retaining clumps of hair of every color of their many nationalities. To help cross one shallow stream, the enterprising Chinese troops used such skulls, so readily at hand, as stepping stones.[40]

Two miles north of Sharaw Ga, a second regiment stumbled into a Japanese outpost, sustaining heavy mortar and machine-gun fire that lasted from noon until dark. The surprise of the attack, to quote the official CBI history, "was complete." It should not have been, for the Chinese commander of the 38th Division, the well-respected General Sun Li-jen, among other things a graduate of the Virginia Military Institute, had for weeks before the advance balked at his orders to advance on the grounds that the Japanese strength in the Hukawng was badly underestimated.[41] Stilwell's G-2, his son Lieutenant Colonel Joseph Stilwell Jr., had, however, reassured the Chinese that they would only encounter ragged bands of Burmese; instead, the regiment had marched into the "well-led, well-entrenched" elements of a veteran Japanese force, the 18th Division, the celebrated "Chrysanthemum unit" that had helped run the British out of Singapore and Malaya.[42] After sustaining significant casualties, the Chinese dug in for what became a fierce battle that lasted for almost a month, in which one of their companies was annihilated, survivors were reduced to tapping jungle vines to quench their thirst, and one of the few Americans present, a liaison officer, was captured.[43] Meanwhile, Stilwell's headquarters continued to insist that the enemy was not present in force and berated General Sun and his troops for passivity, bad tactics, and wasting ammunition.[44] It was these embattled troops that transport pilots like Bob Boody were supplying.

The New Chinese Army trained in India, composed of the two original divisions and a third that was newly formed (the 30th), totaled some thirty thousand men.[45] Commanding the original divisions were the same generals who had led them in the first Burma campaign: General Sun, described as "lean and handsome" and slow and deliberate in manner, and General Liao Yao-hsiang, volatile and stocky, who was a graduate of Saint-Cyr, the French military academy.[46] Some nine thousand of the new army were the remnants of Chiang's elite Fifth Army that had trekked out of Burma into India in 1942. Of these, one division, the 38th, led by General Sun, had arrived at the end of a disciplined march in good condition; the men of the other division, the 22nd, which had been driven in disarray into the far north through the Hukawng Valley, looting and murdering as it went, had stumbled into India in appalling condition, the men covered with festering leech bites, stricken with malaria and dengue fever, and starving.[47]

The other thousands of troops were fresh "recruits" who had been flown to India by transport planes returning over the Hump with their light cargoes of tungsten, tin, and hog bristles. The Nationalist army acquired the new recruits with brutal efficiency. Descending on and cordoning off a neighborhood, they worked their way inward, like beaters on a game hunt, rounding up all males. Ordered to drop their pants, the ambushed men were quickly examined; those with pubic hair were deemed old enough to be in the army.[48] Many American pilots and crew had witnessed the recruiting process. "I have seen a squad of Nationalist soldiers along a path come up to a farmer who was carrying his produce to market and slap and knock him down, take his vegetables from him, tie his hands behind his back—and he was in the army," recalled an officer with the search and rescue unit. "He would never even get to tell his folks he was going. They would march these men miles to the closest army post."[49] "[T]hey were looking for volunteers and they'd see a Chinese 12 or

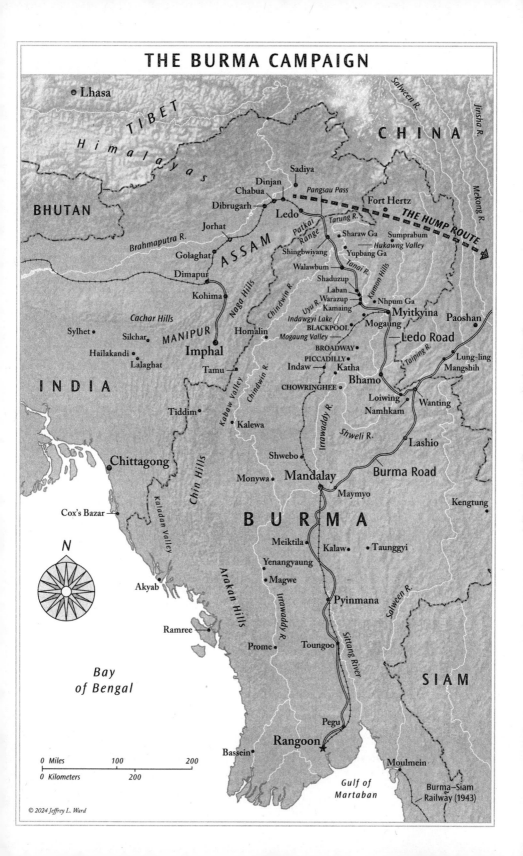

THE BURMA CAMPAIGN

TIBET

Himalayas

Lhasa

CHINA

Salween R.

Jinsha R.

BHUTAN

Sadiya

Dinjan

Chabua

Pangsau Pass

Fort Hertz

Mekong R.

Dibrugarh

Ledo

THE HUMP ROUTE

Jorhat

Patkai Range

Tarung R.

Sharaw Ga

Sumprabum

Brahmaputra R.

ASSAM

Golaghat

Shingbwiyang

Hukawng Valley

Yupbang Ga

Dimapur

Walawbum

Tanai R.

Chindwin R.

Shaduzup

Naga Hills

Kohima

Laban

Kumon Hills

Warazup

Kamaing

Nhpum Ga

Myitkyina

Paoshan

Cachar Hills

Uyu R.

Indawgyi Lake

BLACKPOOL

Mogaung

Ledo Road

Sylhet

Silchar

MANIPUR

Homalin

Mogaung Valley

BROADWAY

Lung-ling

Hailakandi

Imphal

PICCADILLY

Taiping R.

Mangshih

Lalaghat

Tamu

Indaw

Katha

Bhamo

INDIA

Kabaw Valley

CHOWRINGHEE

Loiwing

Wanting

Tiddim

Chindwin R.

Namhkam

Kalewa

Shweli R.

Lashio

Chittagong

Shwebo

Irrawaddy R.

Burma Road

Chin Hills

Monywa

Mandalay

Cox's Bazar

Maymyo

Kengtung

Kaladan Valley

BURMA

Meiktila

Kalaw

Taunggyi

Akyab

Yenangyaung

Magwe

Arakan Hills

Pyinmana

Salween R.

Ramree

Irrawaddy R.

Prome

Toungoo

Sittang River

N

SIAM

Pegu

Bay of Bengal

Rangoon

Bassein

Moulmein

0 Miles 100 200

Gulf of Martaban

Burma–Siam Railway (1943)

0 Kilometers 200

© 2024 Jeffrey L. Ward

14 years old working in the fields and he got recruited," recalled one C-47 pilot based in Chengtu. "They went out and got him and put him in a uniform and gave him a little wooden cup for his food and some chopsticks and brought him to the airport. . . . I felt sorry for them in there, they didn't know what was going on and when the plane took off they didn't know what to do; they opened the door and jumped out even when it was off the ground."[50] One day, the head of the Hump command watched as a plane shed Chinese troops through its open door as it roared down the runway, at the end of which "the plane flew straight up in the air, flipped over on its back and crashed, killing everyone on board." Inside, it was ascertained, the Chinese troops had panicked, some jumping to their death as the plane gathered speed, others running to cover at the rear of the plane and overweighing the tail just as the plane became airborne.[51]

No American crew wanted to fly the Chinese soldiers. Wholly unfamiliar with air travel, let alone in the turbulent weather over the Hump, the new recruits were prone to airsickness and also lacked experience with the improvised latrines, with the result that, on landing, cleanup crews had to aggressively hose down the plane interiors. Plucked raw from villages, often dispatched to India in an almost-naked condition and carrying only cups of rice and chopsticks, they endured the flights huddled and shivering on the planes' cold, metal floors—although one pilot reported that four Chinese soldiers made a fire in the hold of his plane for warmth.[52] Mostly, though, they lay back and passed out at altitude. Oxygen deprivation, the pilots discovered, was an effective method of crowd management. If frightened troops became unruly, pilots would take their planes up to higher altitudes, where, starved of oxygen, the men went quietly to sleep. On arrival in India, they would awake, half-frozen and in silence, then look around and see they were back on planet earth.[53]

Stilwell had given orders to his medical staff to get sick Chinese troops well "as fast as possible by any means, no matter how unorthodox," according to Gordon Seagrave, an American missionary based in Burma who had become famous for the emergency medical treatment he and his stalwart nurses from the Burma hill tribes had provided during the first Burma campaign. Now he was back with Stilwell and charged with establishing field hospitals apace the Chinese advance. Even ahead of any combat casualties, his task was daunting. Tuberculosis, eye diseases, and typhoid were rife, as were venereal diseases; none of the staff had seen syphilitic chancres "so enormous, dirty, or painful" as those the Chinese recruits bore. Once combat casualties began to be brought in, further evidence emerged that, despite months of food and care at the American training center, the symptoms of the men's desperate poverty had not been eradicated. Abdominal wounds revealed cavities filled with roundworms that slipped out through the rents in their torn flesh.[54]

Tempered by hardship and privation and arriving in India at irregular intervals as transport planes returned empty from China, the individual soldiers of X-Force/Chinese Army in India/New Chinese Army were mostly anonymous. A number of photographers captured their well-publicized training exercises at Ramgarh, and there are accounts of Stilwell's pride and satisfaction in what amounted to his little private army—although, according to his chief of staff, publicity photos notwithstanding, he spent little time with them.[55] Yet, insight into who the individuals were or what they felt about the circumstances forced upon them is hard to come by. Given food, medical care, and military pay, they were undoubtedly better treated while training at Ramgarh than at any other time in their lives, and reports made by the American trainers speak of their enthusiasm. "We demonstrate and they copy," according to the Ramgarh infantry officer charged with training them. "They are the greatest mimics in the world and are learning very, very fast."[56] Discipline of the troops, however, was an ongoing challenge. Stilwell had issued orders that no American personnel was to strike a Chinese soldier, but when some were physically abusive and assaulted the long-suffering nurses, American medical staff resorted to administering punitive beatings. General Sun was less squeamish. "Two of our [patients] were taken out & shot today," Dr. John Grindlay wrote in the diary he kept at Ramgarh. "[T]hey were caught in bed together at night—sodomy. Gen Sun is going to have all drivers who smash trucks shot—they do as much harm as a Jap plane—a sensible gesture & one the Chin[ese] will understand."[57]

Stilwell, on hearing that his fervently hoped-for return to the field was already bogged down, arrived in Shingbwiyang in late December to rally his troops. His state of mind is captured in his terse diary entries that spilled into the new year of 1944: "Sun moving very slowly. 3d B[attalio]n. . . . 114 now faced by a Bn well dug in, in depth. The damn fools. His timidity will now costs lives. . . . SUN not moving. Preposterous demands for armor, air support, & art[illery].—Sharaw cleared by fine attack by 113th. . . . Saw Sun & squawked about his slowness & crabbed generally. Told him it would not do. . . . in came T'ang with a long poor-mouth about 'no reserve' & heavy casualties, & could they have the 3d Bn. 112th right away. Offered them a reg[imen]t. of 22d to help them out. They did not appreciate the offer. . . . Sun is just timid & fearful of imagined 'counter-attacks.' . . . Saw Sun—Arrangements delayed. He was stalling as usual. Pinned him to 1/7/44 [two days away] for holding attack & 1/8/44 for south of river. Told him he was responsible for probable increased casualties. Also that I would not put Americans in with him at this rate. He was much at a loss, & had no face left. Unworthy of his men. And Gen. Ta'ng is a bastard trouble-maker."[58]

By now, the failure in his intelligence as to the Japanese presence should have been apparent, but Stilwell does not appear to have processed this. Led by General Sun, the strickened 38th Division recovered to advance and capture Yupbang Ga, which the official army history of the CBI characterizes as one of two "obscure wrecked villages" on the Tarung River.[59] The capture was hailed as "the first major Allied victory in north Burma," and by the end of the first week in January, the CAI held the line of the Tarung River.[60] Celebrating their victory, one company paraded the severed heads of slain Japanese on upheld bamboo poles.[61]

HATRED FOR THE ENEMY IS IMPORTANT, AS THE AIR FORCE'S PSYCHOLOGICAL study of "fatigued pilots" observed; "it protects the ego." Hump pilots, it was noted, lacked this protection, as few had "been out on missions where they have been shot at or seen their friends shot down. They have not the desire to kill the enemy or the hate of the enemy which combat pilots have."[62] For transport pilots and crew, the most direct encounter with the Japanese enemy was on the liaison radio, on which the seductive voice of Tokyo Rose might float to them through the airwaves, reciting with uncanny accuracy the names of those on board and their missions, congratulating men on promotions they did not know they had been given, mocking them for hauling goods to China that would be diverted to the black market, and warning that all captured Hump airmen would be shot.[63] The situation was obviously very different on the ground.

The Japanese had prepared for the encounter by studying their adversaries closely, and their succinct assessments could be read in captured documents:

BRITISH. Stands on formality and gives careful consideration to everything. He has a strong sense of patriotism and nationalism.

AMERICAN. Offhand and "hail fellow well met" in manner and act on the impulse without deep consideration. They are without reserve and take everyone as friends at first meeting.

CHINESE. Have strong desire for material gain and little sense of patriotism, being individualists, and they play fast-and-loose with people. Face saving is important to them so they don't show any emotion in their face. They have a high sense of resignation.

INDIANS. Strong desire for material gain seeking personal advantage to extremes, and they are frightfully obstinate. Little sense of patriotism, but religious with strong sense of rank and caste.

Indians, it was conceded, also had a "high fighting spirit." Best of the whole Allied lot were the Gurkhas, who were "loyal brave agile warlike," and who incidentally were thought to resemble the Japanese. The Gurkha soldier was also observed to "like football" and "rice curry (mixed with mutton)."[64]

The Americans and British had in turn studied Japanese tactics and character since Japan's sweep through Southeast Asia. Tactically, it was observed, their pattern was to strive for air superiority and superiority in numbers. Flanking and rear attacks were their strength, and they traveled lightly and swiftly, moving at night and in careful camouflage through the jungle by day. They followed up early successes with aggressive speed and used tricks, such as waving flags of truce as a ruse and calling out to Allied troops in English in the night, luring them to respond.[65] On learning that Nigerian soldiers were in Burma fighting with the British, the Japanese adapted their usual cry of "Hallo, Johnny, come out" to *"Bakin mutum . . . koma baya"*—Hausa for "Black men . . . go back!"[66] A Tenth Air Force report observed that:

> [t]he Jap is not so small as he is reported and is by no means a weakling. He is tough and tireless and inured to hardships. Not only this, but his national standard of living is lower than ours and thus things that would [be] hardships to us are normal to him. His mentality is not low but he lacks the education of the American soldier. He is cunning and treacherous and will fight to the last man, or move forward in an attack actuated by a fatalistic determination compounded from his peculiar religion and generations of existence where suicide was honorable and preferable to dishonor. To be captured is to be dead, Japanese style.[67]

The Japanese soldier could also be very cruel, and a broad trail of atrocities lay strewn behind their armies' conquests. A few uplifting stories told of acts of compassion performed by individuals, such as the Japanese soldier who had left a handwritten note in a looted Burmese church for the priests: "I am a student of the Society of Mary. I have taken charge of your sacred relics and chalice. I will give them to the first priest I meet on the way."[68] Such small acts of grace, however, were so rare as to startle and were overwhelmed to the point of near irrelevancy by the extent and sadistic savagery of the many acts of cruelty. "They took a long time to die," read placards left beside the mutilated bodies of Australian soldiers.[69] In north Burma, where the hill tribes remained loyal to the British, Japanese troops had stormed through the fragile bamboo settlements murdering, raping, and setting huts on fire. In one Kachin village, the *duwa*, or revered chief, was brought out and made to witness the mass castration of an entire generation of his village's young boys before a compassionate soldier stopped the spectacle.[70] It was known that Japanese military training was infamously brutal, that soldiers accepted slaps and beatings from their officers, but for all that, the atrocities they committed were, as the air force report stated, "something which we cannot understand."[71]

The jungle in which the Allied troops would be operating was still regarded in Western eyes as the domain of the Japanese, an environment to which they were somehow supposedly naturally adapted. Of the Allies, only the Burmese hill tribes—the Kachin, the Chin, the Karen, the Naga, the Kuki—regarded the jungle matter-of-factly, as a place in which people lived and not as an arena of peculiar terror. In early February 1943, the British had attempted to confront this fear with the creation of an elite force trained in jungle guerrilla tactics. The stated mission of this long-range penetration group, dubbed the Chindits—from *Chinthe*, the lion statues guarding Burmese temples—was to disrupt Japanese lines of communication, but its larger purpose was to demonstrate that Europeans, too, could become proficient in jungle lore.[72]

The first Chindits had entered northern Burma in February 1943 with the object of attacking the Mandalay-Myitkyina railway along the Irrawaddy River and harassing enemy garrisons. They were trained and supplied to survive for ninety days in the jungle, and the march to the Irrawaddy took one month. In April, having duly damaged the rail line and caused other disruptions, they began the thousand-mile march out, skirmishing with Japanese forces along the way and relying entirely on supplies dropped by the RAF. Most of their columns broke apart, and remnants of the Chindits were still stumbling back into India through the summer and even into the autumn of 1943. Of the three thousand men of Operation Longcloth, as their venture was code-named, nearly one thousand were killed, and a third of the survivors rendered unfit for future service.[73] The effectiveness and high cost of the expedition was much debated. "As a military operation the raid had been an expensive failure," was Slim's assessment. "If anything was learnt of air supply or jungle fighting it was a costly schooling."[74] Japanese records, however, show that the Chindits disrupted the enemy to the extent that they were taken as a serious threat.[75] Their undoubted greatest achievement was in raising that most mysterious of human forces, morale, and the news that these plucky men had taken the war to the Japanese was much celebrated in the British press.

Now, a year later, in February 1944, a second Chindit expedition was to support Stilwell's Ledo Road campaign. Although differing greatly from the first expedition in scale and logistics, it was the creation of the original mastermind, Major General Orde Charles Wingate, whose unorthodox career and personal eccentricities had made him one of the most controversial officers in the British Army. Wingate was born in 1903, in India, to a family that was distinguished by military service and religious zealotry, both of which characteristics defined him. After graduating from the Royal Military Academy at Woolwich, Wingate gained a posting with the Sudan Defense Force through the good offices of a relative who was governor-general of Sudan. Posted to the Ethiopian borderland, he led patrols to catch ivory poachers—his first taste of irregular, guerrilla-style tactics. This experience was reinforced when, in 1936, he served as an intelligence officer in the British Mandate of Palestine, where he persuaded British and Jewish authorities to authorize him to create and lead a paramilitary unit of volunteers to counter the increasingly aggressive Arab insurgency. The resulting Special Night Squads were successful but also deplored by both British and Zionist authorities for their harsh and undiscriminating tactics, which added to Wingate's reputation for being an unstable zealot. His passionate and publicly voiced support of the Zionist cause discomforted the British authorities to the extent that he was not only relieved of command, but banned from entering Palestine again.[76]

Many sensible people offer testimony to Wingate's extraordinary powers of persuasion, of his ability to silence and bewitch rooms of even skeptical listeners and win them to his cause, but it is difficult to conjure this ability from the evidence he left behind. His long written memoranda reveal his clarity and confidence, but not irresistibly so, and it would seem that his famous persuasive eloquence owed much to his delivery— the fanatical intensity of his expression and his unassailable passion; his eyes and his voice, according to one Chindit, "were sharp as steel and with both of which he seemed to stab anyone to whom he was talking."[77]

Along with his military career, Wingate pursued a variety of interests that included learning both Arabic and Hebrew and making expeditions into the Libyan Desert in search of the lost army of Cambyses and the possibly mythical oasis of Zerzura, doggedly plodding the sands on camel back and foot as new-fangled jeeps adapted for desert travel outpaced him.[78] When war broke out, he returned to Ethiopia, where he led the Gideon Force, another irregular unit, whose mission was to unseat the Italian occupiers and restore the Ethiopian emperor to his throne. The Gideon Force won notable successes, but Wingate's uncompromising manner, cultivated eccentricities, and determined rudeness antagonized many, including his superiors.[79] On campaign in Ethiopia, he never washed, and it was observed by a reporter that his "only ablutions were to lower his trousers and cool his bottom in the occasional waterholes, from which, incidentally, others would have to drink."[80]

Wingate left Ethiopia raging at his superiors, and when the rage burned out he fell into a black depression. His mood was further undermined by the psychiatric side effects of the malaria medication he was taking—Atabrine, the negative effects of which on pilots would be noted— and, in July 1941, he attempted suicide in the Continental Hotel in Cairo. His chosen method was to slit his throat with a hunting knife, but after plunging the knife into his neck he realized he had not locked his door. Stumbling forward, pouring blood, he locked the door, then returned to his task, but, finding the effort of cutting greater than expected, collapsed in unconsciousness. A Colonel Thornhill, enjoying his siesta next door, heard the thump of Wingate's falling body and came out to investigate. The locked door aroused suspicions and, as a result, Wingate was rescued and whisked to a hospital, where he came out of unconsciousness crying to God for mercy. A few days later, he was recovered enough to tell visitors that his mistake had been in not taking a relaxing warm bath beforehand; to cut one's throat with success, one must relax the neck muscles, he had discovered. "His visitors listened in some disquiet," his biographer wrote, "as he illustrated his meaning with graphic gestures." One outcome of this ordeal was that Wingate emerged with the conviction, as he said, "that I am destined for great things."[81] His next great thing had been the first Chindit operation, and now he was back to lead a vastly larger and more complicated second operation in the face of much skepticism against the first.

Training of the second Chindits commenced toward the end of 1943. In Wingate's plan, three groups totaling some twenty-three thousand troops were organized into six brigades, one of which included veterans of Operation Longcloth, although these were the minority, for, as Wingate's biographer observed, "relatively few men could undertake the training, let alone the type of operation, twice."[82] Other brigades were drawn from the Indian Army, from a seasoned division most recently deployed in the Middle East, and from a West African division originally destined for the Arakan offensive.[83] As part of his introductory briefing, Wingate personally gave an account of the first Chindit expedition so that, as one of the men recorded, "we could profit by his experience and come out of the jungle alive." The men were issued solid-green clothing—green down to handkerchiefs and underwear—and given tips on operating in the jungle: never speak above a whisper, never pull off leeches, never drink unsterilized jungle water.[84] So far, so good, as this represented what was by now well-known jungle lore, but other directives were peculiar to Wingate: everyone was to eat one raw onion a day, for example, and only shorts could be worn when it was raining.[85]

The guiding philosophy of the long-range penetration units, as described by Wingate, was "the operation of regular columns of high calibre in the heart of the enemy's war machine, engaging targets he is unable adequately to protect, and thus compelling him to alter his plans, thus causing a situation of which our own main forces are to take advantage."[86] In essence, the Chindits were raiding parties, trained in evasive tactics to sting the enemy and draw him into ambush, and vanish back into the jungle.[87] To be effective, the strikes needed to be coordinated with the actions of the main force they were supporting, for the Chindit units were not equipped for offensive action. In terms of manpower, they were roughly the equivalent of two and a half infantry divisions, but in terms of actual strength they were considerably weaker, about the strength of one standard division, lacking as they did all infantry support such as tanks, heavy guns, and engineers.[88] Since the units' mobility and independence were predicated on being untethered from any land-based supply line, they had to carry all essentials with them—rifles, light machine guns, the heavier Vickers .303 guns, mortar throwers, ammunition, clothing, water, and, following each airdrop, eighteen pounds of rations—all of which amounted to seventy pounds per man. Soaking monsoon rains and river crossings made their sodden burdens even heavier, causing the straps of each man's pack to cut deep into his shoulders.[89]

Training for the ordeal ahead focused on building physical toughness, principally through grueling, endless marches, with everything performed, at Wingate's insistence, at double time. Over twenty weeks and a thousand miles, the Chindits marched through jungle, climbed hills, swam across lakes and rivers, then marched again. In between, they slept in the jungle, in forgotten, ruined temples whose ancient courtyards were padded with tiger pugmarks, and by streams.[90] Discipline was paramount, and all orders were to be obeyed without question or demur, and to this end Wingate informed his officers that, for transgressions that could result in the loss of lives, "they were empowered to flog offenders," which was done with tree branches on more than one occasion.[91] The culmination of the training was a three-week exercise in Central

India, during which, as one Chindit recalled, "we marched 200 miles . . . swam rivers and carried heavier packs than we ever carried in Burma."[92]

Fleets of mules relieved some of the men's burden by carrying the heaviest equipment—the mortars and machine guns, the radios and charging engines—although care of these invaluable, patient, and stoic animals also imposed further burdens, for they, too, required many pounds of grain and fodder. Few men had experience with the animals, yet the muleteers were key elements of the Chindit operation. "We were issued with one hundred mules, which I was told I must train," recalled Richard Hilder, a Chindit who had helped his father on their family farm estate before the war and who, as a former Life Guards officer, was a skilled horseman. Gradually, the mules were trained to accept a saddle, a load, a bridle, to march in track, as he recalled, "all except one mule called Cushy. . . . There was one man who was a Gypsy, who was brilliant. . . . He used to blow into the mules' noses . . . and he took Cushy over and he became one of the best."[93] To ensure silence, the mules were "de-brayed" by veterinarians who cut the animals' vocal cords.[94]

Joining the Chindits as part of the planned integrated long-range penetration groups were three thousand American infantry troops drawn from regiments stationed in the West Indies, the South Pacific, and the continental US, who had volunteered for an unspecified "dangerous and hazardous" mission.[95] On arriving in India, Project Galahad, as the men were collectively called, had been briefed by Wingate, who made high claims about his novel Chindit tactics. The claims prompted the American training officer to take his men aside and remind them that the same tactics had been used by the US Army when fighting in Indian territory, and that they should look on the operation as a continuation of their own history.[96] Nonetheless, the American officers knew of and admired Wingate and were looking forward to cooperating with him, but, as the official history of the CBI states, the command arrangement "caused some protest from CBI Theater officers, who thought it might be taken as an admission that Americans did not know jungle fighting."[97] Chief of the protesting officers was Stilwell. "After a long struggle we get a handful of U.S. troops and by God they tell us they are going to operate under WINGATE!" Stilwell exploded in his diary. General Marshall attempted to calm him, counseling that "[w]e must all eat some crow if we are to fight the same war together."[98] But Stilwell continued to lash out, ultimately wearing down Mountbatten, who agreed to reassign Galahad to Stilwell "because it seemed to mean more to JWS than the bickering was worth."[99] ("You tell General Stilwell he can take his Americans and stick 'em up his arse," was Wingate's official response, before he turned back to apologize.)[100] After several months of a muddled chain of command, the American unit was at last activated as the prosaically named 5307th Composite Unit (Provisional).[101] Other designations would follow. When Stilwell replaced the commander of the new regiment, whom he also disliked, with his friend and colleague from the first Burma campaign, General Frank Merrill, newsmen, searching for some spark of military glamour, dubbed the unit "Merrill's Marauders."[102]

KEY TO THE OPERATION AHEAD, AND INDEED TO THE VERY CONCEPTION OF the mobile units, was the use of aircraft for supply and evacuation.[103] None of this was entirely new. Light planes had been used for both supply and evacuation in the Solomon Islands and New Guinea, for example, and the RAF had supplied and reinforced remote Fort Hertz in the far north and other isolated units in Burma throughout 1943.[104] "Food kickers" like Bob Boody were supporting Stilwell's New Chinese Army, but these troops, with the new Ledo Road unfolding behind them, were not dependent solely on airdrops; indeed, Stilwell's plan was that his army would be mostly supplied by the road. At the time of the Cairo Conference in November 1943, when plans for the long-range penetration brigade were consolidated, the idea that it was possible to supply an army entirely by air transport for weeks and months had never been floated.[105] The attempt to integrate air supply with a ground campaign was Wingate's innovation, although as events turned out it would be used by other agents in the sprawling Burma campaign.

Wingate's air assets for the second, more ambitious Chindit expedition were extraordinary. Originally, he had requested only C-47s for supply drops and light planes capable of operating on short, rough airstrips to evacuate the wounded; the first Chindit expedition had suffered grievously by not having such relief.[106] But Wingate's plans had intrigued General Arnold, who saw an interesting opportunity. Henry "Hap" Arnold had been present at the dawn of aviation, literally, for the Wright brothers were among his flight instructors at their Simms Station flight school in Dayton, Ohio, when Arnold arrived there in 1911—only eight years after the Wrights' first historic flight. Hugely experienced as an airman, deeply interested in science and technological innovation, Arnold had the breathtaking responsibility of commanding US air operations around the world while building a fighting air force from the meager program he had inherited when taking command first of the Air Corps in 1938, and then of the new Army Air Forces in 1941.[107] Now in Burma, Arnold saw an opportunity for bold experimentation. Burma was a physically challenging arena; collaboration there between the Chindits, with their unorthodox tactics, and skilled American pilots might develop useful, innovative surprises.[108] Additionally, no real military objective was at stake given that the Chindits' main mission was to support Stilwell as he covered the building of the Ledo Road. This was a perfect arena in which to experiment. Consequently, Arnold approved for the new aerial task force almost every genre of aircraft flying: thirteen C-47s and other transports, one hundred light planes, thirty P-51 fighters, twelve B-25 medium bombers, half a dozen Sikorsky helicopters, and over two hundred gliders—well might Stilwell gnash his teeth in envy.[109]

The new assets and all their unplanned-for possibilities were made known to the Chindits not by Wingate, but by the leader of the new US Army Air Forces 1st Air Commando, Lieutenant Colonel Philip Cochran. Youthful and handsome, radiating casual confidence and goodwill, he made a memorable first impression on the wary British forces, as witnessed by John Masters, an Indian Army officer and Chindit division chief of staff—and author of one of the finest memoirs of the war, *The Road Past*

Mandalay. When "with expansive good humour" Cochran began to relate all that he had brought with him from America, "[w]e glanced surreptitiously at each other as he enlarged on the marvels of his ships and his men. They would do anything. Any goddam thing we cared to ask for, they'd do it. . . ."[110] Hitherto, Masters reflected, "our relations with our own Royal Air Force had been extremely frustrating. Whatever we asked them to do they declared to be difficult, impossible, or against Air Force policy."[111] Cautiously, Cochran was asked if ground forces would be able to control planes on to a target, something at which the RAF had balked. "Why, sure . . . Hell yes . . ." By the end, "the stolid British audience was frankly disbelieving," Masters wrote. "But his manner, with its evident desire to cooperate, had put us in a good humour." Among themselves, the British agreed that if "nine-tenths of what this chap says is bullshit, we'll still get twice what the R.A.F. is giving us."[112] Proof of Cochran's seriousness came when an injured mule wrangler was swiftly evacuated in an early display of can-do air skill, with the American pilot finessing a light plane landing and takeoff on a four-hundred-foot-long strip of field when absolute minimum safety length demanded a third longer. "The whole force had heard of it within five hours," Masters recalled. "The commanders' hopes and the soldiers' morale rose sky high."[113]

Philip Cochran of Erie, Pennsylvania, was thirty-three years old, with "thick dark hair, wavy and streaked with premature gray, like a movie actor's," as his biographer described it, and indeed he somewhat resembled the young Marlon Brando.[114] The second-born of five sons in a comfortably off Irish Catholic family, Cochran's earliest passion had been for horses and riding. After high school, he eventually attended The Ohio State University, where he supported himself with singing stints in nightclubs, and entered a Reserve Officers' Training Corps. By the time he graduated at age twenty-five with a degree in business administration, he had come to loath both business and administration and decided to apply to the Army Air Corps, although he had never been in an airplane.[115]

By the time the US entered the war, Cochran was a USAAF major and fighter pilot instructor. The following year, he was sent to Tunisia, where

Allied forces were attempting to close Rommel's line of retreat, and here he honed his aerial guerrilla tactics. He also observed the costly blunders when air and ground forces were not coordinated: "At first the ground forces would get into a pickle and call the planes, 'Come and get us out of here,'" he recalled. "They thought the Air Force was the cure-all for their mistakes. When we couldn't pull them out they blamed it on the airplanes."[116]

Cochran was back in the United States at the time General Arnold began soliciting recommendations for command of Wingate's aerial task force, specifying that candidates should be young, skilled, tough, courageous, versatile, and "have a flair for novel ideas."[117] Cochran was one of two officers, both fighter pilots, who emerged at the top of the list of contenders. "He asked me if I wanted a top job," Cochran recalled of his interview with Arnold. "He said he couldn't tell me [what it was], but spoke of the jungle and the roughness of it."[118] The following day, Cochran met with Arnold again, joined by the other pilot contender, a shy, soft-spoken Southerner named John Alison, who had served in China with Chennault's Fourteenth Air Force and who was a good friend of Cochran's since their early days at flight school together. Asked if they wanted the job, both men, with reservations, replied yes. Although Arnold's intention had been to decide between the two men, he never did, and both got the job, officially as co-commanders. Cochran was the older by four months, and in this way seniority and leadership of the 1st Air Commando was amicably if unofficially established.[119]

Regardless of their respective skills, choice of leadership between the two men is unlikely to have really been in question. Alison was deferential and retiring, Cochran was charismatic. Cochran had, as Alison recalled, "instinctive strut and dash."[120] Moreover, he had been a famous fighter pilot before he had ever seen combat. By chance, an old friend of Cochran's from his days as a student at Ohio State was Milton Caniff, a cartoonist whose popular, long-running comic strip, *Terry and the Pirates*, was read by millions in newspapers across the US and by men on all the fronts of battle.[121] In 1941, with the idea that the theme of military aviation would spice his series as the threat of war loomed over the US, Caniff sought out Cochran to learn about military aviation. Cochran was then training P-40 pilots in Groton, Connecticut, and invited Caniff out to look over his operation. Caniff arrived to witness an all-out demonstration of aviation wizardry, as Cochran's commanding officers realized that introducing army aviation into the nationally read comic strip would be a first-rate recruiting asset.[122] Caniff left bedazzled and subsequently paid tribute to his friend with the creation of a new character in his series: smiling, square-jawed air ace Flip Corkin:

> ". . . OH! IS THAT PLANE IN TROUBLE?"
>
> "NO . . . IT'S CAPTAIN CORKIN! HE'S STALLING TO LOSE SPEED—SO HE CAN DROP HIS LANDING GEAR AND FLAPS WITHOUT TEARING THEM OFF!"
>
> "CAPTAIN CORKIN LANDING, SIR!"
>
> "I THOUGHT SO! WHO BUT CORKIN WOULD MAKE A PRACTICE DIVE ON THOSE OBSERVATION AIRCRAFT— WITH ABOUT 200 FEET OF ALTITUDE!"
>
> "HEY, TAFFY! FLIP CORKIN JUST CAME IN!"[123]

Cochran was not impressed with Wingate on first meeting, but when the two men later met and talked closely together in England, Cochran had his own epiphany. "I suddenly realized that, with his radio direction, Wingate used his guerilla columns in the same way that fighter-control headquarters directs planes out on a mission," he said. "I saw it as an adaptation of air to jungle, an application of radio-controlled air-war tactics to a walking war in the trees and the weeds. Wingate had hit upon the idea independently; he knew little about the air."[124]

On the ground in Central India, where the Chindits were training, the flood of arriving equipment was initially welcome and ultimately overwhelming. "The roof fell in on us and our simple plans," Masters wrote.

"Equipment—mainly American—descended upon us in torrents"; guns, clothing, medical supplies, K-rations, walkie-talkie radio sets, VHF radios, air bazookas or rockets, musical instruments for morale. . . . "It was wonderful. It was also awful. . . . We were appalled because we believed that the new force was much too big."[125] As Arnold had hoped, the participation of the 1st Air Commando had indeed unleashed new possibilities. Not only could Wingate's troops be supplied by airdrops, but, it was now realized, with an aerial strike force at their disposal, they could also call in firepower to any given area; they could, in essence, be that "main force" they had originally been intended to support. Cargo-carrying gliders could deliver the heavy equipment and armaments that light planes could not carry into the jungle, where powered transports could not land; gliders could be crash-landed if necessary—these were Cochran's insights.[126] The welter of material assets awakened in Wingate's fertile brain yet more ideas; by airlifting bulldozers and light tractors, it would be possible to construct within the deep jungle pockets of land equipped with landing strips, taxiways, supply-drop areas, storage facilities—in short, "Strongholds" of defense, the name taken from Zechariah (*"Turn ye to the Stronghold, ye prisoners of hope"*).[127]

Strongholds would indeed become an important element of the operation, but other of Wingate's late-arising ideas were not only "innovative" but dangerous, and mere weeks before the Chindit operation was to be launched, he was pumping out memoranda for new plans: airborne, long-range penetration brigades totaling one hundred thousand infantry forces could target Hanoi and Bangkok, occupy the Indo-Chinese peninsula, and join the Americans in the Pacific. . . . The proposal so alarmed Mountbatten that he asked Wingate for assurance that he would attempt no such thing. In the event, the mission remained as originally stated: to help in "a recapture of that part of Burma north of the 23rd parallel which was needed to reopen the land communications with China."[128] To this end, the Chindits had three specific objectives: to cut the communications of the Japanese 18th Division that confronted Stilwell in the Hukawng Valley and prevent it from being reinforced; to facilitate the

Yunnan Chinese forces, or Y-Force, in crossing the Salween into Burma—should Chiang Kai-shek commit to their participation; and to inflict "the greatest possible damage and confusion on the enemy in north Burma."[129]

The start of the second Chindit operation, code-named Thursday, was set at the end of Burma's shorter, less-severe rainy season. One advance brigade was to enter Burma on foot, departing from Ledo, with the objective of capturing and holding two airfields near the town of Indaw on the Myitkyina rail line. Two other brigades were to be flown into jungle clearings in the Indaw area, and three brigades were to be held in reserve for a "second wave," when the first wave was played out.[130] Accordingly, in late January 1944, the two Chindit brigades moved up from their training base to Assam, traveling by train to the head of the Cachar Valley, from where they marched east toward Imphal. The march in was not unpleasant, the days taking them through magnificent scenery, the nights spent sitting around campfires, where officers gathered to hear *Paradise Lost* read aloud (the American Marauder field commander turned to Caesar's *Commentaries*).[131] February was passed encamped near Imphal, studying maps and intelligence reports, and learning, to their surprise, that gliders were to fly in advance groups over the heads of the enemy directly into the jungle.[132] The advance groups, including American engineers, would then carve out airstrips for the powered transport planes to follow, while the Chindits defended the area. At the end of the operation, ten thousand men and sixteen hundred mules would be safely deposited behind Japanese lines in the middle of the north Burma jungle.[133]

The gliders' requirements were minimal: a strip of land several hundred feet long, close to the desired area of operation, on more or less level ground—a rough clearing would do. Cochran's pilots had also finessed the evacuation of the gliders from the jungle. Two long snatch poles were set upright in the ground, fifty feet apart and about two hundred feet in front of the glider. Over them was threaded a towline fastened to the nose of the glider, in which the pilot sat at the ready, with controls set for takeoff. Since the operation was to take place at night, small blue lights sat atop the poles. Aligning with these feeble pinprick signals in the massy darkness, a C-47 flew in low at about 120 miles per hour, dragging a long boom with a hook and catch at the end to snag the towline rig.[134] "[T]he hook caught in the rope, snatched it off the tops of the poles," Masters recorded with awe. "The pilot rammed his throttles fully forward and lifted his nose. The sudden roaring growl of anguish from the engines filled the sky. The glider—jerked from 0 to 80 miles an hour during the stretch of the rope, perhaps a second and a half—rose in the air. The C-47 and the silent glider swept up into the darkness. I repeated the incantation that Mountbatten had made when he first saw this remarkable feat. 'Jesus Christ All Bloody Mighty.'"[135]

Three clearings identified by aerial reconnaissance were designated as landing sites, each named for a major street in an Allied city: Broadway, Piccadilly, and Chowringhee. D-Day for the glider entry was set for the night of March 5—one day short of a full moon—with the C-47 towplanes taking off from the Air Commando base at Lalaghat, Assam, at five p.m.[136] Wingate had already given his men characteristic speeches of encouragement. "You're going to die," he had told them in his rasping, ruthless voice. "Many of you are going to die, or suffer wounds, or near-starvation. All of you will meet hardship worse than anything you have imagined."[137]

Cochran, too, had words of inspiration. His faith in the American pilot was very great. "Our kids are just kind of automatically wonderful," he had previously told reporters in an interview in New York City. "They've got an individual sense of responsibility, a sense of initiative, a native feeling for getting a job done."[138] Speaking now to the assembled pilots sitting quietly on the ground around him, Cochran informed them he had just come from meeting with the British troops; "and I talked to the guy that's got the red flare that you know is going to be shot off if there's too much interference with the first few gliders that land," he told them, beating time on his hand with a map pointer. The guy with the red flare had told Cochran that the flare would be "so deep in my pocket that I doubt if anyone else could find it if I'm killed"—in other words, regardless of what awaited, the Chindits would not be pulling out.[139]

"[I]f those guys have that kind of heart, and have that kind of guts," Cochran told his pilots,

> it's up to us to get them in there so they can do their job and get them in right. Now tonight, your whole existence is going to be jammed up into a couple of minutes and it's going to balance it there. And it's going to take your character to bring it through.[140]

At four thirty, half an hour before the scheduled takeoff, a light plane landed, and a flustered pilot rushed up to Cochran with a sheaf of photographs of the landing zones, "hot from the photo-reconnaissance cell in the Commando."[141] Broadway and Chowringhee were clear, but across Piccadilly there lay symmetrical rows of felled trees. The discovery was entirely due to Cochran's initiative and secret defiance of Wingate's order not to fly over the areas for fear of tipping off the Japanese.[142] Now it seemed that the Japanese had already detected them and sabotaged the site. On being shown the evidence, Wingate, according to Masters, "became highly emotional." What else did the Japanese know? Would there be ambushes in place? To continue with the operation, Wingate said, would be murder. Slim stepped in to calm him down, took responsibility for the decision to go ahead with the operation, and ordered the glider fleets to be diverted to the two clear landing zones.[143] Air and ground command mutually agreed that the number of gliders would be scaled back, and that only Broadway would be used. Springing onto the hood of a jeep, Cochran called to his pilots, "Say, fellers, we've got a better place to go." ("The American colonel showed himself a master of the arts of propaganda," Wingate's British biographer wrote coldly.)[144]

At twelve minutes past six, the C-47s departed, gliders in tow. Sitting with other officers of the 4th Gurkhas, drinking rum, Masters heard the "full, round sound, soft-edged and with a slow pulse," of the approaching C-47s. "We had heard it many times before, but this night we first *heard* it. The black wings swept across the moon, and at the roots of the wings I saw the red glow of the motors."[145] Behind each plane was towed not one, but two gliders. One after the other, the C-47s swept from the darkening field, circled overhead as they struggled to gain a bare 8,000 feet of altitude, then headed east and over the 7,500-foot-high Chin Hills.[146] Disaster followed shortly after. Beyond the Chindwin River, the pilots discovered that the pristine air of Assam had turned to thick haze, in which the gliders floated, dazzled, toward the refracted light of the full moon.[147] Many trials and practice runs had been performed for this moment, and the best pilots had demonstrated that towing two well-balanced gliders in ideal weather was something that could be done; but no test flights had been performed under the conditions the aircraft would actually face—average pilots flying blind in the moon-haze of turbulent mountain air with overloaded gliders in tow.[148]

Only thirty-seven of the fifty-five gliders whisked in glory from the field at Lalaghat arrived at the Broadway clearing.[149] The towropes of some stretched and broke. Others, the C-47 pilots cut adrift, alarmed at their lurching and yawing.[150] Of the gliders that landed in the clearing, all but two or three crashed into one another or into trees. Twenty-four men were killed and as many injured, many of them American engineers sent with the advance party to build the airfields. So began the world's first all-air invasion behind enemy lines.[151] There were, however, no battle casualties, no enemy ambush; the rows of tree trunks across Piccadilly, it was discovered, were not the result of enemy action, but only the casual destruction of teak loggers.[152]

Twenty-four hours after its disastrous beginning, Operation Thursday continued to unfold. The last-minute change of plans ensured that much careful logistical planning was thrown to the wind, and brigade staffs scrambled mightily to reinvent it. Yet the airstrip, some 4,700 feet long, was indeed built, and the C-47s roared into the enlarged clearing, their landing lights eerily illuminating the night and jungle. On March 6, a second operation was launched to Chowringhee, with one of the gliders flown by the former child movie star Jackie Coogan.[153] By midnight of the third night, as one officer described, the airstrip "was like a fair-ground at its extravagant peak, wheels of coloured light circling about in the moonlit sky, cones of brilliant landing-lights flashing across the trees and the strip, red and green beams from the signal lamp near touch down point . . . fiery red of roaring exhausts, clouds of dust whipped up to float across the stars."[154] Men and mules were unloaded to join the brigade that had marched in, light planes successfully evacuated the injured men, and the Chindits dispersed from the landing zones to establish strategic jungle strongholds. So were twelve thousand of Wingate's men disgorged into the jungle.[155]

MEANWHILE, IN LATE JANUARY, THE GALAHAD FORCE HAD SET OUT FROM ITS training camp at Deogarh, to the west of Calcutta, for the Margherita-Ledo railhead in Assam, a departure witnessed by a small cadre of American press.[156] Traveling by rail, the men had enlivened the long journey by shooting out of the train windows at Indian peasants toiling in their fields, and at their cattle; reportedly no one was killed, and so the incident was treated as one of their high jinks.[157] Merrill apart, few officers were happy with the state of the men's training or condition. "Always the optimist, Merrill chose to ignore some basic facts of life," Galahad's deputy commander and Merrill's chief of staff, Colonel Charles Hunter, recorded.[158] In Hunter's view, insufficient attention had been paid to supply—most critical for a mobile unit operating without lines of communication—the men had been equipped in a piecemeal manner, no records had been kept of what they had been given, and the radio operators were still joining the unit as the officers left by air for Ledo.[159]

General Frank Merrill, the ostensible commander of the Marauders, was a former classmate of Hunter's from West Point, where he was known as "Pee-Wee"—he was not physically robust and had a severe astigmatism—and where his yearbook entry predicted a future as "a lawyer, then a politician, and last a soldier." Three years later, in 1932, he graduated with a bachelor's degree in science from MIT. In 1938, he served as an assistant military attaché in Tokyo, where he and his family learned fluent Japanese and remained almost until the outbreak of war. Assigned to General MacArthur's staff in the Philippines as an intelligence officer, he was in Rangoon when Pearl Harbor was attacked.[160] Remaining in Burma, he met and joined up with Stilwell, shortly afterward accompanying him on his walkout as Burma fell. Recently promoted from major to brigadier general and to Stilwell's assistant chief of staff for Plans and Operation, Merrill was down-to-earth with a friendly smile for all, well-liked, courageous, and utterly lacking in combat experience. He was also in ill health and, although only thirty-nine years of age, had suffered a heart attack during the famous Stilwell walkout. Obviously ill-suited for the demands of Chindit-style jungle operations, it appears that he was anointed on account of his unwavering loyalty to Stilwell, but his state of health would have him in and out of the field throughout Galahad operations.[161] Effectively Hunter, not Merrill, would be the force's actual commander in the field.[162] Hunter, after his graduation from West Point, had served in the Philippines and the Canal Zone in Panama, where he had been an instructor in jungle warfare. Back in the States, he ran a combat-training course at Fort Benning, from where he had responded to the call for volunteers for the "hazardous mission."[163] Although a by-the-book officer, he was well-read and learned and had a wry sense of humor, and of compassion: the Chindits might mute their mules, but he refused to silence the mules of Galahad surgically on the principle that "about the only joy in life for a jackass is to bray."[164]

Hunter decided that, in order to complete their physical training, the men and mules would walk instead of drive the 140 miles from Ledo to the head of the Hukawng Valley along the still-evolving Ledo Road.[165] Thus, on February 7, the Marauders set out on the great, raw, jungle-flanked gash that was the road, marching past local laborers, American GIs wielding bulldozers, machine shops, abandoned encampments, a makeshift still, field hospitals, even a portable movie theater, and the wreckage of past traffic. Over the Pangsau Pass, the vista opened to a vast and windswept sky and, to the north, the massive, snow-topped Himalayan ridge that formed the border with China, while ahead, to the southeast, were Burma's jungle-covered hills. The emerging road on which men and mules tramped had once been part of the refugee trail of tears, and one medical unit that was passed en route had assembled a collection of skulls found in the area. The road became increasingly narrow and precipitous, passing through Shingbwiyang and continuing south to the Tarung River, a little beyond Stilwell's headquarters.[166] By this point, the original force of 3,000 was down to about 2,700, nearly one-tenth of its strength having already been lost to dysentery, malaria, and other afflictions.[167]

Following a short meeting with Stilwell, the officers assembled among themselves for a briefing. Their mission, as Hunter reported, was to "pull an 'end run' around the Japanese right or east (our left) flank in order to assist the forward movement of the Chinese who were to drive down the Hukawng Valley."[168] No written orders were produced. With foggy intelligence as to enemy disposition and numbers, aided only by weak aerial photo reconnaissance, and with the awareness, as Hunter put it, that they were "working from an artist's sketch of the campaign rather than from architectural drawings," the sole American ground force on the continent of Asia set forth.[169] On February 24, Galahad's first columns crossed the Tarung and immediately clashed with a Japanese patrol, and so began operating under combat conditions.[170]

Like the Chindits, the Galahad force was defined by a stern timeline, having been "set up to perform one mission of three months' duration and then . . . to be taken out of the lines for rest and hospitalization," as the army historian put it, with a matter-of-fact nod to the extremity of suffering expected.[171] Even with air supply, the men would be living off a diet of K rations, which supplied about three thousand calories a day—wholly insufficient to the needs of men marching daily with heavy packs in mountainous terrain for many hours.[172] Ninety days had been determined as the limit of physical effectiveness; after this, as the first Chindit operation had shown, the men's health broke down, making them yet more vulnerable to the many scourges of the jungle—scrub typhus, amoebic dysentery, malaria, infections, and hosts of other major and minor afflictions. Other practical considerations also converged around the ninety-day mark. The heavy monsoon could be expected in early to mid-May, rendering life in the field yet more hazardous and miserable and also severely constraining the Air Commando's ability to operate and make supply drops.

Two days after the glider fly-in, the Japanese also made their next major move, launching the long-planned Operation U-Go and the invasion of India. Fearful of an Allied invasion of Burma, their aims included establishment of a stronger and better-provisioned defense line to the west of the Chindwin, in India's Imphal plain.[173] The invasion of India had become a personal passion for Lieutenant General Mutaguchi—a passion that dated from the time of Wingate's first Chindit operation: if the British could march from India into Burma across the Chin Hills, Mutaguchi surmised, then the Japanese could surely march from Burma into India; ironically, Wingate's inspiration had been to prove that British forces could operate in the jungle like the Japanese.[174]

With orders to "advance through the hills like a ball of fire," three divisions of the Japanese Burma Area Army advanced toward Manipur State and its capital, Imphal, which was an important Allied base, as well as a Fourteenth Army headquarters.[175] Their objectives were to seize Imphal and, to the north, the town of Kohima and their troves of supplies, cutting the all-weather supply road that climbed and fell through steep, wooded hills to the small town of Dimapur and its railhead, yet farther north. Once Imphal had fallen, Dimapur could be taken, and with it control of the rail line that fed into the line to Ledo, from which all supplies were transported to Assam, destined for the Hump, or for Stilwell's forces.[176] Thus, the Allies found themselves in an extraordinary situation: the New Chinese Army in India, the majority of the Chindits, the entirety of the Marauders, and portions of the Fourteenth Army had been committed to Stilwell's campaign to defend the still-unbuilt Ledo Road against one Japanese division on the premise that China's supply line must be protected at all costs. Meanwhile, the actual supply line through which all goods destined for the Hump had to pass was under direct assault by the main Japanese force in Burma.

Defending this truly vital artery, as well as the gateway to India, would be the task of Slim's Fourteenth Army, now deployed across a nearly seven-hundred-mile front that ran from Fort Hertz in north Burma to the Bay of Bengal.[177] Following the Cairo Conference, the Fourteenth Army was tasked with major offensives in the Arakan and Central Burma. The Arakan campaign—the second—had commenced in January and gone well, with the Fourteenth capturing small ports and other key points and thwarting an enemy advance into Bengal. Caught short of supplies, the Japanese had sustained high casualties, and the campaign had stalled as each side regrouped. At the direct threat on the Manipur front, Slim pivoted toward Imphal. Thus, by the end of March, all Allied forces in the Burma-India arena were engaging with the enemy.

ON THE MORNING OF MARCH 24, WINGATE, DRESSED AS USUAL IN HIS BUSH jacket and massive, old-fashioned pith helmet, flew in the Mitchell bomber that served as his personal transport to the Chindit's old base at Imphal. He was in fact on his way back to Sylhet, his rear headquarters, but had arranged to stop at Imphal for meetings. His meetings concluded, Wingate decided he would visit Cochran at the Air Commando headquarters near Lalaghat before flying on to Sylhet.[178] It was by now evening and dark. The weather was good, with only isolated, easily avoided thunderstorms in the area. At the airfield, Wingate found his five-man crew waiting for him along with his aide-de-camp and two British war correspondents looking for a ride. Wingate, as was his habit, climbed into the copilot's seat beside USAAF lieutenant Brian Hodges. By the time the plane took off, it was dark night—"clear, but very dark," according to one eyewitness.[179] In Lalaghat, Wingate's ultimate destination, the weather was also clear—"the sky starlit, and there was no moon," as Cochran later reported. The short flight, a hop over the hills, should have taken about thirty minutes; but Wingate's plane never arrived.

At around 8:30 p.m., a Captain Richard Benjamin piloting a C-47 bound for the Broadway clearing radioed to Cochran, who was waiting with increasing anxiety for Wingate, to report that he and his copilot could see what appeared to be an aircraft explosion. Flying at eight thousand feet through stratocumulus clouds, Benjamin had broken through the overcast as he crossed the Imphal Valley and seen a fire burning below in the distance. Immediately flying over to investigate, he circled the area at about seven thousand feet, from which height it seemed to him that the flames were about three thousand feet below; in other words, on a ridge. "Flames were shooting up," he stated when later interviewed by investigators of the accident, and there were "those little flickering flareups on the ground . . . almost similar to one of those native fires."

On the following morning, search planes and foot patrols were sent to investigate the crash site, which was easily found. The aircraft, it seemed, had plunged nose-down like an inverted rocket into the ridge and exploded on impact, creating an eight-foot-deep crater. Little of the aircraft itself was to be seen. One wing and an engine could be identified, as could various body parts, but the explosion and impact appeared to have been so great that there was little to retrieve. Those objects that could be identified were poignant and telling: a part of Wingate's iconic pith helmet and some papers he had been carrying, including the beginning of a letter to his wife: "I have been reading the life of Madame Curie and her daughter Eve. . . ."[180]

The subsequent investigation was thorough and inconclusive. No evidence of sabotage was discovered, but there were revealed a number of details that spoke of relaxed protocols in the Air Commando operation. "The pilot did not even report to the watch officer in the first instance," according to the commanding officer of the Imphal airfield, "neither his arrival nor departure was reported." The B-25 was loaded with six hours of gasoline and was carrying ammunition, but it was not at first known whether or not it was carrying bombs (investigation of the site suggested not). Nor was it at first known who or how many passengers there were.

Later reports and accounts would speak darkly of the notorious storms

that so often menaced the region, hinting that this was a factor in Wingate's crash, and that his B-25 was reported to have had a faulty engine.
Yet all contemporaneous accounts from the different vantages of the array
of participants actually involved state that the weather was unproblematic, and no concerns regarding the aircraft had been reported. "Some kind
of material failure" was speculated, with the most likely culprit being a
failed engine; the B-25, it was allowed, did not perform well on a single
engine, and struggled to maintain altitude of more than three to four
thousand feet. At the loss of an engine, the plane would have experienced
a "terrific yaw"—and yet, as the commander of the B-25 Air Commando
section attested, Lieutenant Hodges was a very experienced pilot, "one of
the best in the outfit, and has had no end of single engine practice. I can't
make myself believe," he concluded, "that losing an engine, even on a
dark night, would have thrown him into a spin or thrown him into the
ground that way."

Questioned for his opinion, Cochran, palpably stunned, rebutted each
explanation offered. There was no swath of damage, no trail of shattered
trees, as would be the case if the plane had flown into the ridge in the
dark. The airplane did not fly into the ridge, Cochran stated, "it dove into
the ridge," and from the west, not from the east, the direction it should
have been flying. "I have no conception of what could have happened," he
said. "The pilot was a good pilot and had been picked for the job. He had
enough night time that I know of since joining our outfit to have been
competent. He has flown this district at night before. He had good homing facilities. The weather was clear." Whatever happened had happened
very quickly, in his judgment, for the pilot had not radioed distress. He
had safely traversed the highest ridge—and if he had miscalculated altitude, he would have struck this ridge first. "I have no conception of what
could have caused this accident," he repeated. "I have never heard of a
similar incident in a B-25."

Apart from the crew and passengers, the last person to see Wingate
alive was Sir John Baldwin, Operation Thursday's Allied air commander,
who speculated that this was a case of "human error, i.e. the collapse of

the pilot."[181] There is another possibility, namely the collapse of the passenger in the copilot's seat. Orde Wingate, by his own account, had throughout his life been subject to "attacks of nerves" so extreme as to elicit violent physical reactions—vomiting, speechlessness, collapse, and quasi-paralysis that lasted for days. These attacks were triggered "when he seemed to feel the imminence of death," as he confided to a friend, and Wingate had long been afraid of flying.[182] It is possible that on this very black night, as the bomber headed over the hills, an engine did fail and the plane experienced the expected "terrific yaw"—a yaw that caused the passenger in the copilot's seat to grasp the control stick in fright. But this is speculation.

Among the Chindits, according to their primary historian, regret at Wingate's death "was not universal."[183] "Wingate's death did not seem entirely real," reflected Masters, who had been awakened in the night with the news, "but then nor had Wingate."[184] Selecting a successor was the task of Slim, whose choice fell on Brigadier General Walter David Alexander Lentaigne, known as "Joe," a battle-seasoned Irishman of proven courage, well respected by his fellow Chindits, and who was also, according to Slim's public account in his own memoir, "the most balanced and experienced of Wingate's commanders."[185] Privately, on being asked why he had chosen Lentaigne, Slim was reported to have given "one of his rare, loud laughs: 'Ha! Ha! Because he was the only one who wasn't mad!'"[186] Whether well-chosen or not, Lentaigne lacked Wingate's near-mythic magnetism and direct connections with high command, and the Chindits were to suffer from the lack of their founder's agency. A great ordeal lay ahead, inflicted less by the Japanese than their highest-ranking Allied commander.

8

THE LEDO ROAD

By now, Stilwell and his New Chinese Army were deep in the Hukawng Valley. In early March 1944, his troops—aided greatly by the accompanying Marauders, acting as a regular infantry unit—had captured the village of Walawbum at the southern end of the valley after confused fighting in which the Chinese and American forces had been unaware of each other's location and intentions.[1] Driving the Japanese out and south, the victory effectively flushed the valley and the road to Myitkyina seemed clear.[2]

Despite this success, Stilwell's venture was still dogged by questions of its relevancy. In early January, two months to the day before the capture of Walawbum, the US War Department's Operations Division had submitted an assessment of the "future military value of China Theater."[3] Since, as was now apparent, the central and southwest Pacific were to be the arenas of main activity, efforts in the CBI theater, it was stated, should be limited to giving air support to the Pacific effort. In practical terms, this meant devoting all supplies over the Hump to building up airpower in China, including at the newly built B-29 fields in Chengtu; beyond this, it was recommended, no further efforts should be made to equip Chinese ground forces.[4] Subsequently, Mountbatten and SEAC advocated canceling the north Burma campaign altogether, arguing that it was out of step with developments in the Pacific: a more fruitful approach, they represented, would be an attack against the Dutch East Indies from northern Sumatra, thus opening a way to the South China Sea and ultimately a Chinese port. Furthermore, Chiang Kai-shek was still refusing to commit his Y-Force to crossing the Salween into Burma—an important element of Stilwell's north Burma campaign—and even appeared to be instructing his generals in Burma to drag their feet. In great alarm, Stilwell sent a mission to Washington to forestall the SEAC mission sent by Mountbatten, his superior officer, but unhappily, as the official US Army history reported, "he failed to inform Mountbatten of his decision."[5]

Following exchanges between US and British chiefs of staff, the US held firm, stating that the capture of Myitkyina and its airfield was essential to its plans to expand the Hump and to build up bases in China to support Pacific operations. More to the point, Roosevelt had promised the generalissimo a land route to China and was committed to delivering this.[6] The north Burma campaign was retained, but Mountbatten, exasperated by his deputy's constant insubordination, requested Stilwell's recall. An additional source of irritation was a spate of articles in the US press instigated from Stilwell's end that praised Stilwell and mocked Mountbatten.[7] "Stilwell, as built up by the American press, is something of a hero whose burning desire to beat Japan is being thwarted by the British," Marshall confided to his Anglo allies. This had not been an accidental development, for as early as May 1943, the director of the War Department's Bureau of Public Relations had indicated in a terse memo to his subordinates that "[e]xtensive publicity of Stilwell highly desirable," and that "[i]mportant that prestige of Stilwell be built up."[8] A boost in Stilwell's profile, it was believed, would give him leverage with Chiang Kai-shek. Greatly abetting this building-up process was Stilwell himself, and his cultivation of the media was well known among his military peers. General Albert Wedemeyer, Mountbatten's American chief of staff in New Delhi, recorded how his early view of Stilwell as a "romantic fighting man" had begun to evolve as he witnessed his "vanity, and his acute sense of public relations insofar as the press was concerned. . . . [E]verywhere Stilwell went there was a newspaper correspondent or newspaper photographer present to catch him in brave poses," he observed, "peering between leaves at the enemy, or snuggling close to a gun, always giving the impression of being a field soldier."[9] Fearing a backlash in US public opinion, the British and Marshall dropped the question of recall, but Marshall counseled Stilwell, once again, to repair his relationship with his commander ("I ate crow," Stilwell reassured Marshall).[10]

Stilwell's own state of mind is captured in a memorandum he wrote to himself, one of the daily entries and reflective asides he entered in diaries and notebooks throughout his life. "What are the objections to me? I have assured you that once a decision is made, I will play ball," he wrote, rehearsing what he would say to Mountbatten. "Am I supposed to sink my opinion *before* that time? And help to put over a point of view I do not believe in? Why should I take the opinions of your staff and not my own?"[11] These are extraordinary views for an allegedly professional soldier to hold, and they say a great deal about why Stilwell was disliked and mistrusted by so many of his colleagues. The question of removing Stilwell "came up a number of times," according to George Marshall, speaking in interviews with historians after the war. Stilwell, according to Marshall, "was his own worst enemy," and his "almost pathological tactlessness and rudeness was a major factor in the troubles he had in China."[12]

That Stilwell's rudeness was symptomatic of more than mere bad manners is made clear, again, by his own writing. In a notebook entry dating sometime in the first half of 1943, he set down some thoughts under the heading "Psychology of Command": "A good commander is a man of high character—(this is the most important attribute)—with power of decision—(next most important attribute). He must have backbone." A commander, he goes on to state, is under tremendous pressure—he must show interest in the men whose lives he controls. Many generals "shelter themselves in dugouts & send the soldiers out to get killed. They cover themselves with medals won at the expense of the lives of their men." The long entry concludes with a formula of command:

Character	80%
Power of decision	10%
Technical knowledge	5%
Every thing else	5%[13]

Putting aside entirely all questions of the insightfulness or truth of his formulations, what is most striking about them is their banality. At sixty years of age, and with a lifetime of studying his profession from his days at West Point onward, were these facile ruminations really the best that he could summon? In fact, they were, and in great part for the reason that, prior to coming to Burma, Lieutenant General Stilwell had never been, or led, in combat.

JOSEPH WARREN STILWELL HAD BEEN BORN IN 1883 ON A PLANTATION NEAR Palatka, Florida. His well-to-do father, who had previously dabbled in law, in lumber, and in medicine, eventually moved the family to Yonkers, New York, where he was to become the vice president of the Westchester Lighting Company. Stilwell had been an athletic youth, playing tennis, football, and running track, and seemed destined for Yale, but on his father's authority was diverted to West Point. At age twenty-one, having graduated thirty-second of his 124 classmates and having shown his greatest proficiency in French, he received his commission as a second lieutenant, Infantry.[14]

It was now 1904, the doldrums of peacetime, and Stilwell chose a post in the Philippines, where US forces were most active, battling insurgents in the wake of US annexation of those islands. Apart from a skirmish with a band of rebels, Stilwell saw no action, and fourteen months later was dispatched to West Point as a language instructor. For three years, he taught English, French, and Spanish, and was then transferred to teaching history and a course on tactics. Over the ensuing years, he married, returned to the Philippines, and traveled as much as he could during his summer breaks—including, in 1911, a brief and fascinating trip to China—before taking up duties as language instructor again.[15] Then, at the end of 1917, at the age of thirty-four, Stilwell went to France as a staff officer for intelligence and helped plan the American offensive at Saint-Mihiel.[16] The ensuing battle, while minor, was distinguished among other reasons for being the first US-led offensive in the Great War and the first use of the US Army Air Service. At war's end, Stilwell was awarded the Distinguished Service Medal, a newly created distinction to recognize noncombatants, and praise from the IV Corps chief of staff for being "one of the most capable G-2 officers developed in the war."[17]

After enrolling in the University of California, Berkeley, to study Chinese, Stilwell returned to China in 1920 for further studies, and in late 1926, at the age of forty-three, he returned again to serve as a battalion commander with the 15th Infantry Regiment in Tientsin. Here, he overlapped with Lieutenant Colonel George C. Marshall, executive officer to the 15th and future US Army chief of staff, whose close friendship would direct Stilwell's subsequent career; Stilwell, it was said, was the only professional colleague who ever called Marshall "George."[18] In 1929, at Marshall's invitation, Stilwell was made instructor of tactics at Fort Benning's Infantry School, where he reveled in presiding over all tactical exercises, testing "screw-ball" ideas that challenged his students.[19] Marshall was impressed, stating in Stilwell's efficiency report that he was "qualified for any command in peace or war," that he was "[h]ighly intelligent," "a leader," and—indicating that Marshall's enthusiasm was not necessarily sound—"tactful."[20] In Marshall's later reports, however, as Stilwell's biographer records, a note of caution can be detected: "High principles. Too hardworking. Nervous temperament," and yet "[a]head of his period in tactics and techniques."[21] There were other warning signs that Stilwell's hostile, resentful character wore thin on his colleagues, and Marshall later allowed that he was asked on three different occasions to relieve Stilwell.[22] Marshall's unwavering support was to be both Stilwell's making and his undoing.

Stilwell remained at Fort Benning for four years and was then assigned to San Diego to train the Organized Reserves of the IX Corps area.[23] It was now 1933 and Stilwell, at fifty years of age, was a "Lt.-Col, Infantry." After two years, and at the height of the Depression, when many an officer was hard-pressed for employment, he took a two-year period of leave. The stretch of years after leaving Fort Benning were hard on Stilwell; he noted in his diary that "there will never be a single work of history with me in it," and at times he seemed to be mentally preparing for retirement.[24] But his professional hopes were revived in the summer of 1935 by an unexpected opportunity to serve as a military attaché to China and Siam. He remained mostly in China, based in Peking, for nearly four years, traveling widely amid local people and on local transport, drinking in all that he saw. In many respects, Stilwell was at his best as a traveler. He enjoyed rugged conditions that deterred many Westerners from venturing to out-of-the-way places; he enjoyed studying and learning and recording what he saw and was an astute observer; he seems, too, to have enjoyed the freedom that the anonymity of travel afforded, the ability to make his way under radar, roaming where he wished among people who did not know him. He made a study of China's military forces and their apparent lack of "planned defense against further Japanese encroachment," as he put it in his diary.[25] He met Chiang Kai-shek, briefly, about whom, informed by his travels and observations, he had drawn bleak conclusions, recording that "Chiang Kai-shek is directly responsible for much of the confusion that normally exists in his command."[26]

This remarkable chapter of Stilwell's life ended in the summer of 1939, and after further travels in the East, he returned to the US. For nearly two years, he served as commanding officer of divisions in Texas and California, and in mid-1941 was given command of the III Corps at the Presidio of

Monterey in California. And so the time passed until December of 1941, when Stilwell was asked to report to Washington, DC, for unspecified future service.

Suddenly, his diary records a blur of activities, as his hopes for a commission were raised, then dashed. "'Let's give him this one—or that one,' etc. No one knows where I'm going!" he wrote on December 26. "This AM it was Dakar, this PM it is Casablanca." For a tantalizing few weeks, it appeared that Stilwell was a candidate to lead the American forces of the North African campaign, code-named Gymnast, the precursor to the eventual Torch;[27] simultaneously, his patron, George Marshall, was taking pains to discuss with him "troubles in the Orient Unity of Command," a reference to the contentious relations between Chiang Kai-shek and the British following Wavell's rejection of Chiang's offer of his army as Burma tottered in late 1941.[28] Already, the importance of China as a postwar first power loomed large in Roosevelt's imagination, and a mission to China was being prepared. As Gymnast faded, and after Washington's first choice to lead the China mission declined the position, Stilwell found "the finger of destiny" pointing at him.[29] On January 23, he was asked directly if he would accept the post in China and replied, speaking as a good soldier, "I'll go where I'm sent."[30]

Stilwell had arrived in China with his three distinct responsibilities— a chief of staff to Chiang Kai-shek, administrator of Lend-Lease aid to China, and commander of such American forces as were in China. His role in China, then, was political, not military. Yet it was his last, putative duty that held most meaning for him, and he eagerly took up Chiang's offer to command two of the generalissimo's "crack" armies. It was a bold gesture, for the situation in Burma was dire, with a cold analysis indicating that—lacking airpower, artillery, and a navy—Burma was already lost, but hope and duty induced Chiang, the various British elements, including Burcorps under General Slim, and Stilwell to make a last-ditch effort to push back the Japanese. Hitherto, Stilwell's most significant experience of command had most likely been his five-month service as commanding officer of III Corps in Monterey, California, before he was summoned to

Washington. In Burma, however, he would be leading Chinese troops, whom he knew from his own studies of the Chinese military were inadequately equipped, trained, and provisioned; moreover, while Stilwell was very proficient in Chinese, he communicated to them through an interpreter.[31] Nonetheless, Stilwell had entered Burma with the belief that he would drive the Japanese back to Rangoon.

In the event, Stilwell was routed along with his allies, and the shock of defeat on this, his first command, was clearly crushing. The collapse of Burma, and then Britain's ongoing resistance to the north Burma campaign, on which hung Stilwell's hopes of redemption, exacerbated his already pathological loathing of the British. Many historians have attempted to locate the origin of this hatred, and speculation generally settles around the fact that he abhorred their pomposity, their stuffy traditions of "good form" and appearances; it has been speculated that this may have stemmed from his own parents' love of pomp and hierarchy.[32] His admiring biographer, Barbara Tuchman, writes of his dislike of pretentiousness, of snobs and the rich, and his diaries certainly show many instances to support this. But they also preserve many examples of his mockery and disdain for the poor, the marginalized, the inconsequential. "Stilwell seemed to enjoy the sensation of dislike," Tuchman allows, "and in his diary would work himself up to it, starting out with a reasonably biting remark and then, as if led on by the taste, going on to more and crueler slurs."[33] "Frogs," "limeys," "niggers," "coons," "wops," "googs," "huns," "chinks," "shanty Irish," "hairy little Jew"—even in an era in which such slurs were widely used, their gratuitous frequency in the privacy of his diary is telling, and, as Tuchman concedes, "not commonly used by a man of Stilwell's class and education."[34] "Rubber-legs" was Stilwell's nickname for his president, a cruel reference to Roosevelt's lower-body paralysis from polio.[35] "Peanut" was his habitual and openly contemptuous name for Chiang Kai-shek. Of interest is the fact that the list of slurs does not include the Japanese, his actual enemy. While his diary makes numerous references to Jap attacks, Jap positions, Jap dead, there are throughout the war years, from December 1941 through August 1945, only three overtly disparaging references: "SHWEBO bombed by 27 jap bastards to-day," "stinking jap," and "The japs are dumb."[36] By contrast, the disparagements of the British are too numerous to count, and there is nothing to match the venom of these entries: "These God-damn limies. . . . [T]he bastardly hypocrites do their best to cut our throats on all occasions. The pigfuckers."[37]

The depth of Stilwell's hatred was not known to the British, despite the fact that he went out of his way to taunt them as "cowards," "useless as soldiers," and "yellow."[38] To John Masters (who was so much a fan of most things American as to immigrate to the US and become a citizen after the war), the posthumously published excerpts from Stilwell's diary, with their "consistent pattern of petty disparagement" bespoke "an inferiority complex of frightening dimensions."[39] Tuchman, too, states that groups such as "diplomats" and the "British" made Stilwell feel "uncomfortable"—in other words, out of his depth.[40] For the fact was that, however flawed the individual British commanders Stilwell met in India and Burma, they were "blooded" soldiers all, with the experience—and often scars—of actual combat, which they wore, as was their studied fashion, with irritating nonchalance. Stilwell, in his turn, while admired by his military colleagues, both American and British, for his energy, his courage, his fighting spirit, was also disdained as a commander. "A hopeless crank," was General Alan Brooke's assessment.[41] Lieutenant General Walter Wilson Jr., SEAC's deputy engineer in chief, had known Stilwell at Fort Benning, as had his father, who by coincidence had been Stilwell's Corps commander at Fort Ord, where Stilwell was commanding officer of the 7th Division. "He was one of the finest infantry battalion commanders that we ever had," Wilson recalled, "but quit right there." At Fort Ord, Stilwell had always been "out marching near the front of the point of an infantry maneuver some place. [My father] never found him near the artillery, near the Engineers, near the division logistical side."[42]

In the already confused arenas of India, Burma, and China, Stilwell's antagonism toward his allies—Chiang Kai-shek and the British—added unnecessary complications. It was widely recognized that he was only comfortable with an inner circle of family and close friends whose chief characteristic was loyalty to him; his son, Joseph Stilwell Jr., served as his G-2, or intelligence officer; his son-in-law Colonel Ernest Easterbrook as his headquarters aide; and a second son-in-law, Major Ellis Cox, in the intelligence sector under his son ("Little Joe," according to Stilwell's chief of staff, Haydon Boatner, "was volative and impetuous like his father and both consciously and unconsciously would involve himself in other than intelligence matters").[43] Stilwell's insecurity bred a furtiveness, a seemingly incorrigible compulsion to make "end runs" around his partners and go it alone. This trait had exasperated his superiors when he was in China as a military attaché and lived and traveled where he wanted, in defiance of regulations.[44] Before the second Burma campaign, even his American staff in New Delhi were claiming they "knew little of his plans," while the British were on record for requesting that General Stilwell be instructed that "before any quasi military activities are undertaken by the U.S. Authorities in or from India," the plans be discussed and approved— as opposed to the current practice of presenting "the British with a *fait accompli*."[45] According to Fred Eldridge, his loyal public relations officer, who was very much in Stilwell's inner circle, "[t]here was a lack of co-ordination amongst his various headquarters which caused confusion and conflict. The general had a tendency to render important decisions to subordinate commanders on field trips without letting his staff in on the secret."[46] In early March 1944, ahead of the advance that would eventually see the capture of Walawbum, Stilwell had surprised Slim by sharing with him his plan for a sudden dash at Myitkyina. "I do not know whether he had even discussed it with his staff," Slim recorded. "At any rate he asked me very solemnly not to speak of it to *anyone*, and made it quite clear that that included not only my staff but my superior commanders." The reason, Stilwell alleged, was fear of "leakage," but Slim believed the true reason was that "if the operation did not come off or misfired, he did not want anyone to be able to say he had had a failure." Since the plan depended upon "a good many intervening ifs," Slim duly held his tongue.[47]

By April 1944, the path seemed clear for Stilwell's New Chinese Army to continue its advance through the Mogaung Valley toward Myitkyina. But there were also causes for concerns. On the political front, the US ambassador to China reported that the New Chinese Army's early victories in the Hukawng had induced the Chinese government to issue maps that showed the Hukawng Valley region to be Chinese territory.[48] On the military front, there were looming, inexorable deadlines. April was the last month clear of the impending monsoon, which could fall as early as the first week in May; and the Marauders, who like the Chindits had been on the march since February, had, as Stilwell should have known, only a limited period of usefulness in the field before they would need to be recalled.

THE LEDO ROAD, THE BACKBONE OF THE ENTIRE NORTH BURMA CAMPAIGN, was to run just under six hundred miles from the railhead of the Bengal–Assam rail line at Ledo to connect with the old Burma Road at a point just over the Chinese border. The chosen route climbed out of Assam by way of a pass through the twelve-thousand-foot-high Patkai Range to Shingbwiyang at the head of the Hukawng Valley; crossed the Upper Chindwin River and followed a Japanese-built dry-season road to climb through the Hukawng Valley; descended into the Mogaung Valley; crossed the Irrawaddy near Myitkyina; ran south to the old trading town of Bhamo; then hooked to the northeast to connect with the old Burma Road at Wanting in China; then to Kunming.[49] Apace with the building of the road, and parallel to it, another team was installing a pipeline to carry fuel from a refinery north of Ledo to Myitkyina. This was one of several pipeline projects planned to deliver fuel to transport hubs within India and to China; the most ambitious was to run from the docks of Calcutta to Assam, then along the Ledo and old Burma Road on to Kunming, a distance of 1,800 miles.[50]

Like the old Burma Road, the Ledo Road was cut through some of the most menacing terrain on earth, and although the work was being undertaken with modern equipment and not by hand, progress was slow.

Studies drafted by the CBI's Services of Supply in 1943 had outlined an ambitious schedule. An all-weather road would reach Shingbwiyang by January 1, 1944; Myitkyina by April 1, 1944, ahead of the monsoon; and Paoshan in China by October 1, 1944.[51] The British, who lacked all enthusiasm for the project, had calculated that it would not be operative until January 1945 and of little use to the war effort.[52]

Work went steadily forward in the early months of 1943, but progress ceased with the arrival of the monsoon, and from May until August the road advanced only three miles. Worse, much that had been built was washed away in a river of mud that mired men and equipment, and by September the operation had stalled.[53] Alarmed by these reports, and keenly alert to his loss of face if the project failed, Stilwell had fired the general in charge and brought on General Lewis A. Pick, a military engineer and an expert on flood control.[54] Subsequently, the pace of the road picked up, and as Stilwell's Chinese forces advanced, with engineer reconnaissance parties acting as trailblazers following in their wake to hack traces through the jungle with axes.[55] Behind them came the bulldozers, and behind them the road graders and gravelers. On December 27, 1943, the lead bulldozer had broken out at Shingbwiyang, at the 112-mile mark. Myitkyina was 148 miles ahead, while 160 miles beyond Myitkyina was the Chinese border.[56]

The sense that time had been lost was never overcome, and work proceeded relentlessly around the clock, with teams working at night by the dim light of smudge pots and flaming oilcans.[57] Finding local labor was an ongoing difficulty, given the other competing Allied building projects—airfields, depots, hospitals—all of which, once established, generated yet greater needs for supplies and transport, and the manpower to move them. In Assam, Nepali and Garo Indians worked in clearing the jungle and hauling loads over sodden trails that would have trapped and mired a tractor.[58] Chinese engineering regiments had also been flown over the Hump to Ledo, where it was reported they worked with high morale and pride, although this same pride forbade them to participate in "coolie work" when there were Indian laborers around.[59] Yet, for Captain Charlton "Charles" Ogburn Jr., the communications officer for the Marauders, despite the throngs of local workers with their delicate figures and broad-brimmed hats, the Ledo area "looked like home," for the road was congested with American trucks, American construction equipment, and American labor. [60]

At least two-thirds and perhaps as much as nearly 90 percent of this familiar fifteen-thousand-man-strong American labor was African American.[61] Although given a low profile in the many CBI histories, black troops had been working on the air bases in Assam since 1942.[62] The importation of black personnel to CBI, as in every theater, had been the subject of anxious army memoranda and guidelines. As George Marshall noted in a postwar interview, "[W]hen you are calling on a man to risk his life in the service of his country, he had every right it would certainly seem—to demand the same rights of the other fellow who was risking his life." Yet, he allowed, one could not do away with the "feelings and reactions and customs of the Deep South," so the problem was delicate and "almost insoluble."[63]

It was a particularly delicate problem in those arenas where the Americans were working closely with the British. Roosevelt had frequently declared that the postwar world should see the end of colonialism and the freedom of national self-determination: "I think I speak as America's President when I say that America won't help England in the war simply so that she will be able to continue to ride roughshod over colonial peoples," the president had told his son.[64] The importation of African American units, then, presented two difficulties: the first being that "almost insoluble" problem of balancing individual rights with "the feelings and reactions and customs" of the country, the other being what one might call "the optics" of making passionate declarations for individual rights while practicing apartheid at home.

In Britain itself, which despite its own racial prejudices had no legal color bar, great care was taken by the US authorities to ensure that interactions between black and white personnel would appear in the best possible light. Air force commanding officers stationed in the British Isles, for example, had been instructed to select three of the "most substantial non-commissioned officers as the colored component of what has been designated as a Good-Conduct Committee. The White soldier compo-nent of said committee is likewise of the substantial representative type." The assembled committee members were then to be reminded of "the history of the relationship of the two races in the States and of the desir-ability of only displaying the nice features of same, particularly on for-eign soil."[65]

In Assam, even before the building of the Ledo Road, the ATC had recognized that "non-specialist negroes were urgently needed" to replace both the skilled technical specialists, who due to labor shortage had been co-opted into handling cargo, and insufficient "native laborers." Yet even in the face of a shortage of manpower, the enthusiasm for accepting black troops differed from base to base. Small bases with only one hous-ing area "requested that colored troops not . . . be assigned that base." The greatest apprehension was that the few white women around might cross paths with black soldiers, and air bases in Jorhat and Tezpur re-quested that WAC personnel not be sent to them due to "apprehension on the part of staff officers of race riots if Negro personnel were permit-ted to dance with Red Cross women."[66]

The authorities worked hard to present the illusion of respectful coexistence on the air bases, and the service newsletters were diligent to support this. "1332 B[ase]U[nit] Has Topnotch Group of Negro Soldiers" was one headline from the popular *Hump Express*. Mohanbari air base, the reader learned, had one of the "sharpest and most efficient Negro outfits in the theatre," entrusted with "getting vital war materials over the Hump," while employed in "engineering, bakeries, utilities, engine mod-ifications, plane loading, truck driving, airplane servicing, and other important tasks." The unit was entirely "self-sufficient," having all its own facilities—dispensary, barbershop, dayroom, athletic grounds, and various conveniences; "self-sufficient" was the term of choice for "segre-gated."[67] Despite "numerous 'incidents' and irregularities in the behavior of the colored troops," and some "resentment . . . voiced by the Negroes as to certain racial discriminations," it appeared, at least to the determinedly upbeat ATC historian, that "the Negro soldier seems to have worked out rather well in Assam."[68] And nowhere in Assam, and in Burma beyond, was this labor more needed, and conspicuous, than on the unfolding Ledo Road.

LOOKING DOWN INTO BURMA FROM JUST BEYOND THE PATKAI RANGE, THE road unfurled below in an undulating ribbon of reddish mud that climbed and dropped through jungled hills. The scale of the landscape, of the forest, was not always apparent; an onlooker from this lofty vantage might suddenly realize with a start that the stand of virgin teakwood rising above the distant road was in fact rooted in a two-hundred-foot drop below the road surface. One could "look out, and out, and out over the valleys, the ranges," recorded Reverend Louis Meyer, a US Army chaplain. Yet on some days one might be in actual clouds. "I was up on top of the mountain there, being a young man, in those Himalayan mountains," recalled Willie Yarbrough, a sergeant with the 45th Engineer General Service Regiment. "The clouds were just like dew around me."[69] Monsoon weather roiled the sky in turbulent confusion, yet miles away sunlight shone on a distant range. Soft puffs of mist settled in the valley. On the ground, rain might be only patchy, but the towering trees still dripped water with a steady patter.[70] Behind one's back or before one's eyes, the jungle was always growing. Just beyond Ledo, by the Tirap River, where engineers wrestled to replace a bridge support, clearings that had been leveled and left with stumps the year before were covered with twenty-foot-high growth of jungle bush.[71] Widening the road one day, a soldier of the 1875th Engineer Aviation Battalion, grabbed hold of what he thought was the tail of one of the large lizards found in the jungle—to find it was the tail of a seventeen-foot-nine-inch-long, 125-pound Burmese python.[72] In the monsoon, the land itself shifted and moved beneath the workers. Road banks collapsed, landslides dropped massive boulders, and giant trees suddenly exposed to high winds and floods of rain teetered and fell. Whatever happened in the skies above directed the quality of life below. The rumbling clouds could, with startling suddenness, hurl down hail in lumps large enough to knock a person out; then just as suddenly subside to steady rain.[73] Lightning flashes were powerful enough to light the entire landscape as brightly as did the sun in day.[74] When the rain ceased and the sun came out, depending on where one worked, the smell of Japanese dead sickened the air, and here and there along the forest edges, parts of their bodies could be seen sticking out of the ground.[75] Yet in the dry-season nights, fireflies filled the gulfs of ravines, blinking in dazzling unison out of a darkness that was otherwise complete. "As I stood watching I heard the wail and weep of jackals," Reverend Myers recorded in his diary, "their cries moved through the night from left to right, from far off to nearby and away again. They must travel very fast when on the scent of something dead or dying."[76]

Driving the emerging road in all weather were the quartermaster battalions, also largely African American, ferrying supplies from Ledo to depots, airfields, hospitals, and Allied troops along the way. Driving in the monsoon in Burma, where nine inches of rain could fall in a single night, "was worse than driving on ice," recalled Jeff Jones of the 518th Quartermaster (Truck) Battalion. "The road was often washed away in places or there would be a landslide. Those engineers would go to work in the torrential downpour."[77] Sniper fire erupted from time to time, and, as snipers were not active once darkness fell, night driving was usual. Corporal Charles Pittman, also of the 518th and newly arrived to Assam, described his first run with a convoy, driving with blackout lights in utter darkness, navigating by concentrating on the truck in front of him. By the shifting of gears he knew he was going uphill. "What was really happening was we were climbing almost straight up for six miles," he recalled. After delivering his load, he turned back for the return trip, reaching the bottom of the six-mile stretch as dawn broke. "Then I saw where I was," he recalled. "Like looking down there was nothing. I started think-

ing about the night before and all that time I didn't know there was
nothing on my right side but space for a helluva long distance down. I
broke out in a cold sweat."[78] Those driving in daylight hours often slept
on the roadside, parking their trucks about eight feet apart so as to hang
their hammocks between them.[79]

Home base for engineers and drivers was the ubiquitous *bashas* and
tented encampments mired in mud and mildew. There was little at all in
the way of diversion. "Every day out there in those jungles was like the
day before," recalled Sergeant Yarbrough.[80] Outdoor movies were screened
several times a week, with the projector's light beam swarmed with clouds
of mosquitoes, and from time to time a Japanese soldier snuck through
the darkness to watch the show.[81] Some men drifted off into the nearby
villages, usually in search of women, although these excursions could be
dangerous. A "Negro soldier who was in an engineering detachment . . .
strayed off to some native villages," wrote a field station doctor. "A few
days later his headless body was found in front of the HQ door."[82] A
number of encampments enjoyed musicians who formed pickup bands.[83]
In any case, there was "no spare time," Corporal Greech recalled looking
back on his service in the jungles of north Burma as a combat engineer,
working twelve- to fourteen-hour days. His outfit "smoked a lot of pot"
to get by. "We got it from those Indians up there, the coolies; they came
down with big bags of that stuff. You give them two annas, four annas
and they give you a handful."[84] For lack of other options, attending to
one's duty became a form of entertainment. The heavy-equipment operators "became part of that machine," according to Yarbrough. "They go
up to the edge of the mountain and made that bulldozer go up on its
hind legs and turn it around. . . . [T]hat was their entertainment—to see
how far they could go with that piece of equipment."[85]

Following closely as they did the advance of Stilwell's army, the engineers and drivers were often within hearing distance of skirmishes ahead,
and Japanese snipers were known to infiltrate through the Chinese lines
to shoot at them from high in the trees.[86] Yet, the war—or, more correctly,
the purpose of the war—seemed very distant. Like the pilots flying the

Hump, many of those "driving the Hump" saw too much to accept the heroic narrative that they were building a "vital lifeline" to China. "[S]upplies never reached their destination 100 percent intact," according to Private Clyde Blue from Chicago. "The most lucrative black market in the world was operating right under our noses. Everybody was involved."[87] Amid all the discussion and planning of the new road, no one seems to have raised the point that the original Burma Road had served as a highway for black market traffic, with an estimated three-fourths to two-thirds of all goods vanishing into the countryside between Lashio and Kunming.[88] Stolen goods were passed to Chinese middlemen or taken to villages that served as black market bazaars.[89] Although government-issued firearms were kept locked in the arms depot, the men were armed, for small arms and knives were easy to obtain.[90]

And violent incidents were common, some severe, such as a stabbing during a movie night and even murder. In March 1944, an African American engineer killed a white officer, setting off a lengthy manhunt for the murderer, who had fled to the safety of the forest.[91] Offenders of violent crimes, as well as of such transgressions as disobeying an order, were sent to the Ledo Stockade, a barbed-wire enclosure anchored at each corner by a watchtower and set conspicuously along the road. "They had various kinds of punishment," recalled Blue, who was sentenced to six months of hard labor for disobeying an order. "One of the mildest ones was having a group of men walk around in a circle until their feet had made an ankle deep rut; then they would start a new circle." The most dreaded punishment was confinement in the "sweat box," a two-foot-by-four-foot, cement-sided cell with a corrugated-metal roof and no windows, and designed so that a man could not stand, sit, or lie down, but had to remain in a bent position. "Blacks who spent time in there came out ashy white and whites came out a peculiar blue-white. . . . Few men were able to walk out of this contraption."[92]

"There were endless threats to the health and well-being of human bodies," wrote Ray Peers, who, as commanding officer of the covert guerrilla Detachment 101, was well acquainted with the jungle arena in which the road crews worked. "Fits of depression and illness were an undercurrent of daily life and yet the mood of the engineer battalions was not as mutinous as might be expected."[93] Falling trees and demolition debris, equipment accidents, malaria, leech-bite infections, scrub typhus, heat— all inflicted damage: a favorite saying was that the road was built at the cost of "a man a mile," and according to the final tally of American lives lost, that figure was accurate. The numbers of laborers lost—Indian, Burmese, and Chinese—is unknown.[94] Several hospitals were set up specifically to treat the road workers. The 20th General Hospital from Philadelphia prided itself on being a "League of Nations" hospital, caring alike for Indians, Chinese, and black and white Americans—although in segregated quarters.[95] The 335th Station Hospital at Tagap Ga—mile marker 80 on the road—was an entirely African American operation, although its doctors and nurses made clear they would treat patients of any color.[96] Among their patients were Chinese soldiers who had gone AWOL from Stilwell's army and filtered in from the jungle suffering from malaria, dysentery, Naga sores, and other jungle complaints; the flight from China to India over the Hump had taken only some four hours, and with no sense of the distance traversed they had thought they could walk home.[97]

By the first week in April 1944, the road had progressed as far as Laban, at mile marker 146, just under midway between the Hukawng and the Mogaung Valley, which Stilwell's troops were entering. In Washington, the War Department continued to refine the CBI objectives and in mid-April drafted a list of projects it deemed "timely and feasible," at the top of which was increasing the tonnage over the Hump to twenty thousand tons a month, so as to build a stockpile of supplies for the B-29s and air support of the anticipated big Pacific push.[98] Originally, the B-29s were to have been based in China, but as concerns for security grew it was decided to base them in fields outside Calcutta and stage them from Chengtu, which lay northwest of Chungking. For the north Burma campaign, Mountbatten had succeeded in persuading Chiang to fly two divisions based in China over the Hump to Ledo, to reinforce Stilwell's advancing New Chinese Army;[99] but all attempts to get the generalissimo to commit his Yoke, or Y-Force, troops in Yunnan to cross the Salween River into Burma had so far failed—a matter of growing concern, as the New Chinese Army was approaching Myitkyina, where it was planned the two forces were to meet. This concern goaded Roosevelt into sending Chiang an uncharacteristically blunt message. The fact that Y-Force's Salween front had "remained quiet," the president wrote, had allowed the Japanese to divert part of one division to confront the advance of Stilwell's army and the long-range penetration groups. "It is inconceivable to me," the president continued, "that your YOKE Forces, with their American equipment, would be unable to advance against the Japanese Fifty-Sixth Division in its present depleted strength. . . . To take advantage of such an opportunity, we have, during the past year, been equipping and training your YOKE Forces. If they are to not be used in the common cause our most strenuous and extensive efforts to fly in equipment . . . have not been justified. . . . I do hope you can act."[100] This letter was followed by a message from General Marshall for the Chinese staff that made the president's meaning yet more explicit: unless Y-Force advanced to join the campaign, supplies for it would cease.[101] In mid-April, Chiang at last ordered four of the Yunnan divisions to cross the Salween and enter Burma.[102]

In his letter to Chiang, Roosevelt also referenced the fact that the British were then "ably" battling the Japanese incursion into India, and with it the "strong Japanese threat to the line of communications to China and the supply route which supports your troops in the Mogaung Valley."[103] His sanguine account masked the ferocity of fighting on this new front, where the Japanese were indeed heading for the supply base at Imphal—and also, it was assumed, for the road that ran north from Imphal to the town of Dimapur, from where the Bengal rail line led to Ledo in Assam. If Japanese forces cut the road and seized Dimapur, supplies could not be carried onward either to Stilwell's forces or to other points in Assam and on over the Hump.

———

THE BRITISH, FROM THEIR INTELLIGENCE AND CAPTURED ENEMY PLANS, had surmised that the Japanese intended to attack Imphal from three directions: from the road to the southwest, from Burma to the east, and from the north, so as to cut the Dimapur–Imphal supply road.[104] After considering the limited options available, Slim had decided to meet the attack by directing the action to "ground of our own choosing," namely the vast arena ringed on three sides by wooded ridges and ravines that was the Imphal plain, and "fight a major battle there to destroy the Japanese Fifteenth Army."[105] His strategy was to consolidate and withdraw his forces into the "Citadel" of Imphal, allow the town to be besieged, and thus induce the Japanese to venture farther and farther from their own already-ragged supply lines that now stretched across north Burma to the Chindwin River. Meanwhile, Imphal possessed one of the region's few all-weather airfields, by which his own troops could be supplied.[106]

Air support was central to Slim's plan, and it was put to use early in the series of battles that would rage for five months around Imphal and, farther up the supply road, the British administrative settlement of Kohima. In early March, three Fourteenth Army brigades had been airlifted from the Arakan to Dimapur and Imphal as reinforcements, with Mountbatten diverting twenty C-46s from the Hump to aid the effort.[107] The Japanese, on the other hand, having by this time wholly lost air supremacy, had been forced to withdraw their fighter planes to Rangoon, some seven hundred miles to the south, while their supply bases were similarly distant: it would eventually take six perilous weeks along routes under constant attack for Japanese reinforcements to arrive at Imphal from Bangkok.[108] By contrast, it had taken ten days and 758 sorties to fly the British reinforcements in from the Arakan.[109]

By April, following brutal fighting along the route leading to Imphal from the south, the British had successfully withdrawn into their "Citadel," which, as predicted, was under siege—not a "violent and noisy" one, as one participant recalled, with tanks and bombardments, but "more like a cat watching a mousehole." Completely surrounded, the men "would see the glimmer of fires all around and know every move was watched." Frequently, a nervous sentry would fire at a shadow, triggering a fusillade from every sentry around the perimeter.[110] Some eighty miles up the road, the Japanese were closing in on the settlement of Kohima. Set in the wild and trackless country of the Naga tribal lands, Kohima could only be accessed easily from the road, for the surrounding network of forest trails was known only to local people; the dense forest that lay between the small town and the Japanese lines some 160 miles away across the Chindwin, to the east, represented another of those landscapes that the British had deemed "impossible" to traverse. Nonetheless, it was through this jungled region, and moreover across the north-south-running mountainous "grain" of the land, that the Japanese advanced over twenty days from Burma to Kohima.[111]

Kohima combined a Naga township, the neat, red-roofed bungalows, offices, and warehouses of a British administrative town, and an array of recently built *bashas* for stores, workshops, and other facilities relating to the war, all spread over several ridges, with views of the high peaks that rose in three directions around it.[112] Set on its own ridge at the bend in the road, amid pleasant gardens and a tennis court, was the bungalow of the deputy commissioner.[113] Located only some hundred miles south of the US air base at Jorhat—and forty miles from the Assam rail line—Kohima, with its view of the surrounding terrain, its key pass, its key road, was obviously strategic.[114] Yet it was Dimapur, with its eleven-mile-long, mile-wide supply dump, not Kohima, that had been perceived as the next likely enemy target; in fact the Japanese command had also been torn between the two objectives.[115] As a result, while Dimapur was on the way to being reinforced, Kohima was lightly defended, and by the time the threat to it was perceived and troops ordered to turn back to its defense, the garrison was already cut off and, like Imphal, under siege.[116] Outposts in the hills to the east and southeast, facing the Japanese advance, had been ordered to "fight to the last man." The order was shortly rescinded, but word of this did not reach the outpost at Kharasom, where Captain Jock Young, a young Glaswegian, had dismissed his platoon, announcing, "I will *be* the last man." He was last seen by his departing mates stacking tommy gun magazines and grenades around his bunker.[117]

Of the 2,500 defenders of Kohima, about 1,000 were administrative noncombatants.[118] Against them were two regiments of the Imperial 31st Division, numbering well over 6,000 men.[119] From the first week of April, the garrison was shelled and mortared at every dawn and every dusk, and when darkness fell there followed wave upon wave of infantry attack. As the days wore on, the defenders were driven into tighter and tighter compass, until the garrison was squeezed into a triangle of 700 by 900 by 1,100 yards, and, by April 15, attackers and defenders were lobbing grenades at one another across the district commissioner's tennis court.[120] Water was in short supply and severely rationed.[121] The dead lay rotting in the sun, their stench seeping into the skin, hair, and clothes of the living, who fought, attempted to sleep, and performed every bodily function in their slit trenches. A signaler who had been trapped in Kohima when he came to deliver batteries, found himself in a trench when a Japanese soldier suddenly jumped into it: "We stared at each other in complete amazement before we began to fight," he recalled. "In that confined space there was no room to even use a knife. Desperate, I put my hands round his neck and applied as much pressure as I could muster. Eventually he lay quite still; he had stopped breathing. I had never killed anyone before, least of all with my bare hands. It was an experience that continued to haunt me for many years after the war."[122]

A startling combination of primitive and high-tech warfare defined the two-week siege of Kohima. From the sky, flying as low as 250 feet above the hills and vulnerable to enemy small-arms fire, RAF planes dropped bombs and supplies, while the fighting on the ground was often, as in the Bronze Age, hand-to-hand.[123] At length, the first wave of relief for the defenders appeared at noon on April 18, when Jemadar Mohammed Rafiq, leading the Punjabis, fought through the Dimapur road, followed by a tank detachment. The wounded and noncombatants were evacuated, and the harrowed troops relieved.[124] By April 20, the siege of the rubble and flyblown carnage that was now Kohima was over. Ahead lay another stiff battle of two month's duration, but the back of the Japanese assault had been broken.

Five men at Imphal were awarded the Victoria Cross, Britain's highest military honor, for conspicuous valor in the presence of the enemy, and two at Kohima, and the names of those awarded are telling: Jemadar Abdul Hafiz of the 9th Jat Regiment; Sergeant Hanson Victor Turner of the East Yorkshires; Rifleman Ganju Lama, Naik Agansing Rai, and Subedar Netrabahadur Thapa—the last three of the 7th and 5th Gurkha Rifles; Captain John Niel Randle of the Royal Norfolk Regiment; and Lance-Corporal John Pennington Harman of the Queen's Own Royal West Kent Regiment.[125] Individual officers and men with actual names emerged from the collective term "the Naga," four of whom received the Military Cross: Captain Ralengnao Khathing attached to V Force; and Jemadar Prembahadur Lama, Jemadar Ünilhu Angama, and Jemadar Visai Angami of the Naga Levies.[126]

The Japanese command, for its part, was riven by dissension and its men wrung out, famished, ill, and wounded. "[I]nvalids and the wounded were driven to the front to help supply manpower," according to a Japanese infantry lieutenant. "Even those with broken legs were herded into battle, malaria cases too."[127] They had been provided with few rations beyond what they had carried with them when they set out from the Chindwin on March 15, and had been reduced to eating grass.[128] On the last day of May, deep in the monsoon, Lieutenant General Kōtoku Satō, commander of the 31st Division, acting on his own initiative, ordered what was left of his forces to retreat. To a signal sent by Mutaguchi urging him to fight on—"before a resolute will even the gods give way"—he had signaled back: "It seems Army cannot grasp the real situation: no supplies and men wounded and sick."[129] Leaning on sticks in the piercing cold of the monsoon rain, his men limped in rotting boots and with rotting flesh up and down the mountain ranges back to Burma.[130] By early June, even Mutaguchi realized the invasion of India had failed. The Imperial Fifteenth Army—84,280 strong when it marched into India—retreated with 30,775 men "available for duty," of whom the great majority were in fact sick from malnutrition and wounds—a casualty rate that represented the greatest Japanese losses of the war as a whole thus far.[131] Captured Japanese documents, from official orders to personal diaries, revealed the toll these defeats had taken on morale: "Their diaries contain far less heroics than a year ago," an Indian Army intelligence report noted.[132] Fourteenth Army casualties amounted to 16,667, and their victories on this central front marked the turn of fortunes in the Burma campaign.[133]

BECAUSE THE JAPANESE ADVANCE INTO INDIA DIRECTLY THREATENED THE source of supplies for the New Chinese Army, in early April, when Imphal was under siege and Kohima threatened, Slim flew to Jorhat to meet with Stilwell, whom he found "tired and older" but friendly. Stilwell repeated an earlier offer of a division of his army to meet the crisis, although it would mean stopping his own advance; on the other hand, if the Imphal–Dimapur road supply line were cut, he would be forced to withdraw. Slim refused the offer, confident that his long-game plan was working and knowing that reinforcements were on the way. Furthermore, with Japan's striking force "irretrievably committed" to the battle against his IV Corps, this was, he knew, Stilwell's great opportunity to push on to Myitkyina with his considerable numerically superior advantage.[134]

To the north and east, meanwhile, the Chindits had seen continuous fighting throughout the months of March, April, and May. Their directives had been to cut the supply route of the only enemy division facing Stilwell, and to damage and confuse the enemy. Harried though they were by the enemy, they had successfully disrupted the divisions confronting Slim at Kohima, as well as the division facing Stilwell, and the Japanese command credited their action with having "greatly affected

Army operations and eventually led to the total abandonment of northern Burma."[135]

The Chindits' own survival depended upon close air support, which
had evolved to something of a fine art, using air photographs marked
with a grid system that allowed air and ground forces to identify a common target—an otherwise hugely difficult task in the immense, jungled
landscape that allowed few identifying natural features.[136] In all the tasks
they performed, however, the pilots' improvisational skills continued to
advance and dazzle. Standing at the edge of the jungle, John Masters and
Joe Lentaigne, Wingate's replacement, had watched as men cleared and
leveled a light-plane landing strip for a medical evacuation. Working in
dense ground mist at the end of the strip, sappers were detonating the
last four trees as the two L-1 light liaison planes came in. Three shattered
trees fell, but the fourth did not. A red warning light was fired to tell the
pilots to stay clear, but the planes swung round and continued coming
in, downwind. "They floated on, sinking, their motors purring," recalled
Masters, who with Lentaigne had watched in horror. "Suddenly the lead
plane dipped his right wing sharply and he was among the treetops. Level
again, then left wing down . . . he came on between the trees, spilling air
by violent sideslips, branches and leaves brushing his wings and wheels."
The lead plane burst into the open followed closely by the second, which
was "weaving like a drunken moth" among the trees. "Down, down, and
we were all pressing our feet down against the earth, willing him down."
Touching thirty feet short of the unblown tree, the plane rolled to a stop
with five feet to spare, followed by the second plane.

> The pilots climbed out. They were both smoking cigars. Down the
> strip we were all cheering and clapping. Joe went out, shook the
> lead pilot's hand, and cried, "That was the best landing I've ever
> seen!"
>
> "Thanks General," the sergeant said.
>
> Joe recovered himself, "But why the hell didn't you wait till we'd
> blown down the other tree there?"

The sergeant shook his head in mournful acknowledgement of his fault—"Hell, we could make it."[137]

Little by little, a new element was seeping into this Burmese jungle drama—namely, American-style glamour, and the Chindits, working closely with the Americans, had become highly susceptible to it. Skill accounted for a great part of this glamour, but so it seems did "attitude," which even a pilot whose plane cracked up on takeoff could impart. "Ah shit, I ought to be shot," the American lieutenant of a broken plane said ruefully as he climbed out of the wreck. "This immediately became a favorite expression in the brigade," Masters reported.[138] Enthusiasm for stories of the American West was high, and its supposed lingo had become popular, so that an officer schooled at Eton might say by way of a greeting, "Howdy, buckaroo! Which way you ridin'?" or "There's Japs in them thar hills."[139]

By cutting the communications of the 18th Division, the sole Japanese element confronting Stilwell's advance, the Chindits had added to the hardship of a division that had already been reduced to half its original strength of approximately ten thousand, mostly by malaria and other diseases; by the end of March, with the men's uniforms in tatters and many going shoeless, the men of the 18th were subsisting on a handful of rice each a day and were stricken with beriberi. Nonetheless, on the four occasions when Stilwell's forces had succeeded in cutting off and encircling them, they had managed to slip away into the jungle, regroup, and fight again.[140] Japanese command plans had originally foreseen reinforcing the 18th with another division (the 53rd), which was to have been freed once Imphal was captured, but following Slim's victory and the high toll he had exacted for it, this did not happen. Eventually, reduced reinforcements did arrive piecemeal, so that by mid-May the division was up to a strength of about seven thousand.[141] Meanwhile, Stilwell's forces had also been increased by the addition of the two Chinese Y-Force divisions flown in from Yunnan, bringing his total strength up to five Chinese divisions, or about forty-three thousand men.[142] This did not include the Marauders, or the

supporting Chindits, or the Dah Force (named after the traditional Burmese curved sword)—another special-force element composed of Kachin
guerrillas operating with the Chindits—or elements of the OSS, or the
considerable air support.[143] Knowing this was Stilwell's opportunity,
Slim had encouraged him at their meeting in Jorhat to "push on for
Myitkyina as hard as he could go." Stilwell in turn had replied that his
early plan was still in place, and, depending on the severity of the coming
rains, he hoped to be at Myitkyina on the twentieth of May. He again
asked Slim to tell no one of the plan or proposed date. "I agreed I would
not," Slim recorded. "After all, everyone knew he had been ordered to take
Myitkyina, and whatever his motives in this secrecy I was prepared to
humour him."[144]

MYITKYINA, BEFORE WAR CAME TO BURMA, HAD BEEN A SLEEPY VILLAGE
nestled in a deep, U-shaped bend of the Irrawaddy River. Its position at the
head of all navigation on this major river, the fact that it sat at the end
of a rail line and a road from Rangoon, and its subsequent airstrip had
made it strategic, and since its capture by the Japanese in May of 1942, it
had served as the 18th Division's headquarters. The Allies' slow, steady
advance toward this town had been made by way of the Hukawng and
Mogaung Valleys, but Stilwell's secret plan now called for a strike force
to make a wide hook to the north over the Kumon range, so as to bypass
Japanese defenses in the valleys entirely, and head directly for Myitkyina.[145] Their mission was to seize and hold the five-thousand-foot-long
airstrip, but militarily, as Colonel Hunter recorded, "the most important
objective in north Burma was the city itself" and the Japanese base complex that lay two miles to the east of the airstrip. Once the town was
seized, the whole area could be converted into an Allied base.[146]

The strike force was to be composed of three brigades, each comprised of two Chinese and one Marauder battalion. The Chinese troops
were not drawn from the seasoned New Chinese Army forces that had
doggedly fought and trudged down the Hukawng with the Marauders,

but were elements of the Y-Force army recently airlifted over the Hump from China. Although they, too, had allegedly been trained under Stilwell's program, they were untested and had never operated with Americans.[147] "Those Chinese are nothing but kids," was the shocked view of the Americans when they met the new reinforcements.[148]

For their part, the Marauders were still recovering from an engagement that had tested them severely, for en route to a supply drop they had been ambushed and then besieged over eleven days near a small Kachin village called Nphum Ga set in a tiny forest clearing. After fierce fighting, the battalion that had entered the village 1,100 strong emerged victorious, but with 59 killed, 314 wounded, and 65 suffering from dysentery and malaria and in need of hospitalization. Merrill, too, was hospitalized after suffering another heart attack.[149] Still, the ordeal was over, the victors believed. In the aftermath of the battle, they ate and rested and changed their clothes and waited to be relieved. "When [relief] arrived, we would go into rainy-monsoon quarters somewhere to rest and recuperate and reorganize for the next season," recalled Captain Ogburn of this wistful period. They would be settled, sleeping under a roof, not on the march, have time to read. . . . "Then a grotesque rumor began to be heard," he continued. "The substance of the rumor was the possibility of our being sent against Myitkyina."[150]

The Marauders had trained for jungle operations in all their rigors, but they had not trained for the use to which they were now consistently being put, namely as an infantry assault unit. Having discovered how effectively the Marauders could be employed to make wide, encircling attacks behind the enemy as it faced the advancing Chinese, Stilwell had come to rely on them and this maneuver. These "wide hooks," represented in neat diagrams on paper charts, entailed backbreaking marches, miles and miles slogged through uncut jungle, pushing and pulling their stoic mules up and down mud-slick slopes in enervating heat. Mostly, Stilwell had come to realize that his Chinese troops, despite their training, equipment, and vastly superior numbers, could not be counted on to win any consequential engagement without the Marauders. Now "End

Run," Stilwell's secret plan, entailed the Marauders marching nearly one hundred miles, with mules, up and over the ridges of the six-thousand-foot-high range, through wild, trackless country, hacking trails all the way, to take the airfield. One fact consoled: "This was positively to be the last asked of us," Ogburn recorded. "We had it from General Merrill himself that when we had gained our objective we would be returned at once to India," sent to rest camps, and given furloughs.[151]

Meanwhile, there would be a long and difficult journey. "It was taking more and more effort to keep moving," Captain Fred Lyons recorded of the march to Myitkyina. He had picked up amoebic dysentery, most likely from drinking scummed water that had collected in elephant tracks while he was under siege at Nphum Ga, and had also lost a lot of blood to leeches. "Other illnesses broke out among the men—yellow Jaundice, malaria, stomach disorders—but we kept plugging on." The miles unfolded, always with the nerve-stretching tension of not knowing what lay around each jungled bend. Hill followed hill, and from the crest of one hill the men looked down on the next hill beyond. "Going up, the blood pounding in my head from the strain of hauling on vines and helping pull a mule up the trail," wrote Lyons. "Going down, my heels pounded right up to my backbone, and every step was like beating an open wound." He was draining blood from the dysentery, and one platoon had cut out the seats from their trousers so as to let the diarrhea pass as they marched.[152] Outside of Myitkyina, as Lyons led a patrol along the rail lines, the enemy was sighted in force. Crouched in the bushes, he felt indifferent to the outcome. "All I wanted was unconsciousness."[153]

The capture of the Myitkyina airstrip turned out to be straightforward—"like a service school demonstration," according to the official theater history.[154] Kachin scouts and other patrols ascertained that the garrison was not on alert and only lightly guarded. At ten o'clock in the morning on May 17, Hunter's men attacked, surprising and readily overwhelming such Japanese forces as were there—an estimated seven hundred men. Some hours later, confident that the airport was secured, Hunter sent the arranged code—"Merchant of Venice"—to signal all was clear and reinforcements and supplies could come in.

Stilwell's anxiety as he waited for the message is evoked in the nervous chatter of his diary:

> **Wed. May 17** CLEAR, by God! A break. Japs bombed new field at Warazup at 8:00. No damage—Q. Where were our boys? . . . At 10:50 [message]. "In the Ring" came in. That meant—"AT THE FIELD." Old [Major General William, commanding general of the USAAF and RAF troop-carrying command] flew over at 12:00 & saw nothing. (Hunter getting in place, probably.) We'll just have to sweat it out. . . . MERRILL in at 2:50. Had been over field, which was clear. . . . About 3:30 we got MERCHANT of VENICE (i.e. transports can land.) WHOOPS! Enormous relief to get Merrill's report—at once ordered machinery & reinforcements started. About 3:30 two transports landed. At 4:00, we saw transports and gliders going over. Thereafter, a stream of planes both ways. Told them to keep going all night. We may have the 89th [Chinese Regiment] in by morning. . . .[155]

The enemy that Stilwell and his men had defeated were the Japanese, whose terrible acts of savagery against his compatriots and allies had made this war, for the fighting men, very personal. "[W]e saw atrocities by the Japanese," one Galahad patrol leader reported. "We saw it. Things they had done to us. A young man from the University of Illinois, or Michigan. . . . He was a lieutenant. They captured him and tied him to a tree and shot him, starting with his legs, all the way up his body."[156] Yet at this high point of Stilwell's entire career and the seizure of the only objective of consequence from this enemy, the next line in his diary reads: "WILL THIS BURN UP THE LIMIES!"[157]

The following day, Stilwell's personal plane—with "Uncle Joe's Chariot" written on the nose—touched down at Myitkyina with Stilwell and a dozen US press correspondents. Newsreel footage shows a laughing, re-laxed Stilwell savoring his moment of his triumph. ("We got word from Burma," Secretary of War Stimson recorded in his diary on hearing the news in Washington, "that good old Stilwell had finally reached the en-virons of Myitkyina and had taken the airfield. . . . This campaign which the British were unwilling to take . . . is showing up pretty well.")[158] Off camera, however, Hunter was desperately searching for his next orders. He had urgently requested food and ammunition, but the forty to fifty planes that landed carried only aviation engineers to repair and defend the runway, and aircraft and gliders seemingly bent on their own inde-pendent missions were piling up. Merrill could not be found.[159] The Chi-nese 89th Infantry Regiment arrived with reinforcements as darkness fell, but without a commander. "And where again was Merrill? Was he sick? Was Stilwell sick and not functioning?" Hunter raged. How was it that the Air Corps seemed to be acting entirely on its own initiative?[160] Around noon on May 18, Hunter sent the Chinese 150th Infantry Regi-ment to attack the town, but the commanding officer, misreading his com-pass, set out in the wrong direction and had to return and start again, and the delay caused him to be caught by darkness.[161] On May 19, Merrill arrived for what was to be a brief visit before suffering yet another heart attack, his third, which would remove him permanently from the field.

In this heady period of victory, Stilwell was slow to take in what should have been foreseen. While the Chinese reinforcements got orga-nized, the Japanese began to regroup. Ninety minutes after the airfield had been secured, Colonel Fusayasu Maruyama was bringing in ele-ments of the 56th Infantry Regiment from across the Irrawaddy River, and throughout the night other forces slipped through the gaps in the Allied defenses. Drawing on every element in the vicinity, including con-valescents in the Myitkyina base hospital, Maruyama had by the end of the month increased the number of the garrison's defenders to some 3,500.[162] Meanwhile, on May 20, Hunter again sent the 150th against the town. Pushing into the heart of the city, it took up position on the top floor of a building opposite the rail station, but the battalions following after it were caught in cross fire. In panic and confusion, they opened fire on their own troops, then broke and ran, leaving, as Hunter reported, "close to three hundred of their comrades dead or dying."[163] Thus, after their textbook capture of the lone airfield, Stilwell's forces found themselves confined, as the official CBI history puts it, to "a little island of precariously held territory."[164] To the east was the Japanese garrison, while Japanese forces were dug in on every other side. American planes continued to fly in reinforcements to newly built airstrips until some thirty thousand Chinese troops had been assembled—an overwhelming advantage against a starving and embattled force almost a tenth their size—and the fighting, as Slim put it, "settled down into an untidy, uninspired, ill-directed siege."[165]

There are many readily identifiable causes of the subsequent debacle, from the consistent underestimation of enemy strength by Stilwell's son, to the lurching leadership—the Myitkyina Task Force saw four different commanders over the eventual seventy-eight-day siege—to the unassailable fact that the Chinese forces, to use Slim's tactful words, "lacked sting."[166] Above all else was the complete absence of any strategy. "It is still inconceivable to me," wrote Hunter for the record, "how Stilwell and Merrill could have failed to project their plans beyond the continuation of the attack on the airstrip, to include the city."[167] The state of supplies alone indicated an utter dearth of foresight. On the twentieth of May, according to the official CBI history, "the Allied forces had three days' rations on hand, very little mortar ammunition, and only 350 rounds of 75-mm, shells. . . . By the end of May the quartermaster had no U.S. rations"—this despite the flotilla of incoming aircraft.[168] It is as if Stilwell—and Merrill—had regarded the capture of the airstrip as a "capture the flag" war game; that once the winning team claimed its prize it could stroll back to base amid hearty backslapping for a warm bath and good meal. Within days, awareness of his actual situation began to penetrate Stilwell's consciousness. "Cannon in from Mitch [Myitkyina]. Bad news. Panic in 150th They ran away & had to be taken out," Stilwell wrote worriedly in his diary on

May 21. "What goes on at Mitch? . . . (A bad day, mentally. Good deal of strain & worry. If the troops are undependable, where are we? I'm looking forward to a full stop on this business, Wish it would pour right now.)"[169]

The dawning awareness that, despite every advantage his army enjoyed, he could still lose Myitkyina, brought out the worst in Stilwell's embittered character. "He was extremely caustic to his American commanders, accusing them of not fighting," Slim wrote of this period of "great disappointment to Stilwell." As Stilwell desperately thrashed around for more troops, his terse diary entries indicate the situation in which he found himself and his choices:

> Black Monday. Bad news from Mitch. Now they saw 800 japs got into Charpati* last night. And 200 crossed river from east. McC†
> says "situation is critical." Not a thing I can do. It has rained heavily all A.M. We can't get troops in. Also, the field is in bad shape at Mitch. . . . General air of discouragement down there. And of course corresponding worry here. We've got to sweat it out but it's no fun. [Q. Ask of 36th Br. Div? No. Get Pick's engineers? Yes. At least alert them, & use as replacements for Galahad.][170]

The 36th Division was a veteran, well-rested British force that had, moreover, an American-led Chinese artillery group attached to it, as well as an American engineering company for building landing strips for air evacuation and resupply—but asking for this would mean being bailed out by the British ("No").[171] Yet, as Stilwell now recognized, "replacements for Galahad" were urgently needed, for by this time the Marauders were vanishing, literally, being evacuated at a rate of up to a hundred men a day due to debilitating illness. Increasingly, cases of the deadly

---

*Or Charpate, a village on the Mogaung Road some four miles north of Myitkyina.

†Colonel John E. McCammon, commander of the Myitkyina Task Force for the eight-day period from May 22–30.

scrub typhus were being reported, and some 80 percent of all men suf-fered some form of dysentery.[172] In desperation, Stilwell grasped at the only other Americans anywhere at hand—General Pick's engineers build-ing the Ledo Road; "I will probably have to use some of our engineer units to keep an American flavor in the fight," he wrote to Marshall, and beginning from as early as May 26, two engineer combat battalions (the 209th and 236th) were flown in from Ledo. The realization that the siege of Myitkyina would be lengthy triggered a call for yet more reinforce-ments, and 2,600 volunteers were rushed out from the US without infan-try training. Jack Bell, a reporter from the *Miami Herald*, was in Myitkyina to describe their arrival: this was not a trained infantry outfit, he wrote, "but an assortment of cooks, quartermaster men, artillery men, signal corps men, band men, and some infantry men from one division. They tell, and bitterly, too, how they were herded onto the ship, not knowing who their officers were with no semblance of organization."[173] Officers accompanying them on the planes to Myitkyina later stated on record that the men had set out without having had "their first initiation into the mechanical functioning of the M-1 rifle."[174] Nonetheless, forty days after embarking on the troop ship that carried the men from the US to Bombay, they were disgorged into the monsoon and muddy combat field of Upper Burma.

The engineers, who, in the words of the army's CBI history, "had not seen a rifle since their basic training days," the "New Galahad" battal-ions (also to be known as Mars Force), the weak and ailing remaining Galahad veterans, and the Chinese units, also weakened by their long jungle journey, together now formed a chaotic, semi-trained, yet numer-ically massive army.[175] The monsoon poured down rain, making air sup-ply drops difficult and erratic. Command of the Myitkyina Task Force lurched from officer to officer, and Hunter submitted to Stilwell, in per-son, a formal letter of complaint about the treatment of Galahad and its management.[176] The urgent need to reinforce the Chinese troops had con-tinued unabated, and "American reinforcements of any men who could hold a rifle were rushed in from every possible source," as the official army

CBI history states.[177] This included the convalescent Marauders, who by early June had suffered a complete breakdown, moral and physical, as a unit. They had fought in seven major and thirty-five minor engagements while marching nearly eight hundred miles through jungle, swamp, and mountains; of their one-hundred-day campaign, an estimated sixty days were spent engaging the enemy. Of the original 3,000 men, 1,970 had died, were wounded, or were very ill, with amoebic dysentery claiming the greatest number; of the remainder, only 200 were regarded as fit to remain at Myitkyina.[178] Nonetheless, as the CBI history reports, "[e]xtremely heavy moral pressure, just short of outright orders, was placed on medical officers to return to duty or keep in the line every American who could pull a trigger."[179] One of the doctors, in written testimony forwarded to the surgeon general, described finding, among the men culled from the convalescent wards and delivered to the Myitkyina airstrip, eight "with fevers ranging from 100 to 104 and several men . . . whose wounds were still draining, and one man who had an abdominal operation less than three weeks before and with the skin incision still quite raw," while another, "a veteran of the last war," had clear symptoms of "evident cardiac pathology."[180] On one occasion, Ogburn recalled, when "several hundred of us [had been] loaded in trucks, the medical officers took after the convoy in jeeps, intercepted it, and forced it to return."[181]

Dug in around the Myitkyina airstrips and town were the remnants of the Japanese 18th Division, the "toughest and most experienced fighters in Asia"—the words are Ogburn's; another American officer called them the "magnificent 18th."[182] Reduced to half their strength by casualties and disease, vastly outnumbered, and perilously low on supplies of all kind, their sole advantage was that they held their own base.[183] This was defended by well-placed trenches and raised roads built up around the nearby flooded paddy fields to form breastworks, with houses and railcars for shelter and concealment, and, abutting the town, a deeply flooded field over which their guns had clear sight.[184] Against this, three Chinese regiments were entrenched on the west and southern edges of the town, with Marauders and engineer regiments holding the approaches from the north. The winding Irrawaddy River lay to the east and, at a deep bend in its course, to the south, where American engineers were setting up a ferry operation.[185]

For blocking and holding the outlying supply roads leading into My-itkyina, Stilwell now, despite his aversion to seeking British aid, placed heavy reliance on the Chindits. On the day he had taken the airfield, Slim, recognizing "the need for intimate and daily tactical co-ordination be-tween Lentaigne's and Stilwell's forces," had placed "three mobile Chindit brigades and their stronghold troops"—officially known as the 3rd Indian Division—under Stilwell's direct command.[186] Gloating over the seizure of the airfield, Stilwell had noted this gesture in his diary on May 17: "Radio from Slim, telling me how to run the 3d Ind. Div. Answered po-litely that he could stick the 3d Ind. Div up his ass."[187] But a few days in a fast-moving situation can bring a sea change, and Stilwell now grasped at these brigades.

The Chindit brigades had previously received orders to establish a "block," codenamed Blackpool, south of the town of Mogaung at the junction of the Ledo valley track and Myitkyina roads, so as to cut and hold the rail line that ran through the Mogaung Valley—the "Railway Valley"—from Rangoon to Myitkyina, and to hold it until June 1. By this time, the Chinese forces would have broken through the Japanese front at Kamaing to the north, and the Chindits and Chinese would meet on the Mogaung–Myitkyina line—so it was planned. The Chindits' role would then be over and they could be withdrawn, just as their ninety-day limit was expiring. The campaign called for one brigade, under the command of John Masters, to establish the block and develop it into a stronghold, a second to capture Mogaung, while a third mobile "floater brigade" was to march north to support Masters, to be joined later by a fourth brigade, the West African.[188] The plan marked a departure from the old Chin-dit tactics of operating as independent mobile columns, disappearing guerrilla-style into the jungle when the enemy was stung, and relocating "strongholds" as the need arose; the new orders were offensive, to trap and crush the worn-out Japanese 53rd Division that was advancing from northern Malaya to protect the rail line and reinforce the 18th Division.[189] None of the Chindits knew of Stilwell's secret plan to make a run for Myitkyina.

By May 4, after a two-week march, Masters's brigade had reached the designated area and began the work of creating a fortification at a site overlooking the rail line. Airstrips and shelters had to be built, landing-light cables unfurled and installed, trenches and artillery pits dug. Once the gliders started landing, massive supplies—wire, mortar ammunition, medical supplies, food—had to be unloaded, carried, and stacked. As the men worked, enemy shells fired from the north floated languidly overhead, probing for a response. The expected attack came shortly, frenzied and determined, a sustained onslaught of shelling that began each dusk and lasted until a few hours before the dawn. Like the Marauders, Masters's men were exhausted and greatly reduced in strength from illness, but they rose to engage in a furious battle fought at close quarters with every type of firepower that could be mustered, from rifles to three-inch mortars. Then the Japanese pulled out their heavy guns, and soon the arena "looked like Passchendaele," as Masters recorded, a landscape of shattered trees and crater holes full of water, with the feet and twisted hands of the dead sticking from the earth, and the stench of the dead—hung on wires, draped on trees—overspreading everything. Out of a darkening sky, the monsoon broke. "At night the rain hissed down in total darkness, the trees ran with water," Masters wrote, "and beyond the devastation, the jungle dripped and crackled."[190] Yet, somewhat to Masters's amazement, ten days after the first assault, his brigade was "in sole ownership" of the block and its surrounds.[191] Around him were the many staggering wounded of his brigade; victors for the moment, their position was precarious. If the "floater" brigades arrived, they would be strongly reinforced; if the brigade holding to the north joined him, they could between them crush the inevitable returning Japanese force. If none of these happened—they would be highly vulnerable.

After a peaceful three-day lull, the Japanese returned, not in a frenzy as before, but steadily and purposeful—"professional." The needed support had not come, for the "floater" brigades were trapped elsewhere by rising rivers and the creeks that benignly threaded the jungle in the dry season but became torrents once the rains arrived. The monsoon closed down both land and sky, thwarting even the determined US pilots from making regular supply drops. Then, from down the valley, "above the pop and crackle of small arms fire," as Masters wrote, "I heard the one sound I had been expecting, and fearing, the sharp double crack of heavy anti-aircraft guns. Puffs of yellow-black smoke appeared behind one of the C-47s. They turned for home."[192] At dawn on May 25, the Japanese breached the main perimeter, overwhelming the Gurkhas at their position overlooking the airstrip. Three hours later, coldly assessing his situation, Masters signaled to Lentaigne and Stilwell his intention to withdraw.[193]

The retreat from Blackpool, bearing the wounded through the monsoon as they marched west and north toward the marshlands by the Indawgyi Lake for evacuation harshly revealed the condition of Masters's troops, and in so doing also the wisdom of his decision. As his men limped by him, hopping, carrying and supporting others, a doctor approached Masters. "Will you come with me, sir?" Down the path to which he was directed, Masters came to a group of stretcher-bearers, some also wounded, huddled in dripping stands of bamboo, and on the path itself a line of stretchers, "and on each stretcher," Masters wrote, "a soldier of 111 Brigade." A soldier with only a bloody hollow between his chest and pelvis where his stomach should have been; another with no legs, no hips; another with no left arm, no shoulder, no left breast; another with no face. . . . "I've got another thirty on ahead, who can be saved, if we can carry them," the doctor said. "These men have no chance. They're full of morphia. . . . Not one chance at all, sir, I give you my word of honour." A brutal exchange followed: "Very well. I don't want them to see any Japanese." "We can't spare any more morphia." "Give it to those whose eyes are open." Masters moved on; "one by one, carbine shots exploded curtly behind me. I put my hands to my ears but nothing could shut out the sound."[194]

Stilwell's rage on receiving news that the 111th Brigade had withdrawn was unbounded: it had arrived at the exact moment he had begun to realize his own vulnerability at Myitkyina, and at the moment he was discussing with Lentaigne the necessity of holding Blackpool at all costs to prevent Japanese reinforcement.[195] Why couldn't the Chindits fight like the Marauders, Stilwell demanded of Lentaigne? ("Br[itish] working like hell to give up and get out before the monsoons," Stilwell's son-in-law and executive assistant Colonel Ernest Easterbrook had written in his diary while Masters's brigade was deep in Broadway. "[T]he 'tired 77th' and other two valiant brigades must retire when the weather gets nasty.")[196] Stepping in to smooth over "the Siege of Troy atmosphere, with commanders sulking in their tents," Slim persuaded Stilwell to allow the Chindits time to regroup, and Lentaigne to keep the force on "until Myitkyina falls," which was expected by mid-June.[197]

But Myitkyina did not fall in June, nor in July. The Chindits were not withdrawn, but received orders to move farther north and operate against the Japanese west of Mogaung. An endless parade of events followed, blurred by rain and exhaustion—shelling, hauling supplies, mud, rain, fewer men and fewer stoic mules, failure of air supply, rain, and rain. "What horrified me," wrote Masters, "was the absolute lack of reserve strength in the men's bodies. Beginning about June 1, a man with a cut finger would probably show anemia; then the cut would go bad; then his whole body would droop, and in a day or two, he would die."[198] Men collapsed and died of malaria, of the cold, of jungle sores, of foot rot. On June 27, the Chindits' 77th Brigade captured Mogaung—the first town in Burma to be retaken. Given its position at the junction of the rail line and unfolding Ledo Road, the capture of this key town ensured that the land route to India, such as it was, was open, and the capture of Myitkyina assured.[199]

Like the Marauders before him, Masters urgently requested a medical examination of his men, which, as for the Marauders, Stilwell refused.[200] Mike Calvert, commander of the 77th Brigade, took matters into his own hands, packed up his radio so that no further orders could be received, and marched his men out, prepared to face court-martial.[201] Shortly after, Mountbatten intervened and gave orders that the requested medical assessment take place. From July 17, over three days, "at nameless spots in the jungle," as Masters recorded, every remaining man in his brigade was examined. "The strength of my four and a half battalions then totalled about 2,200 men," he wrote. "Those adjudged fit for any kind of action, in any theatre of operations, numbered 118, being 7 British officers, a score of British soldiers, and 90 Gurkhas."[202]

MYITKYINA FELL AT LAST ON AUGUST 3, AFTER SEVENTY-EIGHT DAYS OF SIEGE, by which time the embattled 18th Division had lost all artillery and was rationing ammunition, since, lacking air support, they could not be re-supplied. Of the division's original strength of 10,000 men, a third had been killed, some 1,800 wounded, and the rest were as weakened with illness as their Allied counterparts.[203] For two months and sixteen days, the Japanese had held up a force as much as ten times their own numbers and which was backed by the most powerful air force in the world.[204] At the end of July, Colonel Maruyama, whose orders had been to secure "vital areas" around Myitkyina, requested of the garrison's commander, Major General Genzô Mizukami, that his regiment be allowed to withdraw east of the Irrawaddy so as to spare their lives. Tasked to defend Myitky-ina to the death, Mizukami had intended to fight to the end, but putting his men ahead of his pride, he agreed. The wounded were evacuated by raft down the Irrawaddy River over three nights, and the garrison was or-dered to withdraw. Retreating with his company to the river, Mizukami halted on an island that fell within the perimeter of the town, remaining there among the trees as the others made their way to the water. Dawn broke as light rain fell, and propped against a tree, facing north-east toward Japan, Mizukami committed ritual suicide. Falling within the strict limits of the town, he had fulfilled his duties as an officer and soldier and defended Myitkyina until his death.[205] Veterans and historians often remark on the fanaticism of the Japanese military, its ruthless dis-regard for casualties or suffering in the relentless pursuit of an objective;

but in these campaigns in Burma, two Japanese generals, at Imphal and at Myitkyina, released their men to live another day. It was the men under Stilwell who had to be wrested from their general's grasp.

Those Marauders who had not been kept in the field were by now convalescing at a rest camp that fell far short of what they had expected, being a rough pasture surrounded by *bashas* "in which cows would not have been stalled at home," as Ogburn wrote. A length of rusty pipe and oil drums made a shower; the heat was stifling; the coolest drink available a "tepid tea."[206] More relevant than the litany of complaints, some of which were petty, was the evident hatred simmering beneath them. Thirty American-trained Chinese divisions were in Yunnan; Stilwell had close to fifty thousand Chinese troops in India and Burma—why then had the Marauders been run so hard? Stilwell had relied on them to make his "end run" and they could justly claim to be responsible for his success; yet questions were being asked in the US press about their moral breakdown. Within the camp, the anger of a few exploded into dangerous violence to the extent that the safety of visitors could not be assured. On one occasion, receiving an urgent summons, Ogburn rushed to the camp's small Red Cross canteen to find two of his enlisted men, fueled by a local brew that was laced with marijuana, "well on the way to demolishing the place. Two horrified Red Cross girls were backed against the far end, while the two drunks hurled plates and shouted obscenities as extreme as I had ever heard."[207] The hatred for Stilwell had become murderous. "I had him in my rifle sights," an enlisted man confessed of an occasion when Stilwell had visited Myitkyina. "I coulda squeezed one off and no one woulda known it wasn't a Jap that got the son-of-a-bitch."[208] The Marauders had not so much broken down as mutinied.

Despite the severe censorship placed on all US press regarding anything to do with China, word of the Marauders' condition seeped out. "Marauders' Morale Broken by Hospital Faults, Promises," ran a *Washington Post* headline on August 6, days after the news that Myitkyina had fallen.[209] Prompted by Hunter's letter and the doctors' reports, a congressional investigation was undertaken, which found that there had been an "almost complete breakdown of morale in the major portion of the unit."[210] The report was not rigorous, however, nor were its findings made public.[211] To head off a looming storm of public inquiry, Merrill himself was flown to Washington for press conferences, which he handled adroitly.[212] Yes, he acknowledged that there had been "a temporary break in the morale of his celebrated jungle fighters," as *The New York Times* (among other press) reported, but the whole business, he gave reassurance, amounted to a "storm in a tea pot" that had already blown over. As for the reports that ill and incapacitated Marauders had been ordered to fight, this had been the result of "misinterpretation of an order for reinforcements"—an order, moreover from a "local commander," meaning Hunter, who was otherwise not mentioned. In any case, Merrill declared, he was "positive that if we had asked for volunteers every one of them would have gone back."[213]

In India and Burma, the facts could not be so easily rearranged. The men who worked on the Ledo Road had vivid memories of seeing the Marauders march out "with long easy strides," and were there to see the depleted Marauders on their return.[214] "The men of this unit I will never forget," recalled Private Blue, 518th Quartermasters (Truck) Battalion. "Their camouflage clothing was torn and dirty; their boots worn. . . . Around the eyes, all of Merrill's men looked alike no matter what their coloring; they had the eyes of dead men. . . . These guerilla fighters took up with blacks in the area. I guess there was a natural empathy; we were at the bottom of the barrel and they had finally reached it. They couldn't stand the griping of the white soldiers about trivials such as the food, pay and their duties. The brief time they were in Assam they spent with us. They seemed to want to talk, to have someone listen to what had happened to them before they choked on it."[215]

Word of what had really happened at Myitkyina was also carried with aircrews over the Hump. "Had an interesting talk at Gaya by a liaison officer between Americans and Chinese," pilot Peter Dominick recorded in his diary. "Face means a lot, so if [the Chinese troops] are ordered to take a certain position they always claim they have whether they actually have or not. The Americans at Myitkyina didn't realize this at first and would rely on the word that the Chinese had captured the position and thereby get outflanked. . . . One of Seagroves' doctors was there as well as one of Merrill's Marauders, so it was pretty interesting."[216] Receiving far less attention was the condition of the Chinese forces, some of whom had been on the march since October 1943. In early June, a divisional commander pointed out that they could muster only 1,000 men between two regiments, and that they were taking casualties, as the official CBI history states, at the rate of "121 on a comparatively quiet day."[217] The capture of Myitkyina cost an estimated 972 Chinese killed and 3,184 wounded, bringing total Chinese casualties for the north Burma campaign to an estimated 2,422 killed and 6,634 wounded.[218]

Stilwell, meanwhile, was in Ceylon, at the relocated SEAC headquarters in Kandy, where he had arrived at the end of July to stand in for Mountbatten, who was away in London. News of Myitkyina's eventual fall reached him there, allowing him to bask in glory. "Radio about Myitkyina," he wrote in his diary on August 4. "Over at last. . . . Thank God. Not a worry in the world this A.M."; but, he continued sourly, "B.B.C. dragged in the God damn chindits on Mitch."[219] Officially regarded, the taking of Myitkyina, as the US Army history summarized events, was "a feat of triumph for the man who had maintained it could be done," adding— since it was easy to forget—that the "town was taken to make possible an intensified air effort from bases in China to support U.S. operations in the Pacific."[220]

Unfortunately, events had overtaken this objective, for in the spring, while China's best-equipped and -trained armies were engaged in Burma, the Japanese had launched a massive offensive—Operation Ichigo, or Operation Number One—striking south from their hub in Hankow to pick off one by one Chennault's Fourteenth Air Force's painstakingly built and stocked forward bases in east China. According to postwar intelligence, the assault on the air bases was motivated in part by the Fourteenth Air Force's successful hampering of the Japanese army's ability to supply Hankow; it was a retaliatory development Stilwell had long prophesied.[221] With few exceptions, such as the heroic defense of the walled city of Hengyang, Chinese forces tasked to defend the air bases had melted away. The Japanese army's conquests left the enemy in possession of a corridor that led from Peking to French Indochina, while also dealing a blow to Allied plans to strike Japan from the mainland.[222]

In July, following the loss of the air bases, the alarmed Joint Chiefs sent Roosevelt a strongly worded memo that warned of the imminent loss of the B-29 staging base at Chengtu. It also reminded the president that the "pressure on us from the Generalissimo throughout the war has been to increase the tonnage over the Hump for Chennault's air in particular"; it was now apparent, however, that "Chennault's air alone can do little more than slightly delay the Japanese advances." The Joint Chiefs' solution was breathtaking: that the president should push Chiang "to place General Stilwell in command of all Chinese armed forces." These would include not only the Nationalist army, but also the growing, well-organized Communist forces in the north, whose headquarters in Yenan American delegations had been warily circling since the summer—an initiative that Stilwell had strongly endorsed.[223] "During this war," the Joint Chiefs' memo stated, "there has been only one man who has been able to get Chinese forces to fight the Japanese in an effective way. That man is General Stilwell."[224] In acquiescence, Roosevelt sent a telegram to the generalissimo stating the urgent need "for the delegation to one individual of the power to coordinate all the Allied military resources in China, including the Communist forces." As a token of his faith in Stilwell, Roosevelt added, Stilwell was being promoted "to the rank of full general," with four stars.[225] The memo marked a complete reversal of American strategy, from the symbolic offer of Lend-Lease supplies with no strings attached, to the demand that an American general command all of China's armies.

Over the next couple of months, Chiang balanced the appearance of compliance with the president's demands against leveraging of his own, including the stipulation that he have full control over Lend-Lease supplies. Of more immediate concern, he also threatened to withdraw his Y-Force troops, then engaged in a battle to regain Lungling, a Chinese town located near the near the junction of the Ledo and old Burma Roads, and the only point on the whole road trace that the Japanese still controlled.[226] The president's stern reply to Chiang's threats, written in a new tone of command, arrived in Chungking on September 19 and was placed in Stilwell's hands. Seeing at a glance that this was as "hot as a firecracker," Stilwell gleefully decided to deliver the message to Chiang himself.[227] Brushing aside pleas from Roosevelt's special representative, Patrick Hurley, to paraphrase the message and tone it done, Stilwell confronted Chiang as he was meeting with a small group of generals, advisers, and members of his National Military Council. Deftly and desperately, Hurley handed Chiang a Chinese-language translation so that he could at least read in privacy Roosevelt's rebuke of him, his armed forces, and his imminent loss of China unless General Stilwell was given "unrestricted command of all your forces."[228]

The ensuing scene has become a set piece in the history of US relations in China: Chiang quietly putting the letter down and inverting his empty teacup on the table. "That gesture still means, I presume, that the party's over?" Stilwell asked, referring to the turning over of the cup, and a Chinese officer nodded yes. Stilwell and Hurley left the room, followed shortly by Chiang's officers. Alone with his brother-in-law, T. V. Soong, so instrumental in this American adventure from the beginning, Chiang burst into "compulsive and stormy sobbing" and declared that Stilwell would have to leave.[229] Chiang had demanded Stilwell's recall on other occasions, but this time he would not back down, despite Roosevelt's reminding him of the "great sacrifices" the Allies had made to support him: "General MacArthur's urgent requirements for air transport have not been met. General Wilson in Italy has not had the transport planes he needs. The situation in Holland now hangs in the balance, and the outcome depends largely upon adequate support by air. . . ." Chiang was not moved, and at last, on October 18, Roosevelt informed him he was "issuing instructions to recall Stilwell."[230] The story for the American public was that Stilwell was leaving China due to a command reshuffle.[231]

The official narrative of both Stilwell's triumph and his downfall at the hands of Chiang Kai-shek has a number of curious details, beginning with Stilwell's visit to Kandy to cover for Mountbatten as Myitkyina fell. Mountbatten's duties had taken him elsewhere before, and it had never been thought necessary for his deputy to "cover" for him—why now? Years after the war, Stilwell's aide-de-camp, Colonel Richard Young, discussing the final days of Myitkyina, stated that by "that time Gen. Stilwell was exhausted, day and night constant problems and so Gen. Marshall said that Gen. Stilwell should get a rest, a few weeks rest, and sent him to Candi [sic] in Ceylon."[232] Was Stilwell, then, showing concerning signs of fatigue? Later events would suggest he was indeed ill at this time, but were there also worries for his mental health?[233] By this time, the reports from Colonel Hunter and the Marauders' doctors were making inroads in the press, and Washington in general. It was highly undesirable, especially in a presidential election year, that the debacle at Myitkyina be exposed. By Marshall's own account, the US press had built up Stilwell to the extent that it was impolitic for his own government to recall him—as a number of Americans in China (including visiting Vice President Henry Wallace) were now urging—and unraveling the narrative that had been so carefully spun would require some care. Did Roosevelt intentionally authorize the memo to Chiang with its wholly unrealistic demands—that Nationalists and Communists join together under the command of Stilwell, whom Chiang detested and mistrusted—knowing that they would be rejected? Was Stilwell's extraordinary promotion to a four-star general—joining the ranks of Marshall, Eisenhower, and Arnold—really to impress Chiang? Or was this an example of an old gambit—that as a prelude to a sensitive firing one kicks the person in question up the stairs? Chiang's demand for Stilwell's recall would serve to demonstrate to the American public the extent of Chiang's intransigence and help the White House distance itself from culpability in the event that China did in fact collapse.[234] In India, Stilwell's replacement, General Albert Wedemeyer, was told that "the British also had something to do with Stilwell's relief."[235] British anger at Stilwell's treatment of the Chindits ran high, and in early November Parliament made the extraordinary motion "to declare

General Stilwell persona non grata in any war theatre where British officers and men are serving."[236] Such threads of evidence suggest that Chiang
Kai-shek's demand was not the sole, or even major, reason for Stilwell's
recall, but the culmination of a process already underway.

THE DRAMA OF STILWELL AND THE OPERATION IN NORTH BURMA TEND TO
obscure the real achievements in this chapter of the extraordinarily difficult Second Burma Campaign. With the victories at Imphal and Kohima, Slim's Fourteenth Army had turned the tide of this long battle and
was in aggressive pursuit of the Japanese across the Irrawaddy. This victory was made possible, however, by what had happened in the air. Sum-
ming up the highlights of the series of operations, Masters singled out the
overall leadership of the US Air Force and RAF: "[I]n supplying China
over the Hump, in getting food and ammunition to divisions and brigades
cut off by the Japanese, in ferrying reinforcements hundreds of miles at
a moment's notice, in keeping the Chindits operating in their scattered
groups all over North Burma—all this in the worst of the monsoon—was
the one faultless operation of the campaign."[237] British memoirs of the
Chindit campaign in particular pay unstinting tribute to the American
airmen. "We would never have come anywhere near to success morally,
physically or materially without the ever-present U.S.A.A.F. who supplied
us, and, in the Mogaung death-trap, probably destroyed more enemy than
we did," wrote Brigadier Mike Calvert, commander of the 77th Brigade
that captured Mogaung. "They used to come over cheerfully again and
again with the quiet drawl, 'What's the target?'"[238]

General Arnold, when briefing Cochran and Alison, the co-commanders
of the newly formed 1st Air Commando, had tasked them to deliver "the
fullest American participation in Wingate's show . . . everything that a
bright airman could think of."[239] True to their orders, the Air Commando
pilots had pulled off a range of landmark innovations in this backwater
campaign. Slim's plan to defeat the Japanese by retreating into Imphal
depended entirely upon air supply, and air supply blunted the Japanese

tactic of encirclement, enabling a surrounded force to stand its ground.[240] Light planes had developed a range of techniques and skills in evacuation of the wounded. The Second Burma Campaign saw the first combat rescue by helicopter—the evacuation from the jungle over two days of a downed American pilot and three wounded British soldiers by a Sikorsky-built R-4.[241]

Both Cochran and Alison had left their briefing convinced that Arnold had also signaled to them a mission beyond his actual words. "General Arnold seemed to say: 'Who can tell? It might turn into an air show,'" Alison recalled. Cochran was more forthright: "I, personally, read into General Arnold's words a thing that actually he never said—'Go over and steal that show.'"[242] And judging by the evidence and tributes, it would seem they did.

9

END OF THE ROAD

The north Burma campaign took a heavy toll on aircraft, mostly on the bombers and fighters, but also to a lesser extent on the transport planes that had been diverted from the Hump to make supply drops. At least fifteen C-46s and C-47s were lost to enemy air fire and to accidents directly related to their missions, for example clipping the trees while attempting a low pass over a target site.[1] In early April, shortly after having been checked out as a C-47 first pilot, Bob Boody had two close encounters with enemy ground fire in two days while supplying the Marauders, returning to base after his second encounter with four bullets in his aircraft's fuselage. But the accident that finally caught him was more banal, and a reminder of the routine hazards of aviation.

On April 5, Boody had already completed one uneventful supply mission into the Hukawng Valley, when he returned to Dinjan to find that a delivery of priority cargo destined for the Marauders had been canceled due to weather. Despite the low-hanging clouds over the Naga Hills, Boody was confident, as he wrote in his diary, "that at least one more flight"—his one-hundred-sixteenth combat mission—"could safely be completed that day before the ceiling closed in."[2] Having assembled his crew, Boody prepared for takeoff, but halfway down the runway realized that the elevator and rudder chocks, used when an aircraft is on the ground to prevent wind-gust movement, had not been removed and the controls were locked—a shocking oversight. Braking quickly, Boody halted the plane, the chocks were removed, and he was cleared by the tower to proceed again. On the second attempt, flying in the first pilot's left seat, Boody pushed the two throttles fully forward with his right hand while holding the control column with his left. His copilot was supposed to tighten a knob behind the throttles to keep them from vibrating backward. But because the copilot did not immediately perform this act, and because the noise of the engine drowned out Boody's voice, Boody signaled with his hand, making "a circling motion with my right index finger to remind him to do so," Boody recorded. "He mistook my circling hand signal for a 'gear-up' signal (right thumb up with fist clenched) and immediately pulled up the landing-gear lever, too soon, before we were airborne."[3]

As the plane hit the runway, both propellers broke off and spun to the right, with the left prop blade cutting through the cockpit and into Boody's leg. "I yelled 'it's gone; I know it's gone!'—before I passed out." Dragged through the hole in the cockpit, Boody was dosed with morphia and taken to the Dinjin infirmary, then rushed by ambulance down a potholed dirt road to the hospital at Chabua. Meanwhile, his fiancée, Jean Parks, was notified and flown to Chabua from the evacuation hospital at Shingbwiyang, where she was stationed.[4]

After seven days in a coma, Boody was awakened to be told that he would either have to have his left foot removed above the ankle or die of gangrene poisoning. He chose to live, and using ice-pack anesthesia, the doctor "from my home-town of Staten Island, N.Y., did the necessary work—I screamed while they were doing it," Boody confided to his diary; "—but I consider them among my very good friends who enabled me to come back up again 'out of the valley of the shadow of death.'"[5] Commuting back and forth from Shingbwiyang to Chabua to be at his bedside was Jean. On the first day of May, Boody woke in the early morning to find her beside him, and hours later she was riding with him in an ambulance to the air base, where he was to be loaded onto a hospital plane bound for Calcutta. And so, planeside and on this cool and rainy day, they had parted.[6]

Throughout the months that transport pilots like Boody were diverted from their normal duties to combat missions, the majority of pilots had continued to deliver their cargos over the Hump. During the long north Burma campaign, transport crews had delivered an average of some twelve thousand tons a month to China. After the fall of Myitkyina, this monthly figure had leapt and in November alone an astonishing thirty-five thousand tons were delivered over the Hump.[7]

"During every hour of every day in November, a fully loaded ICD transport landed on a Chinese airport from India every five minutes," as the India-China Division reported with some self awe. "This round-the-clock record operation produced 8,269 trips to China for the month."[8] During the same ten-month period there had also been 301 major accidents, not including eighty-five bombers lost, many of which were serving as transports by carrying fuel.[9] Few of these accidents and losses were due to enemy action; "[t]he Hump was the arch villain," was the assessment of the ACT historian for 1944. "Pilot error" accounted for the greatest number of accidents, a category that encompassed anything from a pilot becoming hypoxic to getting lost in weather ("nothing could be fairer than to call it pilot error," as the cynical pilots' refrain goes), with the second greatest cause being "Other."[10]

Behind these statistics lay many small epics. A C-46 returning to Chabua from Kunming had engine trouble, causing its five-member crew to bail out over Japanese-held territory, where they were captured (the copilot later died as a prisoner of war); a C-46 carrying a heavy load of ammunition caught fire en route to Kunming—all bailed except the captain, who "rode on in an effort to save the aircraft" and went down with the plane; a C-46 collided in midair with a B-24 bomber coming out of Jorhat; a C-46 en route from Chabua to Kunming and carrying eleven passengers experienced undetermined problems that caused everyone to bail out— all but the radio operator walked out of the jungle, but the copilot was gored by an elephant; a C-46 was caught in a powerful downdraft and the pilot ordered the crew to bail—the badly burned engineer was rescued by a Kachin man named Yo Yin, who took him to a cave in the mountains to recover and hide from the Japanese; a C-46 returning from Kunming got lost in a storm as it came in to land at Misamari, and the crew's last radio contact was recorded:

> **Aircraft #724:** We are at 8,000 feet can you see my lights? Can you see my lights! We are still in rain.
>
> **Tower:** Negative on the lights.
>
> **Aircraft #724:** TC. TC. There's that mountain again (30 second interval) Oh! We may hit it yet (Noise like lightning a few seconds later).[11]

In fact, flying the Hump had become much safer, mostly due to a change in management. In September 1943, Brigadier General Hardin had been replaced by Lieutenant General William Tunner, director of the Ferrying Division of the Air Transport Command, who had helped build the Ferrying Division from its outset. Tunner's father was Austrian, "a newcomer to America," as Tunner described him in his memoir, and had struggled to support his large family. At the age of fifteen, young Tunner received a scholarship to West Point, which he entered at age seventeen. His memoir presents a portrait of a disciplined, detail-oriented, hardworking, businesslike military professional, confident and even complacent. "Major General Tunner played so important a part in the Command's history that it is fitting to stop and take a look at him," a historian of the ATC wrote. "An unusually handsome man, cold in his manner except with a few intimates, somewhat arrogant, brilliant, competent, he was the kind of officer whom a junior officer is well advised to salute when approaching his desk." One can be sure Tunner approved of this characterization, since he reproduced it (at greater length) in his own memoir.[12]

Arriving for the first time in Chabua in early August 1944, Tunner at once noticed great black blotches at the end of the runway. "I knew too well what they were," he recalled. "Each was a lasting memorial to a group of American airmen, the crew of the plane that had crashed and burned on the spot."[13] The next thing he noted was the general slovenliness—of living conditions, sanitation, food, of the personnel's dress and demeanor. The CBI theater, he was made to recall, "was the place to which you ex-iled officers you wanted to get rid of."[14] Off-duty men lounged around or sprawled in front of their *bashas* playing cards or listlessly thumbing through magazines; none greeted him, let alone saluted. The men were unkempt—unshaved and wearing dirty, worn clothing. Diseases such as malaria, dysentery, and upper respiratory infections were rife. Briskly, Tunner embarked on a cleanup campaign, from blasting mosquito-breeding grounds with DDT, to establishing regular inspections of men and their quarters and holding parade drills.[15]

Of more importance, Tunner began to gather statistics, actual data relating to every aspect of the Hump operation. What airfields had the most accidents? What type of aircraft had the most accidents? What was the weather for each accident? Was there a pattern? How many flying hours did each member of a crew have? Who checked out the pilot who had an accident? What had the pilot of an accident been doing in the forty-eight hours previous to an accident? Were pilots flying too much? Were they not flying enough?[16] Out of this mass of statistics came a welter of reforms, from establishing assembly-line efficiency for regular maintenance of air-craft, to adjusting the hours and length of service a pilot had to fly be-fore rotating out. Previously, pilots needed 650 hours to leave, which they would cram into as short a space as possible so as to get home as soon as they could. Tunner's rule called for an increase to 750 hours over a ser-vice period of one year; the rule "didn't make the pilots happy," as Tun-ner conceded, "but with no longer any need to average more than 65 hours per month . . . it kept quite a few of them alive."[17] To address the low morale that was the general state of mind throughout all the bases, Tunner introduced an array of diverting activities as varied as vegetable gardening and theatrical entertainment. These last were mostly amateur shows, but real talent was also discovered and exploited, such as singer

Sergeant Tony Martin, who had performed with Glenn Miller, and pianist Leonard Pennario, then only eighteen.[18] These measures worked to the extent that they made daily life more pleasant and interesting, but they could not eradicate a root cause of a pilot and crew's low morale, which was fear.

A stark expression of this fear came in November with the court-martial of a pilot who refused to fly. Captain John Okenfus, of the 1330th Army Air Force Base Unit in Jorhat, had, on the night of October 23, 1944, refused direct orders to make a flight to China and had stated that he wanted to "quit flying," in his words, "before it was too late."[19] Okenfus had been an experienced airman before coming to India, having learned to fly at Hadley Field in his native New Jersey, where he kept his own open biplane and, according to local press, "did a good deal of barnstorming" in his early twenties.[20] Later, he had worked as a charter pilot for wealthy South Florida families, at first independently, and then in 1941 as a member of a small air-charter business, Midet Aviation Corporation, which operated a triweekly seaplane service between West Palm Beach and the Bahamas.[21] Some seven months after joining Midet, he made unwelcome headlines by crash-landing a Gulfhawk biplane at Hadley Field when the plane's landing gear collapsed. Okenfus had come north to his former home base for the "Newark Airport rededication air show," as the local press reported, adding that he was well known at Hadley Field from his earlier flying days.[22] The Hadley Field crash was not his first publicly reported mishap, for in late 1938, when Okenfus was twenty-three, the regional press had reported more widely on another crash, this one into Newark Bay. The photograph accompanying the story shows a strapping young man—Okenfus was six foot one—standing with rolled-up trousers in shallow water, dredging parts of his plane.[23]

Okenfus had married in 1941 and joined the army in 1942, attached to the Ferry Command. A year after joining, he was in Palm Springs participating in an air show for a war bond fundraiser, delighting onlookers with a demonstration of "the kind of aerial weapons which are being unleashed against the Axis."[24] Then, toward the end of 1943, he made national headlines for piloting a C-87 as "the first flight of the longest air freight line in the world," from Patterson Field to India. The twenty-eight-thousand-mile, round-trip flight had taken twelve days and was the first of what was to be a regular, scheduled airfreight and passenger service—the "Fireball Express"—to overseas bases, ferrying specifically requested equipment and parts, and taking out damaged parts for repair.[25] Speaking to newsmen after the flight, Okenfus reported that he had "hit the tail end of a hurricane" near Puerto Rico, but the "C-87 plowed right through it."[26] So it was that John Okenfus had arrived in Assam in late July of 1944 with a somewhat dashing profile.

Court-martial proceedings began promptly at nine in the morning at Jorhat's on-base Red Cross Enlisted Men's Club, presumably because of the space it offered.[27] Summoned to attend the court-martial were all the officers who had been present to witness Okenfus's willful disobedience of the "lawful command from Lieutenant Colonel William S. Barksdale, Junior, his superior officer, to proceed as a crew member of a military aircraft from Jorhat, India, to Chengtu, China . . . on or about 23 October, 1944." Okenfus's refusal to fly was perhaps not unexpected, for very shortly after his arrival in Assam he had begun, repeatedly, to try to "get off flying status." His first attempt had been made in early August, at which point he had made about six flights over the Hump, when he approached Barksdale with the declaration that "he wanted to quit flying before it was too late." Barksdale had counseled him to "think about it for a couple of days," which Okenfus did, returning two or three days later to declare again that "he wanted to get off flying status." Sent to the flight surgeon for examination, Okenfus received fifteen days of leave, after which he returned to flying. But about a week afterward, he again approached Barksdale, this time over the phone, to say "he did not wish to fly the Hump anymore." This triggered a series of events that might well have induced Okenfus to believe that his bid would be successful. After Okenfus submitted his formal request for Removal from Flying Status, Barksdale informed him that "since undesirable traits of character were involved, his resignation would have to be 'for the good of the service.'"

The undesirable traits, as far as one can judge, seem to be Okenfus's continual complaining and unwillingness to fly. In any case, Okenfus complied, submitting his resignation for the good of the service on September 29, shortly after which his hopes were dashed when the commanding general of the India-China Division, namely General Tunner, directed that "no action would be taken thereon and that accused be restored to flying status."

As commanding officer of the base, Colonel Barksdale had the most official interaction with Okenfus. Barksdale himself had been in Jorhat just three weeks, and his swift assessment of conditions at the base on his arrival reveal a sympathetic attentiveness to the needs of his airmen. Having been received coolly in Calcutta by General Hardin, shortly to be recalled, and "like a cold fish in Jorhat," as he recorded in his diary, he found at Jorhat a "bad setup." Only two days after arrival, he was noting that "pilots are flying as high as 200 hours per month in hump operation. Strain too much." The food was "extremely poor, Everybody losing weight, PX consisted of a 2 x 4 room of toothpaste, shaving cream etc. Messes, looked and were terrible." Encouragingly, morale was not as bad as would be expected. Also shortly following his arrival was "Hardin Day," declared by some functionary to be a celebration of that much-disliked officer, an occasion that Barksdale described in the privacy of his diary as "a gross farce without purpose or meaning." By contrast, noting the day Tunner took over command of the India-China Division—September 1— he recorded an "[a]lmost immediate change in atmosphere."[28]

In short, Barksdale was the kind of officer that a disaffected pilot like Okenfus could have most hoped to find—one sympathetic to the needs of airmen and not at all in the thrall of hidebound officialdom. So far, Okenfus's actions had been within legal bounds; but on being informed that he had been restored to flying status, he had then inquired as to "the consequences if he refused to fly." A legal officer duly briefed him, and Okenfus returned to flight duty long enough to make three flights over the Hump, after which he recommenced his campaign for removal, this time by requesting a transfer to "some other type of flying." Causes of specific fears began to emerge. He would "fly the Hump in the daytime," he told Barksdale, but not at night, "indicating as his reason that he had seen two C-46 planes crash and catch fire in mid air." It is plausible that he had seen such disasters. Between the time of Okenfus's arrival in Jorhat in late July and August 10, the day of his first appeal, there had been a number of incidents matching his description: the wing of a C-46 had caught fire in midair in early August, while on the actual day of his appeal, a Jorhat-based C-46 had crashed into the side of a hill and been consumed in fire; additionally, there had been two similar C-47 crashes, one into the side of a hill, where its horrific fire had been observed by several aircrews passing over.[29]

Complicating Okenfus's case, however, were reports made by other airmen of comments he had made that indicated a more general dissatisfaction and arrogance: only kids out of school who didn't know better or fools flew the Hump; he wasn't going to fly anymore anywhere; he was a fully qualified pilot and was not going to fly as copilot; and so on. Matters had come to a head on the morning of October 22, when Okenfus failed to report for a scheduled flight. On Barksdale's direction, the operations officer, Major Frank Thornquest, presented Okenfus with written orders "to proceed at the proper time on a flight to Chengtu, China." On the afternoon of the following day, an order was prepared that directed that "the following named personnel would proceed to Chengtu, China and return at the proper time," giving the names of Second Lieutenant David L. Dobie as pilot, Okenfus as copilot, and two other members of the crew. Thornquest, accompanied by two other officers, no doubt as witnesses, then took the orders to Okenfus, who was at that time in the tent of a Major Charles McCain. There the orders were either held out to Okenfus, or handed to him, or placed on his lap or stomach where he was reclining— the witnesses it seems were not astute observers—and was asked: "[A]re you going to go or are you not going to go?" to which Okenfus, as all agreed, replied, "Hell no."

Among those listening to the court-martial proceedings was Second Lieutenant David L. Dobie, who, with Alphonse Pecukonis as copilot, had been told to stand by to take the Chengtu flight if, as was by now expected, Okenfus refused to fly. Dobie had begun as a civilian ferry pilot in the early Air Transport Command, and been commissioned to second lieutenant, in his words, because "they just decided they didn't want civilian pilots anymore." Before coming to India, he had delivered a wide variety of aircraft, from the long-range C-54 transports to bombers, to points across North America. Then, in January of 1944, he had been sent to Assam. Arriving in Jorhat, even as late as 1944, he found the base still being "settled." "When we first got there we were in tents. Old G.I tents," he recalled. "Then we got up-graded to British jungle tents, the double walled tents. It was out in the middle of a tea plantation, and it was pretty primitive." By the time of the court-martial, Dobie had been flying the C-87s and bombers full of fuel over the Hump for almost a year and had had his share of "scary times," including flying in lightning so bright it had threatened temporarily to blind him. On one flight over China, he had entered a "terrible, terrible thunderstorm, and hail." The pilot ahead of him lost his windshield and flew for two hours with the hail coming in. The whole crew "got all cut up and beat up," and the captain had a nervous breakdown.[30] In short, Dobie, as a veteran of the Hump at its worst, may not have had a great deal of sympathy for the loud-talking charter pilot from West Palm Beach; and most likely had even less when he and Pecukonis duly proceeded to take the flight Okenfus was afraid to fly.

At the court-martial, "over strenuous objections by the defense," the prosecution presented evidence, admissible under "the so-called character rule," that Okenfus had, over a three-month period, declared "his intent not to fly the Hump," thus demonstrating "the willful nature of the accused's disobedience." Consequently, Okenfus was found guilty of the charges brought against him and was sentenced "to be dismissed the service, to forfeit all pay and allowances due or to become due and to be confined to hard labor for three years." Shortly after, he was shipped back to the States and entered the US disciplinary barracks at Green Haven, in New York.[31]

There is no record of how, or if at all, such a case and verdict affected the pilots who continued to fly through the conditions that Okenfus feared. Refusal to obey orders being in any military circumstances a grave offense, Okenfus's sentence was not unduly severe; still, it stood as a warning to anyone who might have considered balking at taking off into a dark and turbulent night. The force of military discipline and the resolve of pilots, and indeed their crews, was fully tested some weeks later in early January of 1945, when the weather unleashed a protracted storm of a magnitude of ferocity never experienced by any of the pilots before or after, an event referred to by those who survived it as "That Night."

ON THE EVENING OF JANUARY 5, LIEUTENANT CARL CONSTEIN HAD STEPPED outside his *basha* at Chabua to check the weather before turning in; he was scheduled to make a run as copilot across the Hump early the next morning. "It was normal," he recalled, "mostly clear but with the usual cumulus clouds standing like night watchmen over the First Ridge." In the gray dawn light of the following day, he immediately sensed a change. "During the night, the world of the Hump had become something strange and foreign, never seen before." The sky had closed down, as if covered by a "huge gun-metal gray lid." Eyeing the sky as he walked toward the officers' mess with pilot Captain Henry, Constein remarked that it looked like an early monsoon.[32] "No, this isn't a monsoon sky," Henry replied, adding that he didn't like the look of it.[33] Weather forecast stations had been operating for some time in Calcutta and at the B-29 base in Chengtu, and since October 1944 an intrepid Weather Reconnaissance Squadron had been flying hazardous missions over the CBI's often-uncharted terrain and over the sea, gathering data that was supplemented by information from the British fleet in the Bay of Bengal.[34] Yet despite these efforts, a pilot's most useful information still came from the pilot and crew that had flown a route before him.

After filing a flight plan with operations, Constein and Henry climbed into their C-46—"number 634," as Constein would record, the plane etched in his memory—and took off for Chanyi, one of the forward bases northeast of Kunming. Immediately, the plane hit severe turbulence, causing both pilots to grab the control column. Rain and sleet began to strike the aircraft so hard that the sound of impact made it difficult for the pilots to hear each other. "Suddenly we hit an iron wall of even heavier rain," Constein recorded, "jolting us back in our seats." Ice was building on the wings and propellers, and the radio compass needles were spinning "like roulette wheels" as they chased the lightning. The first radio checkpoint, over Shingbwiyang, could not be detected. The turbulence grew more severe, tossing the aircraft wildly, and the indicated air speed jumped from 80 miles per hour to 200, then down again; the pilots were conscious that they were being pushed not only up and down but sideways. "Okay, it sounds crazy," Henry said. "I'm going to make the biggest correction you've ever seen." With winds coming from the south-southwest, instead of the usual west, at at least 100 miles per hour, he hoped to hold his route by pointing off course some thirty degrees south and avoid being driven into the high terrain to the north.[35]

As the day progressed, the weather got worse. When pilots Don Downie and William Hanahan trudged through the rain to Chabua's operation office ahead of their flight, it was beginning to get dark; amazingly, reports of what lay ahead had not come in, or been wholly taken in, and differed somewhat from base to base. "As we filed our flight clearances the big C-46s were landing frequently," Downie recorded. "They were getting back, so things couldn't have been too bad." The tired returning pilots spoke of rough weather and rime ice from ten thousand feet up, but not too bad, and China was "wide open." Taking off in the dusk, Downie piloted the plane through solid but smooth overcast, picking up only rime as he approached his assigned cruising altitude of 14,500 feet. Leveling off, he was mostly concerned about discomfort. This C-46 was an old plane, and rain was leaking into the cockpit. The heater didn't work. Copilot Hanahan was just out of flight school, and this was his first flight under actual instrument conditions.

But as the plane droned on through the rime-thick clouds toward Burma, the weather worsened, and at the First Ridge over the Naga Hills, it unleashed its violence. While the plane lurched, the radio operator tapped Downie on the shoulder to report that he had picked up a Mayday call from a crew that was about to bail out. Switching to the liaison receiver to listen, Downie heard through "crashing static" the radio operator of the stricken plane, his voice nervous but clear; "We are down to 12,000 feet and still dropping. Our left engine is dead." Outside, the heaving darkness of the night pressed against the shaken plane. Shining an Aldis signal light through the window, the pilots could see ice whirling on the propeller hubs and forming a glistening white ring around the carburetor air scoops. That ice was heavy on the wings, they already knew from the drop in aircraft speed. Still, the plane was flying on—but where were they? It had been two hours since they had taken a radio compass reading. "All usable radio frequencies were jammed with distress calls," Downie recorded. The radio compass gave only static, the compass needle was spinning wildly, chasing "scattered lightning discharges through the inky sky." The high peaks were to the north, so to be safe Downie pushed the plane south. At length, they picked up a station known to be fifty miles north of the route—with the compass indicating it was to the south. This, as copilot Hanahan realized, "meant we had flown very close to 14,500ft Mt. Tali while struggling to maintain altitude." Checking his charts, Downie could be more precise: "[S]omewhere about ten minutes back, we had flown three hundred feet above a peak we had never seen."[36]

Piloting a C-87 out of Tezpur to Luliang, pilot Joseph Plosser had also hit the weather over the First Ridge. With propellers spinning off ice and Saint Elmo's Fire, the big C-87 lurched onward over Burma, through the night. "As we approached Myitkyina at our cruising altitude of 18,000 feet," Plosser recalled, "we were suddenly sucked down two or three thousand feet, unable to hold altitude even with the engines set for maximum power. Then just as suddenly, we were propelled upward at 4,000 feet per minute right on through our assigned altitude to 22,000 feet. The turbulence was so violent we were having trouble keeping the airplane right side up.

Everything in the cockpit that was not secured, including a fire extinguisher, was flying through the air."[37]

Thomas Sykes was piloting a C-46 full of fuel drums when severe turbulence hit him, too, around Myitkyina. As whipping winds veered dramatically from an estimated one hundred twenty to over two hundred miles per hour, the plane was batted over the Salween area. Sleet, hail, and snow assailed the aircraft, which was being lifted and dropped two thousand feet up and down. "All four air-ground radio frequencies were Mayday and the radio operator was unable to send any position reports," Sykes reported. Then, as the plane rode at 17,500 feet, a sudden, violent downdraft and "lightning gust" from the south threw it on its side. "We were descending at 4,000ft a minute," Sykes recorded. "Full throttle was applied and after a great struggle, recovery was made at 14,000ft . . . below the minimum safe altitude in that area." The plane was not flying so much as being hurled—from the tops of peaks at twelve thousand feet to above them at twenty-one thousand feet, and from forty-five-degree banks from side to side. "Then things really began to happen," as Sykes recalled. A terrific gust slammed the plane; the crew chief was lifted, striking his head on the ceiling, oil drums broke loose; "suddenly we were on our back. While hanging in my safety belt and with the dirt from the floor falling all around, I realized that it would be impossible to bailout. The co-pilot and I fought the controls until we finally righted the ship at 21,000 feet. We had made a complete 180-degree turn and were headed in the direction from which we had come. We had been in the air quite long and decided our destination must be closer than the point of departure. We turned and bucked our way through the storm and made it."[38]

On the ground in China, pilots and crew thronged the bases' operations. "[Of] course they did not want to return to India through the same weather," Plosser recorded. He had landed in Luliang to find more than the usual number of C-47s, C-46s, and C-87s parked on the ramps. "We listened as one of the pilots told the base commander on the phone that in 20 years of flying with the airlines, he had never flown through weather more violent. Nobody, he said, should be required to fly back until the weather cleared. The base commander told him he could not countermand orders from headquarters," which was in Calcutta.[39] In Kunming, pilots were milling around and swapping stories, "pretty badly shaken up," according to the operations officer.[40]

J. V. Vinyard, who had flown one of the last planes out, departing from Sookerating after dark, arrived in Kunming just before ten o'clock. There had been little hint of the severity of the weather when he departed. Checking in to operations, he had studied the blackboard on which weather was reported and seen "they had taken the chalk and just run it sideways over the whole thing." The entire Hump was covered with chalk, but written below it was "winds estimated at SW 75," which was not too bad. But once airborne, Vinyard had corrected his course for winds from the south that he estimated were coming at 125 miles per hour, yet had still been blown 65 miles north off course.[41] On landing, he went into the base operations and "looked down at the end of the counter and there were a bunch of pilots standing there. There was a guy typing on a typewriter, and I said what's going on down there, and they said, those guys are refusing to go back—and we were told that we could never refuse to fly due to weather. They were saying it would be suicide to turn around and go back because coming into China, you've got all of China—but when you're going back you've got a sixty-mile wide valley. You're going to fly three hours on instruments, with no radio help, and hope that you end up over that dead-end boxed canyon that's only about sixty or eighty miles wide?" In a refrain recited through the night at every base, the operations manager stated he lacked authority to tell the pilots they did not have to fly, but they could sign statements declaring that they had been instructed to fly and refused to do so. "There were five pilots down there signing those letters," Vinyard reported. He had a brain wave: a lost prop governor allowed him to declare "a mechanical," and he was cleared to stay overnight.[42] Shortly afterward, at 10:30 p.m., the word came out that the Hump was closed, and "everybody shouted for joy."[43]

The storm had not blown out the following morning, however, but at least flying would be in daylight. Still, in Sookerating, the assistant operations officer recalled that a United Airlines pilot with twelve thousand flight hours returned from across the Hump "white as a sheet." "That's the worst weather I've ever seen," he said. "Some won't make it."[44]

Reporting on the two-day storm, the *Hump Express*, the weekly newspaper for the air bases, drew on airmen's accounts in the immediate aftermath. "Not all the crews have returned, but most of them flew safely through the hurricane-like storm," it reported. "Those who have returned told about weather conditions as phenomenal as ever have been reported."[45] Each base was attempting to calculate its losses. "This has been a bad day," mechanic Lloyd Gray wrote in his diary from Sookerating on the second day of the storm. "The weather has been full of ice over the Hump. 20 ships from the valley have gone down, we have three confirmed, and two probables." The following day was quiet "after the storm. In the final shakedown we lost two planes, 072 and 559. Fog until eleven, and now clear. weather nice over the Hump."[46] The final tally of losses was much disputed. Initial rumors spoke of as many as thirty-three aircraft downed and 120 lives lost; army ATC airmen were quick to point out that three of the planes belonged to CNAC, which had long bragged about their pilots' superior skills and the fact that "they flew when the birds did not." A later air force historian's computation came up with the more sober figure of nine aircraft lost and thirty-one persons killed or missing; but other investigators came up with different figures still.[47]

Individual pilots followed up with weather officers for insight into what had occurred and learned that a dense occluded front had moved across Africa and India, picking up moisture in the Bay of Bengal as it sped toward Assam, driving winds from the southwest from 100 to 125 miles per hour. Within this system, pilot reports indicated, vicious local wind shifts from every point of the compass had created plane-pitching sheers and turbulence and brought icing and hail up to and above thirty-five thousand feet.[48] The front had moved so quickly that aircraft continued taking off before the worst reports had been received.[49]

DAYS AFTER THE HISTORIC STORM, THERE OCCURRED ANOTHER LANDMARK event, this one highly manufactured. On January 12, a convoy of 113 trucks bearing Chinese and American flags and banners convened outside of Ledo, bound for Kunming. The Ledo Road had not in fact been completed, for there were long stretches that had not been graveled, many bridges were temporary, and indeed the Japanese had not been entirely cleared across the route.[50] But Stilwell had long sworn that the road would be open by January 1945, and Washington had backed him, and face had to be saved.[51] Thus, the convoy gamely set out on its nearly 1,100-mile-long symbolic journey. Four days later, it came to a halt in Myitkyina, where it stopped for a week to avoid heavy fighting farther down the route. The lengthy break allowed the sixty-five-member-strong press and public relations corps covering the event ample opportunity to interview and photograph their subjects.[52] Frank Bolden of the *Pittsburgh Courier*, who had ridden with the convoy from Ledo and would ride with it until its arrival in Kunming, was one of two African American correspondents among the throng.[53] All along the roadside, he noted, "Negro GIs representing engineering and quartermaster complements . . . had gazed upon the convoy which they had helped make possible. Their searching gaze swept from vehicle to vehicle looking in vain for one of their own."[54] Given that almost all drivers on the road were black, as were the road's builders, why was there not a single driver of color on this historic procession? A flurry of embarrassed throat-clearing followed, and at a subsequent press conference, the army explained that the most experienced truck unit had been chosen, which happened to be white. ("There wasn't any unit," Bolden would say later. "It was a pick-up group.")[55] Nonetheless, as Bolden reported, the suspicion was aroused as to whether "Negro soldiers . . . are officially wanted or not wanted in China."[56] A handwritten note lodged between the printed pages of the official CBI history in the papers of General Howard Davidson, commander of the Tenth Air Force at this time, states that "when everything was in readiness to drive the first Convoy over the Ledo road the Chinese issued instructions that negro drivers could not enter China." Eventually, the note continues, "the Chinese . . . finally amended the order when the American authorities agreed to get the negro truck drivers out of China in not more than six days."[57] In the event, the army dispatched eleven black drivers to join the convoy when it lumbered onward to Kunming, which it reached on February 5, twenty-four days after leaving Ledo, and where it was greeted with extravagant celebrations.[58] Chiang, with either great grace or great irony, greeted the convoy's arrival by hailing the fact that the allies had "broken the siege of China"; "Let me name this road," he continued, "after General Joseph Stilwell."[59]

The importance of the road had in any case been downgraded during the summer of 1944, when the US landing on Saipan in the Marianas—within bombing distance of Japan—conclusively indicated that the offensive trajectory of the Pacific War would not be by way of China. Additionally, an analysis of the costs involved, in dollars, manpower, and equipment, revealed that if the originally planned two-way, graveled highway were to run only as far as Myitkyina and to continue from there as a rougher, single-lane road, some twenty-six thousand tons in gasoline and lubricants would be saved—and thirty-five thousand men would be freed for the imminent landing in the Philippines.[60] This math was persuasive, and General Marshall endorsed the single-lane plan on the premise that it would still ensure that "enough equipment to meet the minimum needs of the U.S. sponsored Chinese divisions could be delivered."[61] Thus, while the mission of the US-sponsored Chinese divisions had mainly been to cover the advance of the road, the road, it was now deemed, need only support the US-sponsored Chinese divisions.[62]

The air force and ATC were also doing their own math. Since the taking of Myitkyina, there had been an enormous jump in monthly tonnage over the Hump, from 23,676 tons in August, the month Myitkyina was finally taken, to nearly 35,000 in December. In February and March 1945, the months that saw the first convoy over the Ledo Road, a total of nearly

85,000 tons were delivered.[63] Possession of the Myitkyina airport allowed the Hump traffic to fly a lower route and for the planes to break their journey to refuel from the pipeline laid beside the road. As a result, Myitkyina's obscure airfields, tucked in the bend of the Irrawaddy River, had become one of the busiest airports in the world, with incoming traffic so heavy that transports sometimes had to circle for hours before being cleared for landing.[64] Another factor in the increase of tonnage was the incorporation of the four-engine Douglas C-54 Skymaster into the transport fleet. Faster than the C-46, and with a much longer range, the C-54 had a massive payload of six tons, but, being prone to engine failure in severe or even moderate ice, it had not been used over the Hump until the capture of Myitkyina opened a lower, less ice-prone route.[65] Previously unimaginable equipment was loaded into this aircraft's belly. "We hauled howitzers. We hauled six-by sixes, those huge Army trucks with three rear wheels on each side. We hauled road rollers," Tunner recorded.[66]

Of as great interest to the air force and ATC as the monthly tonnage were those figures that made direct comparison between the Hump and the Ledo Road. Every aspect of the two operations was calculated, from man-hours to supply costs to the monthly haul, and in every regard air transport came out ahead. Air supply, it was estimated, could realistically deliver eighty thousand tons a month to China before the end of 1945, a figure the road would not be able to match, in the most optimistic of circumstances, for well over a year, if then. More to the point, air delivery would require 52,723 air force and Services of Supply troops to achieve this figure, against 73,348 SOS troops required for delivery over the road.[67]

And there were many other practical factors. The single-lane road from Myitkyina to Kunming mandated one-way traffic, with the result that trucks driven into China were left in China, whereas planes could return to India.[68] Road transport, which required a seventeen-and-a-half-day turnaround in the best of circumstances against air transport's nine-hour turnaround, could never accommodate emergency deliveries.

Security on the road, like maintenance, was a chronic problem. "If a truck were stalled and broke down on the road we never saw it again," Corporal Charles Pittman reported, driving for the 518th Quartermaster (Truck) Battalion. "There was a group that was supposed to pick up the trucks, but unless they were literally on the scene when the breakdown occurred the Chinese would come down from the hillsides, strip the truck, then push it over."[69]

Roaming groups of Chinese bandits threatened the slow-moving convoys, and although they were held at bay by elements of the Chinese army, every truck, as one veteran reported, "had at least one Tommy Machine gun and everybody had rifles."[70] One thing the road was doing successfully was continuing to serve as a black market bazaar. A combined British Intelligence and US CID attempt to investigate the traffic of goods convoyed to China resulted in despondent bafflement. "No complete estimate can be made of the tonnage of merchandise seen by the investigators along the Road," the report concluded, but noted that "the innumerable displays in shops and stalls along the Road, to say nothing of the extremely well-stocked shops and stalls in Kunming, contain an aggregate of literally hundreds of truckloads" of merchandise. The Ledo Road, the report concluded, was a "Chinese Army trade route."[71]

Relentlessly, the ATC underscored the overwhelming advantages of air delivery and the irrelevancy of the Ledo Road. And yet, "[t]he Burma Road [was] again put into operation," Tunner wrote. "Fantastic sums were spent on it. As many as twenty engineer battalions were working on it one time. We on the Hump generally had the use of no more than two engineer battalions to build and maintain our bases. . . . But despite all this effort and expense, the maximum amount of supply carried over the Burma Road at its very peak of operation amounted to just six thousand net tons a month. Many of our thirteen bases in India were topping that figure, constantly and without fail." But, he concluded, "[w]e all know now how hard it is to stop a large government project once it is begun."[72] Most galling to the airmen was the refrain recited by the press that the road would at last "break the blockade" to China.[73] If China were indeed blockaded, why were they flying around the clock over the Hump?

BY THE SPRING OF 1945, THE JAPANESE WERE ON THE RUN IN BURMA. TO THE south, the British had cleared the Arakan coast early in the year, and it and its strategic port and airfield were at last securely in Allied hands. By April, the Northern Combat Area Command campaign was over, and the Chinese units were on their way back to China, many by way of the Ledo Road. In the north, the British had also captured Meiktila, the Japanese army's main supply hub some eighty miles south of Mandalay and, at devasting cost to the ancient city, Mandalay itself, where the Japanese had made a ferocious last-ditch stand. On the main central front, Slim's forces had cleared the Shwebo plain that lay between the Irrawaddy and the Chindwin Rivers, crossed the Chindwin, and were in a race against the monsoon for Rangoon, clearing the remnants of Japanese resistance as they met them. "There was a sense of purpose in the air," John Masters wrote. "Burma still contained thousands of the enemy, but they were retreating ahead of us, fighting tenaciously all the while, as only the Japanese can." Individual Japanese soldiers were found crouched in foxholes in the road, holding 250-pound bombs between their legs and stones in hand, ready to strike the detonator when a tank passed.[74]

Encountered now were Allied prisoners of war who had been turned loose or had escaped as the Japanese retreated. "[O]ne day an American flier wandered into our position," reported George MacDonald Fraser, a soldier in the Border Regiment attached to the 100th Indian Infantry Brigade (and later novelist of the Flashman series). The airman had escaped after months of captivity near Rangoon and drifted north. He was, Fraser recorded, "in a fair old state." Presented with hot food for breakfast, he burst into tears and buried his head in the chest of the nearest solider, "and kept repeating, 'Oh boys, boys!'" "Hatred of the Japs," wrote Fraser, "rose a notch higher."[75] It was a hatred that united the multinational Fourteenth Army. "When we found the sort of thing they were doing, we don't spare them any longer," was the summation of an African private with a Gold Coast regiment. "We shot them—we chopped their heads off. We don't allow our officers to see. We just eliminate them."[76] An RAF pilot recalled flying four Japanese prisoners under the supervision of five Gurkhas from a Burma air base to a hospital. On landing, he opened the door to the cargo section. "Just five Gurkhas were there, looking up at me, smoking. I asked: *kishnay* (where) Jap?," he reported. "They just stared at me. I angrily repeated the question. Two of them, with innocent gesticulations, replied: '*Nay mallum sahib.*' (I don't know what you are talking about sir.) The devils had tossed them all out!"[77]

Rangoon was seized on May 3, not by Slim's Fourteenth Army, which was delayed by fierce fighting some forty miles to the north of the city, but by an amphibious assault. The Burmese National Army had switched its allegiance from the Japanese to the Allies after the fall of Mandalay, and it now joined the mopping-up campaigns, along with Burmese guerrillas, the reliable Kachin, and other forces from across the hill tribes. Significant Japanese forces, however, regrouped behind the triumphant advance as it swept south. The most formidable holdout was the Japanese's Twenty-Eighth Army, some thirty thousand strong, which sought refuge in the Pegu Range, where, isolated and unsupplied, they were eventually starved out. When they were forced to make a desperate bid to escape east, across two mighty rivers, toward the Siam border, the RAF unloaded a million and a half pounds of bombs on them.[78] Burma was regained. India was secure. There remained only the task of saving China.

FOLLOWING STILWELL'S RECALL IN OCTOBER 1944, THE WAR DEPARTMENT split the CBI theater in two. Appointed as the senior US officer in the new China theater and, as Stilwell had been, a chief of staff to Chiang Kai-shek was General Albert Wedemeyer, previously deputy chief of staff of the SEAC. General Dan Sultan, Stilwell's deputy theater commander, was given command of the India-Burma theater.[79] Unlike Stilwell, Wedemeyer quickly established a civil working relationship with Chiang Kai-shek. His objectives as he stated were: "A. Create conditions for the effective employment of maximum U.S. resources in the area. . . . B. The Chinese must be required to play an active role in this war."[80] To this end, like Stilwell, Wedemeyer threw himself into an attempt to create thirty-six US trained and equipped Chinese divisions. With these, as he was to tell the Joint Chiefs, "further serious advances of the Japanese in China could be prevented," and a "rebellion in China could be put down by comparatively small assistance to Chiang's central government."[81]

By "rebellion," Wedemeyer was referring principally to the Communists, for while all early efforts to support Chiang Kai-shek had been in the interest of ensuring that China was not lost to the Japanese, it was by now clear that China was more likely to be lost to Chinese elements within China. In the north of the country, the Communists were ensconced within their own state, which was bolstered by both growing popular support and military strength. The state-within-a-state was financed by a calibrated system of taxation that spared the poorest, by boosted production—and by taxation of goods sold to the Japanese. Throughout the war, they had conducted limited guerrilla warfare against the Japanese and rescued and returned downed US airmen in their territory, and US observers had been forced to take note of their high morale, self-sufficiency, and keen sense of mission.[82]

By contrast, Chiang's Nationalist government and armed forces were getting weaker, a fact that had been brutally exposed by the Japanese drive against the American air bases that was begun in the spring of 1944 and continued to the end of the year. Defense of the bases was the responsibility of the Nationalist army, which Chiang (and also Chennault) had long claimed was up to this task. Ragged, starved, and denied critical equipment, the ground forces were further impaired by Chiang's erratic and untimely issuing of commands, without which his generals were forbidden to take any initiative.[83] This was an old pattern, but there were grave new developments. In Henan, a province that had experienced cat-astrophic and largely man-made famine, the people had turned against the Nationalist forces that had come to defend them.[84] "[P]eople of the mountains in western Henan attacked our troops, taking guns, bullets, and explosives, and even high-powered mortars and radio equipment," reported General Jiang Dingwen, who led the defense. "They surrounded our troops and killed our officers. We heard this pretty often." The local people had refused to obey the army's orders to destroy roads so as to thwart the Japanese advance, and had sometimes even gone back under cover of night to repair roads the army had destroyed.[85] "The peasants had waited long for this moment," as journalist Theodore White sum-marized the events he had witnessed firsthand. "They had suffered through too many months of famine and merciless military extortion."[86]

As the Japanese approached, Chiang's generals sent urgent requests for aid, but, in the words of the official history of the CBI (and new China theater), Chiang refused "to let any arms of any sort, Chinese or US Lend-Lease, be sent to the Chinese defending the airfields."[87] Disturbing US intelligence reports stated that the generalissimo had an understanding with the Japanese by which "they would leave him undisturbed in south-west China if he in turn would not interfere while they took the airfields"; circumstantial evidence supporting these charges was the fact that the Japanese army had only two divisions guarding a key Japanese supply base in Hankow, although sixty Chinese divisions were in striking dis-tance of it.[88] Testimonies of Japanese officers after the war indicate a more nuanced situation, with the officers stating that they had indeed engaged in extensive contact with Nationalist commanders known to be disaffected with Chiang, and reassured them that the Japanese drive would not threaten them and their forces but only target the American bases—overtures that suggest that the Japanese command understood Chiang's regime was not secure. Chiang's refusal to aid the defense of the US bases, then, was in turn likely calculated to ensure he did not squander his own forces defending those whose loyalty he doubted. Yet the loyalty of many nominally under his sway was now in doubt.[89] Indeed, shortly after the fall of Hengyang, the walled city that had fought the Japanese offensive so fiercely, representatives of a proposed breakaway provisional government—the Southwestern Government of Joint Defense—approached US consulate officials seeking US backing, without success.[90] There was also the terrible likelihood that any forces Chiang did in fact dispatch might well fail, further revealing his own weakness.

Taken together, the various intelligence indicated the extent to which free China was collapsing. Chiang was now clinging only to the illusion of power and, in Wedemeyer's words, was "impotent and confounded." In the course of daily, face-to-face conferences with the generalissimo, Wedemeyer reported on the Japanese advances and the fact that the Chinese forces, even those that were well equipped and fed, were not fighting, to which Chiang had replied mildly, "[O]f course these were early reports." Writing to Marshall, Wedemeyer vented his frustration: "They are _not_ organized, equipped and trained for modern war. Psychologically they are _not_ prepared to cope with the situation because of political intrigue, false pride, and mistrust of leaders' motives and honesty." The officials surrounding Chiang, Wedemeyer believed, were afraid to report on actual conditions "for two reasons, their stupidity and inefficiency are revealed, and further the Generalissimo might order them to take positive action."[91]

Economically as well as politically and militarily, Chiang's fiefdom was disintegrating. The crushing taxation of the overwhelmingly rural peasant population could not produce revenue to sustain the government, and even the purchasing power of the dollars flowing in could not keep abreast of the outsized inflation. The US was now calibrating more carefully than before the cost of supplying China, and among other things paying closer attention to the steady flow of US commodities into Japanese hands. The Services of Supply had learned, for example, that Red Cross medicines in free China made their way by parcel post from Chiang's capital in Chungking to the Japanese-occupied Shanghai market.[92] As the CBI history tactfully records, Wedemeyer, having had "ample opportunity during his nineteen months previous service in Asia to become aware of the less-publicized problems of that area," requested clear directives with regard to Lend-Lease, the allocation of Hump supplies, "smuggling over the Hump, and black marketing."[93]

That vast, unquantified amounts of supplies ferried over the Hump ended up in the black market trade and even in Japanese hands was another unpublicized fact well known to airmen. Writing in his diary, pilot Peter Dominick reflected on what he saw as the Japanese army's restraint, noting "there is no doubt that they could almost stop this route if they wanted to, but either it isn't worth the effort or instead, as most fellows believe, a good third of what we bring to China ends up in Jap hands through Chinese warlords."[94] The black market was by no means an exclusively Chinese enterprise, and rumors of the participation of US army personnel had shadowed the Hump since the earliest days of the operation. Back in October 1942, the US press was reporting on how "[v]igilant Chinese and Indian customs officials have stamped out numerous smuggling rings that have tried to corrupt the air transport system between China and India." For example, cargo space allotted for war supplies had been appropriated for "items on which smugglers could make fabulous profits." In Calcutta, an American pilot had reportedly been offered $1,000 cash to "carry a 25-pound package to a friend." Also in Calcutta, customs officials had frisked a shady-looking civilian attempting to board a China-bound plane and found $63,000 worth of gold bullion (the equivalent of over a million dollars today), which "might have realized a profit up to 1,000 per cent" in China.[95]

Closer to home, in December 1944, the theater newspaper *CBI Roundup* reported that military police had broken a multinational smuggling and black market ring that had been operating over the Hump since 1942. An estimated $4 million worth of goods (roughly equivalent to $70 million today) that ranged from military supplies to cigarettes had been illicitly moved by a cast of characters that included "members of the U.S. Army, American Volunteer Groups, the famed 'Flying Tigers'; China national Airways personnel, Red Cross members, technical representatives of US aircraft manufacturers and British, Indian and Chinese civilians," some of whom—namely the US Army personnel—were "serving stiff sentences in Leavenworth, Kan." More sobering was the report that a number of the foreign ringleaders "have been executed by the Chinese Government." The criminals had pulled off their crimes with some daring stunts. One USAAF fighter pilot had parachuted from his plane near an air base in China with $10,000 worth of gold bullion and drugs brought from India, leaving his plane to crash.[96]

Exposed around the same time was an audacious plan to have a squadron of Chinese pilots ferry planes from Karachi back to China with some $300,000 worth of drugs, gold, and other valuables stuffed in the aircraft nose and under the floorboards. Chief among the suspects was radio operator Harry Sutter, who was suspected, along with his wife, of being a ringleader of the syndicate, and was also a colleague of General Claire Chennault, who was still in command of the Fourteenth Air Force in Kunming.[97] Complicating the matter was the fact that the wife was one of several women with whom Chennault had had affairs (and in one case a son).[98] This was not the first time that scandal touched Chennault. In the summer of 1943, Stilwell had been notified that "tarts" destined for the Fourteenth Air Force were being recruited in Kweilin and flown to a brothel in Kunming. "Officers pimping," Stilwell had written in his diary. "Hauling whores in our planes.—Sent for Chennault. He knew."[99] Following the scent, Stilwell learned "[m]ore dope on [Kunming] whorehouse & gas-stealing ring," as he jotted in his diary the following day, and confronted Chennault, who stated that the brothel was common knowledge in Kunming ("That whorehouse of mine," he was reported to say; "That's worrying me. The boys have got to get it and they might as well get it clean as get it dirty").[100] Yet he indignantly denied "that any officer was concerned."[101] This last was not true, for a few enterprising air force officers, including Chennault's son Jack, who was based in Sian, China, had been responsible for establishing a small network of brothels to serve the various Chinese bases. Known as "Temples of Love," these facilities were buildings in which all doors and windows were nailed shut, excepting the front door, so that every customer who went in had to come out the same door, where he was intercepted by a medic wielding a "prophylactic injection"; reportedly, the system greatly reduced the Fourteenth Air Force's worrisomely high rate of venereal disease.[102] Stilwell's investigation of the brothel scandal appears to have rattled Chennault. "Letter from Chennault on whore-house indicates he is apprehensive," Stilwell wrote in his diary a few days later. "Does not fully jibe with statements to me."[103] But this particular indiscretion did not gain much traction with anyone else, and he shortly dropped his pursuit. "No hope on whore-house matter," he wrote. "Can't get him."[104]

THE SMUGGLING AFFAIR THAT ERUPTED AT THE END OF 1944 TRIGGERED A closer look at the now-legendary airman. Among other things, Chennault was suspected of taking his pay from China and evading US income tax.[105] None of these matters were publicized, and Chennault, while professing anger and indignation, remained at his post. In early April 1945, with the end of the war in Europe imminent, however, the US War Department decided that the Tenth Air Force should be moved from India to China, where it would become the tactical air force of the China theater under General George Stratemeyer, formerly the commanding general of the India-Burma sector. Chennault's Fourteenth Air Force was to continue its mission of interdicting Japanese lines of communication in the southeast.[106] (The B-29 bombers had been moved from Chengtu to the Marianas in January 1945, a move that had been contemplated as far back as September 1944, in recognition of the fact that if based in China they could neither reach significant Japanese targets nor be adequately safeguarded and supplied.)[107] This clear-cut plan, however, wavered due to confusion over the allotment of tonnage over the Hump that would be required to support two air forces. It is also evident that Wedemeyer was extremely reluctant to break the news to Chennault that he would no longer be the ranking officer in China. In the ensuing conversations between the two men, Chennault aggressively challenged the desirability of the new move and stated that he would stay in China as long as his health allowed; it also emerged that he had expected to be appointed "Theater Commander upon Stilwell's relief."[108] He spoke freely of the past contentions that had overshadowed the CBI, such as his rivalry with Stilwell and his own habit of irregular back-channel communication with Roosevelt through Joe Alsop, but "expressed surprise that his behavior had been considered disloyal."[109] To this last point, the ground soon shifted beneath the feet of everyone in the theater, the US, and indeed the world, with the death of Franklin Roosevelt on April 12.

Chennault fought to the last against his removal. When Arnold, who never entirely trusted Chennault, issued an unambiguous directive to Wedemeyer that stipulated the need for "a senior, experienced air officer, in whom you and I have confidence," Chennault lashed out with a long letter to the War Department.[110] Described by Wedemeyer as being full of "bitter denunciations and vitriolic statements," the letter, sixteen single-spaced, typewritten pages, listed the many ways in which Stilwell's mismanagement had lost east China.[111] The letter had been drafted by Alsop, who pointed out to Chennault that drawing attention to events that the War Department would not wish to have exposed increased the likelihood that charges against him would be dropped.[112] The list was indeed damning and ranged over Stilwell's open contempt toward Chiang Kai-shek; the uselessness of the north Burma campaign, which had been driven by Stilwell's personal ambition; Stilwell's lack of any plan for the defense of China; and the fact that East China and its airfields had fallen while China's best armies were fighting in Burma.[113] Nonetheless, toward summer's end, Chennault at last left China and returned, laden with awards and decorations, to the United States.[114]

"A Hero Leaves the Field"; "Chennault Already a Legend, His Genius Unvarnished by Fate"; "Army Politics Killed Chennault"—newspapers brandished the news across the United States.[115] At "a secret session with the Senate Military Affairs Committee," one widely reproduced syndicated story reported, "[n]ot a Senator present was willing to believe that the resignation of Maj. General Claire Chennault was caused by anything other than Army politics," and there were calls for "senatorial investigation of the incident." After speaking at length about Chinese politics, the senator from Wyoming grilled the undersecretary of war as to whether "the real reason for placing Chennault in a subordinate position to General Stratemeyer was to appease the Communists." It was noted, too, that War Department officials did not attempt to argue about the ability of the former Flying Tiger.[116]

How could they argue? To do so might have entailed digging into the Flying Tigers' inflated record. Also better left buried were the representations that Chennault had made to lure the US into establishing a China-based air force in the first place. Not yet known, but perhaps suspected, was the extent to which the success of the Fourteenth Air Force had also been exaggerated. It had proved most effective, as a granular, postwar US Air Force study determined, when its assault of the Japanese army's lines of communication had been combined with an active ground defense, as in the siege of Hengyang when "the Chinese ground forces were resisting stoutly." On the other hand, events had shown that air action alone "could not halt a ground advance in China." The Fourteenth's "most significant contribution to victory in China" was through its air interdiction campaigns.[117] Yet a tactfully worded theme threads the report like a refrain: "A better conception of the exaggerated nature of these claims may be gained by considering a statistical summary prepared by Fourteenth Air Force. . . ."; "The responsibility for unrealistic claims of shipping sunk by LAB [Low Altitude Bombing] cannot be assigned to any one person. . . . Rather did one error compound another until gross inaccuracy resulted"; "The completely unrealistic contemporary accounts . . ."; "[E]xamination of the evidence available immediately makes it apparent that the Fourteenth Air Force claims were too high. . . ."; "[I]t must be noted again that the claims of motor vehicles destroyed are undoubtedly too large—probably by 50 percent."[118] A couple of specific examples must suffice. The destruction of locomotives was, of all targets, among the easiest to confirm, and it was found that Fourteenth Air Force claims "must be discounted almost completely. . . . The Allied observers reported that some of the locomotives carried on the Japanese books as damaged were, for all practical purposes, destroyed, but if even three times as many were destroyed as the Japanese admitted, the resulting 30 would be a far cry from the 793 reported destroyed by the Fourteenth Air Force Intelligence Summary."[119] Similarly, by the most generous assessment, the "Fourteenth Air Force, with some aid from FEAF [Far East Air Force] and XX Bomber Command" accounted for the total loss of "approximately 238,000 tons" of Japanese ships destroyed in Chinese and Indo-Chinese coastal waters and the Yangtze River, against which, as the study notes, "Fourteenth Air Force claims of 994,389 tons sunk, 441,700 tons probably sunk and 861,600 tons damaged, and 32 naval vessels sunk or damaged seems ridiculously small."[120]

It was to the advantage of every party involved that the rumors of Chennault's participation in smuggling be waved aside. Yet they persisted; "I know nothing about Chennault's so-called connections with illicit traffic and so forth," Wedemeyer wrote to Arnold toward the end of the war, when the rumors were still current; "however, an FBI man named Cooper indicated that Chennault was definitely involved and to a very serious extent."[121] To Marshall, after apologizing for Chennault's vitriolic letter, Wedemeyer summed up: "Either General Chennault is a fine man who has been treated unjustly in the Theater or he is an unscrupulous clever intriguer who is interested in publicity and self aggrandizement."[122]

The convergence of charges and countercharges that swirl around Chennault's retirement serve as a kind of summation of the vexed CBI theater. Chiang could claim that Stilwell had been insubordinate and squandered his best armies. Stilwell could claim that Chiang's leadership was so incompetent that he was in danger of losing his country. Chennault could claim that Stilwell's personal ambition for a land campaign had thwarted his efforts to defend China by air. Stilwell could claim that Chennault had grossly exaggerated his own and his air forces' capabilities and ignored the necessity of a ground force to defend the air bases. And all could claim that better use could have been made of the tonnage transported over the Hump.

Back in October 1944, shortly before the bifurcation of the CBI theater, Washington had weighed the advantages of not aiding China further at all, and terminating operations over the Hump.[123] But to do so, it was concluded, would be bad for Chinese morale, and very possibly bad for US morale as well. Yet there was a sinking feeling that the epic exertions over the Hump had been wasted, and, as Secretary of War Henry Stimson wrote in his diary, might "result in the delay in a victory on the western front over the winter."[124]

In the summer of 1945, even with the war in Europe ended, a long war in the Pacific seemed to lie ahead, and the role for China was even more uncertain. President Truman did not share Roosevelt's fixation on securing China as a great power in the postwar world. Nor had any of the plans to use China in the war against Japan come to fruition—not as an overland route, not as a base for long-range bombers, not as a coastal stronghold for the Pacific fleet—yet still, the Hump operation kept growing. Almost 750 aircraft and 4,400 pilots flying night and day were hauling staggering amounts of fuel and supplies into China—46,394 tons in May; 55,386 tons in June; 71,042 tons in July. B-25 and B-24 squadrons were also serving as airlift transports, as they now had no military targets in China.[125]

THE COUNTRY THAT AMERICAN PILOTS WERE FLYING THE HUMP TO SAVE remained mostly unknown to them. The majority of Air Transport Command airmen were based in Assam, from where they flew mostly round-trip missions. If circumstances forced them to stay in Kunming or other airfields overnight, they tended not to stray far from their bases, with the result that, while they were repeatedly told that they were China's lifeline, China remained mysterious to them.

On days of good weather, a pilot soaring over the glittering foothills of the Himalayas and on over China's vast and magnificent land could still feel a frisson of its mystery and splendor. North of the Able route and high up in the Himalayas was a walled city in the middle of a large plateau—no one knew who inhabited it or what it was called. At the base of the mountain where the Mekong entered its valley, pilots had spotted a large mission complex, said to have been founded by two brothers from St. Louis—but of how they lived and who their mission was for, little was known.[126] "[T]here is an amphitheater, a valley in the 17,000-foot mountains, about five miles long," Peter Dominick recorded in his diary. "The cultivation is almost western in appearances, foliage grows all over, and on the side of the mountain is an orderly town with a huge gold-roofed temple to one side. It's almost a replica of 'Lost Horizon.'"[127]

No one knows this
mountain I inhabit;

deep in white clouds,
forever empty, silent.

HAN SHAN, C. SEVENTH TO NINTH CENTURY[128]

On the ground, from a few privileged perspectives, it was possible to retain some sense of the region's romance. Kunming, Yunnan's capital, was a medieval walled city with cobblestone streets shaded by pepper and eucalyptus trees.[129] As the end of the Burma Road, it was also the beginning of the unknown, as one writer put it.[130] Here was "old China," with its confused, bustling crowds passing in and out of the stone gates, the Mongolian ponies laden with dust-covered vegetables, the imposing Tibetans with their shaggy mules and ponies, the colors of traditional costumes, the babies with their heads swathed in bright silk.[131] Poor workers dressed in rough, patched clothing navigated the stones and traffic while carrying, suspended from shoulder boards, buckets of water and cooked food. Children ran everywhere, laughing, apparently without supervision, and women with bound feet that lacked all flexion walked as with planks, lifting and setting down each foot flatly on the uneven surface.[132] Paul Child, a member of the OSS who was stationed in the city, described walks outside the walls where plum blossoms and jasmine scented the air. From the city's West Gate, one could look down on the roof tiles rolling away below. "God, what a beautiful country—" he wrote after one such outing; "the mud villages with their green-tiled towers, the flocks of black swine, the blue clad people, the cedar smoke, the cinnamon-dust, were all eternally Chinese and connected us with the deep layers of time past."[133]

Yet for most foreigners, the romance quickly wilted. "Kunming," recalled Chennault's amanuensis, Joe Alsop, "was a very lovely, very primitive, and very filthy Chinese city."[134] "A medieval cesspool," according to journalist Theodore White.[135] Its narrow streets consisted mostly of mud, and its sidewalks of beaten mud. Block-like cobblestones formed the few main streets, over which juddered army vehicles, civilian cars, rickshaws, and streams of pedestrian traffic. Motor-driven vehicles tore through the town, horns blaring, spattering mud and scattering people in every direction—for "if they slowed down they would soon be engulfed by the mass of humanity," as a chaplain attached to the US air operations reported.[136] Long Yun, the warlord governor whose province Yunnan was, had made clear he objected to the barring of any of the civilian foot traffic from roads that crossed the US military installations, and yet it was known that mingling amid the throngs of peddlers, beggars, scavengers, and prostitutes were Japanese agents.[137]

In Kunming, and most especially in the rural forward air bases, the Americans were confronted with levels of poverty and filth they had never imagined possible. Human life could be cheap, the Americans learned. Landing in Kunming one day, Bob Boody and his crew had seen "a heavy concrete roller, pulled by hundreds of Chinese coolies, run over and crush to death one of the other coolies who had stumbled at the yoke of the tow rope," Boody wrote in his diary. "The roller continued on, despite undoubted screaming, without interruption—such was the value the indigenous Chinese placed on the life of the individual human being."[138] The poor laborers were admired for their cheerfulness amid their crushing poverty, for their ubiquitous *Ding-hao* greeting (Number One! Thumbs up!), and for their ability to find laughter amid hardship. Yet this cheerfulness often morphed into something darker and beyond the Americans' comprehension: their laughter when a drum of gasoline fell on a companion's foot; the backslapping laughter and cheers from onlookers when a worker ran into the whirring blades of a C-47; or the amusement of pushing companions out of an airborne plane for the fun of seeing them fall.[139] "I have seen airplanes arriving from 'over the Hump' and blow out a tire on the sharp rocks, which constituted our runways, and ground loop into the crowd of coolies working on these trips and kill as many as six at a time," one base commander recalled. "These horrible accidents seemed to amuse the coolies no end. Some would laugh unceasingly at the gasps and antics of their dying comrades."[140]

In the face of Yunnan's poverty, luxuries were everywhere. Kunming, as Theodore White reported, had "the shrewdest banking and commercial speculators in the land," whose talents added to the city's wealth.[141] Shops with stout shutters were said to carry every commodity in the world; there was now a Kodak shop, a Singer sewing machine shop. "It is said that one can buy about anything he wants here in KUNMING because of the Black Market," a base chaplain wrote after visiting the city; "new GE electric ice box down to Cameras, films, Cigarettes, Parker 51 pen and pencil sets, etc." American cigarettes were valued at 1.9 million Chinese dollars a carton and were in constant demand.[142] Restaurants abounded, like the popular Kwang Sueng Yang, which served Cantonese food and had been deemed safe by US medical staff, and where US personnel were led upstairs to the best rooms.[143] Although a thriving center of illegal trade, the city had been cleaned up for the invasion of the Americans. Up until the war, it had been a major hub for opium merchants, and prostitutes had been kept penned in a street chained off at both ends.[144] Yet even in the cleaned-up city, vice thrived and spread, as the range of individuals apprehended in the smuggling ring had exposed. Pilots at one base went on strike, refusing to fly any more drums of gasoline until certain

Red Cross girls in Kunming surrendered their personal sedans.[145] Theft was an intractable problem. Kunming, one pilot recalled, "was full of thieves. There was a guarded car park, which was the only safe place to leave a jeep. If you left it elsewhere not only would all its contents be gone in a few moments but the jeep itself would disappear."[146]

By 1945, some 10,600 US soldiers were based in Kunming, housed in fifteen scattered hostels, and consuming with casual appetite vast quantities of Yunnan's food. "[T]he American army in Kunming have been here over a year, and consume huge amounts," Long Yun had written to the Chinese war minister in 1944, responding to a request to increase the supply of beef to American troops. "Since spring 1943, every single day the Americans have needed nearly thirty oxen every day, over 1,000 chickens, and several thousand eggs, not even counting pigs and sheep. The oxen that plough the fields have all been bought up. It's been a huge and surprising expense." By January 1945, there were 32,956 US troops in China; by August, the number was 60,369.[147]

Away from Yunnan's principal city, Americans found life on the isolated air bases even more primitive and testing.[148] "Everyone was to be confronted with living conditions they had never before in their lives had to contend with," wrote one unit historian.[149] The bases were typically set in a landscape of paddy fields, with the men housed in hostels. Without security fencing, men, aircraft, equipment, and personal possessions were always prey to theft. One camera unit, dispatched to take moving footage of operations at an outlying base in a misguided belief that such images would inspire the American public, found that thieves could penetrate even stoutly bolted rooms. They awoke to find, as one recorded, that "[b]andits had, by some ingenious method, sneaked in and stolen shoes, a pistol, a gas mask, leather flying jackets, mess gear, knives, flashlights, shirts and several clipfuls of cal. .44 ammunition."[150] No personal possessions were safe, and an airman carried anything he valued with him at all times. For reasons of sanitation, most meals were eaten in the hostels, and yet almost everyone lost weight—to dysentery, intestinal disorders, and curdled appetites. "I lost 20 pounds," pilot James Segel recorded of the months he was in China, "and eventually went on a diet of fried egg sandwiches and Spam, when available. Many mornings I dreaded the thought of getting into our C-47, because my growling stomach warned me that I would be racing for the toilet frequently." Flying to China from Assam, he would scrape together as much food as he could for friends in China.[151] In the hostels, the Americans boiled and bottled drinking water for themselves, then kept the bottles locked away.[152]

In Chanyi, the living quarters were built of mud brick and had a high, thin, wooden roof. Four beds were on each side of the single room, divided by a six-foot-wide "hall." In winter, a charcoal-burning stove fashioned from a fifty-gallon gasoline drum heated the room, but due in part to the height of the ceiling most heat was lost, and the men slept in their flying clothes. "I learned that if I sprinkled de-icer alcohol on the bare wood floor, ignited it, the room would warm up quickly," one pilot of this residence reported. Although the field elevation stood at over six thousand feet and there were no mosquitoes, the men slept with netting anyway, to deter the rats. With limited electricity, bridge games at night were played by candlelight—and this was the greatest form of entertainment that could be summoned.[153]

At Luliang, the single water filter that treated water for the base's two thousand personnel was anxiously monitored at all times, for the only source of water, the nearby river, was too filthy to consume even after being boiled. The river, used for washing lice-ridden clothing, bathing, and as a toilet, also carried dead bodies, as the base commander, Howard Stelling, reported, "at a point adjacent to our original water supply." The putrid raw water was pumped into tanks located around the base, from which it was then carried in buckets by local laborers to raised oil drums that served as showers. A visit from the air force surgeon general resulted in one mess hall being put off limits, "since the smell alone caused many soldiers to get up from his meals and rush outside to regurgitate." The living conditions, the ghastly food, the heavy and often dangerous workload, and the lack of any recreational facilities created a "marked depression among the majority of Americans."[154] At all the bases, considerable energy and ingenuity was mustered to devise forms of entertainment and distraction. A few had equipment for showing movies, and there might be pickup sports and card games. One particularly heroic effort drew much admiration—a production of *Oklahoma!* put on entirely by servicemen. "It was a beautiful production," one soldier recalled. "I have never seen another production of Oklahoma I liked better than sitting in the amphitheater on the side of the mountain in Kunming."[155]

The two playwrights in Assam who had written their drama about life on base at Chabua had, however, scored a greater hit. After twenty months in India, they returned to the US and sold their play *The Hump* to producer John Wildberg and director Harry Wagstaff Gribble, identified by the *India-Burma Theater Roundup* (recently renamed from the better-known *CBI-Roundup*) as "the team responsible for the popular play, *Anna Lucasta*." Set in 1943, "when activities of Hump flying were little known," the play was about new fliers and their first mission, and began and ended with "two men moving gear into a locker belonging to two men who didn't come back." In June, *Variety* was reporting that producer Wildberg was in Hollywood working on *Belle Brodie* and "a straight legit play, 'The Hump,'" and that Douglas Dick, an actor formerly with the US Navy, had signed on as lead. So enthusiastic was Harry Gribble, that he had received his copy of *The Hump* at four o'clock one afternoon and had bought the play by six thirty. The producers were hailing it as the "*Journey's End* of World War II," a reference to the bleak classic about life in the trenches of WWI. *The Hump* would surely likewise be a classic and capture for all time the CBI airmen's fear and sense of futility as they lived day-to-day in the shadow of death. Production was slated to begin on August 30, 1945.[156]

THE US AIR FORCE B-29 SUPERFORTRESS THAT ON AUGUST 6 DROPPED AN atomic bomb on the Japanese city of Hiroshima not only ended the war but, in the same flash, also consigned the lumbering efforts of the C-46s and their kind to the irrelevant past. The travails of hauling cargo to

China inspired little awe in the face of airpower's fierce new potency. Yet the end of the war did not end the duties of airmen flying the Hump, for they were co-opted for many tasks in the war's messy aftermath. They were needed to carry POWs rescued from the Japanese to medical centers, and to fly Graves Registration teams into the jungle to search for plane wreckage and the bodies that might be buried nearby.[157] And they flew bodies—of POWs, of airmen disinterred from the jungle and from the Hump base cemetery—to a central burial ground in Calcutta.[158]

The most significant and arduous task was the execution of a massive airlift of Chinese troops and US advisers to points in China. The Japanese had begun a retreat from their positions in south and central China in June and July so as to concentrate their forces in the north, where the Soviets were poised to enter Manchuria. To meet this threat, US transports dropped American-trained Chinese army troops to Luliang and Chanyi for dispersal. These troops fought two aggressive and successful campaigns around the key rail town of Chihkiang and in Hsin-ning, but all other fighting, such as it was, consisted of village skirmishes and outpost clashes. "Having decided to withdraw, the Japanese forces did withdraw at a leisurely and ordered manner," the Chinese Combat Command recorded. "Chinese forces, unwilling to engage in, and unable to see any reason for, costly combat conditions, followed closely but carefully."[159]

Once Japan surrendered, the same "crack troops" were flown by US transports to key points to accept the surrender and serve as occupation forces. Moving fuel for the operation as well as the troops required an elaborate choreography, but eventually 107,000 Nationalist soldiers were moved within an eighteen-day period to Nanking, Shanghai, and Peking from points in central and south China.[160] "Ever since the days of the Flying Tigers, it had seemed to the embattled Chinese that when a miracle had to be worked, U.S. aviators were the men to work it," as *Time* magazine reported the operation. "At war's end, Generalissimo Chiang Kai-shek asked the Army Air Forces to work one more."[161] The operation ensured that Chiang's government was in position to accept the Japanese surrenders ahead of the arrival of the Communist army, which was making its way to the same points on foot. Since at the end of the war the Nationalists controlled only 15 percent of China's geography, the airlift greatly extended Chiang's reach.[162]

Wedemeyer, writing to Marshall five days before the first atomic bomb was dropped, had expressed his concerns about the degree to which China was unprepared for peace. "Frankly, if peace should come within the next few weeks we will be woefully unprepared," he wrote. "The Chinese have no plan for rehabilitation, prevention of epidemics, restoration of utilities, establishment of balanced economy and redisposition of millions of refugees."[163] Air force personnel involved in the various airlifts were in the vanguard of such confusion, the extent and character of which was not widely reported. Many of the Chinese troops, reluctant recruits in the first place, were disinclined to fight at all now that the war was over. In Luliang, soldiers would break and run from their ranks when the time came to board the planes, only to be shot down by their commanding officers. Changing tactics, they embarked the aircraft, but bailed out of the open doors after the planes were about a hundred feet in the air. This, as the base commander reported, "had the same effect as shooting them and the commanders only expressed mild amusement."[164] Half a million Chinese troops deserted to the Japanese during the war, and of the eight million or so total troops "recruited" in the war years, half would never be accounted for, having deserted or died from noncombat-related events, such as disease.[165]

The Americans' final evacuation of their last air bases in China proved to be unnerving and dangerous. "Incidents" between Americans and Chinese were increasing, with a steady growth in what the theater history calls "Chinese depredations on U.S. installations," in which American soldiers had been stabbed, shot, and even killed, hinting that, despite all their efforts and goodwill, the Americans may have overstayed their welcome.[166]

In an extended essay, base commander Howard Stelling recorded "the horrors of my last days at Luliang," where he was to turn over the base and its supplies to the Chinese Air Force station manager. Luliang was also a staging base for the onward transportation to India of Fourteenth Air Force troops still in China, for whom Stelling had set up temporary quarters pending their evacuation. "[O]n several occasions these quarters were raided by the Chinese Army who stole great quantities of these supplies by brute force and in plain view of the American troops," he recorded. "The afternoon before I left, about 50 Chinese troops crowded around my quarters, after which several forced their way into my bedroom and took everything I owned. Similar groups entered the quarters of my staff." Calls to his former friend the garrison commander went unreturned, and he gained a safe exit with a last gift of his flight suit to the groups' ringleader. "Every bit of equipment we turned over to the Chinese had vanished into unknown private caches," he reported. "Good buildings were wrecked for the little pieces of hand-hewn lumber that constituted the flimsy floors."[167]

Significant amounts of matériel, however, were safely stored, as an OSS investigative unit had discovered in November of 1944 during the Japanese drive against the eastern airfields. Tasked with destroying everything of value to the Japanese as the American bases were abandoned, the unit commander followed up on a rumor that the Chinese had buried arms in the hills around the base at Tushan. The rumor, as it turned out, was true, yet he was unprepared for what he found: three massive ammunition dumps comprised of twenty to thirty warehouses, each about two hundred feet long, and crammed with fifty thousand tons of supplies. "There was ammunition of every type—French, Czech, American, Chinese, German, and Russian," wrote Theodore White, who had followed the retreat as a reporter; "there were mortars and thousands of mortar shells, fifty new pieces of artillery and huge quantities of ammunition to supply them."[168] The Japanese were only twenty miles away, and the Chinese forces that were meant to fight them were starved of equipment, yet the cache of arms remained inviolate.

The departure of the Americans from Assam was more decorous than from China. "When they were packing up and bound Stateside we were asked if we needed anything," the wife of a British political officer based in Sadiya recalled. Their small bungalow had sat under a navigational beaming station and, like many residents, they had lived under the throb and roar of Hump traffic for several years. Since there was no sugar available locally, she asked if they had any to spare. "A few days later a truck turned up and deposited not only a huge sack of sugar but big tins of ice cream powder, fruit, Spam (for which they apologized)." The *bashas* and buildings were burned, and equipment was crushed with bulldozers and buried, while the mass of heavy machinery used to build the road was offered to the British government, for a price. After some negotiation, the British agreed to pay, acquiring everything from bulldozers to radios, which they in turn offered for sale, with the result that merchants from all over India converged to bid for the equipment.[169] Thus, in these disparate ways, the Hump's hard-won tonnage was dispersed, and the Hump itself formally closed on November 15, 1945.

According to General Tunner's final assessment, ATC aircraft carried 776,532 tons over the Hump to China between December 1, 1942, and the end of its operation. Far and away the greatest part of this was hauled during Tunner's own fourteen-month-long command, a period that also saw a sharp drop in accidents—to one accident for every four hundred sorties, an improvement of roughly 146 percent compared to estimations of losses during the operation's earliest days.[170] Officially, 594 ATC transport planes were lost over the Hump, with estimates of crew killed or missing ranging from 1,659 to 3,861; an astonishing 1,200 were thought to have survived bailouts over the mountains and jungle.[171] These figures are undoubtedly incomplete, given the less-than-rigorous record-keeping, particularly during early stages of the operation: for one thing, very few reports were filed for aircraft lost before June 1943.[172] CNAC estimates of the ATC's losses were significantly higher and cite 1,404 Army Air Forces planes "totally wrecked." The number of CNAC's own losses—37 planes—is readily known, since CNAC—"[i]n contrast to the Armed

Forces," as one CNAC pilot pointedly wrote—had complete and accurate records of dates, crew lost, plane models, and numbers.[173]

The last of such accidents occurred on September 21, 1945, when a C-46 flying at night out of Misamari, India, encountered engine trouble. With the engine cutting on and off intermittently and the plane rapidly losing altitude, the three-man crew bailed out in the region of Mang Shih, China, near the Burma border. Bad weather prevented a search party from reaching the area for several days, but when the weather cleared rescuers found the site, which the radio operator had flagged with distress panels displayed in a paddy field at the edge of a village. The pilot, James Powell, had hit a tree on landing and broken his leg, and a Chinese girl was killed when the rescue plane dropped medical supplies. In the meantime, the local people had set the pilot's leg with a cast of cow dung. Copilot Edmund Webb, who had bailed out last and lacked sufficient altitude for his parachute to open, was killed.[174]

The last recorded accident involving ATC personnel was not over the Hump but on an inter-India flight, on November 3, 1945, when a C-54 left Chabua loaded with servicemen for Karachi, where they were to embark on passages home. The plane was last reported in the vicinity of Jorhat, after which nothing more from it was heard, but weeks later its wreckage was located on the side of a mountain in Bhutan, well north of the usual course. The reports about its eventual fate are conflicting. The pilot of a second C-54, also flying from Chabua to Karachi and acquainted with many of those killed, was quoted as saying that "a holiday spirit prevailed among all the passengers facing the possibility of an early arrival in the U.S.," and speculated that they might have wanted to go sightseeing in the region of Mount Everest.[175] But the flight was at night, and the eventual accident analysis found the aircraft had been cruising at eight thousand feet, when its right wing struck trees, causing it to crash into a mountainous forest.[176] All forty-four crew and passengers were killed— one of the highest numbers of fatalities of any single-aircraft accident in the CBI theater.

AT WAR'S END, MOST OF THE TOWNS IN BURMA NO LONGER EXISTED. "THE old Bhamo has ceased to be," wrote a priest reporting to his mission superiors. "Not a house is standing. Everywhere there are trenches, shell holes, bomb craters." Katha was destroyed. Myitkyina was destroyed. Mandalay was destroyed. Zaubung was burned; the catalog of damage seemed endless.[177] The country's Civil Government, which included British high officials and Burmese ministers, returned to Rangoon with the expectation of presiding over a leisurely transitional process that would eventually culminate with an independent Burma nestled within the British Commonwealth. To great discomfort, the officials learned that the independence movement, led by General Aung San, the young, high-minded commander of Burma's National Army, had determined on a brisker timeline for the transition and saw no need for Britain's mentoring hand. The Union of Burma became an independent republic on the first day of January 1948; tragically, Aung San was assassinated by political rivals five months before the historic date.[178] Left behind in the eventual settlement were hill people who had fought with the Allies, motivated in part by hatred for the Japanese, but also by the hope that British rule, and the protection it had long accorded them, would continue after the war.

India's independence, long foreseen, came in August 1947 in the form of two riven nations, India and Pakistan. The fate of the Naga people of Assam, who had previously not considered themselves to be Indian, was left unsettled, and many Naga veterans returned to their villages in what was now independent India to discover that no government had made provisions for them.[179]

China, whose economy continued to spiral downward, was clearly destined to resume its civil war. From the distant and prosperous safety of the United States, CBI veterans regarded their "old stomping grounds" with dismay. "India and China are worse off today than at any time during the war," was the assessment of the CBI veteran's newsletter, *Ex-CBI Roundup*. "India has her independence, but the Moslems and Hindus continue to riot and murder. China's economic system has collapsed entirely. The war in Asia goes on."[180]

Left unrealized was Roosevelt's dream of a postwar democratic China standing in solid alliance with the United States and filling the power vacuum in the East that would exist when the European nations surrendered their colonies. This was the dream that had sent not only American airmen over the Hump, but American engineers and British soldiers into the jungle of Burma. The unprecedented air operation, resulting in the world's greatest cargo-carrying airline, was this dream's most tangible achievement.

The larger question is, what did this great achievement achieve? It was a question that many after the war tried to assess, officially and privately. The US Air Force history tackled it by first addressing the conventional claims of the Hump's accomplishments: that by supplying Chennault's command it prevented Chiang Kai-shek's regime from collapsing, that it prevented the Japanese from overrunning all of China, that it saved China as a base for launching attacks against Japanese shipping and instillations. Yet it passes over these contentions with disconcerting swiftness to state that the Hump lift's "[m]ore important" role was as the "proving ground, if not the birthplace, of massive strategic airlift." The Army Air Forces, the history concludes, "demonstrated conclusively that a vast quantity of cargo could be delivered by air, even under the most unfavorable circumstances, if only the men who controlled the aircraft, the terminals, and the needed materiel were willing to pay the price in money and in men."

The question of the value of the airlift was of course one that the airmen of the Hump asked themselves. It was the proud boast of many that supplying China had tied up the Japanese in China, a force that at one time had numbered as many as a million troops. In fact, by 1944, of the twenty-four Japanese divisions in China, ten were stationed in the north to guard the Manchurian border. The fourteen divisions dispersed throughout the rest of China were, in the words of the Japanese leadership, "inferior in quality," being newly organized forces amounting to two hundred ninety thousand men, taking the place of the well-trained, veteran troops who had been sent to the Pacific.[181] In any case, as pilot James Segel, among many others, pointed out, even if China had gone over to the Japanese, "China alone was a major headache to control, as there were many regional warlords with private armies, who were experienced in fighting guerrilla wars. They could keep the Japanese military very busy." His conclusion was that "[o]nce started, the CBI campaign was taken for granted as an essential military operation. But its questionable results indicate that it may have been a terrible waste, costing us dearly."[182] Howard Stelling, commander of the benighted Luliang base, was less analytical but perhaps more eloquent. "I cannot dwell on the military causes and effects of our mission. I must drop that flat before I become utterly confused again."[183]

AFTER BOB BOODY SAID GOODBYE TO HIS FIANCÉE, JEAN PARKS, BESIDE THE hospital plane, he dropped all contact with her. Back in the US, he had a second operation on his damaged leg, resulting in another amputation. He learned to walk and ski on a prosthetic leg, and refused all handicapped services. He married, had children, and became an active participant in his church and an array of civic organizations, including the Freemasons and Sons of the Revolution. Along the way, he continued to fly recreationally and named each of his succession of planes "Little Butch," after his abandoned fiancée. She had continued to write to him, but, as he recorded, "I never could get myself to reply, and to this day I don't know why! Possibly, it was because I felt I was less of a man for the loss of my leg and therefore no longer qualified to be husband and provider to such a wonderful lady. The longer I went without writing, the more difficult it became for me to do so. May God help me and bless her."

In 1987, he came across her name in a newsletter for CBI veterans, and at last contacted her. They met at his home in Staten Island forty-three years since she had seen him safely onto the evacuation plane beside the steaming jungles of Assam. So many shared and improbable memories: dances on the tea estate; the towering forests around the hospital in Shingbwiyang. . . . "It was a happy meeting," his son recalled. Boody died in 2002, at the age of eighty-one, in Staten Island.[184] Jean Seidel, née Parks, died at age ninety-one, having continued to work as a nurse "in numerous hospitals," as her obituary states, "as the Army relocated the family."[185]

The memories of the survivors from across the chaotic CBI theater were long safeguarded by an array of organizations that served as enclaves of shared experience—of tea planters in Assam, of survivors of the exodus from Burma, of the Chindits, of veterans of Kohima, of the pilots and other airmen who flew the Hump. Strikingly, there was never an organization for those who built the Ledo Road. A multivolume history of the CBI from the airman's point of view published by the Hump Pilots Association is dense with reminiscences—of life in the faraway *bashas*, of the cities of the East, plantations of tea, of the jungle and glittering ranges they had once overflown, along with accounts of worst-flight experiences, disasters, and bailouts, often embedded in summations of otherwise ordinary lives.

William N. Hanahan

Enlisted December, 1942, Basic training at Keesler Field. . . . Attended C-46 training at Reno, Nev. Left for Chabua, India, in Dec. 1944. Made 100 round trips over the Rockpile to China bases. . . . [M]emorable event was bailing out over the first ridge near Shingbwiyang and walking out in three days in March 1945. Graduated Ohio University 1951 with a degree in Industrial Engineering and have worked at Goodyear Tire and Rubber Co. in aircraft fuel tanks for the past 25 years. . . .[186]

Many veterans were haunted not so much by their own experiences as by those of lost friends. William Baker, a former pilot who had flown

"That Night" in January of 1945, often talked about a William S. Jones—
"a man whose name Dad has never once forgotten," Baker's daughter said.
"Jones, Dad will say, is still over there. He flew out one night on a routine
flight the night before he was scheduled to go home, and never returned.
I don't think Dad has ever really gotten over that."[187] For Durwood
Kincheloe, who worked in the control tower at Chanyi, the memories
came in dreams: "I could hear airplanes calling for assistance, 'Hey tower,
I'm out of gas, what do I do.' . . . I can hear and see the vision of these boys
calling, wanting help, wanting down and you're trying your best to get
them down and not run into each other."[188]

The aftermath of these disasters, the grief and loss of the families left
behind, remains mostly private, denoted at times by small, inscrutable
notices in local papers, like those that appeared over a succession of years
for Corporal Wesley McCormick:

McCORMICK—Corp. Wesley F. McCormick.
A.A.F., C.B.I. In loving memory of
our son, Wesley, who was killed in the
Burma area, Feb. 25, 1945.
Not just today, but every day,
In silence we remember.
LONESOME MOTHER AND DAD.[189]

Corporal McCormick, flying as navigator on a C-46 out of Sookerating and bound for Luliang, had bailed with the pilot and copilot over the
Hukawng Valley after their plane encountered ice. While the two other
crew members evacuated safely, McCormick did not turn up. A search
party was dispatched and found him. "He had come down in a tree," the
lead rescuer recorded; "but his chute had caught in the upper branches
and allowed him to drop through. . . . Before he could unbuckle his left
leg strap, he had obviously lost his balance and fell forward out of his
seat." He was left hanging upside down, one foot in his strap, his head on
the ground, where red ants found him and began devouring his face and

head. With his handgun, McCormick had tried to shoot and sever the strap around his ankle, and when this did not succeed, he had used the last bullet to shoot himself.[190]

Occasionally, glimpses of private grief are placed before the public. Three years after he had been forced to bail out into the Burmese jungle, Eric Sevareid was back at his father's house in the United States, when out of a snowstorm there arrived the father of Second Lieutenant Charles Felix, the copilot of the plane from which Sevareid had jumped, and who now lay buried on the Patkai Range. Mr. Felix came directly from the train station in wrinkled clothes and with bloodshot eyes, limping on his wooden leg that was a talisman of the last Great War. Charles Felix, Sevareid learned, had been an only child, and his father was tortured by grief and questions; "Why was my son the only one to die?" "I convinced him, I think," Sevareid wrote, "that his son had died instantly and had not suffered."[191]

The most pointed and significant expression of public grief came from Gladys "Chick" Marrs Quinn, whose husband, Lieutenant Loyal Stuart Marrs Jr., had been killed when his C-109 tanker filled with fuel crashed in the Naga Hills as he was flying from Jorhat to Chengtu. Marrs had been considered one of the outstanding pilots based in Jorhat, although he had been in the CBI theater for only a few months.[192] The crash site was located in a rocky ravine, but the force of the explosion had obliterated all trace of the actual wreckage, and of its crew.[193] Loyal was killed at the end of February 1945, and by April, Chick, at age twenty-three, had joined the WACs. Her stated objective was to be sent somewhere in the CBI so as to visit the exact location of where her husband had met his death—his actual grave—but the war ended before this could happen.[194] Instead, she set herself the task of compiling a record of every fatal crash over the Hump. The culmination of nearly a decade of work, her book, *The Aluminum Trail: How and Where They Died*, stands as the most complete document of the Hump's toll of loss.

"The shock of death leaves you temporarily unable to think for yourself," Chick had said in an interview following her enlistment in the

WACs. "You feel you have nothing to turn to, nothing to look forward to. That's when you have to get a grip on yourself and realize that you can't cling forever to memories." But she did cling to memories, and for the entirety of her life. She married again, "a droll fellow," according to her niece, "all engrossed in the flower farm he ran. She helped him out, but she had pictures of Loyal all around the house. Even in later life Aunt Chick was looking back to the Second World War." Chick and Loyal had been high school sweethearts, and their honeymoon in Gulfport, where he was sent for training, according to her niece, was the happiest period of her life.[195] For all her research, it was over forty years before Chick learned the circumstances that had led to her husband's death. Decades later, she made contact with the pilot who had flown Loyal's plane before him. C-109 #2000 had been spraying gasoline out of the trailing edge of a wing, the former pilot now told her, and he had turned back to Jorhat, where his arrival was not welcomed; "in those days," he told Chick, "if you turned back, it was like desertion." The expediting officer ran up the engines, reported that everything was okay, had the tanks topped off, and called another crew. The pilot of the other crew was her husband.[196]

Gladys "Chick" Marrs Quinn died in 2004 and was buried in the same Kentucky cemetery in which her first husband is commemorated. Her memorial marker is brutally succinct:

CHICK
BELOVED WIFE OF
LT L S MARRS JR[197]

Quinn's book has also served to guide ongoing searches for the hundreds of crashed aircraft that still lie undiscovered in the jungles, valleys, and fractured ranges beneath the Hump's old route. Yet so dense is the jungle, so remote the terrain, that even with GPS locators or images from space the wreckage can go undetected. Clayton Kuhles, a private recovery operator with a single-minded passion for the Hump, has discovered the most wrecks, including that of CNAC #58, the C-53 that in 1943 crashed into a mountain slope, and whose two survivors were rescued by Mishmi tribesmen. Kuhles's directions to the site give a taste of the terrain involved: "Cross to E bank of Lohit River on hanging bridge just downstream of Samdul/Minzong. Trek upstream Kallong River to Mishmi village of Bhau. Trek upstream Kallong River to Ghalum River. Trek upstream Ghalum River to Ngat River. Trek upstream Ngat River to Tap River. Trek upstream Tap River and SE up mountain to crash site. Crash site overlooks the Tap River (tributary of Ngat River) and is near India-Burma border." The fuselage of the plane, as he discovered, had been used as a shelter by Mishmi hunters. When Kuhles showed an elderly Mishmi woman a photograph of the two Americans whom as a young woman she had personally tended, she "immediately and joyfully recognized" the men.[198]

ALL ACROSS THIS SAME TERRAIN, THROUGHOUT THE WAR, ANOTHER, AN-cient route had also carried a steady flow of supplies from India to China. Like goods destined for the Hump, those bound for the ancient route arrived by ship in Calcutta, where they were collected by throngs of Tibetan merchants and small traders representing government officials and lamaseries, great and small, back in Lhasa; the Dalai Lama, it was said, had invested part of his private fortune to exploit the once-in-a-lifetime opportunity created by Japan's closing of China's ports.

In Calcutta, the Tibetan traders bought or contracted everything that could be carried by mule: sewing machines, cast-iron cooking ranges, textiles, cases of British and American cigarettes, whiskey and gin, canned goods, toiletries—all were transferred by the merchants onto trains and trucks and sent onward to Kalimpong, an Indian hill town in West Bengal. Here, in the foothills of the Himalayas, the goods were repacked and dispatched by caravan to Lhasa, where they filled the halls of palaces and lamaseries while awaiting professional packers. These expertly sorted the goods, setting the sturdiest articles aside for the yak caravans that would carry them along the rougher, northern route to Tachienlu. The rest were bound for Likiang, the market town that lay beneath the mountain, whose distinctive cleft summit and perpetual plume of snow served Hump airmen as the landmark where they "turned the corner" to the south.

From Likiang, the caravans would travel onward, as they had done for centuries, to Kunming. Weighing each load with care, the packers wrapped the bundled goods in woolen mats and sewed them carefully into wet hides that, shrinking as they dried, compressed the contents into solid masses impervious to damage. Muleteers, and sometimes lowly human porters, wearing broad straw hats and felt blankets as protection against the snow and rain, set out across the roof of the world on the three-month-long journey to Kunming. An estimated 8,000 mules and horses and 20,000 yaks participated in the historic expansion of the normal caravan trade; and when peace came unexpectedly, and the ports in Canton and Shanghai reopened, the caravan traffic immediately receded.[199] "Few people have realized how vast and unprecedented this sudden expansion of caravan traffic between India and China was," wrote Peter Goullart, a longtime European resident of Likiang; "it demonstrated to the world very convincingly that, should all modern means of communication and transportation be destroyed by some atomic cataclysm, the humble horse, man's oldest friend, is ever ready to forge again a link between scattered peoples and nations."[200]

By contrast, most of the aircraft that flew the Hump were deemed obsolete by the end of the war and were not returned to where they had been built. Many air force personnel went home by ship, and most workhorse planes were destroyed, cut into pieces and burned. "They burned all our airplanes," recalled one pilot. "They weren't safe to fly any more. We flew them every day of the week and they wouldn't let us fly home."[201] The exception was the indomitable DC-3/C-47, which still flies the air. "An airplane of refinement and gentle manners," is the testimonial of one Hump pilot; "an honest, faithful machine that flew and flew and flew, always bringing me home again," runs the tribute of another. "There is no life span, as there are DC-3s in use today over 60 years old, with as much as

80,000 hours total time," pilot Segel pointed out in his memoir. "Many aviation experts consider that the creation of the DC-3 was the greatest event in modern aviation."[202]

While the air operation to supply China inspired other historic events, such as the Berlin airlift in 1948 to 1949 (also directed by General Tunner), modern advances have left the epic behind. Military transports today carry payloads of eighty-five tons, against the "giant" C-54's typical six-ton payload, while the payload of the Soviet Antonov An-225 Mriya is an astounding 253 tons.[203] All the elemental features that made the Hump route so formidable are unchanged—the monsoon and winds from Asia still slam against the Himalayas—but aircraft today simply fly above them.

Many man-made landmarks of the Hump's chaotic theater have long vanished. By 1946, the pipeline installed beside the Ledo Road to carry fuel to Myitkyina was being repurposed to irrigate rice fields.[204] Already in 1945, the Ledo Road itself was seen to be disintegrating, and in 1946 an American reporter who had accompanied the road's first convoy returned to find that the jungle was "stretching its green fingers out to take back The Road that had once been part of it. Creepers and weeds were already ankle-high cross sections of the highway. In other places, vegetation came drooping down from overhead. . . . High up I could see where landslides had almost completely erased the thin, man-made scar on the mountainsides."[205]

In Assam, many old tea estates remain, along with new ones, and the US air bases are now used by the Indian Air Force. Local people still remember the Americans and the many goods they left behind—"from steel planking to salt," as one family living near Dinjan recalled. The soldiers seemed fairly young, and "they walked around the villages with beer cans in their hand and shot monkeys that were destroying paddy fields." They also handed out a novel form of candy—sweets in flat, white packets that one could chew for a long time. It was often wondered "how it must have been for these young fellows to come from so far and live in such conditions, away from their family and friends."[206]

The Hukawng Valley Wildlife Sanctuary is now home to the largest tiger reserve on earth, and while there is much encroachment on the buffer zone around it, the land of the reserve itself is little changed from what the pilots of years ago looked down upon with fear and awe. I had the privilege of being there in time of peace and so could dwell upon the pristine rivers, the green shade of the luxuriant trees, the waterfowl, the butterflies, the tiger pugmarks on the river sand.

A few small communities live in the valley. The clusters of neat bamboo and thatched houses that I visited were Naga homes. Beside these, ringing gardens and vegetable plots, stood fences of jagged metal. "The fences are cut from the fuselage of the planes they find in the jungle," my Forest Department companions told me. Ahead of us, beyond the valley, stretched a blue line of mountains that seemed to be always lightly crowned with clouds. One of my companions pointed ahead. "That," he said, "is the Hump."

ACKNOWLEDGMENTS

My first debt of gratitude is to Jeff Arnett and J. V. Vinyard, veteran pilots of the Hump, who shared some of their remarkable experiences with me. Mr. Vinyard was also the last president of the China-Burma-India Hump Pilots Association, whose four volume anthology of both official and private papers is an invaluable resource for the researcher. Additionally I owe great thanks to Richard Hilder, who gave a memorable account of Chindit operations in Burma in the monsoon.

Thanks are also due to a number of people who shared their parents' stories, and in some cases documents. William Barksdale III generously made available boxes of papers of Lieutenant Colonel William Barksdale Jr., who had been commanding officer of the Jorhat air base. Suzanne Baker shared reminiscences and a family history of her father, William Morgan Baker. Lee Boody kindly allowed me to quote from his father Robert Boody's published diary and memoir, and spoke movingly of his last years. Matthew Campanella Jr. told me of his father's historic and extraordinary bailout into the land of the Mishmi. Anne Constein generously allowed me to quote from her father Dr. Carl Frey Constein's two works and vividly evoked his character. Alex Dominick allowed me to quote from the publication of his father Peter Dominick's diary, which

Alex edited, and also shared information of his father's life. Similarly, Dana Downie allowed me to quote from her father Don Downie's account of flying the Hump, a book that is distinguished by the exceptional color photographs that Downie took. John Easterbrook kindly allowed me to quote from the work of his grandfather General Joseph Stilwell. Nell Galloway was generous with her time at the Chennault Aviation and Military Museum. Vance Haynes kindly sent me material about his father, General Caleb V. Haynes, the pioneering "dean of the big ships." I am grateful to Munindra Khaund for his information about Dinjan and family memories of the young airmen. I owe much gratitude to Dawn Balfour, who evoked her aunt Gladys "Chick" Marrs Quinn, historian of the Hump. To Suzanne St. Pierre I am extremely grateful for her generous permission to quote from her father Eric Sevareid's outstanding memoir, *Not So Wild a Dream*. Thanks to Frederick Seidel for recollections of his mother, Mary Jean Parks Seidel.

My thanks to Jim Rumack for sharing his copy of *Situation CBI*, the evocative memoir of the 1880th Engineer Aviation Battalion that his father, Al Rumuck, had played an important role in producing.

Research for this book was greatly aided by Tammy Horton, archivist of the Air Force Historical Research Agency, Maxwell Air Force Base, who supplied scans of thousands of pages of US Air Force documents. My thanks, too, to Archangelo DiFante, also of the AFHRA, and Jeffrey Michalke, of the Air Mobility Command Office. Closer to home, I am deeply grateful to Daniela Accettura, of the Northeast Harbor Library, who provided a steady stream of books and articles through interlibrary loan.

I would like to thank some of the many libraries and archives that provided documents, often when they were short-staffed, through the pandemic. They are: the Anglo-Burmese Library; the Museum of Aviation, Warner Robins, GA; Yale University's Beinecke Rare Book & Manuscript Library; the Burnet County Library, Burnet, TX; the Division of Rare and Manuscript Collections at Cornell University; Columbia University's Oral History Archives; Florida State University's Strozier Library; Florida Gateway College's Wilson S. Rivers Library and Media Center; the

George C. Marshall Foundation of Lexington, VA; the Hoover Institution Library & Archives; the Huntington Library, Art Museum, and Botanical Gardens, which holds both private papers and photographs of medical personnel in the theater; the Imperial War Museums; the Kohima Educational Trust, which runs an excellent series of webinars; Koi-Hai, the association for tea-planters of Assam and Northeast India; the Library of Congress Veterans History Project; Luther Seminary in St. Paul, MN; the National Museum of the Pacific War; the University of Minnesota Libraries' Department of Archives and Special Collections; and the SFO Museum, San Francisco, CA.

And I owe a very great debt of gratitude to Oliver Payne and the late Alan Rabinowitz, who brought me to the Hukawng Valley, and to Saw Htoo Tha Po and his tiger team for taking me around it; and much gratitude is owed to Rob Tizard, from whom I first learned about the Hump. Others who helped in various ways and to whom thanks are due are Richard Lorraine-Smith, Chuck Hodge, Ge Shuya, Florence Reeves, Kim Roseberry, John Snyder, Denys Shortt, Joshua Whitfield, and Morex Arai. I am grateful to Ann Trevor for running down documents in the US National Archives and Records Administration. Thanks, too, for Eric Van Slander, also at NARA.

To Wendy Wolf of Viking, my editorial North Star for many years, the deepest thanks for shepherding every aspect of this book from start to finish. And to Clare Alexander for giving me and this book a safe landing. I would also like to thank key players in the Viking editorial, design, and production team: they are Paloma Ruiz, Rob Sternitsky, Cliff Corcoran, Kim Daly, Anna Scheithauer, Daniel Lagin, and Gabriel Levinson—and David Litman, for going an extra mile for the jacket.

Finally, much gratitude to Frank Blair for unwavering support at home, as well as for his invaluable guidance and instruction—and for those unique insights gained by flying cross-country in a small, experimental plane in turbulence. And lasting gratitude to Mr. Nutkin, most conscientious of assistants, and Miu Miu, who was there to the end.

CREDITS

Grateful acknowledgment is made for permission to reprint excerpts from the following:

Boody, Robert T. *Food-Bomber Pilot, China-Burma-India: A Diary of the Forgotten Theater of World War II*. Staten Island, New York: Robert T. Boody, 1989. Copyright © 1989 by Robert Treat Boody. Used with permission of Lee Boody.

Constein, Dr. Carl Frey. *Born to Fly the Hump* and *Tales of the Himalayas*. Copyright © 2001 and 2002 by Dr. Carl Frey Constein. Used with permission of Anne G. Constein.

Dominick, Alexander S., ed. *Flying the Hump: The War Diary of Peter H. Dominick*. Green Bay, Wisconsin: M&B Global Solutions, Inc., revised ed, 2022. Copyright © 2022. Used with permission of Alex Dominick.

Ethell, Jeff, and Don Downie. *Flying the Hump: In Original World War II Color*. St. Paul MN: Motorbooks, 2004. Copyright © 1995, 2004 by Don Downie and Jeffrey L. Ethell. Used with permission of Dana Downie.

Han Shan. "Cold Mountain" by Han Shan, translated by David Hinton from *Classical Chinese Poetry*, translated and edited by David Hinton. Copyright © 2008 by David Hinton. Reprinted by permission of Farrar, Straus and Giroux. All rights reserved.

Kincheloe, Durwod Chester. "WWII Memories of Durwood Chester Kincheloe," World War II Oral History Series, Burnet County Library System; accessed through National Museum of the Pacific War, Durwood Chester Kincheloe oral history interview, OH2231tr.: 1-27. Used with permission of Herman Brown Free Library.

Marshall, George C. *Papers*, The George C. Marshall Foundation. Used with permission of the George C. Marshall Foundation of Lexington, VA.

Masters, John. *The Road Past Mandalay*. London: Cassell, reprint 2012. Extract by John Masters reprinted by permission of Pollinger Limited (www.pollingerlimited.com) on behalf of the Estate of John Masters.

Sevareid, Eric. *Not So Wild a Dream*. Columbia, Missouri: University of Missouri Press, 1995. Copyright © 1946, renewed 1974 by Eric Sevareid. Used with permission of Suzanne St. Pierre Sevareid, care of Don Congdon Associates, Inc.

Stilwell, General Joseph W. *The Stilwell Papers*, edited by Theodore H. White. New York: Da Capo Press, Inc., 1991. Copyright © 1948; renewed 1975. Used with permission of John Easterbrook.

NOTES

1. PRELUDE

1. Fritsche, 181ff.
2. Quinn, 95.
3. Constein, *Tales of the Himalayas*, 122, as told by Raymond M. Rodgers.
4. USAAF, "Interrogation of PFC (NMI), Kaplan, 12182139."
5. Kelly, 458f.

2. THE BURMA ROAD

1. Mitter, 65f, 59, 52f.
2. Fitzgerald, "The Yunnan–Burma Road," 164.
3. Chang, *Burma Road*, 107.
4. Japan did not officially declare war on China until January 1938—after its conquest of Shanghai and Nanking. Mitter, 146.
5. Plating, 16.
6. Pickler, 36f.
7. Plating, 16, 20f.
8. Tan, 26f. For Marco Polo's account, see his *Travels*, 161ff., and notes, 380.
9. For a survey of the long interest in a Mandalay to Yangzte rail line, and its many false starts, see Croizier.
10. Fitzgerald, *The Tower of Five Glories*, 2, 4; Rosinger, 19.
11. Fitzgerald, *The Tower of Five Glories*, 10f.
12. For opium trade, Goullart, 205; for Chiang Kai-shek's fears, Mitter, 206, 252.
13. Fitzgerald, *The Tower of Five Glories*, 210.
14. The two principal sources for the building of the road are Tan Pei-Ying, and Fitzgerald, "The Yunnan–Burma Road." This section follows closely Tan's account, 38ff.
15. Tan, 42.
16. Tan, 56.
17. Tan, 143; but see Smith, *Burma Road*, 160ff., for his haunting description of the symptoms of arsenic poisoning in the young tin miners of Kochiu (Gejiu), situated

about 150 miles south of Kunming, which included their skin becoming green and their faces and bodies grotesquely swollen.

18. Tan, 149.
19. Tan, 105ff.; the quotation is on 112f.
20. Tan, 93.
21. Tan, 57f.
22. This section closely follows Tan, and the song lyrics are taken verbatim from Tan, 52.
23. Tan, 10; "so small . . . buffalo" being a direct quote.
24. Tan, 151.
25. Fitzgerald, "The Yunnan–Burma Road," 171.
26. "drive . . . into the sea," quoted from Harvey, 22.
27. For the downfall of Thibaw, Thant Myint-U, 12, 18–22, 156–62; and Harvey, 21ff.
28. The composition of the government and its strengths and weaknesses are variously described in Maung Htin Aung, 297; Harvey, 82ff.; and Thant Myint-U, 215f.
29. Thant Myint-U, 166, and Harvey, 49; for the remittance of income to England or India, Maung Htin Aung, 273.
30. Taw Sein Ko, 49f.
31. Thant Myint-U, 3ff., chapter titled "The Fall of the Kingdom," especially 20ff.
32. Goodall, 83f.; Thant Myint-U, 19.
33. Population statistics, McLynn, 7.
34. Migration: Thant Myint-U, 185; Harvey (who breaks down the numbers per year), 71. For the Chettiars: Thant Myint-U, 185; Harvey, 55f.; Charney, 10f.
35. Furnivall, "Burma Fifty Years Ago: Little Picture of Progress," *Guardian Magazine* (Rangoon) 5, no. 10 (October 1958): 29–30; quoted in Charney, 23.
36. Taw Sein Ko, 50, 322ff.
37. Scott, *Burma: A Handbook*, 26ff.
38. Gribble, 18.
39. Many works discuss this mixture of wizardry and religion; see for example Taw Sein Ko, 167ff. and 173ff. For a modern survey of this magical landscape, see Patton.
40. Quote from Harvey, 73. For fuller accounts of this extraordinary rebellion, see Thant Myint-U, 209f.; Charney, 13ff.
41. The frontier described and government policy discussed in: Thant Myint-U, 194ff.; Scott, *Burma: A Handbook*, 146ff., with detailed description of British government organization in the hill areas; Harvey, 11f. and 84f.; Taw Sein Ko, 7ff., on the hill tribes and their lapse into "savagery"; Charney, 37f., on the ethnic minorities' fear of the Burmans. See also Burma, Frontier Areas Committee of Enquiry, 7ff. The quotes of the civil servant is from Harvey, 86; the number of British officers in the Chin Hills follows Harvey, 85.
42. Seppings, 2.
43. Thant Myint-U, 210ff.; for vivid records of missionary life, see Morse; Seagrave, *Burma Surgeon*; Fischer.
44. Forbes, 20.
45. Campagnac, 262, who gives a haunting reminiscence across many years of a beloved padauk tree in his Rangoon garden.
46. A wonderfully vivid snapshot of the city just before the war is given in Chin Y. Lee, *A Corner of Paradise*, a memoir of his service with the Saopa of Mang Shih, a Shan state near the Burmese border.
47. Charney, 26.

48. Khin Yi, 86ff., 106.
49. This section closely follows Charney, 32; see also Maung Htin Aung, 277.
50. Thakin Nu, 1f.
51. Thant Myint-U, 229.
52. Thant Myint-U, 218.
53. Plating, 18.
54. Craw, 241.
55. Smith, *Burma Road*, 305ff., for a description of Lashio; shop supplies given at 309f. Smith was an adventurous travel writer and later a member of the OSS (Dunlop, 87f., offers a cameo of him on the job).
56. Lunt, 53.
57. Chang, *Burma Road*, 13f.; the quote is on 14.
58. Quote is from Lee, 53; his book is laced with descriptions of the upheaval caused by the presence of the Chinese truckers.
59. Chang, *Burma Road*, 8.
60. Borg, 155.
61. For timeline: Chetwode, Keeling, et al., state that the road was kept open in the summer of 1939, "except for a short time," due to the rains, 172; the quote is from Craw, 241.
62. Craw, 241, 243.
63. Craw, 242.
64. For the car make, Smith, *Burma Road*, 225; the journey and accident, 264, 316ff.
65. Chetwode, Keeling, et al., 173.
66. Smith, *Burma Road*, 257.
67. Roxby, 171.
68. Craw, 242; and see Thorne, 80, citing the US military mission to China findings.
69. Outram and Fane, 629.
70. Mallory, 627.
71. Wang Jing-wei had once been seen as the natural successor to Sun Yat-sen, and had played a significant role in China's revolutionary struggle.
72. Paraphrasing Taylor, *The Generalissimo*, 174f.
73. Chiang's threat of capitulation, Taylor, *The Generalissimo*, 174f.; see also a summary of this exchange with Ambassador Nelson T. Johnson, Romanus and Sunderland, I.9.
74. Dreifort, 279ff.
75. Japan's request and Churchill's reply, Plating, 24; qualification of the road closure and quote regarding banned supplies, Craw, 245.
76. Mitter, 235.
77. "Mr. Lauchlin Currie to President Roosevelt," FRUS Diplomatic Papers, 1941, The Far East, Volume IV, Document 57: 81–95, with quotes from 82f., 83, 86, 92.
78. Romanus and Sunderland, I.13f.
79. Romanus and Sunderland, I.15f.
80. Romanus and Sunderland, I.26f.
81. Romanus and Sunderland, I.29f.
82. On Toungoo, Ford, *Flying Tigers*, 57ff. The AVG is discussed in the following chapter.
83. Dawes, 1.
84. Goodall, 31ff.
85. Thant Myint-U, 223.
86. Glass, 130.

87. Slim, 5; Ford, *Flying Tigers*, 105, 108.
88. Dawes, 3.
89. Ford, *Flying Tigers*, 110.
90. Campagnac, 272.
91. Pearn, 7.
92. Tinker, 4ff. The tragic saga of what would amount to one of the great refugee evacuations of the war is told in many personal memoirs by survivors, as well as by the official "The Rangoon Civil Evacuation Scheme," prepared by B. R. Pearn.
93. Goodall, 37. This is the best single work for an overall evocation of the exodus, drawing as it does on firsthand sources in the form of letters, diaries, and memoirs, as well as official papers; it is supplemented by the author's own descriptions from her travels to many of the key places named. The papers of Jean Melville, whom Goodall cites in this section, are in the Imperial War Museum, Documents, 17492.
94. Tinker, 5; prohibition of male Europeans, Pearn, 16.
95. Expected reinforcements, Lunt, 81; logistics of supply, Foucar, 179.
96. Collis, 50.
97. For the Chinese-British impasse, Romanus and Sunderland, I.53ff.; also McLynn, 20f.; Tuchman, 286ff.
98. Lunt, 81; and Collis, 52ff., elaborating on Wavell's reasoning.
99. Romanus and Sunderland, I.55.
100. Eight hundred British soldiers, Goodall, 32; strength of Burma division, Callahan, 29; characterization of the Burma Rifles, Lunt, 47ff.
101. Lunt, 48.
102. Lunt, 70ff.
103. Collis, 44.
104. Romanus and Sunderland, I.66f.
105. Romanus and Sunderland, I.70f.
106. Tuchman, 314f.
107. Romanus and Sunderland, I.74.
108. Romanus and Sunderland, I.36f.
109. Romanus and Sunderland, I.43f.
110. Van de Ven, *War and Nationalism*, 21ff.
111. Thakin Nu, xxv (introduction by Furnivall), 2.
112. Goodall, 35.
113. Van de Ven, *War and Nationalism*, 23.
114. Campagnac, 275.
115. Goodall, 65.
116. Pearn, 10.
117. Glass, 138.
118. Campagnac, 277.
119. The letter is quoted in Glass, 139; Campagnac, 277, also describes the young officer and his death.
120. Glass, 138.
121. Goodall, 65.
122. Collis, 104ff.
123. Campagnac, 320.
124. Quoted from Goodall, 42; Tyabji's papers are in Cambridge University's Center of South Asian Studies. Tyabji's memoir, with photographs and commentary, is also

presented online by Amitav Ghosh, amitavghosh.com/exodus-from-burma-1941-42
-a-memoir-by-captain-nadir-s-tyabji-part-1.

125. Campagnac, 277.

126. Pearn, 23f.

127. Collis, 128f.

128. Romanus and Sunderland, I.109.

129. This account was posted by Amitav Ghosh on his website, having been given to
him by someone he met while on a book tour. It is one of only a handful of known
accounts of the exodus made by Indian survivors: amitavghosh.com/exodus-from
-burma-1941-a-personal-account.

130. Romanus and Sunderland, I.84f.

131. Romanus and Sunderland, I.97.

132. Collis, 122.

133. For a succinct account of events at Toungoo, Van de Ven, *War and Nationalism*, 32;
Romanus and Sunderland unfold this episode in detail, I.105ff.

134. Romanus and Sunderland, I.127f.

135. Slim, 62, 67.

136. McLynn, 34f.; Tuchman, 340f.

137. Van de Ven, *War and Nationalism*, 32f.; Romanus and Sunderland, I.127ff.; for a detailed account of events leading to the fall of Lashio, see especially 131f.

138. Lunt, 221.

139. Van de Ven, *War and Nationalism*, 32.

140. USAAF, "Memo for the Chief of the Air Staff: Subj: Alternative Supply Line to
China, 2 February 1942, fr. War Dept."

141. Brookes, 58f.

142. Pearn, 71. China National Aviation Corporation (a joint Chinese-American venture) could make two flights a day. The USAAF had been generous with their time,
but on many days was unable to take any passengers at all. Answering an urgent
appeal from the US Tenth Air Force in New Delhi, thirty Pan American Airways
pilots and technicians based in Ghana volunteered their assistance. The primary
duty of RAF planes was to carry out the military sick and wounded.

143. Brookes, 68f.

144. Pearn, 72.

145. Brookes, 72.

146. Brookes, 69–72. The following section and paragraph continue to follow Brookes
closely.

147. Brookes, 85.

148. Pearn, 72; Lieutenant Colonel A. D. Stoker of the Royal Army Medical Corps, who
was at the Myitkyina airfield as the planes were being loaded, reported that, before
the bombs were dropped, the two Japanese planes circled overhead "shooting
crackers as a warning to the crowds below to disperse; and added, harshly, that
"[i]njuries were confined to those foolish people who stayed staring at the planes
and did not take cover"; Stoker, 13.

149. Pearn, 74.

150. Pearn, 75.

151. Tyson, 23.

152. Brookes, 101.

153. Whitworth, 315; Tyson, 56.

154. Whitworth, 315.
155. Pearn, 78.
156. Tyson, 58.
157. McPhedran, 67.
158. Tyson, 58.
159. Pearn, 78, quoting an unnamed evacuee.
160. Pearn, 78.
161. Goodall, 187.
162. Brookes, 133.
163. McPhedran, 45; Goodall, 178.
164. Tyson, 58.
165. Tyson, 52, 54.
166. Tyson, 98; the official report gives a slightly different figure of 20,160 refugees; Pearn, 82.
167. Campagnac, 288.
168. McPhedran, 97.
169. Geren, 41.
170. Tyson, 68.
171. Tyson, 83.
172. Brookes, 117.
173. Pearn, 88.
174. Pearn, 90.
175. Baird-Murray, 50f., 58, 60.
176. Pearn, 71.
177. Goodall, 53.
178. Pearn, 71.
179. McLynn, 38.
180. McPhedran, 52.
181. Plating, 80.

3. THE AIR

1. Grant, *Flight*, 49.
2. Grant, *Flight*, 36f.
3. Gunston, 8, 12.
4. Gunston, 22; blood on the windshield, Grant, *Flight*, 87.
5. Grant, *Flight*, 22f., 26ff.
6. Grant, *Flight*, 103.
7. Gunston, 37; Grant, *Flight*, 108f.
8. Cooke, 269f. An exception was the de Havilland DH-4, which was not bought, but built under license from the British company.
9. Quoted from Cooke, 269; these hours are broken down as follows: 13,000 fighter flights, some 6,600 observation flights, over 1,100 bombing missions.
10. The "old guard" speaker is General John J. Pershing; the air advocate is Captain Robert Webster; Faber, 183f.
11. O'Neil, 23.
12. O'Neil, 25; Grant, *Flight*, 108.
13. O'Neil, 155.

14. Faber, 191f.
15. Gunston, 42.
16. Grant, *Flight*, 169f.; Gunston, 56f.
17. Peattie, 18ff.
18. Peattie, 89.
19. Peattie, 27. The London Naval Treaty of 1930, shorthand for the Treaty for the Limitation and Reduction of Naval Armament, tied up loose ends left by the Washington Naval Treaty eight years earlier; while the earlier treaty limited tonnage for warships, the second sought to regulate other forms of naval craft, including submarines.
20. Pickler, 2; for the British attempts, Leary, *The Dragon's Wings*, 5.
21. Leary, *The Dragon's Wings*, 13ff.
22. Leary, *The Dragon's Wings*, 30.
23. Gully, 5.
24. Leary, *The Dragon's Wings*, 33; Pan American interest, Leary, *The Dragon's Wings*, 73.
25. Leary, *The Dragon's Wings*, 126f.
26. Leonard, *I Flew for China*, 196.
27. Leary, "Wings for China," 449.
28. Tuchman, 168.
29. Leary, "Wings for China," 450.
30. Leary, "Wings for China," 451f.; quote on 454.
31. Leary, "Wings for China," 458.
32. Pickler, 14; Bridgeman, 199.
33. Leary, "Wings for China," 461.
34. Chennault, *Way of a Fighter*, 55.
35. Bond, 254f.
36. Leary, *The Dragon's Wings*, 135.
37. Leary, *The Dragon's Wings*, 135.
38. Leary, *The Dragon's Wings*, 135.
39. The account of discussions in the US about the aerial route closely follows Leary, *The Dragon's Wings*, 136.
40. Plating, 30.
41. For the breakdown of Bond's report, Leary, *The Dragon's Wings*, 138ff.
42. Young, Arthur, "Air Freight Service into China," May 8, 1941, 3, 14.
43. The description of the flight closely follows the report made by Young, "First Flight India-China, via Tibetan Border," 1-5.
44. Bond, 272.
45. Young, Arthur, "First Flight India-China," 4f.
46. Bond, 272f. It has been claimed that the first Hump route was flown by CNAC pilot Xia Pu in the same month of November 1941; see Yufu, 16. This claim does not accord with any other CNAC document, memoir, or report. William Bond is unequivocal in stating that the flight flown by senior CNAC pilots Sharp and Woods was the first over the Hump. Veteran CNAC pilot Captain Moon Fon Chin clarifies this point in detail: Chin, 78ff. Plating suggests that Xia Pu's flight in 1941 may have been one of several reconnaissance flights conducted by CNAC at this early stage, and that his route was probably south of the "classic" high Hump route later necessitated by the presence of Japanese fighters; Plating, 38.
47. Plating, 40ff.

48. Crouch, 231.

49. Soong, T. V., "Memorandum for the President," January 30, 1942, Joseph Warren Stilwell papers, Box 20, folder 7, Hoover Institution Library & Archives; for commentary, see Romanus and Sunderland, I.77f.

50. Leary, *The Dragon's Wings*, 150. Leary notes that Soong was speaking of a Sadiya-to-Myitkyina route—not the eventual, notorious Hump route—and that this could be flown at "10,000 to 12,000 feet, a comfortable altitude for a DC-3." Nonetheless, Soong's characterization of this as "comparatively level" is quaint, to say the least.

51. McHugh, "Military Correspondence," Letter to the Honorable Frank Knox, Secretary of the Navy, February 20, 1942, 4.

52. USAAF, "Memo for the Chief of the Air Staff: Subj: Alternative Supply Line to China, 2 February 1942, fr. War Dept."

53. Tuchman, 297.

54. Stilwell, *Diaries*, February 9, 1942.

55. Stilwell, *Diaries*, January 27, 1942.

56. Stilwell, *Diaries*, February 9, 1942; the US Army Air Forces had been created in June 1941, to which the original Air Corps was now subordinate.

57. "Telegram from President Roosevelt to Generalissimo Chiang Kai-shek, Washington, February 9, 1942," FRUS, Diplomatic Papers, 1942, China, Document 16, 13.

58. Romanus and Sunderland, I.78f.

59. Weaver and Rapp, *The Tenth Air Force 1942*, 20.

60. Weaver and Rapp, *The Tenth Air Force 1942*, 12.

61. Arnold, "Lewis H. Brereton to Lt. General H. H. Arnold, Chief of Army Air Forces," March 6, 1942, The Papers of Henry H. Arnold, Box 199, Folder 4.

62. The 1st Ferry Group was activated on March 7, 1942, shortly before the SS *Brazil* sailed.

63. White, *Ten Thousand Tons by Christmas,* 23. This memoir by USAF Colonel Edwin Lee White (Ret.), who traveled to India as a member of the first wave of the Ferry Command, is the best source available for the voyage out and the early days in India and is followed closely for this section.

64. White, *Ten Thousand Tons by Christmas*, 27ff.

65. Craven and Cate, VII.118.

66. Scott, *The Day I Owned the Sky*, 49; see also Tunner, 20.

67. In a nice quirk of fate, I had for some years unwittingly been in correspondence with Haynes's son, a distinguished archaeologist, on an entirely unrelated matter. It was a pleasant shock to put the names together, and I am grateful to Vance Haynes for furnishing me information about his father.

68. Partly quoted by Yerkey, 94. The full text of the memorandum, dated February 21, 1942, can be read on the online catalog page of Alexander Historical Auctions, where the document came up for auction in the spring of 2021: alexautographs.com/auction-lot/gen-henry-h-arnold-orders-col-caleb-v-haynes-to-m_50C4400A55/.

69. Scott, *God Is My Co-Pilot*, 50.

70. Vaz, 294.

71. Vaz, 287.

72. For the remarkable life of Merian Cooper and his air force career, see Vaz, *Living Dangerously*. Robert Lee Scott's life is told (in places more accurately than in his own works) in Coram, *Double Ace*.

73. Scott, *God Is My Co-Pilot*, 83.

74. Yerkey, 99; Vaz, 288; Scott, *God Is My Co-Pilot*, 83. All accounts suggest different dates and reasons for pulling the mission.
75. Segel, 149.
76. Weaver and Rapp, *The Tenth Air Force 1942*, 35.
77. Scott, *God Is My Co-Pilot*, 85.
78. Weaver and Rapp, *The Tenth Air Force 1942*, 36.
79. Downing, 272f.
80. Segel, 48, 53.
81. Spencer, *Flying the Hump*, 43.
82. Weaver and Rapp, *The Tenth Air Force 1942*, 34, 63n, 141.
83. Weaver and Rapp, *The Tenth Air Force 1942*, 34, who cite two planes on this first mission; for description of the DC-3, Cunningham, 3. The famous Doolittle Raid was an audacious air raid on Tokyo and other main-island targets in retaliation for the bombing of Pearl Harbor. Led by US Army Air Forces Lieutenant Colonel James Doolittle, sixteen B-25 crews launched off the aircraft carrier USS *Hornet*. When the carrier was spotted by enemy scouts, the bombers had to launch earlier and farther from their targets than planned. The bombers succeeded in hitting the home island but inflicted little damage—yet demonstrated that Japan could be struck from the air. On return from the mission, they were supposed to refuel in Nationalist-held parts of East China, and continue on to Chungking, from where they could fly west to Kunming and pick up fuel ferried over the Hump, and thence to India. But on account of the longer-than-planned flight out and bad weather, the crews ran out of fuel and bailed or ditched in East China, or the sea (and in one case in the Soviet Union). Crews that landed in China were rescued and taken to safety by local officials and villagers, who then paid a terrible price for their generous actions. Japanese forces swept through the regions, torturing and killing tens of thousands of people and putting villages to the torch. For reasons of secrecy, Chiang Kai-shek was given only short notice of the raid and predicted there would be retaliation. Taylor, *The Generalissimo*, 208f.
84. Leary, *The Dragon's Wings*, 152.
85. Scott, *God Is My Co-Pilot*, 86.
86. Lunt, 272.
87. Crouch, 273.
88. Scott, *God Is My Co-Pilot*, 103ff.
89. Scott, *God Is My Co-Pilot*, 105.
90. One of the few passengers on board was Jimmy Doolittle, who helped haul refugees onto the plane. For the whole dramatic event—from takeoff in Chungking, to diversion from Kunming to an airstrip due to enemy fire in the area, to the second diversion to Myitkyina—see Chin, 91–96.
91. White, *Ten Thousand Tons by Christmas*, 52.
92. Romanus and Sunderland, I.164.
93. Brereton's mission, Brereton, 130–37, with quote on 130f. For the rumors, for example, Plating, 93.
94. Craven and Cate, I.512f.
95. Stilwell, *Diaries*, June 24, 1942.
96. Romanus and Sunderland, I.169ff., for the Chinese minutes of the meeting; the quotation is at I.171.
97. McHugh, "Military Correspondence," Letter to the Honorable Frank Knox, Secretary of the Navy, July 9, 1942, 7.

98. For FDR's China background, and his fondness for talking about it, see Butow, "A Notable Passage to China."

99. Doenecke and Stoler, 28.

100. Stilwell, *Black and White Books*, July 1, 1942, 65.

101. Romanus and Sunderland, I.172.

102. Romanus and Sunderland, I.224.

103. "Mr. Lauchlin Currie to President Roosevelt," FRUS Diplomatic Papers, 1941, The Far East, Volume IV, Document 57.

104. McHugh, "Military Correspondence," Letter to the Honorable Frank Knox, Secretary of the Navy, February 20, 1942.

105. Plating, 67.

106. Bond, 273.

107. Leary, *The Dragon's Wings*, 135.

4. THE HUMP

1. Ethell and Downie, 116f.

2. Constein, *Born to Fly the Hump*, 54f.

3. Hall, *A Goldstar Century*, 102.

4. Segel, 70f.

5. Spencer, *Flying the Hump*, 27ff.

6. Pocock, 59.

7. Hilton, 49.

8. Plating, 52. While many accounts of the Hump give anecdotal examples of the weather hazards, Plating breaks down the systems and phenomena into hard data points, and this section follows him closely.

9. Plating, 52.

10. Lowry, 1.

11. Romanus and Sunderland, I.77.

12. Plating, 56f.; Craven and Cate, VII.324f.

13. Plating, 58f.

14. Ethell and Downie, 115.

15. Plating, 59.

16. Segel, 70, 73.

17. Shaver, 199.

18. Shaver, 199.

19. Roberts, Oral History.

20. Mitchell, 19.

21. For Assam, Plating, 57; for Burma, Moser, 136, 139.

22. USAAF, Eastern Air Command, Southeast Asia, "Memo from Weather Cdr, for Air Marshal, Commanding Base Air Forces SE Asia."

23. USAAF, Eastern Air Command, Southeast Asia, "Memo from Weather Cdr."

24. Constein, *Born to Fly the Hump*, 63.

25. White, *Ten Thousand Tons by Christmas*, 98.

26. King, *Flying the Hump to China*, 95.

27. Weaver and Rapp, *The Tenth Air Force 1942*, 56f.

28. USAAF, "Air Transportation to China under the Tenth Air Force; April–November 1942," 26ff.

29. Gunston, 87.

30. Weaver and Rapp, *The Tenth Air Force 1942*, 142, note 71.

31. Segel, 72.

32. Grant, *Flight*, 148f.

33. Laben, Oral History.

34. Hall, *A Goldstar Century*, 97f.

35. Crouch, 273.

36. Tuchman, 353, puts a characteristic spin on this scene: "'General Arnold sent us to rescue you, Sir.' Gaunt and haggard from the strain of the last days, Stilwell looked through his rimless glasses at the 'fly boys' and declined the privilege. The aviators gasped. . . .'"

37. Taylor, *The Generalissimo*, 204f.

38. Taylor, The *Generalissimo*, 205.

39. Stilwell, *Diaries,* May 6, 1942.

40. Thompson, "Walk a Little Faster," 170.

41. Between 1971 and 1974, Henrietta Thompson, a graduate student at the University of Maine, tracked down all survivors in every country of Stilwell's company for interviews. Her fascinating narrative, "Walk a Little Faster: Escape From Burma with General Stilwell in 1942" (presented as a thesis for her MA), gives background on all the participants.

42. Vorley, 99.

43. Thompson, "Walk a Little Faster," 195.

44. What emerges from Thompson's narrative, "Walk a Little Faster," is that those who were fit—which included Seagrave's nurses and Stilwell—did not suffer unduly. Those who did suffer, like Stilwell's aide, Frank Merrill, who had a heart attack, and Seagrave, who was overweight, were not in good physical condition. There are a number of firsthand accounts of the trek: journalist Jack Belden's *Retreat with Stilwell*; *Wrath in Burma* by Fred Eldridge, Stilwell's US Army press relations officer; Gordon Seagrave's *Burma Surgeon*; and *Walkout with Stilwell*, written by Stilwell's aide, Frank Dorn.

45. Stilwell, *Diaries*, May 21, 1942.

46. Taylor, *The Generalissimo*, 207.

47. Whitworth, 318. Lambert's extraordinary survey journey is described in Lambert, "From the Brahmaputra to the Chindwin."

48. Scott, *God Is My Co-Pilot*, 105. Back in New Delhi, Stilwell recorded in his diary the comments of Brigadier General Earl Naiden, chief of staff to Brereton, the Tenth Air Force's commander: "Naiden's remark 'Came over the mountains just to save his face.'" Stilwell, *Diaries*, May 26, 1942.

49. Stilwell, *Diaries*, June 4, 1942. For a succinct overview of Stilwell's use of the Chinese forces, Mitter, 254ff.; and a detailed analysis of Stilwell's management of the key campaign at the town of Tounggoo, Van de Ven, *War and Nationalism*, 31ff.

50. Stilwell, *Diaries*, June 15, 1942.

51. Stilwell, *Diaries*, July 26, 1942.

52. Tuchman, 393ff.

53. Romanus and Sunderland, I.182f.

54. Romanus and Sunderland, I.192; Eldridge, 132.

55. Tuchman, 393f.

56. Tuchman, 366.

57. Leary, *The Dragon's Wings*, 155. In view of the AAF failures, in July 1942 Arnold and others recommended that CNAC be allowed to take over the entire Hump

operation (M. X. Quinn Shaughnessy, adviser to China Defense Supplies, to Louis A. Johnson, President Roosevelt's personal representative in India, forwarded by Johnson to Secretary of State; telegram dated April 16, 1942, FRUS, Diplomatic Papers, 1942, China, Document 590, 676f). Stilwell, however, adamantly objected. While fully recognizing the many shortcomings of the air forces' efforts, he argued that military personnel should not be placed under civilian authority in a combat arena. Furthermore, given the Chinese government's majority ownership of CNAC and that the airline was "thoroughly mixed up in Chinese internal politics," he was wary of it coming under Chiang's control; Plating, 94. Romanus and Sunderland, I.173, 66n, cites Madame Chiang's claim that the generalissimo had the "authority to divert CNAC Lend-Lease planes to the Chinese Air Force." Bond, 331ff., gives a detailed and lively account of his own attempts to convince Stilwell that CNAC should take over the Hump operation.

58. Plating, 82.
59. Craven and Cate, IV.416f.
60. Craven and Cate, IV.414f.
61. USAAF, "Air Transportation to China Under the Tenth Air Force; April–November 1942," 18.
62. Japanese Monograph No. 64, 28; Romanus and Sunderland, I.234.
63. Romanus and Sunderland, I.232f.
64. An inner-circle network of air-warning stations had been established in the Brahmaputra Valley in the summer of 1942, and in early October 1942, an intrepid team of Americans and British special forces set out for the Naga Hills and into Burma on the dangerous mission to establish a more effective outer net. Phillips, *KC8 Burma*, 14.
65. Scott, *God Is My Co-Pilot*, 110ff.
66. Details of the flight taken from *The Salt Lake Tribune*, September 13, 1942, 2; other coverage given, for example, in *The New York Times*, September, 13, 1942, 26.
67. Weaver and Rapp, *The Tenth Air Force 1942*, 78.
68. Biographical facts are drawn from the following: For George Humphrey Hadley, US Consular Reports of Births, 1910-1949; World War II Draft Cards Young Men, 1940-1947; World War II Army Enlistment Records, 1938-1946 (Service Number 11008656); *Post-Star* (Glens Falls, New York), December 29, 1945, 7. For Harold J. Folkers, World War II Draft Cards Young Men, 1940-1947; *Wichita Eagle*, May 8, 1928, 3; *Wichita Beacon*, September 18, 1934, 15; *Wichita Eagle*, August 1, 1937, 2; *Wichita Eagle*, August 12, 1937, 5; *Wichita Eagle*, October 12, 1942, 5; *Wichita Eagle*, December 2, 1942, 5.
69. Weaver and Rapp, *The Tenth Air Force 1942*, 78.
70. Weaver and Rapp, *The Tenth Air Force 1942*, 110f.
71. The specific difficulties of night flying are described in USAAF, India-China Division, Air Transport Command, "A History of the India China Wing for the Period June through December 1943," 159f, 163f.
72. Phillips, *KC8 Burma*, 10.
73. Dmitri, 72f.; Phillips, *KC8 Burma*, 10.
74. Craven and Cate, IV.432f.
75. Romanus and Sunderland, I.225; for the role of Chiang and General Ho in pushing for more divisions, see Stilwell, *Black Notebook*, June 25, 1942, 22. The figures are based on Stilwell's statement that the Chinese divisions would be brought up to "a total strength of 10,000 each." FRUS, Diplomatic Papers, The Conferences

at Washington and Quebec, 1943, "Combined Chief of Staff Minutes," Document 36, 72.

76. Romanus and Sunderland, I.222f.
77. Romanus and Sunderland, I.225f.
78. Romanus and Sunderland, I.227.
79. McLynn, 133.
80. Romanus and Sunderland, I.244.
81. McLynn, 133.
82. Romanus and Sunderland, I.227.
83. Thorne, 226.
84. Thorne, 227f.
85. Churchill, 785f.
86. Thorne, 175; Roosevelt's message was sent to Chiang in a telegram from Owen Lattimore, Chiang's former political adviser, with a preface that indicated that the thoughts and words were Roosevelt's: FRUS, Diplomatic Papers, 1942, China, "Draft of Letter from Mr. Owen Lattimore to Generalissimo Chiang Kai-shek," Document 158, 185f.
87. For a withering assessment of Hornbeck's actual knowledge of China, Seagrave, The Soong Dynasty, 404.
88. Herzstein, 21f.; quote from 1.
89. Stowe, 63f.
90. Stowe, 65f.
91. Stowe, 68f.; for the postwar revelations of Soong family profiteering, Seagrave, The Soong Dynasty, 406–9.
92. Stowe, 76f.
93. Finney, 103–6.
94. Byrd, 60; Dwiggins, 197f.
95. Byrd, 59.
96. Byrd, 64.
97. Smith, "Claire Lee Chennault," 62; and Chennault's own account, Way of a Fighter, 3.
98. As so often with Chennault's biography, it is difficult to pin down exact facts, and there are different accounts of the agency that brought him to China. See Byrd, 61f.; Chennault, Way of a Fighter, 31; Ford, Flying Tigers, 7ff.
99. Ford, Flying Tigers, 10.
100. Byrd, 30n, 77, 376.
101. The little-known story of Vincent Schmidt and the Fourteenth International Squadron is told by Bridgeman, 56; 200–208. For regional press, "American Ace Heads International Group in First Air Foray," Hong Kong Telegraph, February 25, 1938. Eileen Bigland, who rode with and reported on the first convoy of buses to travel the old Burma Road, rubbed shoulders with the international pilots in Kunming, where the state of the airfields and lack of planes kept them grounded and playing endless games of crap; Bigland, 214f.
102. Byrd, 105ff.; cable quoted on 106. For a detailed examination of the many attempts to create an international aviation force, including Chiang's overtures to the RAF in February 1939, see Buchan, A Few Planes for China. Drawing on a wealth of unexamined source material, including personal papers in her possession, Buchan describes how the International Aviation Force, or IAF (as the British called it), was to have joined with the regionally understrength RAF in the event Singapore was attacked.

103. McHugh, "The History and Status of the First American Volunteer Group," 9f.
104. Ford, *Flying Tigers*, 31.
105. Ford, *Flying Tigers,* 42, 44.
106. Chennault, *Way of a Fighter*, 106.
107. Ford, *Flying Tigers*, 49.
108. Chennault had dinner with the first group of volunteers, which did not include pilots, in Rangoon in late July; Chennault, *Way of a Fighter*, 107. For his diary, Buchan, 150ff. See also Ford, *Flying Tigers*, 160.
109. Chennault, *Way of a Fighter*, 111f. Possibly Chennault was drawing on his experience in the slow-moving P-12E trainer he had used for stunt flying.
110. Ford, *Flying Tigers*, 201, 206. Olga Greenlaw, in her informative and personal account of living and working with the AVG while her husband, Harvey Greenlaw, served as Chennault's chief of staff, gives an intriguing, if biased, description of the AVG's actual working chain of command in a letter to historian Riley Sunderland: "If my note suggests that Greenlaw and not Chennault was responsible for the tactics used by the A.V.G., it is because Greenlaw was the only one in the Group who knew anything about [tactics]. He was the only West Point graduate and the only one who had any real training and who had actual experience in training pilots for combat. . . . Chennault and Greenlaw prepared the courses. Later, at the pilots meetings or conferences, the General delivered the lectures. Naturally, as in any organization, the 'head man' gets all the credit, as General Chennault does for the training of [the] A.V.G. and their combat tactics, and [that] is as it should be." Greenlaw, 187.
111. Byrd, 152.
112. Ford, *Flying Tigers*, 307.
113. Ford, *Flying Tigers*, 309.
114. See once again Ford, *Flying Tigers*, 198f., 311. Ford explores the rumor at some length, both in his book (pages above) and on his website: danfordbooks.com/tigers/claiming.htm. The sources of the rumor that he cites are compelling, being varied, multinational, and detailed. Ultimately, however, he rejects them, largely on the grounds that, as he contends, the AVG did not, at this early stage, securely know about the bonuses offered for downed Japanese planes, nor had walking-around money to pay off the RAF. However, eyewitness accounts describe the AVG pilots' outspoken boasting about the bonuses they were to receive well before they had come close to seeing combat. See, for example, Stowe, 140f., who gives a colorful, first-person account of discussing bonuses with an AVG airman in Burma: "'You mean to say you don't get any bonus?' exclaimed the dark lynx-eyed flier from Spokane. 'What in hell do you go to places like Burma and China for?'"
115. "Battle of China: Blood for the Tigers," *Time* (December 29, 1941): 19.
116. Ford, *Flying Tigers*, 99f.
117. "Flying Tigers in Burma," *Life* (March 30, 1942): 27–32.
118. Cal Tinney, "Man of the Week," *Detroit Free Press,* July 12, 1942, 43.
119. Shores, I.251.
120. Romanus and Sunderland, I.252.
121. Byrd, 78.
122. Byrd, 21. Similarly, while Chennault is usually credited with the "boom and zoom" dive tactic deployed against the Japanese, he had learned the tactic from the Russians, while the RAF had also used it in the battle for Singapore (Ford, *Flying Tigers*, 307f.; and Preston-Hough, 130). As a point of interest, while no adequate warning

system existed throughout Burma, Rangoon was served by the Burma Observer Corps and radar unit (Preston-Hough, 153).

123. Ford, *Flying Tigers*, 15; Byrd, 87.
124. Craven and Cate, IV.422.
125. Romanus and Sunderland, I.252f.; Byrd, 172f.
126. "When I describe my role as back-room boy, I mean that I advised General Chennault—and sometimes my friend T. V. Soong—on approaches to Washington, that I drafted for Chennault any paper having to do with politics, and that I did my best to bring Chennault's problems before the leading authorities in Washington"; Alsop, 208f.; Byrd, 174.
127. The letter is reprinted in a number of sources, including Chennault's own memoir: *Way of a Fighter*, 212–16. That used here is found in McHugh, "Military Correspondence," "Appendix 'A' to Report No. 10/42 from Naval Attaché, Chungking, Dated 11 October 1942."
128. For a summation of the lengthy letter, Romanus and Sunderland, I.253.
129. Byrd, 176.
130. Tuchman, 373.
131. Arnold, "General Air Situation in the China-Burma Area, Statement by General H. H. Arnold," April 1943, Box 199, Folder 4.
132. Chennault, *Way of a Fighter*, 235f.
133. Romanus and Sunderland, I.250.
134. USAAF, "Air Transportation to China Under the Tenth Air Force; April–November 1942," 18f.
135. The last moments of CNAC #60 are pieced together principally by the intrepid on-site investigations of Clayton Kuhles, miarecoveries.org/pdf/C-47DL-41-18556-CNAC-60-Site-Report.pdf; and by a report made by the Chinese People's Liberation Army to the Joint POW/MIA Accounting Command (now the Defense POW/MIA Accounting Agency): PLA Archives Department, "The Achievement Document of Military Archives Cooperation Between the Peoples Republic of China and the United States of America, 2013.09-2014.08," 10ff., found at: dpaa.mil/Portals/85/Documents/ChinaReports/china_archival_report_201309-201408.pdf; and by independent researchers posting to the CNAC website: cnac.org/jamesbrowne01.htm.
136. USAAF, "Air Transportation to China Under the Tenth Air Force; April–November 1942," 25.
137. See for example, Wigington, 99; Segel, 162f.
138. Segel, 161f.
139. The meteorological phenomenon now known as supercooled large droplets (SLD) was only identified in the 1980s; see for example, Marcia K. Politovich, "Aircraft Icing Caused by Large Supercooled Droplets," *Journal of Applied Meteorology* 28, no. 9 (September 1989): 856–68.
140. Ethell and Downie, 117.
141. Hanks, 39f.
142. Quinnett, 179.
143. Whelan, 271.
144. Closely following Plating, 102–4.
145. Plating, 105.
146. More specifically, it would be directed from Gravelly Point, Arlington, Virginia; Plating, 110.

147. Craven and Cate, IV.415.
148. The allocation of Lend-Lease supplies to the receiving nations was directed by the US Office of Lend-Lease Administration; and by the Munitions Assignments Board, a body comprised of and under the Anglo-American Combined Chiefs of Staff that allocated from pooled Anglo-American munitions. (For a glimpse into the politics behind this powerful agency, see Romanus and Sunderland, I.158f.). Lend-Lease allocations for China were on occasion more freely directed by the president himself.
149. Romanus and Sunderland, I.259f.
150. Stilwell, *Black and White Books*, No. 2, January 8, 1943, 168.
151. Stilwell, *Diaries*, January 18, 1943.
152. Romanus and Sunderland, I.270f.
153. Romanus and Sunderland, I.272, I.274.
154. The Combined Chiefs of Staff were the heads of the individual services—army, navy, air forces—of both the United States and Britain, and service advisers to the president and prime minister, respectively. In the interest of day-to-day communication and cooperation, a British Joint Staff Mission, under Dill, operated in Washington.
155. Arnold, *Global Mission*, 411.
156. Arnold, *Global Mission*, 411; Huston, I.487.
157. Huston, I.488.
158. Huston, I.489; Taylor, *The Generalissimo*, 161f.
159. Tuchman, 429. Stilwell describes Huang Shan's position and lookout, noting it "would be a grand place to bum around in during peace time." Stilwell, *Black and White Books*, No. 2, April 1, 1942, 40.
160. Arnold, *Global Mission*, 420.
161. Huston, I.491.
162. Huston, I.491; Arnold, *Global Mission*, 419.
163. Huston, I.492.
164. Stilwell, *Diaries*, February 7, 1943.
165. Huston, I.492f.
166. Huston, I.494.
167. Huston, I.495; Tuchman, 430.
168. Huston, I.495.
169. Huston, I.496.
170. Stilwell, *Black and White Books*, No. 2, [undated], 189.
171. Tuchman, 430; Romanus and Sunderland, I.277.
172. Romanus and Sunderland, I.279; USAAF, India-China Division, Air Transport Command, "ATC Statistics on Hump Tonnage 1942–1945."
173. Arnold, "Memorandum For General Marshall, Lieut. Gen. Arnold," The Papers of Henry H. Arnold, February 24, 1943, Box 199, Folder 4.
174. Weaver and Rapp, *The Fourteenth Air Force to 1 October 1943*, 7.
175. Stilwell, *Diaries*, February 20, 1943.
176. Chennault, *Way of a Fighter*, 154f.
177. Tuchman, 404.

5. THE VALLEY OF DEATH

1. Appropriation of city and location of New Malir is described by Major General Syed Ali Hamid, "Karachi as the GI's Saw It," *Friday Times* (Karachi), June 21, 2019.

2. For details of life in New Malir, Lichty, Second Section, 1; and USAAF, Karachi American Air Base Command, "Historical Record and Activities of U.S. Army Air Forces in Area of Karachi, India," which includes photographs.

3. Boody, 17.

4. Boody, 19.

5. Lichty, Second Section, 1.

6. For example, an order for three hundred copies of *Under the Greenwood Tree* is found in: USAAF, R. W. Dieterich, "Letter to Commanding Officer, 5320th Defense Wing, 4 January 1944"; USAAF, Karachi American Air Base command, Miscellaneous Correspondence.

7. Peacock, 1.

8. Peacock, quotes on 3, 4–5; diagrams of bamboo usage, 7.

9. "Record of Lectures Given by Lt. E. H. Peacock on 15th, 16th, & 17th December 1942," Karachi Air Base Command (July 1942–January 1944); USAAF, "Historical Record and Activities of U.S. Army Air Forces in Area of Karachi, India."

10. For a brief description of the journey, White, *Ten Thousand Tons by Christmas*, 79f.

11. Segel, 68f.

12. Phillips, *KC8 Burma*, 8f.

13. Ethell and Downie, 38.

14. Ethell and Downie, 29.

15. Report on the first bailout, *Yank* 2, no. 40 (March 24, 1944): 4.

16. "Twenty-three days in the Burma Jungle," *CBI Roundup*, December 31, 1942; and "Additional Background Information from Matt Campanella," which accompanied the original article when it was reprinted in 2006 (copyright Carl Warren Weidenburner). My account follows these articles closely. Further information kindly provided by Matthew J. Campanella Jr.

17. The Dafla are properly known as Nyishi.

18. See for, example, Min Thu, 1f. For the theory that the term "Kachin" may be a Burmese corruption of *Ye-jen*, see Carrapiett, vii; and Wang, xiv.

19. Thu, 1.

20. See for example, Carrapiett, 4.

21. Seng, 6.

22. Carrapiett, 4.

23. Air Headquarters, *Under the Greenwood Tree*, 5.

24. Majumder, 14, 44.

25. Fürer-Haimendorf, 97ff.; Swedien, 44ff., gives a chilling account of the raids and of an instance of the sacrifice of children, accompanied by a horrifying photographic record of captured children's heads.

26. Majumder, iii.

27. Bower, 64.

28. The lengthy account that follows is drawn primarily from Rosbert, "Forty-Six Days to Dinjan," 52–65. Additional details are drawn from a later book by Rosbert that bizarrely combines a memoir of the key events of his life as a pilot with recipes he picked up from travels across the world; Rosbert, *Flying Tiger Joe's Adventure Story Cookbook*. Rosbert was interviewed in 2001 for the Vietnam Archive Oral History Project at Texas Tech University. A transcript of the interview can be found at: Interview with Joseph Rosbert, OH0026, April 13, 2001, Joseph Rosbert Collection, Vietnam Center and Sam Johnson Vietnam Archive, Texas Tech University, vietnam.ttu.edu/virtualarchive/items.php?item=OH0026, accessed November 8, 2021.

29. Rosbert, "Forty-Six Days to Dinjan," 52f.

30. Rosbert, *Flying Tiger Joe's*, 114.

31. Wallace, 15.

32. For visibility ahead, Ramsden, 56; jungle acoustics, Schweitzer, 4.

33. See for example, Phillips, *KC8 Burma*, 53f.; Peers, 115.

34. Fraser, 157, describes an encounter with such a centipede.

35. Durant, 6.

36. Wade, 46f.

37. Wade, 31; Kingdon-Ward, *Himalayan Enchantment*, 134.

38. Constein, *Tales of the Himalayas*, 89, as told by Ted Hendrick.

39. Dunlop, 143.

40. Tunner, 100f.

41. White, *Ten Thousand Tons by Christmas*, 168ff.

42. Ramsden, 92.

43. Dickinson, 29.

44. Sevareid, 307.

45. "Snake Victim's Arm May Be Saved by Neurologist," *Long Beach Press-Telegram*, November 7, 1949, 15. The surgeon who saved him was Dr. Ormond Julian, later to make history by performing the world's first heart bypass.

46. Dunlop, 116, 120.

47. One such character outside the scope of this story was Arthur Mansfield Nuttall, the son of an English officer posted to Assam, whose English wife abandoned him and her family to return to England. When his father died, Arthur was raised by the former household servants in their jungle village until he was recognized and "rescued" by well-meaning Englishmen. He was sent off to St. Paul's School in Darjeeling, where he rebelled and bolted back to the Naga Hills. He entered the tea industry first as an expert elephant handler in charge of a work herd clearing the jungle, and over the years worked for and was fired by a number of estates. Nuttall's background is given in a wonderfully romantic account by Ann Poyser, who, as the Anglo-Indian child of a "Tribal" mother and absent English father, was raised by nuns until the age of sixteen, when she was told by the Sisters that she had to accept an arranged marriage with an older man. Refusing, she was exiled to her mother's village, where one day Arthur Nuttall came, having been summoned by the Pengaree Tea Estate to handle a rogue elephant. Having successfully led the elephant back to the jungle, he caught sight of Ann watching in her school uniform. Approaching her, he asked why she wasn't in school, and tearfully she told him her story. He left, but returned days later to report that he and a parish priest had gone together to remind the Sisters of their religious duty, and that Ann was to return and finish her schooling, which was now paid for. Ann never saw Nuttall again; Mitchell, 305ff.

48. Milton's own reminiscences are reported by Bill Beattie in the Koi-Hai newsletter, June 2003: www.koi-hai.com/Default.aspx?id=490686. An account of the epic retreat is given by Jack Barnard, *The Hump*.

49. Dunlop, 218ff.

50. Dunlop, 37. The story of Father Stuart is well told by Dunlop, 29ff.

51. Kingdon-Ward, *Himalayan Enchantment*, ix.

52. Pearn, 87.

53. "Explorer Talks to ICD Pilots on Himalayas," *Hump Express* 1, no. 18 (May 17, 1945): 5.

54. Chasie and Fecitt, 156f.

55. Thomas, *The Naga Queen*, 167f.

56. In this section, I was greatly aided by a lecture titled "V Force—Defending the Gates of India 1942-1944," given by Robert Lyman on October 7, 2021, for the Kohima Educational Trust; see also Lyman's book *Among the Headhunters*. Bower, 177, describes the duties assigned to the V Force units.

57. Phillips, *KC8 Burma*, 14, 37ff. Phillips's memoir gives a detailed account of the hardship suffered, original naiveté, and growing expertise of these pioneering teams. In July of 1942, an intrepid Captain James Arthur Kehoe from Kentucky (although described in the US Serviceman's newsletter *CBI Roundup* as "a thin, wiry Irishman"), who was assigned to British Intelligence in Karachi, made a five-hundred-mile tour on foot of the Naga territory, surveying the country for lookout sites; he also appears to have made more extensive travels by jeep; "Americans Clubby with Head Hunters," *CBI Roundup* 1, no. 9: 1; "The Extraordinary Life of James Arthur Kehoe, Kentucky's 31st Adjutant General," *Defense Visual Information Distribution Service*, Courtesy Story, Kentucky National Guard Public Affairs, January 8, 2020. Kehoe's tour was aggressively promoted with stories appearing in *Time* ("Kehoe of the Head-hunters," *Time* [May 31, 1943], 68–70), as well as local press.

58. Dunlop, 119.

59. The estimate of bailout numbers is based on Peers's reckoning that the 125 airmen Detachment 101 rescued in just under a year (1943) represented 25 to 35 percent of all men who had bailed over the Hump (Peers, 146). For aircraft and crew numbers, Plating, 116f.

60. Plating, 116.

61. Peers, 86f.

62. Political officers passed on information about missing flights to their junior officers, who then contacted the people of the hills with whom they were in direct contact, but as the wife of one officer recalled, "Lost aircraft were located but never with their living crews." Allen, *"Missy Baba"*, 102.

63. Segel, 227.

64. Constein, *Tales of the Himalayas*, 89, as told by Ted Hendrick.

65. Spencer, *Flying the Hump*, 66f.

66. Gann, 213.

67. Vincenti, 725.

68. White, *Ten Thousand Tons by Christmas*, 126ff.

69. Gann, 214f.

70. Gann, 258.

71. Gann, 258ff.

72. Plating, 66.

73. Craven and Cate, VII.24.

74. The specifications of all CBI aircraft are given in "CBI Aircraft," *China Airlift—"The Hump,"* I.146–67.

75. Spencer, *Flying the Hump*, 105.

76. Following closely Craven and Cate, VII.4f., VII.25.

77. USAAF, India-China Division, Air Transport Command, "A History of the India China Wing for the Period June through December 1943." The lengthy list of defects is given over many pages.

78. Plating, 69.

79. Plating, 69.

80. Craven and Cate, VII.24.
81. White, *Ten Thousand Tons by Christmas*, 130f.
82. Spencer, *Flying the Hump* 105.
83. Tuchman, 440f.; Romanus and Sunderland, I.323.
84. Chennault, *Way of a Fighter*, 225f.
85. For minutes of the key sessions, FRUS, Diplomatic Papers, The Conferences at Washington and Quebec, 1943, "Combined Chief of Staff Minutes," Document 35, 52–66, and Document 36, 66–77.
86. Stilwell, *Diaries*, May 14, 1943.
87. Romanus and Sunderland, I.329ff.; Plating, 131f.; FRUS, Diplomatic Papers, The Conferences at Washington and Quebec, 1943, "Combined Chiefs of Staff Minutes, May 14, 1943," Document 36, 73.
88. USAAF, India-China Division, Air Transport Command, "ATC Statistics on Hump Tonnage 1942-1945."
89. Spencer, *Flying the Hump*, 72f.
90. Segel, 207.
91. Quinn, 10. Decades after the crash, former CNAC pilot Fletcher Hanks set out to look for the remains: Hanks, *Saga of CNAC #53*.
92. Segel, 211.
93. La Farge, 118–23, gives lengthy extracts from this report. For a detailed statement of Project 7's ambitious goals and failures, USAAF, "A History of the India China Wing for the Period June through December 1943" ("Project Seven Begins"), 38.
94. Craven and Cate, VII.126f.
95. Spencer, *Flying the Hump*, 73; Craven and Cate, VII.128.
96. Spencer, *Flying the Hump*, 75f. Details of the crashes are in Quinn, 23, 54.
97. Peers, 146.
98. Sevareid, 250-99. The description of the ordeal follows Sevareid closely throughout.
99. Sevareid, 251.
100. Sevareid, 252f.
101. Sevareid, 253f.
102. Severied, 254f.
103. Severied, 255ff.
104. Sevareid, 254, 258.
105. Sevareid, 259f.
106. Sevareid, 275.
107. Sevareid, 264f.; for details of Flickinger's army career, USAAF, "Biography: Flickinger, D.D."
108. Sevareid, 282; enthusiasts of Agatha Christie will recognize the opening sentence of *The Incredible Theft*.
109. Sevareid, 282.
110. Sevareid, 269, 273, 275, 281.
111. Sevareid, 282f.
112. Sevareid, 292.
113. Sevareid, 292.
114. Sevareid, 294f.
115. Sevareid, 295.
116. Sevareid, 297f. The full menu is given in a letter by John Davies to his wife, quoted in Lyman, 211.
117. The word "coolie" is derived from *kuli*, meaning "wages," in many South Indian

languages. The term was widely used throughout Asia, and in India and China in particular, to refer to a day laborer. The translation of the Chinese characters for the word is "bitter strength." The term was adopted by English speakers, although it is not used today.

118. Sevareid, 298.
119. Sevareid, 299.
120. Sevareid, 270f.
121. Sevareid, 257.
122. Schweitzer, 25.
123. USAAF, HQ India China Wing, Air Transport Command, A-2 Section, "Intelligence Bulletin: Tips on Bailing Out."
124. Peers, 146.
125. Details come from two stories, both by Search and Rescue participants: Blossom, 51–54; Johnson, 54–58.
126. Spain, 507. For the reports of Lieutenant George Porter's death, *Freemont News-Messenger*, March 30, 1943, 1; and *Freemont News-Messenger*, April 2, 1943, 3.
127. Johnson, 56; Tunner, 79.
128. Tunner, 79.
129. Sevareid, 265.
130. Tunner, 97f.
131. Schweitzer, 138. These official statistics render Detachment 101's claims of having rescued "one hundred and twenty-five" airmen all the more questionable.
132. Quinn, 16; Defense POW/MIA Accounting Agency, Personnel Profiles, dpaa-mil .sites.crmforce.mil/dpaaProfile?id=a0Jt0000000XesEEAS. The profile is of pilot Second Lieutenant Omer E. Huntington but has links to the other service members.
133. USAAF, HQ India China Wing, Air Transport Command, "Weekly Information Report," August 13, 1943, Box 04040508, ICD Documents, Air Mobility Command History Office (AMCHO).
134. A crew of six had been on board, and in July the families of each man had been duly notified that their son was missing. The military's eventual determination that all the men were dead, however, trickled in to the different families at different times. Copilot Robert Dixon, possessed of movie-star good looks, was declared dead in October 1945, after his parents had traveled from New York to Washington, DC, to make inquiries. The family of crew chief Sergeant Floyd Jones Jr.—whose hometown paper in Gustine, California, had reported on every stage of his military career and letters home from India—received a "personal letter" in early August 1944 that suggested that Jones "might be among those being held in a Japanese prison camp"; but a year later, in September 1945, the family was informed that he was dead. The pilot of the lost plane had been Second Lieutenant Omer E. Huntington, who received his wings in December 1942, before getting married on New Year's Day, after which he headed out to India.

6. NIGHT FLIGHT

1. Quinn, whose work is the primary chronicle of all aircraft losses, states that the plane was en route from China to India; however, all news coverage, including that of 1945, when the crew was officially declared to be dead, states the aircraft was leaving Jorhat for China; see below for sources. The Defense POW/MIA Accounting Agency (DPAA), which searches for missing American military personnel from all

eras of combat, also states that the plane was flying from India: dpaa-mil.sites
.crmforce.mil/dpaaProfile?id=a0Jt0000000XfGMEA0.

2. George to Arnold, August 13, 1943, Box 04040508, ICD Documents, Air Mobility
Command History Office (AMCHO).

3. Background for the individual crew members is found as follows: For Perry, *The
Tampa Tribune*, August 18, 1943, 2, and *The Tampa Tribune*, November 21, 1945, 8,
when his probate cleared; for Tennison, DPAA site as above and World War II
Army Enlistment Records, 1938–1946, John T. Tennison Jr.; for Funk, World War II
Army Enlistment Records, 1938–1946, John W. Funk, and *Los Angeles Times*, Sep-
tember 27, 1945, 2, reporting news that he "was disclosed to have been killed in the
Asiatic theater of war"; for Lenox, *Hartford Courant,* August 19, 1943, 2; and for
Johnson, World War II Army Enlistment Records, 1938–1946, Donald A. Johnson.

4. Quinn, 20; and military correspondence with pilot Samuel Anglin Jr.'s family
posted on the CNAC website, cnac.org/anglin01.htm; the date and direction of
the aircraft confirmed by details on his grave marker: findagrave.com/memorial
/186326287/samuel-clarke-anglin.

5. Toland, 444.

6. Toland, 441ff., tells the story of his death in dramatic detail. US code breakers had
intercepted and decoded a message indicating Yamamoto's itinerary and schedule, allowing for the ambush that killed him; the news of his death was withheld
from the US press for fear of tipping off the Japanese that their "unbreakable" code
had been broken.

7. Toland, 445f.

8. Japanese Monograph No. 64, 10, 19. In June 1942, the Imperial Japanese Army's 5th
Air Division in Burma was placed under the reorganized 3rd Air Army, under
Lieutenant General Noboru Tazoe; former division commander, Lieutenant Gen-
eral Hideyoshi Obata, was promoted as commander in chief of the 3rd.

9. Japanese Monograph No. 134, 4f., 10f.

10. Japanese Monograph No. 134, 32.

11. Japanese Monograph No. 134, 29f.

12. Japanese Monograph No. 134, 39; Trager, 32f.

13. Japanese Monograph No. 134, 37.

14. Slim, 231; Japanese Monograph No. 134, 24f.

15. Japanese Monograph No. 64, 10f.

16. Japanese Monograph No. 64, 15f.

17. Japanese Monograph No. 64, 11.

18. Shaver, 203, gives a firsthand account of such an incident. Plating, 147, suggests
that the spartan conditions in which the Japanese in north Burma lived and operated limited such interference.

19. Slim, 128.

20. Slim, 153f., 156.

21. FRUS, Diplomatic Papers, The Conferences at Washington and Quebec, 1943, Document 393, 906–9.

22. The most succinct distillation of these plans is given in the telegram sent by Roosevelt and Churchill to Chiang Kai-shek to report on the determinations made in
Quebec: FRUS, Diplomatic Papers, The Conferences at Washington and Quebec,
1943, Document 527.

23. FRUS, Diplomatic Papers, The Conferences at Washington and Quebec, 1943, Document 431, 983, 986.

24. FRUS, Diplomatic Papers, The Conferences at Washington and Quebec, 1943, Document 213, 433–4.

25. FRUS, Diplomatic Papers, The Conferences at Washington and Quebec, 1943, Document 380, 879.

26. FRUS, Diplomatic Papers, The Conferences at Washington and Quebec, 1943, Document 430, 974.

27. McLynn, 183, 185f.

28. McLynn, 190.

29. McLynn, 191.

30. McLynn, 187. A précis of the history of pykrete is given in "The Tale of Habbakuk Ice Cube Carrier of World War II," *National Defense Transportation Journal* 13, no. 1 (January–February 1957): 42.

31. Romanus and Sunderland, I.364.

32. FRUS, Diplomatic Papers, The Conferences at Washington and Quebec, 1943, Document 382, 883.

33. Romanus and Sunderland, I.364.

34. Romanus and Sunderland, I.346; Plating, 141.

35. Tuchman, 474.

36. Following closely Romanus and Sunderland, I.377.

37. Stilwell, *Diaries*, October 8, 1943.

38. USAAF, India-China Division, Air Transport Command, "ATC Statistics on Hump Tonnage, 1943–1945," 2.

39. Plating, 147.

40. Plating, 141ff.

41. Craven and Cate, VII.129; Hardin became commander of the India-China Wing Eastern Sector—newly created and representing yet another hopeful reconfiguration of the same elements. Eastern Sector managed the Assam-China Hump operation, as opposed to the Western Sector, which was responsible for the trans-India ferry. The Eastern Sector included Jorhat, Tezpur, Chabua, Sookerating, Mohanberi, Misamari, Moran, Golaghat, and Fort Hertz. The Western Sector included Karachi, Agra, Ondal, Gaya, Banchi, and Lalmanirhat. Brigadier General Earl Hoag replaced General Alexander as commander of the India–China Wing, based in New Delhi. Calcutta was headquarters of the Western Sector, Chabua of the Eastern Sector. The China Sub-Sector was headquartered in Kunming; White, *Ten Thousand Tons by Christmas*, 233f.

42. White, *Ten Thousand Tons by Christmas*, 132.

43. White, *Ten Thousand Tons by Christmas*, 132; and Tunner, 63. Hardin's "no weather on the Hump" declaration is lodged in Hump lore and mentioned every time Hardin is introduced, but as Plating suggests, it may be apocryphal (Plating, 144)—it seems that no one who knew Hardin can quite bring themselves to refute it. For what it's worth, *Time* magazine presents the declaration as a direct quote: "So Hardin drafted a curt order: 'Effective immediately, there will be no more weather over the Hump.'" "Aviation: Storm Ahead—but No Weather," *Time*, November 12, 1945, 85.

44. Devaux, n.p.

45. Ethell and Downie, 34f. Trucks, jeeps, see Spencer, *Flying the Hump*, 48; Devaux, n.p.; Segal, 191f. For Madame's possessions, Seagrave, *The Soong Dynasty*, 391; for her piano, Scarano, 17.

46. Ethell and Downie, 37; La Vove, 129.

47. Devaux, n.p.

48. A handy photograph of the tower can be seen in White, *Ten Thousand Tons by Christmas*, 98.
49. Drunken movement of the C-46, Ethell and Downie, 37; Segal, 171.
50. La Vove, 131.
51. Segal, 172.
52. Constein, *Tales of the Himalayas*, 109, as told by George L. Wenrich.
53. Segal, 172.
54. Devaux, n.p.
55. Ethell and Downie, 34.
56. Dominick, 75.
57. White, *Ten Thousand Tons by Christmas*, 134.
58. Devaux, n.p.
59. Devaux, n.p.
60. Dominick, 22.
61. Constein, *Born to Fly the Hump*, 55.
62. Phipps, 65.
63. Kelly, 459.
64. Devaux, who was not a pilot, marveled as an aside that pilots fresh from the States "could come in on the top of that stack of planes; follow the ranges and the instructions, and let down through 20,000 feet of pea soup fog and often storms full of violent turbulence and lightning."
65. Ethell and Downie, 41.
66. Ethell and Downie, 41.
67. Ethell and Downie, 42. McClain, 257, gives a personal account of such sabotage and the consequences of flying with unfiltered fuel.
68. Constein, *Born to Fly the Hump*, 57.
69. Ethell and Downie, 43.
70. Ethell and Downie, 31f.
71. Stelling, 142.
72. Ethell and Downie, 43.
73. Engs, 75.
74. Ethell and Downie, 46; Devaux, n.p.
75. Craven and Cate, VII.122; Plating, 116, walks through Arnold's math: assuming 70 percent availability of the fleet at any given time, after allowing for repairs and maintenance, would ensure ninety operational aircraft available to make two round trips each over the Hump, for a total of 1,800 monthly round trips—enough to meet the 4,000-ton monthly quota.
76. Craven and Cate, VII.122f.; 128.
77. Craven and Cate, VII.131f., cites thirty-eight major accidents over the Hump in November; crashes are recorded in USAAF, India-China Division, Air Transport Command, "Chronological List of Aircraft Crashing on Hump Route," 4–9.
78. Craven and Cate, VII.128.
79. USAAF, Aircraft Accident and Incident Reports, (44-8-23- 501), MICFILM 46245.
80. USAAF, Aircraft Accident and Incident Reports, (44-9-15-520), MICFILM 46255.
81. USAAF, Aircraft Accident and Incident Reports, (44-9-15-505), MICFILM 46255.
82. Quinn, 34.
83. USAAF, Aircraft Accident and Incident Reports, (44-10-3-504), MICFILM 46263.
84. Shores, 3.104; Japanese Monograph No. 64, 10f.
85. Shores, 3.104; Quinn shows two losses on each of these days.

86. Plating, 149; quote from Japanese Monograph No. 64, 19.
87. Stilwell specifically links the October losses to the introduction of night flying: Stilwell, *Black Book*, 69. The first night flight across the Hump had been accomplished back in September 1942, when Captain John Payne, a highly skilled pilot who had been handpicked for the assignment, had flown round trip from Chabua to Kunming and back. Information about John Payne and details of the first flight can be found in chapter 4, "The Hump." Segal, 147f., quotes *CBI Roundup*, September 17, 1942 (inaugural edition), hailing the flight.
88. For the first predawn flights, Bundy, 85. Allegedly the first "working" night flight was flown by John Nelson from Sookerating to China on October 17, 1943. Nelson claimed that "We caught hell when the word came out what we had done, as night flying over the Hump at that time was a NO! NO!"; Spencer, *Flying the Hump*, 91. Night flying becomes standard operational practice; USAAF, India-China Division, Air Transport Command, "A History of the India China Wing for the Period June through December 1943," 159f.
89. Segel, 59f.
90. USAAF, India-China Division, Air Transport Command, "Medical History of the India China Wing and India China Divisions, Air Transport Command, December 1942–December 1945," 51f. The pilot of this particular crash may also have been suffering from anoxia.
91. FAA, *Airplane Flying Handbook*, chapter 11, "Night Operations," 1–14, faa.gov/sites/faa .gov/files/regulations_policies/handbooks_manuals/aviation/airplane_handbook /12_afh_ch11.pdf.
92. Craven and Cate, VII.129.
93. White, *Ten Thousand Tons by Christmas*, 223f.
94. USAAF, India-China Division, Air Transport Command, "A History of the India China Wing for the Period June through December 1943," 160.
95. Interview with Jeff Arnett.
96. Constein, *Tales of the Himalayas*, 93, as told by Roland E. Speckman.
97. Interview with Jeff Arnett.
98. Interview with J. V. Vinyard.
99. Leary, *The Dragon's Wings*, 153.
100. Ramsey, 179ff.
101. Dominick, 118, 121. These passages are quoted from a short story Dominick wrote titled "'The Rock Pile': Based on a Flyer's Diary," appended to his actual diary. It is evident that the fictive element is very thin, serving perhaps to give him cover to write intimately of his experiences.
102. Constein, *Born to Fly the Hump*, 65.
103. Devaux, n.p.
104. Bundy, 87; Gray, *Diary*, October 17, 1943.
105. Miller, 85.
106. Constein, *Tales of the Himalayas*, 93 as told by Roland E. Speckman.
107. Bundy, 87.
108. Shaver, 203.
109. The account below is taken solely from Wade, *Five Miles Closer to Heaven*.
110. Wade, 24.
111. Wade, 25.
112. Wade, 29.
113. Townsell, 112, 117.

114. Devaux, n.p.
115. Sevareid, 247.
116. Spencer, *Flying the Hump*, 55.
117. Sevareid, 247.
118. McBride, 146.
119. King, *Flying the Hump*, 57; White, *Ten Thousand Tons by Christmas*, 80.
120. Dmitri, 86.
121. Biographical details taken from Marshall's obituary; Rauner Library, Dartmouth College, Box 5, Letters to Administrators, Folder 3, WWII Letters 1941–46, Howard Edward Marshall, Class of 1940, 1941.
122. *Albany Democrat*, October 4, 1921, 1.
123. *News-Pilot* (San Pedro, California), June 17, 1943, 7.
124. Myron G. Woodworth, World War II Army Enlistment Records, 1938–1946. His early career can be traced through reviews of "Little Theater" productions in California and Tennessee; for example, *Oakland Tribune*, November 16, 1934, 23; *Oakland Tribune*, January 18, 1935, 16; *Elizabethton Star* (Elizabethton, TN), July 28, 1940, 2.
125. I have been able to locate only one copy of the play, at the New York Public Library: *The Hump* by Howard E. Marshall and Richard Woodworth, New York Public Library, NCOF + p.v. 296.
126. Marshall and Woodworth, excerpted from 1, 21f., 24, 26.
127. An account of this friction in the Hump's early days is given by Plating, 93, and Ethell and Downie, 21. Spencer, *Flying the Hump*, 127, cites total pay for second lieutenant at a slightly lower figure, $367 a month.
128. Ethell and Downie, 22.
129. Plating, 171ff.
130. King, *Flying the Hump*, 57.
131. Plating, 158f.
132. Leighton, 216f.; White, *Ten Thousand Tons by Christmas*, 225ff.
133. Devaux, n.p., served as a Link Trainer operator and describes these systems in some detail.
134. Dominick, 79.
135. Gray, *Diary*, October 17, 1943, and October 19, 1943.
136. Craven and Cate, VII.131f.
137. Pope, "Brand of Fear," 187.
138. Dominick, 85.
139. Constein, *Tales of the Himalayas*, 87, as told by Lawrence D. Edmonson.
140. Constein, *Born to Fly the Hump*, 61.
141. Constein, *Born to Fly the Hump*, 29.
142. Constein, *Born to Fly the Hump*, 73ff.
143. Constein, *Born to Fly the Hump*, 78.
144. White, *Ten Thousand Tons by Christmas*, 134. Cases of hypoxia and studies of the phenomenon based on blood draws are discussed in USAAF, India-China Division, Air Transport Command, "Medical History of the India China Wing and India China Divisions, Air Transport Command, December 1942–December 1945," 51–54.
145. Mays, 1090.
146. Hanks, 142.
147. The pilot in question was based in Dum Dum, the air base outside of Calcutta, which in turn supplied the bases in Assam, and the court-martial cites his many "flights up to the valley and back." War Department, Branch Office of the Judge

Advocate General, with the United States Forces India Burma Theater, (199) Board of Review, CM IBT 351, "United States v. James A. McPherson, 0-510073, First Lieutenant, 1305th Army Air Force Base unit, ATC," quotes from 2, 4.

148. USAAF, India-China Division, Air Transport Command, "Medical History of the India China Wing and India China Divisions, Air Transport Command, December 1942–December 1945," 56.

149. USAAF, India-China Division, Air Transport Command, "Medical History of the India China Wing," 57.

150. USAAF, India-China Division, Air Transport Command, "Medical History of the India China Wing," 59–60.

151. Greiber, 1083.

152. Greiber, 1084.

153. USAAF, India-China Division, Air Transport Command, "Medical History of the India China Wing," 60.

154. Peterson, 819.

155. Peterson, 819.

156. There are many accounts of these rest camps; see, for example, Hodell, 254–56; Dominick, 36–39.

157. Devaux, n.p.

158. Greiber, 1085f.

159. Segel, 185f.

160. Dawless, *The Ledo Road and Other Verses from China-Burma-India.* This little booklet also contains doggerel verses about flying the Hump: "Last night I flew across the Hump / And cut my transport's final roar / Upon an Elysian landing field. . . ." Read at cbi-theater.com/verses/Verses_Main.html.

161. Huston, II.85.

162. Huston, II.84.

163. Romanus and Sunderland, II.57f.; summarized in McLynn, 216.

164. Romanus and Sunderland, II.62.; FRUS, Diplomatic Papers, The Conferences at Cairo and Tehran, 1943, Document 265, 336–45.

165. FRUS, Diplomatic Papers, The Conferences at Cairo and Tehran, 1943, Document 255, 312f.

166. FRUS, Diplomatic Papers, The Conferences at Cairo and Tehran, 1943, Document 255, 313.

167. For Chiang's views and presentation, Taylor, *The Generalissimo*, 246.

168. FRUS, Diplomatic Papers, The Conferences at Cairo and Tehran, 1943, Document 265, 342.

169. FRUS, Diplomatic Papers, The Conferences at Cairo and Tehran, 1943, Document 265, 342.

170. FRUS, Diplomatic Papers, The Conferences at Cairo and Tehran, 1943, Document 265, 342f.

171. Stilwell, *Black Book*, 92.

172. FRUS, Diplomatic Papers, The Conferences at Cairo and Tehran, 1943, Document 265, 343.

173. Stilwell, *Diaries*, November 23, 1943.

174. Stilwell, *Diaries*, November 23, 1943.

175. Romanus and Sunderland, II.63.

176. McLynn, 224. Taylor, *The Generalissimo*, 249–52, characteristically seeks to defend Chiang, giving a lengthy and labored explanation of how each party other than

Chiang had mistaken what had been agreed to, but in light of the other sources does not convince.

177. Romanus and Sunderland, II.65.

178. Huston, II.87.

179. Taylor, *The Generalissimo*, 246.

180. Tuchman, 485.

181. Taylor, *The Generalissimo*, 247, 249, drawing on Chiang's diaries.

182. Taylor, *The Generalissimo*, 249, 252.

183. Romanus and Sunderland, II.63.

184. Roosevelt, *As He Saw It*, 142.

185. FRUS, Diplomatic Papers, The Conferences at Washington and Quebec, 1943, Document 53, 138.

186. FRUS, Diplomatic Papers, The Conferences at Cairo and Tehran, 1943, Document 360, 489.

187. FRUS, Diplomatic Papers, The Conferences at Cairo and Tehran, 1943, Document 438, 676.

188. White, *The Stilwell Papers*, 251f.

189. Tuchman, 495.

190. Dorn, 75f.

191. Dorn, 77f. A similar revelation was made by Colonel Carl F. Eifler, the unbalanced senior OSS officer for the CBI who was stationed in India, in his memoir, published in 1975—four years after Dorn's. Eifler claimed that Stilwell told him that in order to proceed "in a logical way it would be necessary to get Chiang Kai-shek out of the way" (Moon and Eifler, 145f.). Eifler, who was recalled when his dangerously erratic behavior bordered on the insane following a head injury, appears to have been a pathologically competitive individual and was besotted with film noir–inspired ideas of spycraft. I believe it is likely that he was made aware of Dorn's report and felt the need to make a similar claim. Allegedly, his own inquiries led to a plan to use botulinus toxin.

192. Romanus and Sunderland, II.80.

193. USAAF, India-China Division, Air Transport Command, "ATC Statistics on Hump Tonnage 1942–1945," 2.

194. USAAF, India-China Division, Air Transport Command, "A History of the India China Wing for the Period June through December 1943." Quotes and examples are taken from 139–47, but the catalog of defects is lengthier. See also White, *Ten Thousand Tons by Christmas*, 232.

195. Plating, 162.

196. USAAF, India-China Division, Air Transport Command, "A History of the India China Wing for the Period June through December 1943," 452.

197. Dominick, 64.

198. Gray, *Diary*, November 9–11, 1943.

199. Plating, 151.

200. Plating, 150ff.

7. NUMBER ONE AIR COMMANDO

1. Boody, 19.

2. Boody, 24.

3. Boody, 25f.
4. Boody, 23.
5. Boody, 26.
6. Boody, biographical material, 1, 3; adages: viiC, frontispiece, iiiB.
7. Mary Seidel obituary, *Reading Eagle* (Reading, PA), October 15, 2009.
8. Boody, 12.
9. Boody, 26.
10. Quinn, 45.
11. Boody, 26f.
12. Quinn, 99f.
13. FRUS, Diplomatic Papers, The Conferences at Cairo and Tehran, 1943, Document 360, 488.
14. Romanus and Sunderland, II.71.
15. Romanus and Sunderland, II.74f, 77.
16. Stimson, *Diaries,* January 19, 1944.
17. Romanus and Sunderland, II.77.
18. Stilwell, *Diaries,* December 18, 1943.
19. Romanus and Sunderland, II.74f.
20. Romanus and Sunderland, II.77.
21. Romanus and Sunderland, II.78; Stilwell, *Diaries,* December 18, 1943.
22. Romanus and Sunderland, II.80.
23. Romanus and Sunderland, II.48; the December advance was calculated to position the troops ahead of the actual offensive, which was to begin in March 1944.
24. Tuchman, 477f.
25. Eldridge, 186f.
26. The First Burma Campaign being the Allies' fight for Burma in 1942.
27. The objectives of the operations are most succinctly described by Slim, 214.
28. Slim, 248f.
29. Slim, 249.
30. Slim, 249f., 251.
31. Lewin, 51; Anthony Mills, "Student's Interlude," *Blackwood's Magazine* 239, no. 1448 (June 1936): 845–64; quote from 849.
32. Slim's background is drawn from Lewin, 1–10.
33. Lewin, 82, 103ff.
34. Masters, 162; the comparison with Xerxes's army was made by Churchill (see Fraser, xiii).
35. Lewin, 41; Slim, 185f.
36. Slim, 250f.
37. Slim, 205.
38. Tuchman, 508.
39. Slim, 206f.; Tuchman, 509.
40. Seagrave, *Burma Surgeon Returns,* 27f., 72f; Stone, 119.
41. Romanus and Sunderland, II.32, on Sun's background. For the failure of intelligence, Romanus and Sunderland, II.45. Stilwell's failure of intelligence is somewhat masked by the historians' choice of terminology: "Compounding the intelligence and reconnaissance failure was the reluctance of Chih Hui Pu to admit that the enemy was present in strength." Chih Hui Pu, meaning General Headquarters, was the name that the Americans had given to the American-staffed Northern

Combat Area Command headquarters. On the pattern of American historians using the Chinese name when referring to CAI failure, see Taylor, *The Generalissimo*, 654, 42n. Tuchman, 471, also describes the faulty intelligence.

42. Romanus and Sunderland, II.45f.; Japanese Monograph No. 131, 15.
43. Romanus and Sunderland, II.47.
44. Romanus and Sunderland, II.46, II.48.
45. Tuchman, 500.
46. Eldridge, 140.
47. Eldridge, 143.
48. Tunner, 126.
49. Eubank, 34f.
50. Babcock, 14f.
51. Tunner, 126.
52. Fisher, 11f.
53. Spencer, *Flying the Hump*, 124.
54. Seagrave, *Burma Surgeon Returns*, 30, 44, 47.
55. Brigadier General Boatner, Stilwell's chief of staff and deputy commander of the Chinese Army in India, states that "in the six months or so I was at Ramgarh, J[oseph]W[illiam]S[tilwell] visited us about four times. . . . His total time there with me did not exceed 10 hours"; Boatner, "Barbara Tuchman's Stilwell."
56. Eldridge, 142.
57. Lathrop, *A Surgeon with Stilwell*, 140, 147.
58. Stilwell, *Diaries*, January 2–5, 1944.
59. Romanus and Sunderland, II.121, II.44ff.
60. Romanus and Sunderland, II.124f.; Liang, 175.
61. Tuchman, 504, quoting Boatner.
62. USAAF, India-China Division, Air Transport Command, "Medical History of the India China Wing and India China Divisions, Air Transport Command December 1942–December 1945," 60.
63. Spencer, *Flying the Hump*, 83; for the black market, White, *Ten Thousand Tons by Christmas*, 232.
64. [British] Special Forces Pamphlet, *Through Japanese Eyes*, n.d., Document 5584, Imperial War Museum.
65. USAAF, *10th Air Force Narrative of Events in Malaya and the Philippines, 1941–1942*, 8f.
66. Phillips, *Another Man's War*, 84; the badge of the 81st (West African) Division was a black spider representing Ananse, a magical, shape-shifting animal spirit from Ashanti mythology, depicted on a yellow background; Phillips, *Another Man's War*, 47.
67. USAAF, *10th Air Force Narrative of Events in Malaya and the Philippines, 1941–1942*, 8f.
68. Fischer, 91.
69. Toland, 439.
70. Dunlop, 28.
71. On treatment of Japanese troops, Toland, 301; USAAF, *10th Air Force Narrative of Events in Malaya and the Philippines, 1941–1942*, 10.
72. Sykes, 360ff.; on the Chindits' name, Sykes, 378.
73. A good, very succinct overview of the first Chindits is given in Jowett, 30.
74. Slim, 162f.
75. Japanese Monograph No. 134, 22, 27.
76. Wingate's life story is told in a number of both pro-Wingate and anti-Wingate biographies. His first biographer, Christopher Sykes, is pro-Wingate but mostly

does not edit out the dark corners. For the facts referred to in this text, see Sykes 19, 21ff., 42ff., 53f., 58ff., 71f., 102, 109, 148ff., 262ff. For a deeper examination of his Special Night Squad tactics, see Bierman and Smith, 122ff. Glimpses of Wingate are caught in autobiographies as diverse as those of Moshe Dayan and Wilfred Thesiger.

77. Durant, 2.
78. On languages, Sykes, 55, 127; on expeditions, 71ff., and discovery of the dread motor car, Sykes, 80.
79. On Gideon, Sykes, 262ff.
80. Thesiger, 330.
81. Sykes, 331ff.
82. Sykes, 485.
83. Bidwell, 46f.; Phillips, *Another Man's War*, 130f.
84. Captain Fred O. Lyons, "Here's What Happened! Merrill's Marauders in Burma." The original interview was published by the *Tampa Tribune* (Mortimer, 216).
85. Latimer, 157.
86. Bidwell, 51.
87. Bidwell, 52.
88. Masters, 140.
89. Bidwell, 53f.
90. Bidwell, 55; Masters, 140ff.
91. Bidwell, 246f.; the issue continued to raise eyebrows after the war; "Flogging Order by British Major Alleged," *Sydney Morning Herald*, July 6, 1946, 1.
92. Durant, 2.
93. Hilder; and author's interview.
94. Bidwell, 53f.; Masters, 141.
95. Romanus and Sunderland, II.34f.
96. Hunter, 5.
97. Romanus and Sunderland, II.34f.
98. Tuchman, 462; and Romanus and Sunderland, II.35.
99. Boatner claimed to have heard this from Mountbatten personally; Boatner, "Comments on 'Crisis Fleeting,'" 13.
100. Hunter, 10; on a pedantic note, Hunter has Wingate saying "ass," but British sources amend the quote to "arse," which seems most likely.
101. Romanus and Sunderland, II.35.
102. Romanus and Sunderland, II.146.
103. Latimer, 156.
104. Thomas, *Back to Mandalay*, 27; PRO AIR 41/36, Air Historical Branch, "R.A.F. Narrative: The Campaigns in the Far East," Vol. III, India Command, September 1939–November 1943, 140, National Archives, UK.
105. Paraphrasing Saunders and Richards, 314; for early examples of air supply, including Slim's experiments in the early 1930s, see Lewin, 54.
106. Bidwell, 64; Thomas, *Back to Mandalay*, 54.
107. Daso, 3, 44f.
108. Paraphrasing Thomas, *Back to Mandalay*, 27.
109. Craven and Cate, IV.504.
110. Masters, 144.
111. Masters, 143.
112. Masters, 144.

113. Masters, 144f.

114. Thomas, *Back to Mandalay*, 12.

115. Biographical information drawn from Okerstrom, 53f.; Cochran's *New York Times* obituary: "Col. Philip G. Cochran, War Hero and Model for 2 Cartoon Figures," *New York Times*, August 27, 1979, sec. D, 7; and Thomas, *Back to Mandalay*, 46f.

116. Thomas, *Back to Mandalay*, 36ff.; quote from 38.

117. Thomas, *Back to Mandalay*, 29.

118. Thomas, *Back to Mandalay*, 31.

119. Thomas, *Back to Mandalay*, 46f.; for Cochran and Alison's friendship, 55f. General Arnold activated Cochran's Air Commando Operations in mid-September of 1943, following his meeting with Wingate in Quebec: USAAF, "Chronological History of Project 9 (Cochran)," 1.

120. John Allison [*sic*], Maj. General, USAFR, "Phil Cochran: The Most Unforgettable Character I've Met!" Air Commando Association, specialoperations.net/Col Cochran.htm.

121. Thomas, *Back to Mandalay*, 14.

122. Thomas, *Back to Mandalay*, 32; Thomas's account, which was published in 1951, closely follows a syndicated news story that appeared in March 1943; for example, see *The Kansas City Times*, March 3, 1943, 18.

123. Caniff, 67.

124. Thomas, *Back to Mandalay*, 76.

125. Masters, 139; Thomas, *Back to Mandalay*, 89, 91, 99, completes the equipment list.

126. Thomas, *Back to Mandalay*, 81.

127. Zechariah 9:12; for Wingate's strongholds, Sykes, 495, 497, 512f.

128. Sykes, 510f.

129. Slim, 259.

130. Slim, 259.

131. Masters, 164; Hunter on confronting a shaky bridge over a fast-flowing, sixty-yard-wide river recalled Caesar's *Pons a Caesare in Rhenu Factus*; Hunter, 24.

132. It is not wholly clear when this decision was made and made known to the participants. Some accounts have Arnold saying, "Wingate marched into Burma the first time. I want him to fly in and fly out," but are vague as to when and where this was said; see, for example, Bidwell, 64. Wingate's biographer gives a thorough and convincing account (and rebuts a more colorful account given by Lowell Thomas) quoting correspondence from Wingate that Cochran won Wingate over to the idea in New Delhi in November 1943 (Sykes, 485f.), and a week later one finds Mountbatten confidentially pitching the use of gliders to the Combined Chiefs of Staff in Cairo (FRUS, Diplomatic Papers, The Conferences at Cairo and Tehran, 1943, Document 255, 313). Yet Masters, who was "on the spot," states the decision was made when the men were encamped outside Imphal, indicating that he and other officers did not previously know of the plan; Masters, 165.

133. Masters, 165.

134. Thomas, *Back to Mandalay*, 102; Masters, 186.

135. Masters, 186.

136. Bidwell, 102; Masters, 171, describes the moon.

137. Masters, 146.

138. The interview, conducted in New York City, was widely syndicated: see, for example, the *Clarion-Ledger* (Jackson, MS), June 10, 1943, 9.

139. Chinnery, 19.

140. Cochran's speech was filmed by the United States Army Pictorial Service Signal Corps for publicity purposes, as part of a film titled *The Stilwell Road*, and is widely available online. The transcript used here is that of the Silent Wings Museum, Lubbeck, Texas.
141. Bidwell, 104.
142. Bidwell, 104f.
143. Masters, 170; Bierman and Smith contest the allegation that Wingate became "emotional," 381ff., on which point the sources are conflicted.
144. Sykes, 517.
145. Masters, 171.
146. Okerstrom, 198.
147. Constein, *Tales of the Himalayas*, 62f., as told by Frank Wenrich, gives a marvelous glider pilot's account.
148. Thomas, *Back to Mandalay*, 208; for the significant overloading, Okerstrom, 197, 199f.
149. Okerstrom, 213.
150. Bidwell, 107.
151. Okerstrom, 213.
152. Masters, 172.
153. Thomas, *Back to Mandalay*, 262; Richard "Dick" Cole, Doolittle's copilot on the Tokyo Raid, flew a C-47 tow plane to Broadway but lost the gliders en route.
154. O'Brien, 81.
155. Chinnery, 22.
156. Hunter, 62.
157. Ogburn, 64.
158. Hunter, 12.
159. Hunter, 12f.
160. Mortimer, 38f.
161. Ogburn, 57ff.; Bidwell, 85.
162. McMichael, 45.
163. McMichael, 46.
164. Hunter, 7.
165. Hunter, 19.
166. The description of the march to Shingbwiyang and the Tarung closely follows Ogburn, 71-75.
167. Bjorge, 12, states the number was 2,750; USAAF documents state 2,700; USAAF, "Interesting Histories: China-Burma-India, Tenth Air Force, 1943-1945," 2.
168. Hunter, 27.
169. Quotation from Hunter, 30; and paraphrasing Hunter, 20.
170. Hunter, 30f.
171. Matloff, 327.
172. Hunter, 16.
173. Allen, *Burma*, 153f.
174. Allen, *Burma*, 153.
175. Quotation from Slim, 298; a ball of fire was the badge of the Japanese Burma Area Army's 15th Division; Latimer, 189. For crossing of the Chindwin, Japanese Monograph No. 134, 71f., 79, 97.
176. Slim, 170.
177. Slim, 169f.
178. The Air Commando headquarters were divided between two airports some ten

miles apart; Lalaghat, with its longer airstrip, was used for transports, bombers, and gliders; Hailakandi, for fighters and light planes; Okerstrom, 116f.

179. All details that follow are taken from the investigative report of the crash, which drew on an array of interviews: USAAF, "Investigation of and Report on the Airplane Accident Which Resulted in the Death of General Wingate, 24 March, 1944."

180. Sykes, 532.

181. Williams, "Excerpts from 'An Appreciation,'" 227.

182. Sykes, 70, and 503, quoting a letter to his wife in which Wingate tells her that his "old dislike of flying is quite gone"; and Bierman and Smith, 148.

183. Bidwell, 157.

184. Masters, 204. In death as in life, Wingate caused controversy. British military tradition is to bury the dead where they fall; US tradition is to bring the bodies home. Wingate's site of death had been duly marked and a solemn religious service performed over his de facto grave. Later, US authorities retrieved the remains of the US crew, and along with them the remains of Wingate, his ADC, and the two journalists; all remains were buried together in Arlington National Cemetery. Wingate's family was not consulted or notified of the removal. When it was discovered, there was a storm of protest in Britain, with Wingate's sister writing to Churchill, asking, "If an American general, say Patton, had been killed in a plane flown by a British crew, would the Americans ever have allowed his body to be transported back to Britain and put into an RAF cemetery?" (Bierman and Smith, 377f.). Wingate remains the only non-American combatant buried in Arlington.

185. Slim, 269.

186. Bidwell, 162.

8. THE LEDO ROAD

1. Romanus and Sunderland, II.147, 154.

2. Romanus and Sunderland, II.160.

3. Following closely Romanus and Sunderland, II.82.

4. Romanus and Sunderland, II.82.

5. The account of SEAC's reservations about the north Burma campaign closely follows Romanus and Sunderland, II.161.

6. Romanus and Sunderland, II.162f.

7. Van de Ven, "Stilwell in the Stocks," 253; Boatner, "Barbara Tuchman's Stilwell," 10, points out that Fred Eldridge, Stilwell's public relations officer and later the editor of the theater magazine *CBI Roundup,* exerted "great influence in building up the 'image' of JWS."

8. Casey, 189, 342, 2n for sources.

9. Wedemeyer, *Wedemeyer Reports!,* 197.

10. Van de Ven, "Stilwell in the Stocks," 253.

11. Quote in Romanus and Sunderland, II.169f.

12. In July 1949, CBI historians Charles Romanus and Riley Sunderland interviewed George Marshall and then made a typescript record of their debriefing of each other, sometimes paraphrasing Marshall, sometimes apparently quoting him directly. Marshall, George C., "Marshall Interviews," 11:30–1:30, July 6, 1949.

13. Stilwell, *Black Book,* 1–5.

14. Biographical information is taken from Tuchman, 16–23.

15. Tuchman, 26f., 28–33, 56.

16. Tuchman, 58, 63.
17. Tuchman, 73.
18. Tuchman, 127.
19. Tuchman, 154.
20. Tuchman, 154.
21. Tuchman, 160.
22. Tuchman, 160.
23. Quoting Tuchman, 172.
24. Tuchman, 172.
25. Tuchman, 188.
26. Tuchman, 240.
27. Stilwell's candidacy, Craven and Cate, II.45.
28. Stilwell, *Diaries*, January 1, 1942.
29. Stilwell, *Diaries*, January 14, 1942.
30. Stilwell, *Diaries*, January 23, 1942.
31. "Discussion between Mr. Sunderland and Mr. Romanus on the Interview with General George C. Marshall, 11:30-1:30, 6 July 1949," 22.
32. McLynn, 47.
33. Tuchman, 156.
34. Bidwell, 33, gives a handy list of these slurs, to which can be added those found in Stilwell's diary entries of July 30, 1942, and August 9, 1942; Tuchman, 157.
35. Stilwell, *Diaries*, November 9, 1943, and October 1, 1944.
36. Stilwell, *Diaries*, April 29, 1942, and June 27, 1945.
37. Stilwell, *Diaries*, August 9, 1944.
38. See, for example, Bidwell, 32.
39. Masters, 155. Excerpts from Stilwell's diaries and correspondence were edited by Theodore White and published as *The Stilwell Papers* in 1948. The edited selections exclude Stilwell's most troubling diction and thoughts, retaining Stilwell's "pungent" wit and forthrightness. Stilwell's own character is revealed by his diaries in the raw, available online through the Hoover Institution's website: hoover.org/library -archives/collections/diaries-general-joseph-w-stilwell-1900-1946.
40. Tuchman, 160.
41. Alanbrooke, 479.
42. Wilson, 79.
43. Boatner, "Barbara Tuchman's Stilwell," 30, who cites incidents.
44. Tuchman, 231f.
45. Stilwell's staff's ignorance of his plans, Romanus and Sunderland, I.248; British request, FRUS, Diplomatic Papers, The Conferences at Washington and Quebec, 1943, Document 211, 425.
46. Eldridge, 166.
47. Slim, 255.
48. FRUS, Diplomatic Papers, 1944, China, Volume VI; Ambassador in China (Gauss) to the Secretary of State, March 24, 1944, Document 39, 44f.
49. USAAF, "The Campaign in Northern Burma and the Construction of the Ledo Road," January 15, 1945, 1.
50. Romanus and Sunderland, II.11, 15, 472.
51. Anders, *The Ledo Road*, 78f.
52. Anders, *The Ledo Road*, 75.
53. Brockbank, 80.

54. Stilwell's replacement of General Arrowsmith, and the underhanded way in which he went about this, was criticized even by his supporters; see Anders, *The Ledo Road*, 82ff. Anders, who is admiring of Stilwell, offers by way of explanation that Stilwell was tired and ill.

55. USAAF, "The Campaign in Northern Burma and the Construction of the Ledo Road," January 15, 1945, 1.

56. Ogburn, 70f.

57. Stevens, 401.

58. Keeler, 365.

59. Anders, *The Ledo Road*, 38, 48f., 81.

60. Ogburn, 69.

61. Koerner, 7, and note on 334f. In a close study of the Ledo Road and its builders, historian Nancy Brockbank noted that "[m]ost authors writing military history generally did not identify black units" and it was therefore possible to read even the most thorough and comprehensive history of the road without knowing that the American workers were in fact black. She found that files relating to the black engineers of the Ledo Road were "missing from the National Archives" and that there was a dearth of personal material, such as diaries or memoirs, to fill out the experience (Brockbank, 7ff.). Oral histories, such as those preserved by the Library of Congress's Veterans History Project, provide some information, as do the writings of two African American journalists who followed the road for the *Pittsburgh Courier* and the *Chicago Defender*; see below in text.

62. Army Air Forces Policy Studies: No. 9, "Abstracts of Policy-Making Messages Affecting Air Operations in the China-Burma-India Theater, 1 January 1942 to August 1943," 30 ("Labor Troops needed even if they have to be sent piecemeal. White preferred. Cannot rely on local Indian labor. . . . One colored Engineer Company stationed in Assam is now loading and unloading all freight going into and out of China"); and 17 ("Second Jap attack on Dinjan-Chabua took place today. Conduct of American forces including colored engineer units was magnificent").

63. The George C. Marshall Foundation of Lexington, VA, Tape 17M, Interview with General George C. Marshall, February 20, 1957: "Demobilization Problems, 1945; African-American Soldiers; Relations with FDR," 16.

64. Roosevelt, *As He Saw It*, 25.

65. A list of pointers was also offered: "Whites must respect girls going with negroes. Negroes must respect girls going with white soldiers and civilians. Neither race must interfer[e] with or cut in on soldiers of the other race in company with girls. One race must not attend dances given for the other race. . . . In hostels, and dormitories, where beds are available, whites and negroes should ask to be given accommodation with their own race. . . . Negroes must preserve the honor and integrity of the race through good behavior and avoidance of any act that might lead to arguments or brawls, whites must acknowledge this and respect this, and conduct themselves in such manner as to avoid any argument, quarrel, or brawl"; USAAF, "Colored Troops," Headquarters Eighth Air Force, ETOUSA, August 28, 1942.

66. USAAF, *A History of the India-China Division, Air Transport Command, Year 1944*, vol. 3, 700f., 703f., 704f.

67. *Hump Express*, April 26, 1945.

68. USAAF, *A History of the India-China Division, Air Transport Command, Year 1944*, vol. 3,

705f. Plating, 204f., quotes correspondence from an ICD-based African American clerk complaining of discriminatory promotions, discipline, and of racial slurs.

69. Willie Percy Yarbrough Collection (AFC/2001/001/97802).
70. Keeler, 370f.
71. Keeler, 408.
72. King, *Building for Victory*, 118f.
73. Keeler, 297.
74. Weber, 6.
75. Paul J. Wooten Collection (AFC/2001/001/67357).
76. Keeler, 289.
77. Motley, 119.
78. Motley, 121.
79. James W. Spencer Collection (AFC/2001/001/12292).
80. Willie Percy Yarbrough Collection (AFC/2001/001/97802).
81. Mosquitoes in light, King, *Building for Victory*, 121f. Japanese watch show, Motley, 133.
82. Engs, 47.
83. James W. Spencer Collection (AFC/2001/001/12292).
84. Greech, Oral history.
85. Willie Percy Yarbrough Collection (AFC/2001/001/97802).
86. Peers, 18.
87. Motley, 131.
88. Romanus and Sunderland, I.45; Craw, 242.
89. For Chinese middleman, Motley, 131; black market bazaars, Koerner, 107.
90. Motley, 121.
91. Brendan Koerner's *Now the Hell Will Start* tells the story of this manhunt, 125; and at 139–43 give a vivid evocation of the incident.
92. Motley, 134f.
93. Peers, 18.
94. Anders, *The Ledo Road*, 114f.
95. Magoon, 17.
96. Dan Burley, "Surgeon from Harlem Hospital Talks N.Y. with Dan in Burma," *Amsterdam News*, 1945; the article is reproduced, along with others written about the 335th that were clipped and kept by Carl Scarborough Jenkins, a battalion surgeon with the hospital; the articles can be read at 335thstationhospital.org. Other information is gleaned from various sites such as Geraldine Seay, "The Ledo Road: African American Soldiers and Nurses in WW2 Burma," medium.com /afro-asian-visions/the-ledo-road-african-american-soldiers-and-nurses-in-ww2 -burma-31728ce64844; and "African Americans and the Ledo Road," ledoroad .com. The first site also posts a letter from the National Archives: "This letter is in reply to your recent request to the National Archives for unit information about the 335th Station Hospital. We have carefully searched our holdings and were unable to locate any records relating to that hospital."
97. Salyer, 16.
98. Matloff, 445f.
99. Slim, 271.
100. Romanus and Sunderland, II.310.
101. Romanus and Sunderland, II.312.

102. Matloff, 440.
103. Romanus and Sunderland, II.310.
104. Allen, *Burma*, 188f.
105. For the plain, wonderfully evoked, Allen, *Burma*, 194; for Slim's strategy, Slim, 290–94.
106. Slim, 293; Latimer, 195.
107. Latimer, 199.
108. Evans and Brett-James, 194.
109. Latimer, 199.
110. Allen, *"Missy Baba,"* 90.
111. Allen, *Burma*, 230.
112. Latimer, 236f.
113. Allen, *Burma*, 228.
114. Allen, *Burma*, 228.
115. Allen, *Burma*, 229; the extent of dissension among the Japanese command is explored by Moore, "Japanese Command Crisis in Burma, 1944," which also cites Mutaguchi's private dream of riding a white horse in Roman-style triumph through New Delhi.
116. Chasie and Fecitt, 202.
117. Latimer, 259f.
118. Regarding the number of defenders and noncombatants, see Latimer, 498, 6n.
119. Allen, *Burma*, 234f.
120. Allen, *Burma*, 235ff.
121. Allen, *Burma*, 235; the water shortage could have been mitigated: the garrison was equipped with canvas tanks that should have been both filled and buried, but were not.
122. Latimer, 265.
123. On airdrops, Latimer, 267f.; Allen, *Burma*, 236.
124. Chasie and Fecitt, 249–53.
125. For Imphal, see Evans and Brett-James, 283, 308, 310, 312f., 314f. For Kohima, see kohimaeducationaltrust.net/news-and-events/webinars/valour-at-kohima-the-story-of-the-two-victoria-cross-recipients-at-the-battle-of-kohima-1944, with images of the original War Office citations.
126. Chasie and Fecitt, 251–53.
127. Latimer, 304.
128. Latimer, 262, 266.
129. Allen, *Burma*, 289.
130. Tamayama and Nunneley, 176f.
131. Japanese Monograph No. 134, 164.
132. General Headquarters, India, Military Intelligence Directorate, *Japanese in Battle*, 2nd ed. (New Delhi: Government of India Press, 1944), 3.
133. Allen, *Burma*, 637ff., gives a detailed breakdown and points out that the Indian sepoys accounted for the greatest losses in the British counteroffensive.
134. Slim, 272.
135. Japanese Monograph No. 134, 149f.
136. USAAF, "First Draft Supreme Allied Commander's Despatches: Part III Operations by Northern Combat Area Command," 2.
137. Masters, 209f.
138. Masters, 215.

139. Thomas, *Back to Mandalay*, 171.

140. Fuwa, 48, 56f.

141. Original strength, Fuwa, 60; estimated total strength, Ogburn, 79.

142. Romanus and Sunderland, II.202f.

143. Fuwa, 59; Slim, 271.

144. Slim, 272f.

145. Slim's account refers only to "a plan," but he was given no details. Hunter, however, claims that after the battle of Nphum Ga, to keep "officers and men busy," he, Hunter, had directed his staff to make a "study" for a possible Myitkyina task force, which he understood Stilwell was "seriously thinking of organizing." After duly questioning the Kachin, local villages, and the unfailingly knowledgeable Father Stuart, they came up with the idea of coming to Myitkyina from over the Kumon range; the Kachin, however, advised that the Kumon hills would be unmanageable for mules in the monsoon. Somewhat to Hunter's surprise, the plan was adopted, and he had the impression that apart from this study no detailed plans had in fact been made (Hunter, 84–87). Boatner states his belief that "the NCAC [Northern Combat Area Command] at Shaduzup never was consulted nor participated in any prior planning"; Boatner, "Barbara Tuchman's Stilwell," 36.

146. Hunter, 104f. Anders, "The Engineers at Myitkyina," 466, describes the runway with an engineer's zeal as being 4,800 feet long by 75 feet wide, with a "Telford base of 6-to-8-inch river stones beneath a 3-inch layer of crushed rock," surfaced with asphalt for about two-thirds of its length, and pocked with eroding bomb craters.

147. Hunter, 87; Boatner, "Barbara Tuchman's Stilwell," 39, on the new troops' lack of experience.

148. Ogburn, 201.

149. Romanus and Sunderland, II.188–91; this official account does not explore the muddled leadership that complicated this ordeal, for which see Ogburn's long account, 170–91; and Hunter, 72, on finding Merrill.

150. Ogburn, 193f.

151. Ogburn, 200; Hunter's recollection was more specific: "Merrill held a meeting of the Galahad staff and the battalion commanders. . . . At this meeting it was explained that should we succeed in capturing the airstrip Galahad personnel would be relieved and flown to an already selected site where a rest and recreational area would be constructed"; Hunter, 88.

152. Romanus and Sunderland, II.230.

153. Captain Fred O. Lyons, "Here's What Happened! Merrill's Marauders in Burma."

154. Romanus and Sunderland, II.226.

155. Stilwell *Diaries*, May 17, 1944.

156. Denzler, 21.

157. Stilwell *Diaries*, May 17, 1944.

158. Stimson, *Diaries*, May 18, 1944; see also Stimson, *Diaries*, January 19, 1944.

159. Hunter, 115f. For the number of aircraft landing on the night of May 17–18, Taylor, "Air Supply in the Burma Campaigns," 26.

160. Hunter, 117.

161. Hopkins, 444f.

162. Romanus and Sunderland, II.232f.

163. Hunter, 119, 123.

164. Romanus and Sunderland, II.235.

165. Slim, 275.

166. Slim, 275. The underestimation of enemy numbers was so consistent that Hunter and others at the time and later have wondered if this was done deliberately so as not to scare the Chinese: see for example Hunter, 151; and Diamond, 67.

167. Hunter, 128f., who adds he has "General Boatner's word as chief of staff of Stilwell's headquarters the plan was never discussed with him."

168. Romanus and Sunderland, II.238.

169. Stilwell Diaries, May 21, 1944.

170. Stilwell Diaries, May 20, 1944.

171. Characterization of the 36th, Diamond, 67. Stilwell's failure to use the 36th Division has been the subject of heated discussion, conveniently encapsulated in an exchange between historian Scott R. McMichael and Riley Sunderland, the latter being one of the two joint authors of the US Army's three-volume history of the China-Burma-India theater. In an article for the US Army War College quarterly magazine Parameters, McMichael examined and praised the role of Colonel Charles Hunter for stepping into the leadership vacuum of the Myitkyina campaign. Amid his numerous criticisms of the higher command's inept management of the campaign, he cites Stilwell's refusal "to accept the offer of an excellent British division," the Indian 36th (McMichael, 53). His article provoked much comment, some of which was published at length in a subsequent issue (Parameters XVII, no. 1 [1987]: 97–111). Writing to rebut McMichael's most contentious statements was Riley Sunderland, who gave a lengthy account of why (a) reference to Stilwell's rejection of the 36th had been omitted from his (Sunderland's) own history, and (b) why it was not true Stilwell had in fact rejected the division, pointing out that on May 27, Stilwell had sent a request to Mountbatten through General Daniel Sultan, his deputy theater commander, for a British parachute regiment. Sultan reported back that the regiment was at that time engaged in the defense of Imphal, but that the 36th Indian Division, then in the Arakan, was in the process of converting from an amphibious assault unit to a standard, three-brigade division, of which "the first brigade . . . might be ready by the end of June," and the whole by the middle of July (100). McMichael's response is as follows: "Even though, as Mr. Sunderland notes, this excellent division was not immediately available to Stilwell, it could have been available within a month if Stilwell had pressed for it with his usual singlemindedness. If called for, the 36th Division could certainly have done a far better job against the Japanese than the dilatory, unaggressive Chinese. The 36th did, in fact, fly into the Myitkyina airfield in July [when the fight for the town was still raging], but it was sent south under British command, rather than against Myitkyina. . . . But Stilwell never asked for it. He elected to keep it a Chinese-American effort, not wanting to share any credit with the British" (109). This was also Hunter's view at the time (Hunter, 138). What is clear from Stilwell's own diary is that on May 22 he considered asking for the 36th and, as it seems, in the same moment decided against this ("No")—and in fact never did.

172. Romanus and Sunderland, II.237.

173. Casey, 209.

174. Hunter, 148f., reproducing the written testimonial of the officers in question. Ogburn, 230f., cites other testimonies. Stone, 310, gives the medical assessment that the replacements were "all the misfits in the Army. Many of the men had extremely low IQs and many were physical wrecks." The text goes on to list the ailments, from blindness in one eye, to deafness due to neural pathology, to "bony deformities."

175. Romanus and Sunderland, II.241.

176. Hunter, 130; Hopkins and Jones, 522–24, reproduces the letter.

177. Romanus and Sunderland, II.237.

178. Romanus and Sunderland, II.240, gives a breakdown of the casualties; Ogburn, 227, on the remaining Marauder strength.

179. Romanus and Sunderland, II.240.

180. Stone, 374f.; this book reprints the full medical report. On the origin of the report see, too, Hopkins and Jones, 589.

181. Ogburn, 229.

182. Boatner, "Barbara Tuchman's Stilwell," 41.

183. The condition of the 18th is eloquently evoked in the postwar interrogations of Colonel Maruyama and Lieutenant General Tanaka; USAAF, Howard C. Davidson Collection, "The North Burma Campaign."

184. Closely following Ogburn, 233.

185. Anders, "The Engineers at Myitkyina," 446, 448.

186. Slim, 275.

187. Stilwell, *Diaries*, May 17, 1944.

188. Bidwell, 222ff.; Masters, 219f., which also gives his reservations concerning the order, questioning among other things the wisdom of establishing another block close to the front line when a block to the rear, held by the 77th Brigade, was already operating successfully.

189. Latimer, 251.

190. Masters, 245; Master's account of the Blackpool battle is "tracked" by Bidwell through the log of a Royal Artillery officer that gives "the day, the exact time and the details of every event, including the missions fired, with range, bearing and ammunition expended, the supply drops, the enemy shelling, the casualties and the course of the final battle"; Bidwell, 233.

191. Masters, 247.

192. Masters, 251.

193. Bidwell, 237.

194. Masters, 259.

195. Romanus and Sunderland, II.221; Bidwell, 241.

196. Easterbrook, *World War II Diaries*, May 18, 1944.

197. Slim, 279f.; Masters, 267f.

198. Masters, 268, 277.

199. The capture of Mogaung, strategically as important as the capture of Myitkyina, became the subject of another contentious debate. It was intended that the 77th Brigade be supported by a Chinese force, but when this did not turn up, the 77th's commanding officer, "Mad" Mike Calvert, dispatched a patrol to find it, also sending a signal to Lentaigne to warn that owing to casualties and sickness he could not hold his position indefinitely; the message was conveyed to Stilwell, who promised to "speed up the Chinese" (Calvert, *Prisoners of Hope*, 215). On the evening of June 18, the patrol returned announcing the arrival of the 1st Battalion of the Chinese 114th Regiment. It is noteworthy that, unusually among the Allies, Calvert was an admirer of the Chinese soldier; he had been in Shanghai when the city fell to the Japanese in 1937–38 and spoke some Cantonese. He had a rare and nuanced view of Chinese fighting methods and an appreciation of why Chiang Kai-shek's army would not "take part in mammoth battles in which the fate of China could be changed in a day" (Calvert, *Prisoners of Hope*, 224). His impression of the 1st Battalion's commander, Major P'ang, and on-record comments about him

428 NOTES TO PAGES 316-320

are highly complimentary: "He was a true soldier, and any soldier in the world would have got on well with him" (Calvert, *Prisoners of Hope,* 221). The battle for Mogaung raged for sixteen days, with the Chindits taking the town, and the Chinese force mopping up on the outskirts (Bidwell, 271ff., who, among other sources, quotes from a long letter written by a machine-gun platoon commander to his family describing the action at the time). On the evening of June 24, while mopping-up operations continued, the BBC News announced that Chinese-American forces had captured Mogaung; the source of this misinformation was Stilwell's office. The news enraged the Chindits and embarrassed the Chinese. Calvert writes: "Colonel Li, on hearing of it a day or two later, through one of the Hong Kong Chinese, came straight to my H.Q. and, in front of the American lieutenant-colonel and [liaison officer], apologized for the announcement" (Calvert, *Prisoners of Hope,* 238). Famously, this was followed by Calvert's own report to Lentaigne, to be passed to Stilwell, "Mogaung having been taken by Chinese, 77 Brigade proceeding to take Umbrage" (Calvert, *Prisoners of Hope,* 244).

200. Masters, 278f.
201. Calvert, *Prisoners of Hope,* 246f.
202. Masters, 281.
203. Fuwa, 60; Romanus and Sunderland, II.220.
204. Following Bidwell's tribute, 280.
205. Allen, *Burma,* 381–85, who vividly evokes the retreat and pointedly draws comparison between Mizukami and Stilwell.
206. Ogburn, 240.
207. Ogburn, 241f.
208. Ogburn, 246.
209. Mortimer, 197.
210. Ogburn, 238.
211. Mortimer, 200f.
212. By contrast, Colonel Hunter, who alone could tell the story of the Marauders and of the campaign from start to finish, had been relieved of duty when Myitkyina fell and sent home by boat—slow boat, as his supporters pointed out, and so was not available for comment.
213. *The New York Times,* August 26, 1944, 7.
214. King, *Building for Victory,* 115.
215. Motley, 132f.
216. Dominick, 81f.; Masters also reports on this face-saving tendency: "Where were the Chinese who were supposed to be co-operating in this attack from positions 393425, 488410, and 410400? Well, actually they weren't within miles of those places. They'd only said they were there to please Stilwell," (Masters, 277). Dominick reports that in the same conversation it was claimed that the "Americans actually captured Myitkyina once when the Japanese surrendered. As they came out under a white flag the Chinese shot them anyhow so the Japs naturally ducked back and dug in"—but no other source mentions this.
217. Romanus and Sunderland, II.243.
218. Romanus and Sunderland, II.253, cites the figures for Myitkyina and the striking discrepancy between the numbers of American and Chinese sick—980 and 188, respectively—attributing it to the Chinese soldiers' practice of boiling all water and cooking all food, 254. For casualties for the north Burma campaign from fall 1943 through mid-April 1944, II.188.

219. Stilwell, *Diaries*, August 4, 1944.

220. Romanus and Sunderland, II.256.

221. Romanus and Sunderland, II.316.

222. Romanus and Sunderland, II.372f.

223. Accompanying a search and rescue team dispatched to Yenan to liaise with the Communists, who were picking up downed US airmen, was an American officer who had been born in China and spoke Chinese. Unexpectedly, he met Mao Tse-tung on the trip north. "He was very cordial. While he was visiting, he kidded us a little about America's being an imperialist country. When he was talking, his dialect was about the accent of the Shanghai area, so I could understand him. I hadn't told anyone that I was from China. I was a military officer and I didn't see that it was anyone's business. But after we had talked for a few minutes . . . Mao said, 'I see that one of our visitors understands Chinese.' I didn't know who he would be talking about except me. I answered, in Chinese, that I was born in Shanghai. He got up, reached across the table, stuck out his hand and said, in Chinese, 'old-time friend, old-time friend.' I thought at the time he was pretty sharp to see through my poker face." Eubank, 18.

224. Romanus and Sunderland, II.381ff.

225. Romanus and Sunderland, II.383f.

226. Romanus and Sunderland, II.329, II.352.

227. Stilwell, *Diaries*, September 19, 1944.

228. Romanus and Sunderland, II.444ff.

229. Following Taylor, *The Generalissimo*, 287–89, who makes use of Chiang's own diary.

230. Romanus and Sunderland, II.468.

231. Casey, 217.

232. Young, Richard, Oral History, 12f.

233. After the war, in October 1946, it was discovered that Stilwell had stomach cancer, which had metastasized to his liver; Tuchman, 633.

234. Plating, 197.

235. Wedemeyer, *Wedermeyer Reports!*, 275.

236. "Briton for Ban on Stilwell," *The New York Times*, November 4, 1944, 6.

237. Masters, 288.

238. Calvert, *Prisoners of Hope*, 241.

239. Thomas, *Back to Mandalay*, 54f.

240. Allen, *Burma*, 195.

241. McGowen, 34ff., which gives accounts of other dramatic rescues in Burma; and Chinnery, 29f.

242. Thomas, *Back to Mandalay*, 55.

9. END OF THE ROAD

1. For the individual accidents, Quinn, 87ff., 105, 108, 115, 120, 130, 145, 161, 169ff., 178, 198.

2. Boody, 44.

3. Boody, 45; Boody's crash serves as a good example of why fixed crews are desirable. In a fixed crew, pilot and copilot have clearly assigned duties, each knowing his own part in the ritual pre-check, so that something as basic as the removal of the highly visible, bright-red gust chocks would not slip between the cracks. Similarly, the copilot's misreading of Boody's hand signal was due to lack of familiarity

between pilot and copilot; Boody exonerated his copilot for the error, stating, "I had not used that hand signal, before, with him" (45). The incident also speaks to poor oversight and poor higher management in allowing any discretion for pre-flight procedures.

4. Boody, 45ff., with illustrations of the crashed plane on 45-A.

5. Boody, 46.

6. Boody, 46; for weather, Gray, *Diary*, May 1, 1944.

7. USAAF, India-China Division, Air Transport Command, "ATC Statistics on Hump Tonnage, 1942–1945," 2. Other documents give slightly different figures.

8. USAAF, "Operations," *A History of the India-China Division Air Transport Command, Year 1944*, vol. 1, 23.

9. USAAF, India-China Division, Air Transport Command, "Major Accidents to ICD Aircraft," *A History of the India China Wing for the Period June through December 1943*, 452–57; and USAAF, *A History of the India-China Division Air Transport Command, Year 1944*, vol. 1, 603ff.

10. USAAF, *A History of the India-China Division Air Transport Command, Year 1944*, vol. 1, 605.

11. Quinn, 48, 54, 74, 86, 103, 106.

12. Tunner, 26, in turn quoting LaFarge.

13. Tunner, 43.

14. Tunner, 51.

15. Tunner, 57, 90–92.

16. Tunner, 68.

17. Tunner, 94, 90.

18. Tunner, 108f.

19. For these and following details of the court-martial, "United States v. Captain John L. Okenfus, 0-905324, Air Corps, 1330th Army Air Forces Base Unit, Air Transport Command," *Holdings and Opinions, Board of Review, Branch Office of the Judge Advocate General, China-Burma-India, India-Burma Theater*, vol. 2, Judge Advocate General's Department (Washington, DC: Office of the Judge Advocate General, 1943–1946), 339–49.

20. "Pilot of Plane on Longest Flight Known at Hadley," *Courier-News*, December 11, 1943, 7.

21. One finds Okenfus advertising his services in the *Miami Herald* in 1940 ("Young Man, licensed pilot with plane and car wants work"), "Wanted Positions," *Miami Herald*, March 21, 1940, 29; "New Air Service Inaugurated Here," *The Palm Beach Post*, February 2, 1941, 13.

22. The incident received wide local coverage: *The Daily Home News*, September 18, 1941, 1; "Pilot Escapes Injury When Plane Upsets," *Courier News*, September 18, 1941, 1, 19.

23. Among others notices, "Too Bad!," *Daily News*, November 5, 1938; *Brattleboro Reformer*, November 11, 1938, 3.

24. "Ferrying Service Gets Local Pilots," *The Palm Beach Post*, February 27, 1942, 8; "Bomber Drive," *The Desert Sun*, February 26, 1943, 1ff.

25. "Ohio-to-India Airline Operates," *The Galveston Daily News*, December 9, 1943, 6; and "Dayton, India Linked by Air Freight Route," *Journal Herald*, December 9, 1943, 1, among many others; for an overview of the "Fireball Express" service, Orth, 68.

26. *The Staley Journal* (Decatur, Illinois), January 1944, 38.

27. John Anthony Pope Collection (AFC/2001/001/73071); "Bingo, Dancing, Feature

Show, at G.I. Party," *CBI Roundup* 1, no. 51 (September 2, 1943); William S. Barksdale Jr. Papers, by kind permission of William Barksdale III.

28. All quotations from "A journal of William S. Barksdale Jr.," by kind permission of William Barksdale III.

29. Quinn, 195f., 198, 202.

30. Dobie, 3, 5ff.

31. For the sentence, "United States v. Captain John L. Okenfus, 0-905324, Air Corps, 1330th Army Air Forces Base Unit, Air Transport Command," 339–49. For the place of punishment, "Court Martial Appeal Studied," *Courier-News*, May 1, 1946, 10.

32. In his memoir, Dr. Carl Constein writes of pilot Captain Henry, "unfortunately I didn't record his first name" (81). Among the short autobiographical notices given in the Hump Pilot Association's four-volume history, there is a John A. Henry, who, like Constein, was based at Chabua, and who includes among his chosen memories "THAT NIGHT of Jan. 6-7-45 when . . . we lucked out in guessing we should turn south," and landed safely at Chanyi, as did Constein and his "Captain Henry." HPA, vol. 1, 428.

33. Constein, *Born to Fly the Hump*, 80f.; the account of this flight follows Constein closely.

34. Taylor, "2nd Weather," 142f.

35. Constein, *Born to Fly the Hump*, 81ff.

36. Downie's story is told in Ethell and Downie, 107–14, and in Downie, "The Wildest Night," *Flying Ace*, October 1945, 45 and 69; the story was also reprinted in the Hump Pilot Association's anthology, vol. 1, 175f. Copilot Bill Hanahan's account appears in Ethell and Downie, 114, and Constein, *Tales of the Himalayas*, 125ff.

37. Constein, *Tales of the Himalayas*, 154, as told by Joseph B. Plosser.

38. Sykes's account is given in Ethell and Downie, 117f.; and in an interview shortly after the ordeal: "Hump's Worst Weather Bats Planes About," *Hump Express* 1, no. 2 (January 25, 1945).

39. Constein, *Tales of the Himalayas*, 154f, as told by Joseph B. Plosser.

40. Constein, *Tales of the Himalayas*, 35, as told by Harvey Borkenhagen; Calvert, Oral History, 7.

41. Interview with J. V. Vinyard.

42. Interview with J. V. Vinyard.

43. Constein, *Tales of the Himalayas*, 35, as told by Harvey Borkenhagen.

44. Ethell and Downie, 120.

45. *Hump Express* 1, no. 2 (January 25, 1945).

46. Gray, *Diary*, January 7–8, 1945.

47. Quinn cites nine aircraft lost and forty killed; this record, when it errs, errs in underestimation.

48. An eyewitness account of the height of the clouds was made by a pilot flying to Kunming behind the weather; Spencer, *Flying the Hump*, 157.

49. Constein, *Born to Fly the Hump*, 88; Ethell and Downie, 121.

50. Anders, *The Ledo Road*, 213; for fighting on the road, Koerner, 268.

51. Stilwell had in fact stated that the road could be open "by January '44" (FRUS, Diplomatic Papers, The Conferences at Washington and Quebec, 1943, Document 35, 63), and even more categorically that it "should be operating by the middle of 1944" (FRUS, Diplomatic Papers, The Conferences at Washington and Quebec, 1943; "The Commanding General, United States Forces, China, Burma, India [Stilwell] to the Secretary of War [Stimson], Document 64, 166).

52. Brockbank, 133.
53. Stevens, 398, 403. The second correspondent was Denton Brooks of the *Chicago Defender*.
54. Bolden, "Ledo Road Diary," *Journal and Guide*, March 17, 1945, 1.
55. Stevens, 403, based on interviews with the journalists; Bolden, 1.
56. Bolden, 1.
57. USAAF, Howard C. Davidson Collection, "China Burma India Theater of Operations," Part III: the handwritten note follows VII.8. Madame Chiang Kai-shek's racism was notorious. Eric Sevareid reports on "the well-marked trail she left behind her" into Assam. A soldier at the Chabua base asked him: "What kind of a dame is she? She wouldn't sign a bill I handed her because it had a picture of a Negro girl on it." Sevareid, 230.
58. Stevens, 403.
59. Tuchman, 612.
60. Romanus and Sunderland, II.387.
61. Romanus and Sunderland, II.388.
62. Romanus and Sunderland, II.380.
63. USAAF, India-China Division, Air Transport Command, "ATC Statistics on Hump Tonnage, 1942–1945."
64. Taylor, "Air Supply in the Burma Campaigns," 29.
65. Plating, 200.
66. Tunner, 128.
67. USAAF, "Combined Study by Headquarters, Services of Supply, India-Burma Theater & Headquarters, Army Air Forces, India-Burma Theater of the Comparative Costs in Personnel and Equipment of Delivering 80,000 Tons per Month to Kunming by Road and by Air." See, too, USAAF, HQ India-China Division, Air Transport Command, "Investigation Regarding Hump Flying."
68. An experiment to train Chinese drivers who could end their journey in Kunming failed, for the Chinese conscripts arrived in poor physical condition, and the volunteers, if that is indeed what they were, deserted. More seriously, the four-week crash course did not turn out proficient drivers. One early Chinese-manned convoy setting out from Ledo arrived at the Pangsau Pass thirty-eight miles away with only sixty-six of its original ninety vehicles operational. Accidents and mistreatment of the vehicles proved too frequent and too costly, and reluctantly the Services of Supply appropriated a veteran Chinese motor regiment with long experience in Burma along with drivers from the US Engineer and Quartermaster battalions. These made the long journey into Kunming, from where they were flown back to India over the Hump. Motley, 121f.; Romanus and Sunderland, III.316.
69. Motley, 121.
70. Weskamp, 19.
71. Romanus and Sunderland, III.364.
72. Tunner, 129f.
73. See for example, a *Time* magazine interview with Stilwell defending the road: "[T]he Ledo Road fulfills two U.S. objectives: 1) to get at least some supplies to blockaded China; 2) to set up a situation in which Japs are killed." "Battle of Asia; A Difference of Opinion," *Time*, February 14, 1944, 33.
74. Masters, 310f.
75. Fraser, 155; Fraser's searing memoir is one of the most memorable personal accounts of the war. The incident he describes may be the same incident that is re-

corded in USAAF documents that tell the story of how two American airmen who had been captured after bailing over the Hump were released as the Japanese retreated. On a forced march from Rangoon, the Japanese commandant leading the march turned to them and said, "What you have been waiting for for three years has now come. You are free." As the airmen walked north, a scout contacted the Fourteenth Army, who took them in and saw that they were flown to Calcutta; USAAF, India-China Division, Air Transport Command, "Weekly Summary (28 April–5 May 1945)."

76. Phillips, *Another Man's War*, 85.
77. Hall, *A Goldstar Century*, 97.
78. There are many sources for this sweeping summation of an always complicated campaign; Slim's own account strikes a balance between accuracy, clarity, and readability. An excellent succinct account is found in Philip Jowett's *Images of War: The Battle for Burma, 1942–1943*, illustrated with well-chosen photographs from the campaign; from 137ff. For the RAF's final air assault, Saunders and Richards, 362f.
79. Romanus and Sunderland, III.5.
80. Romanus and Sunderland, III.6.
81. Romanus and Sunderland, III.338, quoting from a report made by Admiral Leahy, who was present at the meeting.
82. Mitter, 277f.
83. Mitter, 320.
84. Theodore White gives a searing firsthand account of the devastating famine—and of how he successfully skirted Henry Luce's censorship of any news that reflected badly on the Kuomintang to file his report for *Time* (for which accomplishment Madame Chiang Kai-shek demanded that White be fired). White, *In Search of History*, 154.
85. Mitter, 320.
86. White and Jacoby, 178.
87. Romanus and Sunderland, III.8.
88. Romanus and Sunderland, III.8f.
89. Romanus and Sunderland, II.9; and Taylor, *The Generalissimo*, 272.
90. Romanus and Sunderland, II.408ff.
91. USAAF, "The Situation in China or the Thankless Job," *A History of the India-China Division Air Transport Command, Year 1944*, vol. 3, 880f.
92. Romanus and Sunderland, III.8, III.12.
93. Romanus and Sunderland, III.21.
94. Dominick, 23.
95. *Miami Herald*, October 11, 1942, 45.
96. "Hump Smuggling Ring Exposed by Army," *CBI Roundup*, December 21, 1944.
97. Byrd, 277f.; Samson, 41, describes Sutter as "a marvelously bilingual man," noting that he was Swiss and his wife Indian-Chinese.
98. Samson, 289.
99. Stilwell, *Diaries*, June 24, 1943.
100. Samson, 154.
101. Stilwell, *Black Book*, 18.
102. Eubank, 37f.
103. Stilwell, *Diaries*, June 29, 1943.
104. Stilwell, *Diaries*, July 2, 1943.
105. Byrd, 263.

106. Romanus and Sunderland, III.342f.; the events related to Chennault's eventual relief are also covered by Byrd, from 275.

107. Plating, 187–90, gives an overview of the ill-fated B-29 plans in China; for a blow-by-blow account, Craven and Cate, V, 131 onward, chapter 5, "Exit Matterhorn."

108. Romanus and Sunderland, III.344; Arnold, "Chennault's Retirement," The Papers of Henry H. Arnold, Container 199, File China 1944–1945.

109. Byrd, 276.

110. Byrd, 279.

111. Arnold, "Chennault's Retirement," The Papers of Henry H. Arnold.

112. Byrd, 280, citing personal correspondence with Alsop.

113. Arnold, "Chennault to Lieutenant General A. C. Wedemeyer," The Papers of Henry H. Arnold, July 6, 1945, Container 199, File China 1944–1945.

114. Byrd, 280.

115. The stories appear in a number of publications, for example: "A Hero Leaves the Field," The Herald-Journal, July 25, 1945, 2; "Chennault Already a Legend, His Genius Untarnished by Fate," The Buffalo News, July 23, 1945, 2; "Army Politics Killed Chennault," The Knoxville Journal, July 26, 1945, 4.

116. "Army Politics Killed Chennault," 4.

117. Taylor, Air Interdiction in China, 84f.

118. Taylor, Air Interdiction in China, 9f., 32, 44, 52, 80.

119. Taylor, Air Interdiction in China, 70.

120. Taylor, Air Interdiction in China, 11.

121. Arnold, "Wedemeyer to Arnold," The Papers of Henry H. Arnold, August 3, 1945, Container 199, File China 1944–1945. Repeated submission of FOIA requests to the FBI for information in Chennault's file yielded the response that "we were unable to identify records subject to the FOIPA that are responsive to your request."

122. Arnold, "Wedemeyer to Marshall," The Papers of Henry H. Arnold, August 4, 1945, Container 199, File China 1944–1945.

123. Tuchman, 599.

124. Tuchman, 599; Stimson, Diaries, October 4, 1944; see also Stimson, Diaries, January 19, 1944.

125. Planes and pilots, Plating, 227; tonnage figures, USAAF, India-China Division, Air Transport Command, "ATC Statistics on Hump Tonnage, 1942–1945," 2.

126. McGuire, 19.

127. Dominick, 35.

128. "Han Shan" (Cold Mountain), translated by David Hinton; Hinton, 221.

129. Samson, 43.

130. Conant, 178.

131. Conant, 178.

132. Gooding, 279f.

133. Conant, 183; Paul Child would later marry Julia Child, née McWilliams, also in the OSS.

134. Alsop, 167.

135. White and Jacoby, 160.

136. Gooding, 279.

137. USAAF, "The Situation in China or the Thankless Job," 890f.

138. Boody, 28.

139. Among the many reports of such incidents: Fessler, 112; Constein, Born to Fly the

Hump, 58; Tunner, 125; Constein, *Tales of the Himalayas*, 120, as told by Raymond M. Rodgers.

140. Stelling, 142.
141. White and Jacoby, 160; Mitter, 284.
142. Rosinger, 20.
143. Greenlaw, 54.
144. Quoting White and Jacoby, 160.
145. Constein, *Tales of the Himalayas*, 79, as told by Jim Segel.
146. White, *Ten Thousand Tons by Christmas*, 110.
147. Mitter, 340.
148. The recordkeeping at these Fourteenth Air Force bases was slipshod and scanty, as an ATC historian laments: USAAF, India-China Division, Air Transport Command, "A History of the India China Wing for the Period June through December 1943," 137. There are, however, numerous firsthand accounts of day-to-day life at the various bases, as below.
149. USAAF, "History of the 16th Combat Camera Unit 1 May 1943 to 31 December 44," 24.
150. USAAF, "History of the 16th Combat Camera Unit 1 May 1943 to 31 December 44," 28.
151. Segel, 131.
152. White, *Ten Thousand Tons by Christmas*, 106.
153. Lazzara, 317.
154. Stelling, 142–46.
155. Englert, 10.
156. "ATC Officers Sell Drama, 'The Hump,'" *India-Burma Theater Roundup* (formerly *CBI Roundup*) III, no. 30 (April 1945); for national press, for example, "Two Officers' Play to be Staged," *Democrat and Chronicle*, May 20, 1945; *Variety*, June 13, 1945, 2; and *Variety*, June 20, 1945, 47.
157. For example, "Search for Lost Planes in Burma," *Ex-CBI Roundup*, May 1947, 12.
158. POW remains, see for example the extraordinary story of the crash in May 1946 of a Tenth Air Force plane carrying the remains of forty-three POWs recently discovered by the Army Graves Registration Service in southern Burma. Debriefing of the crash revealed that the pilot disliked flying over water and diverted in a storm to avoid doing so, and so ran out of fuel; eleven men were killed in the crash. Clayton Kuhles, "Crashed Aircraft Site Report," for C-47B #43-48308, MIA Recoveries Inc, miarecoveries.org; Constein, *Tales of the Himalayas*, 162, as told by A. H. Miller.
159. Romanus and Sunderland, III.38.
160. Plating, 233; *Time*, below, gives slightly different figures of numbers and days.
161. "The Big Lift," *Time*, November 12, 1945, 25.
162. Plating, 233f.
163. Romanus and Sunderland, III.390.
164. Stelling, 149; Plating, 225.
165. McLynn, 123.
166. Romanus and Sunderland, III.390.
167. Stelling, 149f.
168. White and Jacoby, 196.
169. Allen, *Missy Baba*, 102, 107.
170. The accident rate is assessed in various ways, including by sorties flown, by accidents

per one thousand hours, by comparing the final month's toll with that of the early years. Plating, 226; Tunner, 116, 134.

171. Catalogs of the losses are given in USAAF, India-China Division, Air Transport Command, "Chronological List of Aircraft Crashing on Hump Route," 1–114, which cites a total of 834 aircraft lost over the Hump, including bombers, fighters, light-evacuation aircraft, and British Spitfires. Of these, 585 were transport losses, but this does not include the B-25 bombers that were used to transport fuel. Quinn appeared to work from this list, and her *The Aluminum Trail* mostly accords with this tally. Hanks, a CNAC pilot who includes a table of losses in his memoir (and makes a convincing case for CNAC having run the superior airlift operation) estimates 702 ATC planes lost and gives the highest estimated casualty count (Hanks, 258). Correll, 71, gives recent estimates, including bailouts.

172. Quinn, 475f.

173. Hanks, 252f.

174. For basic information, giving only the surnames of the crew, Quinn, 472. Further information about the men and the incident can be culled from: "James Powell Listed Missing," *Des Moines Tribune*, October 2, 1945, 9; "James Powell," in *China Airlift—"The Hump,"* vol. 1, China-Burma-India Hump Pilots Association, 509; Edmund J. Webb, US National Cemetery Interment Control Forms, accessed at ancestry.com/discoveryui-content/view/1889212:2590?tid=&pid=&queryId=48d7b 867361a4e36fc7268a987643b5a&_phsrc=KVq4&_phstart=successSource.

175. Quinn, 473f.

176. "Crash of a Douglas C-54G-5-DO Skymaster in Chhukha," Bureau of Aircraft Accident Archives, citing aircraft #45-0528: baaa-acro.com/crash/crash-douglas-c-54g-5-do-skymaster-chhukha-44-killed.

177. Fischer, 79.

178. His daughter, Aung San Suu Kyi, served as state counselor of Myanmar and leader of the National League for Democracy until 2021.

179. Chasie and Fecitt, 90ff., 107f.

180. "Chaos in India and China Two Years after War Ends," *Ex-CBI Roundup* 1, no. 7 (September 1947): 1.

181. Japanese Monograph No. 72, 14, 17. Stilwell, on the eve of his departure in October 1944, correctly stated that there were "[t]wenty-four Japanese divisions" in China at that time, but he did not break these down by geographical region; Arnold, "CG to US Army Air Forces, China, Burma and India to War Department, The Papers of Henry H. Arnold, October 10, 1944, Container 199, File China 1944-1945.

182. Segel, 251, 255.

183. Stelling, 146.

184. Boody, 48, 61; and interview with Lee Boody, Robert Boody's son.

185. *The News & Observer*, October 15, 2009, 18.

186. "William N. Hanahan," in *China Airlift—"The Hump,"* vol. 1, China-Burma-India Hump Pilots Association, 420; Hanahan flew as copilot with Don Downie on the night of the great storm.

187. Information from author's interviews with Suzanne Baker, from a family biography of her father, and from a recorded interview with William Morgan Baker, conducted and kindly made available by Chuck Hodge.

188. Kincheloe, 18.

189. *Chicago Tribune*, February 25, 1949, 32; *Chicago Tribune*, February 25, 1950, 16.

190. Wesley McCormick's death is cited by many, evoked as perhaps the worst fate that could befall one in the jungle; the facts of his death were not publicized and perhaps, one hopes, his family never knew them. Quinn, 373f.; Diebold (the rescuer), 163ff.

191. Sevareid, 349f.

192. Lt. Marrs's skills are attested to by radio operator Douglas Devaux: When he learned from his base commander that he could choose a permanent pilot, Devaux narrowed his selection down to two: Lt. Loyal Marrs and Lt. Ed Schumacher. Devaux, n.p.

193. Quinn, 372f.

194. "Widow of Officer Killed Flying Hump Joins W.A.C.," *Courier-Journal*, April 26, 1945, 17.

195. Interview with Dawn Balfour.

196. Quinn, 475ef.

197. Quinn's obituary appears in the *Lake City Reporter*, December 5, 2004, kindly provided by the Florida Gateway College Library. For her grave marker: findagrave.com/memorial/84342793/gladys-marrs-quinn.

198. MIA Recoveries, Inc., "Crashed Aircraft Site Report, for C-53DO #42-15890 aka CNAC #58." Another remarkable search is that of Fletcher Hanks, a former CNAC pilot, who repeatedly attempted to find the wreck of CNAC #53, a C-53 that crashed on March 11, 1943, as it returned from China carrying tungsten ore. For decades, its remains lay on a ridge of the mountains only four miles from the Ledo Road, on the Pimaw Pass close to the Burma border, visible from the air and the object of many searches to retrieve its "hidden treasure," the tungsten ore. Hanks had joined a party to search for the plane in 1944, unsuccessfully, and eventually found it, at age eighty, in 1997, buried in azaleas, bamboo, and vines, and with a tree growing through it. Hanks, especially 151, 159. See, too, the CNAC website, cnac.org/hanks01.htm.

199. Goullart, 150–54, 180; Fitzgerald, *The Tower of Five Glories*, 200–203.

200. Goullart, 154.

201. Romer, 19.

202. Segel, 226.

203. The aircraft recently made headlines: Jeffrey Gettleman, "One Ukrainian War Casualty: The World's Largest Airplane," *The New York Times*, April 22, 2022.

204. Fischer, 88.

205. See for example, Engs, which has a lengthy account of driving the road in 1945; 85–123. Richardson, "The Jungle's Victory" describes the road in 1946. This story first appeared in the *New Republic*, and was reprinted in the July 1951 issue of *Ex-CBI Roundup*: cbi-theater.com/junglesvictory/junglesvictory.html.

206. Muhindra Khaund, "A Glimpse of Dinjan, Assam," pxley.com/a-glimpse-of-dinjan-assam/; and author's correspondence with Mr. Khaund.

BIBLIOGRAPHY

Aida, Yuji. *Prisoner of the British: A Japanese Soldier's Experience in Burma.* London: Cresset Press, 1966.

Air Headquarters. *Under the Greenwood Tree—or How to Acquire Burm-ease.* India: Air Forces in India, 1944.

Alanbrooke, Field Marshal Lord. *War Diaries 1939–1945.* London: Phoenix, 2002.

Allen, Joan. *"Missy Baba" to "Burra Mem": The Life of a Planter's Daughter in Northern India, 1913–1970.* London: Chameleon Press, 1998.

Allen, Louis. *Burma: The Longest War, 1941–45.* London: Phoenix Press, 2000.

Alsop, Joseph W. (with Adam Platt). *"I've Seen the Best of It": Memoirs.* New York: W. W. Norton & Company, 1992.

Anders, Leslie. "The Engineers at Myitkyina." *Military Engineer* 44, no. 302 (November–December 1952): 446–50.

Anders, Leslie. *The Ledo Road: General Joseph W. Stilwell's Highway to China.* Norman, OK: University of Oklahoma Press, 1965.

Arnold, H. H. *Global Mission.* Blue Ridge Summit, PA: TAB Books, 1989.

Arnold, Henry Harley. "The Papers of Henry H. Arnold." Box 199, Library of Congress, Manuscript Division. Read on AFHRA Microfilm Reel 28238.

Astor, Gerald. *The Jungle War: Mavericks, Marauders, and Madmen in the China-Burma-India Theater of WWII.* Hoboken, NJ: John Wiley & Sons, 2004.

Babcock, Kenneth. Ken Babcock Oral History Interview (OH01808trs): 1–29. National Museum of the Pacific War.

Baird-Murray, Maureen. *A World Overturned: A Burmese Childhood 1933–1947.* New York: Interlink Books, 1998.

Barber, Jack. *The Hump: The Greatest Untold Story of the War.* London: Souvenir Press, 1960.

Bayley, Christopher, and Tim Harper. *Forgotten Armies: The Fall of British Asia, 1941–1945.* Cambridge, MA: Belknap Harvard, 2004.

Belden, Jack. *Retreat with Stilwell.* Garden City, NY: Blue Ribbon Books, 1944.

Bhattacharji, Romesh. *Lands of Early Dawn: North East of India.* New Delhi: Rupa Co., 2002.

Bidwell, Shelford. *The Chindit War: Stilwell, Wingate, and the Campaign in Burma: 1944.* New York: Macmillan, 1979.

Bierman, John, and Colin Smith. *Fire in the Night: Wingate of Burma, Ethiopia, and Zion.* New York: Random House, 1999.

Bigland, Eileen. *Into China.* London: Collins, 1940.

Bjorge, Gary J. "Merrill's Marauders: Combined Operations in Northern Burma in 1944." *Army History*, no. 34 (Spring/Summer 1995): 12–28.

Blossom, W. R. "Bill." "Capt. John L. 'Blackie' Porter's Search and Rescue Squadron at Chabua" in *China Airlift—"The Hump,"* vol. 3, China-Burma-India Hump Pilots Association, 51–54. Paducah, KY: Turner, 1992.

Blum, John Morton. *From the Morgenthau Diaries: Years of War, 1941–1945.* Boston: Houghton Mifflin, 1967.

Boatner, Haydon L. "Comments on 'Crisis Fleeting' by James H. Stone." Unpublished typewritten manuscript, n.d., Haydon L. Boatner papers, Box 1, Collection no. 74020, Hoover Institution Library & Archives.

Boatner, Maj. Gen. H. L., USA Ret'd. "Barbara Tuchman's Stilwell and the American Experience in China, a Statement Thereon for the Record." University of Minnesota Libraries, Archives and Special Collections: Mss032.

Bolden, Frank E. "Ledo Road Diary," *Journal and Guide.* Nine-part weekly series from March 17, 1945–May 5, 1945.

Bond, W. Langhorn. *Wings for an Embattled China.* Edited by James E. Ellis. Bethlehem, MD: Lehigh University Press, 2001.

Boody, Robert T. *Food-Bomber Pilot, China-Burma-India: A Diary of the Forgotten Theater of World War II.* Staten Island, NY: Robert T. Boody, 1989.

Borg, Dorothy. "Yunnan-Burma Road Enters Trial Stage." *Far Eastern Survey* 8, no. 13 (1939): 155–56.

Borge, Jacques, and Nicolas Viasnoff. *The Dakota: The DC 3 Story.* New York: Vilo, 1982.

Bower, Ursula Graham. *Naga Path.* London: John Murray, 1952.

Brereton, Lewis H. *The Brereton Diaries: The War in the Air in the Pacific, Middle East and Europe, 3 October 1941–8 May 1945.* New York: William Morrow, 1946.

Bridgeman, Brian. *The Flyers: The Untold Story of British and Commonwealth Airmen in the Spanish Civil Wars and Other Air Wars from 1919 to 1940.* Upton-upon-Severn, UK: Self Publishing Association, 1989.

[British] Special Forces Pamphlet. *Through Japanese Eyes,* n.d., Document 5584, Imperial War Museum.

Brock, Horace. *Flying the Oceans: A Pilot's Story of Pan Am, 1935–1955.* Lunenburg, VT: Stinehour Press, 1978.

Brock, Horace. *More about Pan Am: A Pilot's Story Continued.* Lunenburg, VT: Stinehour Press, 1980.

Brockbank, Nancy E. "The Context of Heroism: The African American Experience on the Ledo Road." Masters Thesis, Eastern Michigan University, 1998.

Brookes, Stephen. *Through the Jungle of Death: A Boy's Escape from Wartime Burma.* New York: John Wiley & Sons, 2000.

Brown, A. Sutherland, and William Rodney. "Burma Banzai: The Air War in Burma through Japanese Eyes." *Canadian Military History* 11, no. 2 (2002): 53–59.

Browne, Horace A. *Reminiscences of the Court of Mandalay: Extracts from the Diary of General Horace A. Browne, 1859–1879.* Woking: Oriental Institute, 1907.

Buchan, Eugenie. *A Few Planes for China: The Birth of the Flying Tigers.* Lebanon, NH: ForeEdge, 2017.

Bundy, Wendell D. "The Hump and Posterity" in *China Airlift—"The Hump,"* vol. 2, China-Burma-India Hump Pilots Association, 85–88. Paducah, KY: Turner, 1996.

Burma, Frontier Areas Committee of Enquiry 1947. *Report Presented to His Majesty's Government in the United Kingdom and the Government of Burma*. Rangoon: Govt. Printing and Stationery, 1947.

Butow, R. J. C. "A Notable Passage to China: Myth and Memory in FDR's Family History." *Prologue* 31, no. 3 (Fall 1999).

Byrd, Martha. *Chennault: Giving Wings to the Tiger*. Tuscaloosa, AL: University of Alabama Press, 1987.

Byroade, Henry. Henry Byroade Oral History Interview by Niel M. Johnson. Harry S. Truman Library and Museum, National Archives (September 1988). trumanlibrary .gov/library/oral-histories/byroade.

Callahan, Raymond. *Burma 1942–1945*. Newark: University of Delaware Press, 1979.

Calvert, Jim. Jim Calvert Oral History Interview (OH00629tr): 1–21, National Museum of the Pacific War.

Calvert, Michael. *Prisoners of Hope*. Revised edition. London: Leo Cooper, 1996.

Campagnac, Charles Haswell. *The Autobiography of a Wanderer, in England & Burma*. Edited by Sandra Campagnac-Carney. Raleigh, NC: Lulu, 2011.

Caniff, Milton. *Terry and the Pirates*. Volume 8 (1941–1942). Hong Kong: Flying Buttress Classics Library, 1992.

Carrapiett, W. J. S. *The Kachin Tribes of Burma: For the Information of Officers of the Burma Frontier Service*. Rangoon: Govt. Printing and Stationary, 1929.

Casey, Steven. *The War Beat, Pacific: The American Media at War Against Japan*. New York: Oxford University Press, 2021.

Cavert, H. Mead. "Midwest China Oral History and Archives Collection." (1979). *China Oral Histories*. 13.

Chaikin, Rosalind Bryon. *"To My Memory Sing": A Memoir Based on Letters and Poems from Sol Chick Chaikin, an American Soldier in China-Burma-India During World War II*. Monroe, NY: Library Research Associates, 1997.

Chan, Won-Loy. *Burma: The Untold Story*. Novato, CA: Presidio Press, 1986.

Chang, C. T. *Burma Road*. Singapore: Malaysia Publications, 1964.

Chang, Jung. *Big Sister, Little Sister, Red Sister: Three Women at the Heart of Twentieth-Century China*. New York: Alfred A. Knopf, 2019.

Charney, Michael W. *A History of Modern Burma*. Cambridge, UK: Cambridge University Press, 2009.

Chasie, Charles, and Henry Fecitt. *The Road to Kohima: The Naga Experience in the Second World War*. 2nd ed. United Kingdom: Infinite Ideas Limited, 2020.

Chennault, Capt. C. L., A. C. *The Role of Defensive Pursuit*. Maxwell Field, Montgomery, AL: Air Corps Tactical School, 1935.

Chennault, Claire Lee. *Way of a Fighter: The Memoirs of Claire Lee Chennault*. New York: Putnam, 1949.

Chetwode, Philip, E. H. Keeling, Patrick Fitzgerald, Dudley Stamp, Ernest Wilton, Gerald Samson, and C. G. Seligman. "The Yunnan-Burma Road: Discussion." *Geographical Journal* 95, no. 3 (March 1940): 171–74.

Chin, Captain Moon Fon. Oral History Interview [transcript]—1999.244.0042. SFO Museum, San Francisco, CA.

China-Burma-India Hump Pilot's Association, *China Airlift—"The Hump,"* 4 vols. Paducah, KY: Turner, 1981–97.

Chinnery, Philip D. *Any Time, Any Place: A History of USAF Air Commando and Special Operations Forces*. Annapolis, MD: Naval Institute Press, 1994.

Chung, Rebecca Chan, Deborah Duen Ling Chung, and Cecilia Ng Wong. *Piloted to*

Serve: Memoirs of Rebecca Chan Chung: World War II in China with Flying Tigers, U.S. Army and China National Aviation Corporation. Self-published, 2012.

Churchill, Winston. *The Hinge of Fate.* Boston: Houghton Mifflin, 1950.

Clemons, Walter L. Oral History Interview by William Tilt. Walter L. Clemons Collection (AFC/2001/001/73256), Veterans History Project, American Folklife Center, Library of Congress (April 2009).

Clifford, Francis. *Desperate Journey.* London: Hodder and Stoughton, 1979.

Coffey, Thomas M. *Hap: Military Aviator.* New York: Viking Press, 1982.

Collis, Maurice. *Last and First in Burma (1941–1948).* New York: Macmillan, 1956.

Conant, Jennet. *A Covert Affair.* New York: Simon & Schuster, 2011.

Constein, Dr. Carl Frey. *Born to Fly the Hump: The First Airlift.* Self-published, 1st Books Library, 2000.

Constein, Dr. Carl Frey. *Tales of the Himalayas: Letters from WWII Airmen Who Flew the Hump and from Other Veterans of the CBI.* Self-published, 1st Books Library, 2002.

Cooke, David C. *Sky Battle: 1914–1918: The Story of Aviation in World War I.* New York: W. W. Norton, 1970.

Coram, Robert. *Double Ace: Robert Lee Scott Jr., Pilot, Hero, and Teller of Tall Tales.* New York: St. Martin's Press, 2016.

Correll, John T. "Over the Hump to China," *Air Force Magazine* (October 2009): 68–71.

Craven, Wesley Frank, and James Lea Cate, eds. *The Army Air Forces in World War II: Volume One, Plans and Early Operations: January 1939 to August 1942.* Chicago: University of Chicago Press, 1948.

Craven, Wesley Frank, and James Lea Cate, eds. *The Army Air Forces in World War II: Volume Four, The Pacific: Guadalcanal to Saipan: August 1942 to July 1944.* Chicago: University of Chicago Press, 1950.

Craven, Wesley Frank, and James Lea Cate, eds. *The Army Air Forces in World War II: Volume Five, The Pacific: Matterhorn to Nagasaki, June 1944 to August 1945.* Chicago: University of Chicago Press, 1953.

Craven, Wesley Frank, and James Lea Cate, eds. *The Army Air Forces in World War II: Volume Six, Men and Planes.* Chicago: University of Chicago Press, 1955.

Craven, Wesley Frank, and James Lea Cate, eds. *The Army Air Forces in World War II: Volume Seven, Services Around the World.* Chicago: University of Chicago Press, 1958.

Craw, Henry. "The Burma Road," *Geographical Journal* 99, no. 5/6 (May–June, 1942): 238–46.

Croizier, Ralph C. "Antecedents of the Burma Road: British Plans for a Burma-China Railway in the Nineteenth Century," *Journal of Southeast Asian History* 3, no. 2 (September 1962): 1–18.

Crozier, Brian, and Eric Chou. *The Man Who Lost China: The First Full Biography of Chiang Kai-shek.* New York: Charles Scribner's Sons, 1976.

Crouch, Gregory. *China's Wings: War, Intrigue, Romance, and Adventure in the Middle Kingdom During the Golden Age of Flight.* New York: Bantam Books, 2012.

Cunningham, Ed. "ATC, India China Wing," *Yank* 2, no. 40 (March 24, 1944): 2–4.

Dallek, Robert. *Franklin D. Roosevelt: A Political Life.* New York: Penguin Books, 2018.

Daso, Dik Alan. *Hap Arnold and the Evolution of American Air Power.* Washington, DC: Smithsonian Institution Press, 2000.

Dawes, E. M. Private Papers, Document 21835, Imperial War Museum.

Dawless, Smith. *The Ledo Road and Other Verses from China-Burma-India.* Washington, DC: Enterprise Services, 1951, cbi-theater.com/verses/Verses_Main.html.

Denzler, Edward G. Edward G. Denzler Oral History Interview (OH01842trs): 1–25, National Museum of Pacific War.

Devaux, Douglas F. "China, Burma, and India from the Back Seat: Memories from the China-Burma-India Theater Flying the 'Valley' and the 'Hump.'" Self-published, 2001. cbi-theater.com/backseat/backseat.html.

Diamond, Jon. "Blunder or Deception? Stilwell at Myitkyina." *WWII History* 12, no. 7 (December 2013): 24–27, 67.

Dickinson, Wesley H. "On 'Spitting' Cobras." *Herpetologica* 3, no. 1 (November 21, 1945): 28–30.

Diebold, Lieutenant William. *Hell Is So Green*. Guilford, CT: Lyons Press, 2013.

Dmitri, Ivan. *Flight to Everywhere*. New York: McGraw-Hill, 1944.

Dobie, Dave. Dave Dobie Oral History Interview (OH 00095.tr): 1–10, National Museum of the Pacific War.

Dod, Karl C. *The Corps of Engineers: The War Against Japan*. The United States Army in World War II: The Technical Services. Washington, DC: Office of the Chief of Military History United States Army, 1966.

Doenecke, Justus D., and Mark A. Stoler. *Debating Franklin D. Roosevelt's Foreign Policies, 1933–1945*. Lanham, MD: Rowman & Littlefield, 2005.

Dominick, Alexander S., ed. *Flying the Hump: The War Diary of Peter H. Dominick*, 2nd ed. Green Bay, WI: M&B Global Solutions, 2022.

Dorn, Frank. *Walkout with Stilwell in Burma*. New York: Thomas Y. Crowell, 1971.

Downie, Don. "The Wildest Night" in *China Airlift—"The Hump,"* vol. 1, China-Burma-India Hump Pilots Association, 175–78. Dallas, TX: Turner, 1981.

Downing, Mrs. V. Private Papers, Document 3810, Imperial War Museum.

Dreifort, John E. "Japan's Advance into Indochina, 1940: The French Response." *Journal of Southeast Asian Studies* 13, no. 2 (September 1982): 279–95.

Dun, General Smith. *Memoirs of the Four-Foot Colonel*. Ithaca, NY: Department of Asian Studies, Cornell University, 1980.

Dunlop, Richard. *Behind Japanese Lines: With the OSS in Burma*. Chicago: Rand McNally, 1979.

Durant, Captain N. Private Papers, Document 4885, Imperial War Museum.

Dwiggins, Don. *The Air Devils*. Philadelphia: J. B. Lippincott, 1966.

Easterbrook, Ernest F. *World War II Diaries*, Easterbrook (Ernest Fred) papers, Box 11, Folder 1. hoover.org/library-archives/collections/world-war-ii-diaries-ernest-f-easterbrook-1944-45.

Eldridge, Fred. *Wrath in Burma*. Garden City, NY: Doubleday, 1946.

Elsey, George M. *Roosevelt and China: The White House Story: "The President and U.S. Aid to China—1944."* Wilmington, DE: Michael Glazier, 1979.

Englert, Robert. Robert Englert Oral History (OH00942trs): 1–17, National Museum of the Pacific War.

Engs, Ruth Clifford, ed. *The Field Hospital That Never Was: Diary of Lt. Col. Karl D. Macmillan's [sic] MD, 96th Field Hospital in China-India-Burma Theater 1945, WWII*. Bloomington, IN: Magic Farm, 2015.

Ethell, Jeff, and Don Downie. *Flying the Hump: In Original World War II Color*. St. Paul, MN: Motorbooks, 2002.

Eubank, Dillard Marion, "Midwest China Oral History Interviews." *China Oral Histories*. Book 32. St. Paul, MN: Midwest China Center, 1980. digitalcommons.luthersem.edu/cgi/viewcontent.cgi?article=1028&context=china_histories.

Evans, Lieutenant-General Sir Geoffrey, and Antony Brett-James. *Imphal: A Flower on Lofty Heights*. London: Macmillan, 1964.

Faber, Lt. Col. Peter R., "Interwar U.S. Army Aviation and the Air Corps Tactical School: Incubators of American Air Power," 183–238, in *The Paths of Heaven: The Evolution of*

Airpower Theory, edited by USAF Colonel Phillip S. Meilinger. Maxwell Air Force Base, AL: Air University Press, 1997.

Fellowes-Gordon, Ian. *Amiable Assassins*. London: Panther Books, 1958.

Fergusson, Bernard. *The Wild Green Earth: The Battle for Burma*. Barnsley, UK: Pen & Sword, 2015.

Fessler, Diane Burke. *No Time for Fear: Voices of American Military Nurses in World War II*. East Lansing, MI: Michigan State University Press, 1996.

Fielding-Hall, H. *The Soul of a People*. London: Macmillan, 1908.

Finney, Robert T. *History of the Air Corps Tactical School, 1920–1940*. Washington, DC: Center for Air Force History, 1992.

Fischer, Edward. *Mission in Burma: The Columban Fathers' Forty-Three Years in Kachin Country*. New York: Seabury Press, 1980.

Fisher, Leroy. Leroy Fisher Oral History Interview (OH01525trs): 1–39, National Museum of the Pacific War.

Fitzgerald, C. P. *The Tower of Five Glories: A Study of the Min Chia of Ta Li, Yunnan*. London: Cresset Press, 1941.

Fitzgerald, Patrick. "The Yunnan–Burma Road." *Geographical Journal* 95, no. 3 (March 1940): 161–71.

Forbes, Capt. C. J. F. S. *Legendary History of Burma and Arakan*. Rangoon: Government Press, 1882.

Ford, Daniel. *Flying Tigers: Claire Chennault and His American Volunteers, 1941–1942*. Durham, NH: Warbird Books, 2016.

Ford, Daniel. *Tales of the Flying Tiger*. Durham, NH: Warbird Books, 2016.

Foucar, Colonel E. C. V., MC. *First Burma Campaign: The Japanese Conquest of 1942*. Barnsley, UK: Frontline Books, 2020.

Fraser, George MacDonald. *Quartered Safe Out Here: A Recollection of the War in Burma*. Pleasantville, NY: Akadine Press, 2001.

Frillman, Paul, and Graham Peck. *China: A Remembered Life*. Boston: Houghton Mifflin, 1968.

Fritsche, Carl H. "The Day We Rode the Storm" in *China Airlift—"The Hump,"* vol. 1, China-Burma-India Hump Pilots Association, 181–83. Dallas, TX: Turner, 1981.

Fuller, John F. *Thor's Legions: Weather Support to the U.S. Air Force and Army, 1937–1987*. Boston: American Meteorological Society, 1990.

Fürer-Haimendorf, Christoph von. *The Konyak Nagas: An Indian Frontier Tribe*. London: Holt, Rinehart and Winston, 1969.

Fuwa, Hiroshi. "Japanese Operations in Hukawng Valley," *Military Review* xlii, no. 1 (January 1962): 48–63.

Gann, Ernest K. *Fate Is the Hunter: A Pilot's Memoir*. New York: Simon & Schuster, 1986.

General Headquarters, India, Military Intelligence Directorate. "Japanese in Battle," 2nd ed. New Delhi: Government of India Press, 1944.

Geren, Paul. *Burma Diary*. New York: Harper & Brothers, 1943.

Gilhodes, Charles. *The Kachins: Religion and Customs*. Bangkok: White Lotus, 1996.

Glaser, Patricia. "African Americans in the 'Forgotten Theater' of World War II." *Folklife Today* (blog), American Folklife Center & Veterans History Project, Library of Congress, July 29, 2019, blogs.loc.gov/folklife/2019/07/african-americans-in-the-forgotten-theater-of-world-war-ii/.

Glass, Leslie. *The Changing of Kings: Memories of Burma, 1934–1949*. London: Peter Owen, 1985.

Goodall, Felicity. *Exodus Burma: The British Escape Through the Jungles of Death 1942*. Stroud, UK: History Press, 2017.

Gooding, Ernest A., Jr. "The Adventures of the Hump Flying Meg Wa Padré (American)" in *China Airlift—"The Hump,"* vol. 2, China-Burma-India Hump Pilots Association, 275–80. Paducah, KY: Turner, 1996.

Goullart, Peter. *Forgotten Kingdom*. London: Readers Union, 1957.

Grant, Ian Lyall. *Burma: The Turning Point: The Seven Battles on the Tiddim Road Which Turned the Tide of the Burma War*. Barnsley, UK: Le Cooper, 2003.

Grant, R. G. *Flight: the Complete History of Aviation*. Revised edition. New York: Penguin Random House, 2017.

Gray, Lloyd S. *Diary*. Personal Collection of SSgt. Lloyd S. Gray, Call #168.7223-1, IRIS #01066894, in USAF Collection, AFHRA, Maxwell AFB, Montgomery, AL.

Greech W. Oral history interview with Greech, W., 1980. "Addicts Who Survived Oral History Collection." Catalogue Record 11663619. Columbia Center for Oral History, Columbia University.

Greene, Jesse W. Sr. Jesse W. Greene, Sr. Collection (AFC/2001/001/74431). Veterans History Project, American Folklife Center, Library of Congress.

Greenlaw, Olga. *The Lady and the Tigers*. Edited by Daniel Ford. San Bernárdino, CA: Warbird Books, 2012.

Greiber, Major M. F., MC. "Psychiatric Casualties in Pilots Flying the China Hump Route." In *Neuropsychiatry in World War II: Volume II Overseas Theaters*. Edited by Lieutenant General Hal B. Jennings Jr., 1083–86. Washington, DC: Department of the Army, 1973.

Gribble, R. H. *Out of the Burma Night: Being the Story of a Fantastic Journey Through the Wilderness of the Hukawng Valley and the Forest Clad Mountains of the Naga Tribes People at the Time of the Japanese Invasion of Burma*. Calcutta: Thacker Spink, 1944.

Gully, Patti. *Sisters of Heaven, China's Barnstorming Aviatrixes: Modernity, Feminism, and Popular Imagination in Asia and the West*. San Francisco: Long River Press, 2008.

Gunston, Bill. *History of Military Aviation*. New York: Sterling, 2003.

Gurumurthy, Krishnan. "Exodus from Burma, 1941: A Personal Account, Parts 1, 2 & 3." Edited by Amitav Ghosh, June 21, 2011. amitavghosh.com/exodus-from-burma-1941-a-personal-account.

Hall, Colonel E. Foster, MC. "The Graves Service in the Burma Campaigns." *Journal of the Royal United Service Institution* 92 (February 1, 1947): 240–44.

Hall, Ian. *A Goldstar Century: 31 Squadron RAF 1915–2015*. Barnsley, UK: Pen & Sword Books, 2015.

Hall, Russell E. "Transport Facilities in China's Defense: II China's Domestic Transport System," *Far Eastern Survey* 6, no. 22 (November 5, 1937): 253–57.

Hamilton, J. A. L. *81 (West African) Division and the "Disaster" at Kyauktaw*, LBY K. 02/1494, Imperial War Museum.

Hanks, Fletcher. *Saga of CNAC #53*. Bloomington, IN: AuthorHouse, 2004.

Hanwell, Norman D. "China Driven to New Supply Routes." *Far Eastern Survey* 7, no. 22 (November 9, 1938): 258–60.

Harris, Robert Harding. Robert Harding Harris Collection (AFC/2001/001/43875). Veterans History Project, American Folklife Center, Library of Congress.

Harvey, G. E. *British Rule in Burma: 1824–1942*. London: Faber and Faber, 1946.

Headquarters—India China Wing, Air Transport Command, Station #1. "Restricted: Weather Conditions from Lalmanir Hat to Kunming" in *China Airlift—"The Hump,"* vol. 1, China-Burma-India Hump Pilots Association, 183–87. Dallas, TX: Taylor, 1981.

Herzstein, Robert E. *Henry R. Luce, Time, and the American Crusade in Asia.* New York: Cambridge University Press, 2005.

Highly, Lyndell T. "Letters From China, 1943–1944." Collection Box 1443, Folder 002, Identifier 1998.122. Special Collections and Archives, Kent Library, Southeast Missouri State University.

Hilder, Richard Waterhouse. Sound, Catalogue no. 19599, Imperial War Museum.

Hilton, James. *Lost Horizon.* New York: Pocket Books, 1939.

Hinton, David, trans. and ed. *Classical Chinese Poetry: An Anthology.* New York: Farrar, Straus and Giroux, 2008.

Hodell, Mel. "Jungle Rest Camp" in *China Airlift—"The Hump,"* vol. 2, China-Burma-India Hump Pilots Association, 254–56. Paducah, KY: Turner, 1996.

Hopkins, James E. T., and John M. Jones. *Spearhead: A Complete History of Merrill's Marauder Rangers.* Revised edition. Lindenhurst, NY: Merrill's Marauders Association, 2013.

Hunter, Colonel Charles N.(Ret.). *Galahad.* San Antonio, TX: Naylor, 1965.

Huston, Major General John W., ed. *American Airpower Comes of Age: General Henry H. "Hap" Arnold's World War II Diaries,* vol. 1 and 2. Maxwell Air Force Base, AL: Air University Press, 2002.

Jacobs, Julian. *The Nagas: Hill Peoples of Northeast India.* Revised edition. London: Thames & Hudson, 2012.

Japanese Monograph No. 58. *The Record of Burma Operations, Part II.*

Japanese Monograph No. 64. *Burma Air Operations Record, January 1942–August 1945.*

Japanese Monograph No. 72. *Army Operations in China, January 1944–August 1945.*

Japanese Monograph No. 131. *Burma Operations Record, Operations in Hukawng Area (August 1943–July 1944).*

Japanese Monograph No. 134. *Burma Operations Record, 15th Army Operations in Imphal Area and Withdrawal to Northern Burma.*

Japanese Monograph No. 148. *Burma Operations Record, The 33rd Army Operations.*

Johnson, David C. "Blackie's Gang: Search and Rescue in the CBI 1943–1945" in *China Airlift—"The Hump,"* vol. 3, China-Burma-India Hump Pilots Association, 54–58. Paducah, KY: Turner, 1992.

Jowett, Philip. *Images of War: The Battle for Burma, 1942–1945.* Barnsley, UK: Pen & Sword, 2021.

Kahn, E. J. *The China Hands: America's Foreign Service Officers and What Befell Them.* New York: Viking, 1975.

Kaminer, James Heath. James Heath Kaminer Collection (AFC/2001/001/51577). Veterans History Project, American Folklife Center, Library of Congress.

Kawlu Ma Nawng. *The Kachins of the Hukawng Valley.* Translated with notes by J. L. Leyden. Bombay: Times of India Press, 1941.

Keeler, Louis, MD. *The Chalice: Letters and Diary of Rev. Louis Meyer.* West Conshohocken, PA: Infinity Publishing, 2009.

Kelly, Joseph B. "Memoirs of World War II (An Odyssey, Chiefly Concerning the China, Burma, India Theater)." *Penn State International Law Review* 21, no. 3 (2003): 449–75.

Khan, Yasmin. *India at War: The Subcontinent and the Second World War.* Oxford, UK: Oxford University Press, 2015.

Khin Yi. *The Dobama Movement in Burma (1930–1938).* Ithaca, NY: Southeast Asia Program, Cornell University Press, 1988.

Kincheloe, Durwood Chester. WWI Memories of Durwood Chester Kincheloe. World

War II Oral History Series. Burnet County Library System. Accessed through National Museum of the Pacific War, Durwood Chester Kincheloe Oral History Interview (OH2231tr), 1–27.

King, Steven C. *Flying the Hump to China: How Getting the Flying Bug Got This Pilot into the World's First Airlift Flying Gas to China in WW II*. Bloomington, IN: AuthorHouse, 2004.

King, William Collins. *Building for Victory: World War II in China, Burma, and India and the 1875th Engineer Aviation Battalion*. Lanham, MD: Taylor Trade, 2004.

Kingdon-Ward, Frank. *Himalayan Enchantment: An Anthology*. Edited by John Whitehead. London: Serindia, 1990.

Kingdon-Ward, Frank. "Report on the Forests of the North Triangle, Kachin State, North Burma." *Journal of the Bombay Natural History Society* (August–December 1954): 1–17.

Koerner, Brendan I. *Now the Hell Will Start: One Soldier's Flight from the Greatest Manhunt of World War II*. New York: Penguin Books, 2009.

Kuhles, Clayton. MIA Search and Recovery Missions Worldwide, miarecoveries.org /#:~:text=What%20we%20do...,in%2DAction%20(MIA).

Laben, George J. George J. Laben Collection (AFC/2001/001/34441). Veterans History Project, American Folklife Center, Library of Congress.

La Farge, Oliver. *The Eagle in the Egg*. Cambridge, MA: Houghton Mifflin, 1949.

Lambert, T. D. "From the Brahmaputra to the Chindwin." *Geographical Journal* 89, no. 4 (April 1937): 309–23.

Larrabee, Eric. *Commander in Chief: Franklin Delano Roosevelt, His Lieutenants, and Their War*. Annapolis, MD: Blue Jacket Books, Naval Institute Press, 1987.

Lathrop, Alan K. "The Employment of Chinese Nationalist Troops in the First Burma Campaign." *Journal of Southeast Asian Studies* 12, no. 2 (September 1981): 403–32.

Lathrop, Alan K. *A Surgeon with Stilwell: Dr. John H. Grindlay and Combat Medicine in the China-Burma-India Theater of World War II*. Jefferson, NC: McFarland, 2018.

Latimer, Jon. *Burma: The Forgotten War*. London: John Murray, 2004.

Lattimore, Owen. *China Memoirs: Chiang Kai-Shek and the War Against Japan*. Tokyo: University of Tokyo Press, 1990.

Launius, Roger D. "An American in Asia, 1942–1946: Lloyd S. Gray and the Hump Airlift." *Journal of Third World Studies* 4, no. 2 (Fall 1987): 27–46.

La Vove, Arthur. *Hump Drivers: An American Pilot's Account of Flying Over the Himalayas During WWII*. Atglen, PA: Schiffer Military, 2021.

Lazzara, Peter J. (Pete). "And Then There Was Chanyi . . ." in *China Airlift–"The Hump,"* vol. 2, China-Burma-India Hump Pilots Association, 314–18. Paducah, KY: Turner, 1996.

Leary, William M., Jr. *The Dragon's Wings: The China National Aviation Corporation and the Development of Commercial Aviation in China*. Athens, GA: University of Georgia Press, 1976.

Leary, William M., Jr. "Wings for China: The Jouett Mission, 1932–1935," *Pacific History Review* 38, no. 4 (November 1969): 447–62.

Lee, Chin Y. *A Corner of Paradise*. London: Four Square Books, 1962.

Leighton, Bob. "Project 7" in *China Airlift–"The Hump,"* vol. 1, China-Burma-India Hump Pilots Association, 216–17. Dallas, TX: Taylor, 1981.

LeMay, Curtis E., and MacKinlay Kantor. *Mission with Le May: My Story*. Garden City, NY: Doubleday, 1965.

Leonard, Royal. *I Flew For China: Chiang Kai-Shek's Personal Pilot*. Garden City, NY: Doubleday Doran, 1942.

Lewin, Ronald. *Slim: The Standardbearer: A Biography of Field-Marshal the Viscount Slim.* Ware, UK: Wordsworth Editions, 1976.

Liang, Chin-tung. *General Stilwell in China, 1942–1944: The Full Story.* New York: St. John's University Press, 1972.

Lichty, Private R. D. "Passage to India: The Trip by Convoy, Charleston, S.C. to Karachi, India, 27 May–23 July 42." Call #810.13-1, IRIS #01026714, in USAF Collection, AFHRA, Maxwell AFB, Montgomery, AL.

Lin, Hsiao-ting. "War or Stratagem? Reassessing China's Military Advance Towards Tibet, 1942-1943." *China Quarterly*, no. 186 (June 2006): 446–62.

Losonsky, Frank S., and Terry M. Losonsky. *Flying Tiger: A Crew Chief's Story.* Algen, PA: Schiffer, 1996.

Lowry, George E. "The Hump—Rocks in those Clouds!" 40th Bomb Group Association, *Memories,* no. 12, November 1986. Call #146.002-36, IRIS #01108166, in USAF Collection, AFHRA, Maxwell AFB, Montgomery, AL.

Lunt, James. *"A Hell of a Licking": The Retreat from Burma, 1941–2.* London: Collins, 1986.

Luto, James. *Fighting with the Fourteenth Army in Burma: Original War Summaries of the Battle Against Japan.* Barnsley, UK: Pen & Sword Military, 2013.

Lyman. Robert. *Among the Headhunters: An Extraordinary World War II Story of Survival in the Burmese Jungle.* Philadelphia: Da Capo Press, 2016.

Lyons, Capt. Fred O. "Here's What Happened! Merrill's Marauders in Burma." *Ex-CBI Roundup,* July 1991. Interview by Paul Wilder, first published by *The Tampa Tribune,* 1945. marauder.org/article1.htm.

Ma, Yufu. *Hump Air Transport.* Beijing: China Intercontinental Press, 2004.

Magoon, Christopher. "The 20th General Hospital: The Reach of Formalized Medicine During World War II." *Pharos* (Autumn 2016): 15–21.

Majumder, Surendra Nath. *Ao Nagas.* Calcutta: U. Ray & Sons, 1925.

Mallory, Walter H. "The Burma Road." *Foreign Affairs* 17, no. 3 (April 1939): 625–27.

Marshall, George C. George C. Marshall Papers, The George C. Marshall Foundation of Lexington, VA.

Marshall, George C. "Marshall Interviews of July 1949," Records of the Army Staff, Office of the Chief of Military History, Background Files to the Study "Stilwell's Mission to China" 1940-1955. Record Group 319, Entry (P) 75, National Archives Identifier 2163532, Box 9, National Archives.

Marshall, Rev. Harry Ignatius. *The Karen People of Burma: A Study in Anthropology and Ethnology.* Columbus, OH: University at Columbus, 1922.

Marshall, Howard E., and Richard Woodworth. *The Hump* (1944). New York Public Library, Lincoln Center of Performing Arts: Call no. NCOF+p.v. 296.

Masters, John. *The Road Past Mandalay.* London: Cassell, 2012.

Matloff, Maurice. *Strategic Planning for Coalition Warfare, 1943–1944,* United States Army in World War II: The War Department. Washington DC: Office of the Chief of Military History, Department of the Army, 1959.

Maung Htin Aung. *A History of Burma.* New York: Columbia University Press, 1967.

Maung, Mya. "On the Road to Mandalay: A Case Study of the Sinonization of Upper Burma," *Asian Survey,* vol. 34, no. 5 (May 1994): 447–59.

Mays, Lieutenant Colonel John R. S., MC. "Consultant's Composite Report of Toxic Psychoses Due to Atabrine, India-Burma Theater." In *Neuropsychiatry in World War II.* vol. 2, *Overseas Theaters.* Edited by Lieutenant General Hal B. Jennings Jr., 1087-94. Washington, DC: Department of the Army, 1973.

McBride, John D. "Collected Stories" in *China Airlift—"The Hump,"* vol. 3, China-Burma-India Hump Pilots Association, 146–48. Paducah, KY: Turner, 1992.

McClain, William F. "Pete." "Bailout" in *China Airlift—"The Hump,"* vol. 1, China-Burma-India Hump Pilots Association, 257–58. Dallas, TX: Turner, 1981.

McClure, Glen E. *Fire and Fall Back: Casey Vincent's Story.* San Antonio, TX: Barnes Press, 1975.

McDonald, William C., Jr. "The Chennault I Remember." *Air Power Historian* 6, no. 2 (April 1959): 88–93.

McDonald, Yong Hui V. *Tornadoes of War: Inspirational Stories of Veterans and Veteran's Families.* Brighton, CO: Sora Productions, 2012.

McGowen, Stanley S. *Helicopters: An Illustrated History of Their Impact.* Santa Barbara, CA: ABC-CLIO, 2005.

McGuire, Joseph. Joseph McGuire Oral History Interview (OH01529tr), National Museum of the Pacific War: 1–26.

McHugh, James. "The Burma Road Diary." James M. McHugh Papers, 1930–1965. Collection Number 2770, Box 11, Folder 4. Kroch Library, Cornell University.

McHugh, James. "The History and Status of the First American Volunteer Group." James M. McHugh Papers, 1930–1965. Collection Number 2770, Box 4, Folder 5. Kroch Library, Cornell University.

McHugh, James. "Military Correspondence, 1934, 1937–1946." James M. McHugh Papers. Collection Number 2770, Box 1, Folder 9. Division of Rare and Manuscript Collections, Cornell University.

McLynn, Frank. *The Burma Campaign: Disaster into Triumph.* New Haven, CT: Yale University Press, 2011.

McMichael, Scott R. "Common Man, Uncommon Leadership: Colonel Charles H. Hunter with Galahad in Burma." *Parameters: Journal of the US Army War College* 16, no. 2 (1986): 45–57.

McPhedran, Colin. *White Buttrflies.* Canberra: Pandanus, 2002.

Miller, Stan. "Nature's Peace" in *China Airlift—"The Hump,"* vol. 3, China-Burma-India Hump Pilots Association, 85. Paducah, KY: Turner, 1992.

Mitchell, David. *Tea, Love and War: Searching for English Roots in Assam.* Leicestershire, UK: Troubador, 2019.

Mitter, Rana. *Forgotten Ally: China's World War II.* Boston: Mariner Books, 2014.

Moon, Thomas H., and Carl F. Eifler. *The Deadliest Colonel.* New York: Vantage Press, 1975.

Moore, J. H. Major, ed. "Japanese Command Crisis in Burma, 1944." *Army Journal,* no. 271 (December 1971): 10–23.

Morse, Gertrude. *The Dogs May Bark: But the Caravan Moves On.* Edited by Helen M. Morse. North Burma Christian Mission: College Press Publishing, 1998.

Mortimer, Gavin. *Merrill's Marauders: The Untold Story of Unit Galahad and the Toughest Special Forces Mission of World War II.* Minneapolis: Zenith Press, 2013.

Moser, Don. *China-Burma-India.* New York: Time-Life Books, 1978.

Motley, Mary Penrick. *The Invisible Soldier: The Experience of the Black Soldier, World War II.* Detroit: Wayne State University Press, 1987.

Murphy, James B., and David E. Jacques. "Death from Snakebite: The Entwined Histories of Grace Olive Wiley and Wesley H. Dickinson." *Bulletin of the Chicago Herpetological Society,* special supplement, 2006.

Nalty, Bernard C., ed. *Winged Shield, Winged Sword: A History of the United States Air Force. Volume 1: 1907–1950.* Washington, DC: Air Force History and Museums Program, 1997.

Newton, William H. D. Private Papers of Major W. H. D. Newton, Documents 11216, Imperial War Museum.

Nunneley, John. *Tales from the King's African Rifles.* London: Cassell & Co., 2000.

O'Brien, Terence. *Out of the Blue: A Pilot with the Chindits.* London: Arrow Books, 1989.

Ogburn, Charlton Jr. *The Marauders.* New York: Ballantine Books, 1974.

Ogden, Alan. *Tigers Burning Bright: SOE Heroes in the Far East.* London: Bene Factum Publishing Ltd., 2013.

Okerstrom, Dennis R. *Project 9: The Birth of the Air Commandos in World War II.* Columbia: University of Missouri Press, 2014.

O'Neil, Paul. *Barnstormers & Speed Kings.* Alexandria, VA: Time-Life Books, 1981.

Orchard, John E. "Transport Facilities in China's Defense: I. Overland Routes into China." *Far Eastern Survey* 6, no. 22 (November 5, 1937): 251–53.

Orser, Joseph Andrew. *The Lives of Chang & Eng: Siam's Twins in Nineteenth-Century America.* Chapel Hill: University of North Caroline Press, 2014.

Orth, David. "The Fireball Express" in *China Airlift—"The Hump,"* vol. 1, China-Burma-India Hump Pilots Association, 68. Dallas, TX: Turner, 1981.

Outram, Frank, and G. E. Fane. "Burma Road, Back Door to China." *National Geographic* LXXVIII, no. 5 (November 1940): 629–58.

Pandey, S. N. "Tribal Uprising in North East-India During the British Rule: Kuki and Naga Revolts in Manipur." *Proceedings of the Indian History Congress* 56 (1995): 545–50.

Patterson, Richard. *Tales from Life & the Battle of Kohima.* Middletown, DE: Self-published, 2022.

Patton, Thomas Nathan. *The Buddha's Wizards: Magic, Protection, and Healing in Burmese Buddhism.* Revised edition. New York: Columbia University Press, 2020.

Peacock, Captain H. "Jungle Craft." *Journal of United Service Institution of India* LXXIII, no. 310 (January 1943): 1–11.

Pearn, B. R. The Rangoon Civil Evacuation Scheme. (Synopsis for publication.) BURMA. Burma Defence Council. [Rangoon], 1941. Found in B78/40(b); War: compilation of official history of the war: War Diary Jun–Oct, Dec 1941 with documents attached. IOR/M/3/808, British Library.

Peers, William R., and Dean Brelis. *Behind the Burma Road.* New York: Avon Books, 1963.

Pei-Ying, Tan. *The Building of the Burma Road.* New York: McGraw-Hill, 1945.

Peterson, Colonel Donald B., MC USA (Ret). "China-Burma-India Theater." In *Neuropsychiatry in World War II: Volume II Overseas Theaters.* Edited by Lieutenant General Hal B. Jennings Jr., 819–47. Washington, DC: Department of the Army, 1973.

Phillips, Barnaby. *Another Man's War: The Story of a Burma Boy in Britain's Forgotten African Army.* London: Oneworld Publications, 2014.

Phillips, Bob. *KC8 Burma: CBI Air Warning Team, 1941–1942.* Manhattan, KS: Sunflower University Press, 1992.

Phipps, Monzell J. "Staff Sergeant Pilots Flew 'China Airlift—the Hump" in *China Airlift—"The Hump,"* vol. 2, China-Burma-India Hump Pilots Association, 62–65. Paducah, KY: Turner, 1996.

Pickler, Gordon K. "United States Aid to the Chinese Nationalist Air Force, 1931–1949." (PhD diss., Florida State University, 1971).

Plating, John D. *The Hump: America's Strategy for Keeping China in World War II.* College Station: Texas A&M University Press, 2011.

Pocock, William S., Jr. "52nd Air Service Group; Jungle Rescue" in *China Airlift—"The Hump,"* vol. 1, China-Burma-India Hump Pilots Association, 58–59. Dallas, TX: Turner, 1981.

Politovich, Marcia K. "Aircraft Icing Caused by Large Supercooled Droplets." *Journal of Applied Meteorology* 28, no. 9 (September 1989): 856–68.

Polo, Marco. *The Travels.* London: Penguin Random House, 2016.

Pope, Jack. "Brand of Fear" in *China Airlift—"The Hump,"* vol. 1, China-Burma-India Hump Pilots Association, 187–89. Dallas, TX: Turner, 1981.

Pope, John Anthony. John Anthony Pope Collection (AFC/2001/001/73071). Veterans History Project, American Folklife Center, Library of Congress.

Preston-Hough, Peter. *Commanding Far Eastern Skies: A Critical Analysis of the Royal Air Force Air Superiority Campaign in India, Burma and Malaya, 1941–1945.* Warwick, UK: Helion & Company, 2015.

Quinn, Chick Marrs. *The Aluminum Trail: China-Burma-India, World War II, 1942-1945: How & Where They Died.* Privately printed, 1989.

Quinnett, Paul. "It Seemed a Lifetime" in *China Airlift—"The Hump,"* vol. 1, China-Burma-India Hump Pilots Association, 179. Dallas, TX: Turner, 1981.

Rabinowitz, Alan. *Life in the Valley of Death.* Washington, DC: Island Press, 2008.

Raghavan, Srinath. *India's War: World War II and the Making of Modern South Asia.* New York: Basic Books, 2016.

Ramamurthy, Stephanie. "Remembering Burma: Tamil Migrants & Memories." (MPhil diss., School of Oriental Studies, University of London, 1994).

Ramsden, A. R. *Assam Planter: Tea Planting and Hunting in the Assam Jungle.* London: John Gifford, 1945.

Ramsey, Wm. H. "The First Thunderstorm" in *China Airlift—"The Hump,"* vol. 1, China-Burma-India Hump Pilots Association, 179–81. Dallas, TX: Turner, 1981.

Richardson, Dave. "The Jungle's Victory," *Ex-CBI Roundup,* July 1951. Read at cbi-theater .com/junglesvictory/junglesvictory.html.

Roberts, David Neal. Oral History. Catalogue no. 14842, Imperial War Museum.

Romanus, Charles F., and Riley Sunderland. *Stilwell's Command Problems,* vol. 2, United States Army in World War II: China-Burma-India Theater. Washington, DC: Department of the Army, Office of the Chief of Military History, 1956.

Romanus, Charles F., and Riley Sunderland. *Stilwell's Mission to China,* vol. 1, United States Army in World War II: China-Burma-India Theater. Washington, DC: Department of the Army, Office of the Chief of Military History, 1953.

Romanus, Charles F., and Riley Sunderland. *Time Runs Out in CBI,* vol. 3, United States Army in World War II: China-Burma-India Theater. Washington, DC: Department of the Army, Office of the Chief of Military History, 1959.

Romer, Jim. Jim Romer Oral History Interview (OH00939tr), National Museum of the Pacific War: 1–23.

Rooney, David. *Mad Mike: A Life of Brigadier Michael Calvert.* Barnsley, UK: Pen & Sword, 2006.

Roosevelt, Elliott. *As He Saw It.* New York: Duell, Sloan and Pearce, 1946.

Roosevelt, Elliott, and James Brough. *An Untold Story: The Roosevelts of Hyde Park.* New York: Putnam, 1973.

Rosbert, Captain C. Joseph. "Forty-Six Days to Dinjan" in *More About Pan Am.* Edited by Horace Brock, 52–65. Lunenburg, VT: Stinehour Press, 1980.

Rosbert, C. Joseph. *Flying Tiger Joe's Adventure Story Cookbook.* Franklin, NC: Giant Poplar Press, 1985.

Rosbert, C. J. "Only God Knew the Way." As told to William Clemons in *China Airlift—"The Hump,"* vol. 1, China-Burma-India Hump Pilots Association, 170-75. Dallas, TX: Turner, 1981.

Rosbert, Joseph. Interview with Joseph Rosbert by Stephen Maxner. Joseph Rosbert
    Collection. Vietnam Center and Sam Johnson Vietnam Archive, Texas Tech Univer-
    sity (April 2001). OH0026. vietnam.ttu.edu/virtualarchive/items.php?item=OH0026.
Rose, David MacNeil Campbell. Private Papers of Lieutenant Colonel D. M. C. Rose
    DSO, Documents 3931, Imperial War Museum.
Rosinger, Lawrence K. "Yunnan: Province of the Burma Road." *Far Eastern Survey*, 11,
    no. 2 (1942): 19–23.
Roxby, P. M. "The Burma Road." *Geography* 25, no. 4 (1940): 170–71.
Ruppenthal, Karl M. *Over the Hump to Chiang Kai-Shek*. Self-published, 2014.
Russell, S. Farrant. *Muddy Exodus: A Story of the Evacuation of Burma, May 1942*. London:
    Epworth Press, 1943.
Salyer, John. "Memoirs of John M. Salyer, M.D., Col., U.S. Army retired," annotated
    version. United States Army, 73rd Evacuation Hospital papers, 1943–1985, Box 1,
    Folder 1, Huntington Library.
Samson, Jack. *Chennault*. New York: Doubleday, 1987.
Sanda, Sao. *The Moon Princess: Memories of the Shan States*. Bangkok: River Books, 2008.
Saunders, Hilary St. G., and Denis Richards. *Royal Air Force 1939–1945: Volume III, The
    Fight Is Won*. London: Her Majesty's Stationary Office, 1954.
Scarano, Patrick. Patrick Scarano Interview: 1–19. Veterans Oral History Program, New
    York State Military Museum and Veterans Research Center.
Schweitzer, Sergeant George F., Historical Technician, India China Division Historical
    Section: Calcutta, India. "The Story of Search and Rescue in the India China Divi-
    sion, Air Transport Command: December 1942 to December 1945." Call #312.04-1,
    IRIS #00181452, in the USAF Collection, AFHRA, Maxwell AFB, Montgomery, AL.
Scott, Sir J. G. *Burma: A Handbook of Practical Information*, 3rd ed., rev. London: Daniel
    O'Connor, 1921.
Scott, Robert Lee, Jr. *God Is My Co-Pilot*. Reynoldsburg, OH: Buckeye Aviation Book
    Company, 1989.
Scott, Robert Lee, Jr. *The Day I Owned the Sky*. New York: Bantam Books, 1988.
Seagrave, Gordon S. *Burma Surgeon*. New York: W. W. Norton, 1943.
Seagrave, Gordon S. *Burma Surgeon Returns*. New York: W. W. Norton, 1946.
Seagrave, Sterling. *The Soong Dynasty*. New York: Harper & Row, 1985.
Segel, James P. *Flying the Hump to China—The Early Days: The Humble Beginnings of the First
    Airlift*. Self-published, 2017.
Seng, Z. Brang. *Duwa Zau June: The Legacy of a Kachin Warror*. Self-published, 2017.
Seppings, Alwyn Henry. "Burma Memoir 1924–48." IOR/Mss/Eur/D/1028, British Library.
Sevareid, Eric. *Not So Wild a Dream*. Columbia, MO: University of Missouri Press, 1995.
Shaver, John V. "Memories of a Hump Pilot" in *China Airlift—"The Hump,"* vol. 1, China-
    Burma-India Hump Pilots Association, 198–206. Dallas, TX: Turner, 1981.
Shores, Christopher, and Brian Cull, with Yasuho Izawa. *Bloody Shambles: Volume One:
    The Drift to War to the Fall of Singapore*. 1992; London: Grub Street, 2007.
Shores, Christopher, and Brian Cull, with Yasuho Izawa. *Bloody Shambles: Volume Two:
    The Defense of Sumatra to the Fall of Burma*. London: Grub Street, 1993.
Shores, Christopher. *Bloody Shambles. Volume 3, Air War for Burma: The Allied Air Forces
    Fight Back in South-East Asia, 1942–1945*. London: Grub Street, 2005.
Sinclair, William Boyd. *Confusion Beyond Imagination: China-Burma-India in World War II
    in a Series of Ten Books. Book Two: Those Wild Blue Characters Over the Hump from Wings
    to Shoes*. Coeur d'Alene, ID: Joe Whitely, 1987. First published 1956 by Cassell and Co.
    (London).

Slim, Field-Marshal Viscount William. *Defeat Into Victory: Battling Japan in Burma and India, 1942–1945.* New York: Cooper Square Press, 2000.

Smith, Nicol. *Burma Road.* New York: Garden City, 1942.

Smith, Robert M. *With Chennault in China: A Flying Tiger's Diary.* Atglen, PA: Schiffer Military/Aviation History, 1997.

Smith, William. "Claire Lee Chennault: The Louisiana Years." *Louisiana History: The Journal of the Louisiana Historical Association* 29, no. 1 (Winter 1988): 49–64.

Spain, James F. "John L. 'Blackie' Porter" in *China Airlift—"The Hump,"* vol. 1, China-Burma-India Hump Pilots Association, 507. Dallas, TX: Turner, 1981.

Spencer, James W. James W. Spencer Collection (AFC/2001/001/12292), Veterans History Project, American Folklife Center, Library of Congress.

Spencer, Otha C. *Flying the Hump.* College Station: Texas A&M University Press, 1994.

Starks, Richard, and Miriam Murcutt. *Lost in Tibet: The Untold Story of Five American Airmen, a Doomed Plane, and the Will to Survive.* Guilford, CT: Lyons Press, 2004.

Stelling, H. C. "Mama-Foofoo (Starvation in Silk Pants)" in *China Airlift—"The Hump,"* vol. 2, China-Burma-India Hump Pilots Association, 141–50. Paducah, KY: Turner, 1996.

Stevens, John D. "Black Correspondents of World War II Cover the Supply Routes." *Journal of Negro History* 57, no. 4 (October 1972): 395–406.

Stilwell, General Joseph W. *Black Book, 1943 June–1944 January 22.* Joseph Warren Stilwell Papers, Box 36, Folder 3. Hoover Institution Library & Archives.

Stilwell, General Joseph W. *Black and White Books, No. 1, 1941 December 11–1942 January 28.* Joseph Warren Stilwell Papers, Box 36, Folder 1. Hoover Institution Library & Archives.

Stilwell, General Joseph W. *Black and White Books, No. 2, 1942 February 8–1943 April 18.* Joseph Warren Stilwell Papers, Box 36, Folder 2. Hoover Institution Library & Archives.

Stilwell, General Joseph W. *Diaries.* Joseph Warren Stilwell Papers, Boxes 39 and 41 [transcripts]. Hoover Institution Library & Archives. Available online at digital collections.hoover.org/advancedsearch/Objects/archiveType%3AItem%3BseriesId%3A56295.

Stilwell, General Joseph W. "Letters from Claire Lee Chennault to Joseph W. Stilwell, 1944 April–May." Joseph Warren Stilwell Papers, Box 22, Folder 3. Hoover Institution Library & Archives.

Stilwell, General Joseph. "Letters from Frank Dorn and T. F. Taylor, 1944." Joseph Warren Stilwell Papers, Box 21, Folder 8. Hoover Institution Library & Archives.

Stilwell, General Joseph W. "Reports on Frank Merrill's Marauders," Joseph Warren Stilwell Papers, Box 30, Folder 1, Hoover Institution & Archives.

Stimson, Henry Lewis. Henry Lewis Stimson Papers (MS 465). Manuscripts and Archives, Yale University Library.

Stoker, A. Desmond. "A Journey from Burma." Private Papers, Document 1072, Imperial War Museum.

Stone, James H., ed. *Crisis Fleeting: Original Reports on Military Medicine in India and Burma in the Second World War.* Washington, DC: Office of the Surgeon General, Department of the Army, 1969.

Stowe, Leland. *They Shall Not Sleep.* New York: Alfred A. Knopf, 1944.

Sunderland, Riley, and Charles F. Romanus. *Stilwell's Personal File, China-Burma-India, 1942–1944,* vols. 1–5. Wilmington, DE: Scholarly Resources, 1976.

Swedien, Bea Anderson. *Under the Red Blanket.* London: MX Publishing, 2011.

Sykes, Cristopher. *Orde Wingate: A Biography.* Cleveland, OH: World Publishing, 1959.

Symington, Andrew. *A Journey of an Unknown Englishman to Hukong Valley of Burma: The Unpublished Diary of Andru Symington from 10th December 1891 to 11th March 1892.* Edited by Nilamani Sen Deka. Nalbari: Journal Emporium, 2012.

Tamayama, Kazuo, and John Nunneley. *Tales by Japanese Soldiers, of the Burma Campaigns, 1942–1945.* London: Weidenfeld & Nicolson, 2000.

Taw Sein Ko. *Burmese Sketches.* Rangoon: British Burma Press, 1913.

Taylor, Bill. "2nd Weather Reconnaissance Squadron (Medium)" in *China Airlift—"The Hump,"* vol. 1, China-Burma-India Hump Pilots Association, 142–43. Dallas, TX: Turner, 1981.

Taylor, Jay. *The Generalissimo: Chiang Kai-shek and the Struggle for Modern China.* Cambridge, MA: Harvard University Press, 2011.

Taylor, Dr. Joe G. "Air Interdiction in China in World War II." USAF Historical Studies No. 132. Maxwell AFB, Montgomery, AL: Air University USAF Historical Division Study, 1956.

Taylor, Dr. Joe G. "Air Supply in the Burma Campaigns." USAF Historical Studies: No. 75. Maxwell AFB, Montgomery, AL: USAF Historical Division, 1957.

Taylor, Col. Thomas H., USA (Ret.). *Rangers Lead the Way.* Paducah, KY: Turner, 1996.

Thakin Nu. *Burma Under the Japanese.* Edited and translated by J. S. Furnivall. London: Macmillan, 1954.

Thant Myint-U. *The River of Lost Footsteps: A Personal History of Burma.* New York: Farrar, Straus and Giroux, 2006.

Thesiger, Wilfrid. *The Life of My Choice.* New York: W. W. Norton, 1987.

Thomas, Lowell. *Back to Mandalay.* New York: Greystone Press, 1951.

Thomas, Vicky. *The Naga Queen: Ursula Graham Bower and Her Jungle Warriors, 1939–1945.* Stroud, UK: History Press, 2012.

Thompson, Henrietta. "Walk a Little Faster: Escape from Burma with General Stilwell in 1942." (master's thesis, University of Maine, 1992).

Thompson, Virginia. "Transit Duty on the Burma Road." *Far Eastern Survey* 10, no. 18 (September 1941): 213–15.

Thorne, Christopher. *Allies of a Kind: The United States, Britain, and the War Against Japan, 1941–1945.* London: Hamish Hamilton, 1978.

Thorp, Ellen. *Quiet Skies on Salween.* London: Jonathan Cape, 1945.

Tidey, George. *Trek from Burma.* London: Society for the Propagation of the Gospel in Foreign Parts, 1944.

Tinker, Hugh. "A Forgotten Long March: The Indian Exodus from Burma, 1942." *Journal of Southeast Asian Studies* 6, no. 1 (1975): 1–15.

Tizzard, F. G. Private Papers of Captain F. G. Tizzard, Documents 22383, Imperial War Museum.

Toland, John. *The Rising Sun: The Decline and Fall of the Japanese Empire, 1936–1945.* New York: Modern Library, 2003.

Townsell, Lt. G. Marshall. "Intelligence Bulletin #6," Headquarters, India China Wing, Air Transport Command, Station #1, in *China Airlift—"The Hump,"* vol. 2, China-Burma-India Hump Pilots Association, 112–18. Paducah, KY: Turner, 1996.

Trager, Frank N., ed. *Burma: Japanese Military Administration, Selected Documents, 1941–1945.* Translated by Won Zoon Yoon. Philadelphia: University of Pennsylvania Press, 1971.

Tuchman, Barbara. *Stilwell and the American Experience in China.* New York: Grove Press, 1970.

Tulloch, Major-General Derek. *Wingate in Peace and War.* London: Macdonald and Company, 1972.

Tunner, William H. *Over the Hump.* New York: Duell, Sloan and Pearce, 1964.

Tyson, Geoffrey. *Forgotten Frontier.* Calcutta: W. H. Targett, 1945.

U Min Thu. *Glimpses of Kachin Traditions & Customs.* Yangon: U Htun Hlaing, 2002.

Underbrink, Robert. *Somewhere We Will Find You.* Bennington, VT: Merriam Press, 2012.

USAAF. *A History of the India-China Division Air Transport Command, Year 1944*, vol. 1. Call #312.01-V.1, IRIS #00181448, in the USAF Collection, AFHRA, Maxwell AFB, Montgomery, AL.

USAAF. *A History of the India-China Division, Air Transport Command, Year 1944*, vol. 2. Call #312.01-V.2, IRIS #00181449, in the USAF Collection, AFHRA, Maxwell AFB, Montgomery, AL.

USAAF. *A History of the India-China Division, Air Transport Command, Year 1944*, vol. 3. Call #312.01-V.3, IRIS #00181451, in USAF Collection, AFHRA, Maxwell AFB, Montgomery, AL.

USAAF. *A History of the India-China Division, Air Transport Command, Year 1945.* Call #312.01, IRIS #00181451, in the USAF Collection, AFHRA, Maxwell AFB, Montgomery, AL.

USAAF, "A History of the India China Wing for the Period June through December 1943," Call #312.01, IRIS #00181446, in the USAF Collection, AFHRA, Maxwell AFB, Montgomery, AL.

USAAF, Air Force Safety Agency, Aircraft Accident and Incident Report, Call #MICFILM 46245, IRIS #00877192, in the USAF Collection, AFHRA, Maxwell AFB, Montgomery, AL.

USAAF, Air Force Safety Agency, Aircraft Accident and Incident Report, Call #MICFILM 46255, IRIS #00877202, in the USAF Collection, AFHRA, Maxwell AFB, Montgomery, AL.

USAAF, Air Force Safety Agency, Aircraft Accident and Incident Report, Call #MICFILM 46263, IRIS #00877210, in the USAF Collection, AFHRA, Maxwell AFB, Montgomery, AL.

USAAF. "Air Transportation to China Under the Tenth Air Force, April–November 1942." Call #312.04-3, IRIS #00181455, in the USAF Collection, AFHRA, Maxwell AFB, Montgomery, AL.

USAAF. "Abstracts of Policy-Making Messages Affecting Air Operations in the China -Burma-India Theater, 1 January 1942 to August 1943." No. 9 of Army Air Force Policy Studies. Call #103-9, IRIS #00467728, in USAF Collection, AFHRA, Maxwell AFB, Montgomery, AL.

USAAF, Assistant Chief of Air Staff, Intelligence, Historical Division. "The Fourteenth Air Force to 1 October 1943" (Short Title: AAFRH—90). Call #101-109, IRIS #00467693, in the USAF Collection, AFHRA, Maxwell AFB, Montgomery, AL.

USAAF. "Biography: Flickinger, D. D." File 4167 AAF Base Unit (Air Base). Call #MICFILM 23236, IRIS #00893412, in the USAF Collection, AFHRA, Maxwell AFB, Montgomery, AL.

USAAF. "Chronological History of Project 9 (Cochran)." Intelligence Data and Memoranda—CBI Theater. Call #142.0411-9, 1, IRIS #00115242, in the USAF Collection, AFHRA, Maxwell AFB, Montgomery, AL.

USAAF. "Colored Troops 1942-1943," Headquarters Eighth Air Force, ETOUSA. Call #519.765-1, IRIS #00217874, in USAF Collection, AFHRA, Maxwell AFB, Montgomery, AL.

USAAF. "Combined Study by Headquarters, Services of Supply, India-Burma Theater & Headquarters, Army Air Forces, India-Burma Theater of the Comparative Costs in Personnel and Equipment of Delivering 80,000 Tons per Month to Kunming by Road and by Air." Call #825.461-1, IRIS #00266737, in USAF Collection, AFHRA, Maxwell AFB, Montgomery, AL.

USAAF. Eastern Air Command, Southeast Asia, "Memo from Weather Cdr, for Air Marshal, Commanding Base Air Forces SE Asia." Call #820.9081-1, IRIS #00266101, in USAF Collection AFHRA, Maxwell AFB, Montgomery, AL.

USAAF. "First Draft Supreme Allied Commander's Despatches: Part III Operations by Northern Combat Area Command." Call #168.7266-64, IRIS #01095406, in USAF Collection, AFHRA, Maxwell AFB, Montgomery, AL.

USAAF. "Historical Record and Activities of U.S. Army Air Forces in Area of Karachi, India." Call #828.08 vol. 1, IRIS #00266923, in the USAF Collection, AFHRA, Maxwell AFB, Montgomery, AL.

USAAF. "History of the 16th Combat Camera Unit 1 May 1943 to 31 December 1944." Call #UNIT/0016/COMBAT CAMERA, IRIS #00038422, in USAF Collection, AFHRA, Maxwell AFB, Montgomery, AL.

USAAF. "History of the Air Transport Command's China Wing, October 1943–June 1945." Call #312.01, IRIS #00181447, in the USAF Collection, AFHRA, Maxwell AFB, Montgomery, AL.

USAAF. "History of the India-China Ferry Under the Tenth Air Force, March to November 1942." Call #830.04-4, IRIS #00267074, in the USAF Collection, AFHRA, Maxwell AFB, Montgomery, AL.

USAAF, Howard C. Davidson Collection. "The North Burma Campaign." Call #168.7266-60, IRIS #01095402, in USAF Collection, AFHRA, Maxwell AFB, Montgomery, AL.

USAAF, HQ India China Division, Air Transport Command. "Investigation Regarding Hump Flying." In Personal Collection of W. H. Tunner. Call #168.7158, IRIS #01038153, in USAF Collection, AFHRA, Maxwell AFB, Montgomery, AL.

USAAF, HQ India China Wing, Air Transport Command, A-2 Section. "Intelligence Bulletin: Tips on Bailing Out," September 4, 1943. Call #312.606, 1, IRIS #00181545, in the USAF Collection, AFHRA, Maxwell AFB, Montgomery, AL.

USAAF, India-China Division, Air Transport Command. "A History of Hump Operations, January 1, 1945–March 31, 1945." Call #312.04-2, IRIS #00181454, in the USAF Collection, AFHRA, Maxwell AFB, Montgomery, AL.

USAAF, India-China Division, Air Transport Command. "A History of the India China Wing for the Period June Through December 1943." Call #312.01, IRIS #00181446, in the USAF Collection, AFHRA, Maxwell AFB, Montgomery, AL.

USAAF, India-China Division, Air Transport Command. "ATC Statistics on Hump Tonnage, 1942–1945." Call #312.3081-2, IRIS #00181528, in the USAF Collection, AFHRA, Maxwell AFB, Montgomery, AL.

USAAF, India-China Division, Air Transport Command. "Chronological List of Aircraft Crashing on Hump Route." Call #312.3912-2, 1–114, IRIS #00181544, in USAF Collection, AFHRA, Maxwell AFB, Montgomery, AL.

USAAF, India China Division, Air Transport Command. "Medical History of the India China Wing and India China Division, Air Transport Command December 1942–December 1945." Call #312.740, IRIS #00181547, in USAF Collection, AFHRA, Maxwell AFB, Montgomery, AL.

USAAF, India China Wing, Air Transport Command. "Search and Rescue Activities." Call #312.755-2, IRIS #00181557, in the USAF Collection, AFHRA, Maxwell AFB, Montgomery, AL.

USAAF. "Interesting Histories: China-Burma-India, Tenth Air Force, 1943–1945."

Call #830.309-3, IRIS #00916088, in the USAF Collection, AFHRA, Maxwell AFB, Montgomery, AL.

USAAF. "Interrogation of PFC (NMI), Kaplan, 12182139." Air Transport Command, Ditching and Survival Narratives. Call #312.756-1, 1, IRIS #00181560, in USAF Collection, AFHRA, Maxwell AFB, Montgomery, AL.

USAAF. "Investigation of and Report on the Airplane Accident Which Resulted in the Death of General Wingate, 24 March, 1944." Call #825.7501-1, IRIS #00266793, in the USAF Collection, AFHRA, Maxwell AFB, Montgomery, AL.

USAAF, Karachi American Air Base Command. "Miscellaneous Correspondence," Call #828.168, IRIS #00266927, in the USAF Collection, AFHRA, Maxwell AFB AL.

USAAF. "Memorandum for Chief of the Air Staff: Subj: Alternative Supply Line to China, 2 February 1942, fr. War Dept." Call #142.0411-7, IRIS #00115240, in the USAF Collection, AFHRA, Maxwell AFB, Montgomery, AL.

USAAF. "Pacific Strategic Intelligence Section, Japanese-Burmese Relations." Call #180.2043-8, May 9, 1945, IRIS #01039786, in the USAF Collection, AFHRA, Maxwell AFB, Montgomery, AL.

USAAF, "10th Air Force Narrative of Events in Malaya and the Philippines, 1941-1942," Call #830.309-4, 8f., IRIS # 00916089, USAF Collection, AFHRA, Maxwell AFB, Montgomery, AL.

USAAF. "The Campaign in Northern Burma and the Construction of the Ledo Road," January 15, 1945. Call #812.947-3, IRIS #00264880, in USAF Collection, AFHRA, Maxwell AFB, Montgomery, AL.

USAAF. "The Situation in China or the Thankless Job." *A History of the India-China Division Air Transport Command, Year 1944*, vol. 3. Call #312.01, 878–940, IRIS #00181450, in the USAF Collection, AFHRA, Maxwell AFB, Montgomery, AL.

USAAF. *The Story of Search & Rescue in the India China Division, Air Transport Command, December 1942 to December 1945.* Call #MICFILM 34918, IRIS #01038158, in USAF Collection AFHRA, Maxwell AFB, Montgomery, AL.

USAAF. "The Tenth Air Force 1943." US Air Force Historical Study No. 117. Call #101-117, IRIS #00467701, in the USAF Collection, AFHRA, Maxwell AFB, Montgomery, AL.

USAAF. "The Tenth Air Force, 1 January–10 March 1943." US Air Force Historical Study No. 104. Call #101-104, IRIS #00467688, in the USAF Collection, AFHRA, Maxwell AFB, Montgomery, AL.

US Department of State. Foreign Relations of the United States (FRUS), Diplomatic Papers. Washington, DC: US Government Printing Office, 1956. history.state.gov /historicaldocuments/roosevelt-fd.

Van de Ven, Hans J. "Stilwell in the Stocks: The Chinese Nationalists and the Allied Powers in the Second World War." *Asian Affairs* XXXIV, no. III (November 2003): 243–59.

Van de Ven, Hans J. *War and Nationalism in China, 1925–1945.* London: Routledge Curzon, 2003.

Vaz, Mark Cotta. *Living Dangerously: The Adventures of Merian C. Cooper, Creator of King Kong.* New York: Villard, 2005.

Vincenti, Walter G. "The Davis Wing and the Problem of Airfoil Design: Uncertainty and Growth in Engineering Knowledge." *Technology and Culture* 27, no. 4, *Special Issue: Engineering in the Twentieth Century* (October 1986): 717–58.

Von Tunzelmann, Alex. *Indian Summer: The Secret History of the End of an Empire.* New York: Henry Holt, 2007.

Vorley, J. S., and H. M. Vorley. *The Road from Mandalay.* Windsor, UK: Wilton 65, 2002.

Wade, Harry F. *Five Miles Closer to Heaven: An Adventure by Parachute over the Jungles of India*. Oconomowoc, WI: The Ligurian Pamphlet Office, 1945.

Wallace, Captain I. A. "The Arakan: The Diary of a Junior Officer, 32 Battery Mountain Artillery," Private Papers of Captain I. A. Wallace, Documents 6985, Imperial War Museum.

Wang, Zhusheng. *The Jingpo Kachin of the Yunnan Plateau*. Tempe, AZ: Arizona State University Program for Southeast Asian Studies, 1997.

Watson, George M., Jr. "Building Air Power" in *Winged Shield, Winged Sword: A History of the United States Air Force*. Vol. 1: 1907–1950. Edited by Bernard C. Nalty. Washington, DC: Air Force History and Museums Program, United States Air Force, 1997.

Weaver, Herbert, and Marvin A. Rapp. *The Fourteenth Air Force to 1 October 1943 (Short Title: AAFRH-9)*. United States Air Force Historical Study, No. 109. Washington, DC: AAF Historical Office, 1945.

Weaver, Major Herbert, and Sergeant Marvin Rapp. *The Tenth Air Force 1942*. Army Air Forces Historical Study, No. 12. Manhattan, Kansas: Sunflower University Press, 1980. First published 1944 by AAF Historical Office (Washington, DC).

Weber, Ethel H. "My Diary of Experiences in India and Letter to Elizabeth Crahan." United States Army, 73rd Evacuation Hospital papers, Box 2, Folder 1, Huntington Library.

Webster, Donovan. *The Burma Road: The Epic Story of the China-Burma-India Theater in WWII*. New York: Harper Perennial, 2004.

Wedemeyer, General Albert C. *Wedemeyer Reports!* New York: Devin-Adair Company, 1958.

Wedemeyer, General A. C. USA (Ret.). et al. "Commentary & Reply: On Stilwell and Galahad in Burma." *Parameters: Journal of the US Army War College* XVII, no. 1 (Spring 1987): 97–111.

Weskamp, Herman. Herman Weskamp Oral History Interview (OH00125trs): 1–38, National Museum of the Pacific War.

Whelan, Joseph R. "Bailout" in *China Airlift—"The Hump,"* vol. 1, China-Burma-India Hump Pilots Association, 271–73. Dallas, TX: Turner, 1981.

White, Edwin Lee, Col. USAF (Ret.). *Ten Thousand Tons by Christmas*, 2nd ed. St. Petersburg, FL: Valkyrie Press, 1977.

White, Theodore H. *In Search of History: A Personal Adventure*. New York: Harper & Row, 1978.

White, Theodore H., ed. *The Stilwell Papers*. New York: Da Capo Press, 1991.

White, Theodore H., and Annalee Jacoby. *Thunder Out of China*. Boston: Da Capo Press, 1980.

Whitworth, Brigadier Dysart. "The Evacuation of Refugees and the Chinese Fifth Army from the Hukawng Valley into Assam, Summer, 1942." *Journal of the Royal Central Asian Society* 30, no. 3–4 (February 2011): 311–21.

Wigington, Don. *It's Hangar Flying Time*. San Antonio, TX: Bounds Publishing Company, 1990.

Williams, Douglas O., F/Lt. (Ret.). "Excerpts from 'An Appreciation of General Wingate'" in *China Airlift—"The Hump,"* vol. 2, China-Burma-India Hump Pilots Association, 226–27. Paducah, KY: Turner, 1996.

Williams, J. H. *The Spotted Deer*. London: Rupert Hart-Davis, 1957.

Wilson, Lieutenant General Walter K., Jr. *Engineer Memoirs*. Washington, DC: US Government Printing Office, 1984.

Wooten, Paul J. Paul J. Wooten Collection (AFC/2001/001/67357). Veterans History Project, American Folklife Center, Library of Congress.

Yarbrough, Willie Percy. Willie Percy Yarbrough Collection (AFC/2001/001/97802). Veterans History Project, American Folklife Center, Library of Congress.

Yerkey, Gary G. *A Pilot's Pilot: Gen. Caleb V. Haynes and the Rise of American Air Power 1917–1944*. Washington, DC: GK Press, 2018.

Young, Arthur. Arthur N. Young Papers. "CNAC Chungking file, 1941," Box 103. Hoover Institution Library & Archives.

Young, Richard. Richard Young Oral History Interview (OH00947trs): 1–17, National Museum of Pacific War.

PERIODICALS AND NEWSPAPERS

In addition to local US newspapers cited in the endnotes, the following military and veteran publications were also useful:

CBI Roundup: accessible at cbi-theater.com/roundup/roundup.html.

CBIVA Sound-off: newsletter of the China-Burma-India Veterans Association. Compilation of many issues at: cbi-theater.com/soundoff/soundoff.html.

Ex-CBI Roundup

Hump Express: accessible at cbi-theater.com/hump_express/humpexpress.html.

SEAC: The Services' Newspaper of South East Asia Command

The China Lantern: some issues accessible at cbi-theater.com/lantern/lantern-home.html.

INDEX

Page numbers in italics indicate maps.